INTERRELATIONS OF LITERATURE

Edited by

Jean-Pierre Barricelli and Joseph Gibaldi

THE MODERN LANGUAGE ASSOCIATION OF AMERICA

NEW YORK   1982

Copyright © 1982 by The Modern Language Association of America

Library of Congress Cataloging in Publication Data
Main entry under title:
Interrelations of literature.
  Bibliography: p.
  Includes index.
  1. Literature—Addresses, essays, lectures.
I. Barricelli, Jean-Pierre. II. Gibaldi, Joseph,
1942-
PN45.8.I56 1982   809   82-7956
ISBN 0-87352-090-4   AACR2
ISBN 0-87352-091-2 (pbk.)

Published by The Modern Language Association of America
62 Fifth Avenue, New York, New York 10011

Contents

Preface

The approaches to literary study are many. Some scholars, we know, prefer to study literature as an entity unto itself, as a single, coherent, self-contained, self-existent art, just as some choose to study a literary work within the frontiers of a single, self-sufficient, national language. Such centripetal approaches, however, while of value, tend to deny literature its centrifugal spirit — its tendency not only to cross international borders, both artistically and intellectually, but also to intersect with other forms of art and knowledge. Primarily under the aegis of comparative literature, the study of letters has become progressively more interdisciplinary as well as interliterary. Through this important development in modern scholarship, literature is being restored to its pristine position as a central cognitive resource in society, as its most faithful and comprehensive interpreter. It is an art but more than an art, for, while being itself, literature extends outside itself to forms of human experience beyond disciplinary boundaries, making it evident that the rigid separation of disciplines by myopic specializations can in the long run lead only to a counterproductive and paralyzing isolation. Literature, as the hub of the wheel of knowledge, provides the logical locus for the integration of knowledge. It is with this conviction that we have approached the preparation of this volume.

The interrelations of literature have been discussed for years, in fact for centuries (if one wishes to go back to Gotthold Ephraim Lessing, the Italian Renaissance theorists, Horace), and more recently by scholars like, on the one hand, the demurrer Cornelis de Deugd, who endorsed literary study that crossed the boundaries of nations but not the boundaries of literature itself, and, on the other hand, such advocates and practitioners of interdisciplinary study as Karl Vossler, Ernst Robert Curtius, Mario Praz, Theodore Meyer Greene, Helmut Hatzfeld, and René Wellek. In 1967 the Modern Language Association took a significant step forward by publishing *Relations of Literary Study: Essays on Interdisciplinary Contributions*, edited by James Thorpe. That volume, sponsored by the MLA's Committee on Research Activities, contained seven essays, written by seven distinguished scholars, each of which treated a specific literary interrelation: "Literature and History" (Rosalie L. Colie), "Literature and Myth" (Northrop Frye), "Literature and Biography" (Leon Edel), "Literature and Psychology" (Frederick C. Crews), "Literature and Sociology" (Leo Lowenthal), "Literature and Religion" (J. Hillis Miller), and "Literature and Music" (Bertrand H. Bronson).

Because of the unprecedented interest in interdisciplinary study during the succeeding decade, and the proliferation of interdisciplinary scholarship that followed in its wake, the Committee on Research Activities decided at the end of the 1970s that the time was right for a new collection of essays that would reflect the current state of interdisciplinary literary study. Assigned the task of preparing the volume, we consulted widely with scholars and teachers and developed plans for a volume that of necessity differs significantly from its predecessor, which in its own right will continue to remain among the classic contributions to literary scholarship.

The present volume almost doubles the number of interrelational studies. Essays on the relations between literature and myth, psychology, sociology, religion, and music are here joined by essays on eight new topics: the interrelations of literature with linguistics, philosophy, politics, law, science, folklore, the visual arts, and film. (Since history and biography have already been treated in another MLA volume, *Introduction to Scholarship in Modern Languages and Literatures*, edited by Joseph Gibaldi [New York: MLA, 1981], it was decided to omit these topics from the present work.) Only limitations of space have dictated the omission of studies involving such other disciplines as economics, anthropology, dance, and theater.

Although they will doubtless be of substantial interest to specialists, these essays are introductory in nature and are intended for an audience of nonspecialists, particularly students, who need considerable guidance in this increasingly important and increasingly complex area of humanistic learning. For this reason, we have insisted that the essays, as much as possible, be organized symmetrically and focused internationally and that each contain the following: an enunciation of the nature and value of the interrelation; a historical overview of the interrelation, including a history of the relevant scholarship; a selection of methodological analyses; a discussion of major issues; a consideration of prospects for contemporary research; and a brief though basic bibliography. Our starting and concluding focal point being *literature*, we have emphasized the primary source — the intellectual work of art — and have allowed only passing consideration, except where inevitable, of the secondary source — the criticism, and the criticism of criticism. For terminological problems, a selective glossary appears at the end of the book.

We are grateful for the cooperation and understanding we have received from all the contributors. We also wish to express our appreciation to the many scholars who served as readers of the essays, lending their valued judgment and expertise, as well as to the members of the sponsoring Committee on Research Activities and the MLA headquarters staff for their un-flagging support of the project and their timely editorial and administrative assistance: Walter S. Achtert, Hazard Adams, John Algeo, C. L. Barber, David Bleich, Leo Braudy, Gerald L. Bruns, Joel Conarroe, James C. Cowan, Frederick C. Crews, Peter Demetz, William B. Edgerton, Sigmund Eisner, Frederick Garber, Ronald Gottesman, Judy Goulding, Jean H. Hagstrum, Wayland D. Hand, S. K. Heninger, Jr., Sarah N. Lawall, Samuel R. Levin, A. Walton Litz, Leonard Manheim, Leo Marx, Gita May, Patricia Merivale, J. Hillis Miller, John Neubauer, Eric S. Rabkin, H. Blair Rouse, Jeffrey L. Sammons, Roslyn Schloss, Egon Schwarz, Charles T. Scott, Roger Shattuck, Stuart M. Tave, Madeleine B. Therrien, Karl D. Uit-ti, Mario J. Valdés, Robert K. Wallace, Ian Watt, and Carl Woodring.

With colleagues such as these and more, aware of the consequence of pursuing the field of literature in its numerous interrelations, the future of this scholarly, academic, and culturally vital orientation is assured. And our growing into a society more conscious of the full significance of the fact of literature becomes a possibility. The challenge remains, however, to develop for interdisciplinary studies of this kind successful pedagogical approaches and structures. It is our hope that the present volume will assist in this task.

J.-P. B.

J.G.

1

Literature and Linguistics

Jonathan Culler

I

"Above everything else, poetry is words," wrote Wallace Stevens. If so, then linguistics would seem to have a close and vital relation to literature; but many have contested Stevens' claim, and many more have disagreed about its implications. Undoubtedly, literature is words in that words are what the reader or listener encounters, but does it follow, as the linguist Roman Jakobson argues, that the study of literature or poetics is therefore a subdivision of linguistics, which is "the global science of verbal structure"?[1] Or is it rather the case, as the critic F. W. Bateson claims, that for the native speaker the linguistic analysis of the language of a work is not a necessary part of the study of literature, except in rare instances?[2]

Everyone would agree that to appreciate a literary work one must understand its language, and thus when reading literature from times and places not our own, we need linguistic information. In reading Geoffrey Chaucer we need a glossary to tell us the meaning of words, but beyond this, as William G. Moulton suggests, "we also want to know . . . how Chaucer's rhymes and rhythms actually sounded; and this, in turn, leads us to the linguist's full apparatus for phonological analysis: his phonemes and allophones, his shifts and splits and mergers. Much of this apparatus was developed in the first place by scholars who wished to understand literary works more fully."[3]

Classical and medieval texts are often accompanied by linguistic commentary, but this application of linguistic expertise to literature is generally seen as compensatory: to help modern readers who lack the knowledge and sensitivity to language that the author's contemporaries would have had. Neither the defenders nor the opponents of an intimate and necessary relation between linguistics and literature wish to take this as the exemplary case, for the kind of linguistic information necessary for the understanding of a linguistically strange work is often best presented in ad hoc glosses or notes and has only a distant relation to the analytical methods and concepts of contemporary linguistics, which are what the proponents of a relation between linguistics and literature usually have in mind.

1

No one denies that one must understand the language in which a work is written; nor does anyone deny that all the effects of literature are achieved through language. But the same could be said, for example, of history: if you are to read a history of Spain, you must know the language in which it is written, and what you learn about Spain you learn through the language of the work. Some critics would argue that while novelists, like historians, must cope with language, the principal objects of their art are characters, actions, and ideas, not words and sentences per se. An analysis focused exclusively on language would miss what is most important in the novel. Other critics maintain that writers — especially the poet but also the novelist and playwright — are different from the historian in that language is their subject as well as their medium. They investigate its imaginative possibilities, testing its limits, engaging through their works in an exploration of and reflection on its power to persuade or incarnate. Insofar as literature calls attention to itself as language, it would seem to invite the application of the concepts and methods developed in linguistics for the analysis of language.

One might be tempted to seek a compromise by positing a continuum along which literary works could be placed: at one pole works that do not seem concerned with language but simply use it to present actions, characters, and ideas; at the other pole, works that seem to be language reflecting on itself. Linguistics would have little to do with the works at one end and a lot with those at the other. This scheme, whatever its attractions, would not satisfy our disputants. In the first place, they would disagree about how to classify writers and works: no novelist seems more intensely concerned with characters, actions, and ideas than Charles Dickens, yet his writing flaunts its linguistic virtuosity. Moreover, the defenders of linguistic analysis would argue that works that seem not to call attention to their own language are precisely those that most require linguistic analysis, whereas their opponents might claim that when a work does make language one of its themes, readers can understand it without the intervention of a linguist, just as they understand novels about despair or financial disaster without the assistance of psychiatrists or economists.

No compromise formulation is likely to satisfy our disputants, who disagree both about the importance of language to literature and about the relevance of linguistic analysis to the language of literature. Instead of seeking a settlement, let us try to clarify the debate by noting the three major sources of confusion.

1. Discussions of the topic "literature and linguistics" often take the form of surveys of language devices prominent in literature. These inventories of rhetorical figures and other patterns of language can be informative without making a case for the utility of the discipline of linguistics in literary studies. The devices or techniques they survey, though linguistic in the sense that they are resources of language, can be identified and appreciated without any specialized linguistic knowledge. Thus, the examples presented by

advocates of linguistics in literary studies are likely to seem irrelevant to those who are skeptical about this relation. Many effects are linguistic in that they are due to identifiable uses of language, but this does not in itself demonstrate the importance of linguistics to students of literature, who are likely to be convinced of its importance only if linguistic analysis can shed light on phenomena that would otherwise remain mysterious. The examples in Section 3 will illustrate claims that some kinds of analysis relevant to literary studies require a knowledge of linguistics.

2. Confusion also arises because those who are most enthusiastic about the relation between linguistics and literature may be the most vociferous in their critique of linguistics. Actually, this position is explicable and even appropriate. Linguistics has concentrated for the most part on the phonological and syntactic systems of languages and has made the sentence the largest unit with which it attempts to deal. One can thus praise the achievements of linguistics within these limits, while pointing out that most of the effects of interest to literary critics involve relations among sentences or larger sections of discourse and therefore lie beyond the scope of linguistics. Those who wish to affirm the pertinence of linguistics to literary study are often led to reply that linguistics must and shall develop techniques for analyzing discourse and describing the semantic structure of entire texts.

We can thus see that the relation between linguistics and literature is a reciprocal process, not simply a matter of applying linguistics to literature. Focus on literary material may lead to an enrichment and expansion of linguistics. No linguistics can be adequate to language if it cannot describe the way in which sentences interact to form coherent (or incoherent) texts; it ought in principle to be able to describe the effects achieved by the most elaborate, sophisticated, and self-conscious productions of language—. literary works. Those who call most emphatically for the linguistic analysis of literary language may be not so much defenders of contemporary linguistics as advocates of a new linguistics of discourse.

3. Finally, confusion in debates about the relation between linguistics and literature stems from the assumptions, seldom directly expressed, about the nature of literary study itself. The skeptics often appear to assume that the understanding of individual works is the only possible goal of literary study and that, unless a linguistic analysis can lead to new and valid interpretations of a work, it is irrelevant. But there is no reason to think that linguistics should be a tool of interpretation. Its own relation to language is different. Linguists do not try to discover the meaning of sentences, much less to develop new meanings or interpretations. They attempt to describe the system of rules that enables sentences to have the form and meaning they do. If a linguistic analysis were to suggest a new meaning for a sentence, that would be evidence that the analysis was wrong.

What are the implications for literary studies of this basic fact? Can it help critics to see the narrowness of their assumptions? Once one begins to think about what linguistics does and can do, one may gain a more comprehensive view of literary studies. First, one might expect that in discussion of individual works linguistics could help explain what is responsible for a particular effect and would thus contribute to a criticism that seeks to account for the meanings works have for readers rather than propose yet one more interpretation. Second, linguistics will be central to descriptions or theories of any aspect of literary discourse: a theory of meter, a theory of metaphor, a description of period style, an account of the evocative power of sound patterns, a discussion of the nature of semantic coherence. Such projects, which belong to poetics or the theory of literature, cannot but make use of linguistics; but to demand that linguistics help to produce new interpretations of individual works involves a misunderstanding of both linguistics and literary criticism.

The discussion that follows will first sketch in the most cursory fashion the history of relations between linguistics and literature and then proceed to detailed examples of the kind of interaction that now takes place and may be expected in the future.

II

In classical times linguistics and literature were closely associated. Rhetoric, that comprehensive discipline, encompassed both, and linguistic study was essentially the study of the language of the best authors. Dionysius Thrax of the first century B.C., who composed the earliest surviving linguistic description of Greek, wrote that "grammar is the practical knowledge of the general usages of poets and prose writers."[4] Two of the six parts of his grammar were accurate reading aloud with regard for prosody and "the appreciation of literary compositions, which is the noblest part of grammar." Until the late Middle Ages appreciation of classical authors was the accepted purpose and context of linguistic work. Although the speculative grammarians, or *modistae*, of the thirteenth and fourteenth centuries paid less attention to literature and concentrated on the integration of grammatical analysis with philosophical theory, the orientation toward literature survived until the end of the Renaissance: linguistic analysis was linked with commentary on the language of classical texts.

The rise of historical linguistics or comparative philology in the nineteenth century began the dissociation of linguistics and literature. The effort to work out the historical affiliations of languages, to reconstruct primitive Indo-European forms, and to establish the laws governing sound changes diverted attention from the literary aspects of texts and suggested the possibility of a distinct linguistic discipline with its own goals. However, some linguists, such as the German Wilhelm von Humboldt, conceiving of each language as a system with its own *innere Sprachform*, connected language with literature by arguing that the literature of a people was the product of the distinctive spirit of its language, whose system the linguist was attempting to describe. Moreover, many comparative philologists continued to see their work on the history of the language as part of a general philology and thus related to the study of literary texts.

The twentieth century has witnessed the emergence of linguistics and literary criticism as separate disciplines. Linguistics has come to be not so much a store of knowledge about language as a series of attempts to describe one or more levels of the language system as explicitly and rigorously as possible. Linguistics has thus focused on problems not directly related to literature, and literary criticism has also had a series of goals of its own. Various rapprochements have been attempted, but in a context of fundamental and continuing separation. Linguists have from time to time worked on literary texts and attempted to show the relevance of their knowledge and methods, and students of literature have taken from linguistics concepts that seemed applicable to the problems that interested them. We can group these attempts into several general movements or schools of thought and sketch them briefly in rough chronological order.

1. Philology

Today "philology" usually means the study of the language of ancient texts, but before modern literature became an object of academic study, philology was a discipline of greater scope, encompassing language and literature, an *Altertumwissenschaft*, or science of antiquity, whose goal was a knowledge of past cultures. The glorious period of philology, when it covered much of the humanities and social sciences, was roughly the years of 1860–1915. Since then things have changed.

The philological ideal of a comprehensive discipline that studies literary works to increase its understanding of language and that brings to literature a profound knowledge of the language and culture of a period has remained alive in classical and medieval studies. However, in postmedieval studies comprehensive knowledge has come to seem a personal ideal rather than a goal that could define a discipline. The view that knowledge is the result of systematic method has doubtless contributed to the development of distinct activities in the area once covered by philology: synchronic linguistics, diachronic linguistics, textual criticism, intellectual history, literary biography, literary criticism, each defined by its own methods and objects of knowledge. In this process scholars such as Ernst Robert Curtius, Erich Auerbach, and Leo Spitzer, who began as philologists, have emerged through their writings as masters of other disciplines. Curtius and Auerbach turned away from new developments in linguistics to concentrate on cultural history and literary criticism, while Spitzer became associated with a particular integration of linguistics and literature, stylistics.

Partisans of philology would argue that such disciplinary distinctions are unfortunate and artificial, dividing a philology that should remain unified. They claim that there are virtues to a philological approach that recognizes the dialectic between the history of a language and the subtle manifestations of that history in literary works. For example, the American philologist Karl Uitti has argued that the description and understanding of Old French is not a linguistic problem but requires full literary appreciation of texts. Discussing the suffix *ois* and the playful proliferation of such forms in Rutebeuf, he writes, "Clearly, Rutebeuf's poem documents the true vitality and the complexity of a linguistic fact in Old French, but, I repeat, the documentation depends on the reader's active understanding. One would get nowhere by merely recording and classifying -*ois* forms in Rutebeuf's work." Unlike linguistics, which attempts to reconstruct a system and is interested in a moment of a text only in relation to the system, "philological activity is ideally *ad hoc*" ("Philology: Factualness and History," in Chatman, *Literary Style*, pp. 124, 122).

This is a formulation on which linguists and literary critics might agree. If philology works in ad hoc fashion and provides glosses on the language of literary texts, both groups can then use this information in the projects of reconstruction and interpretation that interest them. But whether or not one takes philology, so conceived, as the ideal, it no longer holds sway. Today philology is most often a particular way of relating the study of language and the study of literature: by analyzing texts as illustrations of the history of the language.

2. Stylistics

Stylistics, which came into being in the early twentieth century, is often seen as the modern and restricted version of the discipline of rhetoric. It studies the expressive resources of language and their use in different sorts of discourse. Stylistics is sometimes considered a branch of linguistics, treating a particular aspect of language, and sometimes a parallel discipline with roughly the same internal divisions as linguistics: phonology, morphology, syntax, and semantics. Two orientations are generally distinguished: a stylistics of *la langue* or the language system and a stylistics of *parole* or of particular discourses. The first, associated with the French stylistician Charles Bally, attempts to provide an inventory of the expressive resources of a given language (also see Ullmann, *Language and Style*). It will classify, for example, the various nuances or implications that can be expressed by inversion of noun and adjective in French: *un immense travail* instead of *un travail immense*, or *les blanches fleurs* instead of *les fleurs blanches*.

While stylistics of *la langue* identifies the linguistic options of writers or speakers — the expressive choices they must make in enunciating propositions — the stylistics of *parole* seeks to identify the distinctive features of individual styles. Benedetto Croce, who insisted on the link between inner intuition and outer expression, was an eminent proponent of this orientation, but its best-known practitioner is doubtless Leo Spitzer, philologist turned critic, whose linguistic sensitivity helped him identify unusual constructions in a work that he could correlate with its author's artistic vision. Reading *Bubu de Montparnasse* (1905) by Charles-Louis Philippe, Spitzer noted what he thought were odd uses of *à cause de* and *parce que*, as in "Les réveils de midi sont lourds et poisseux. . . . On éprouve un sentiment de déchéance *à cause des* réveils d'autrefois" 'Noontime awakenings are heavy and sticky. . . . One feels a sense of discomfort *because of* former awakenings.' Spitzer calls this tendency to use causal conjunctions to connect associations "pseudo-objective motivation." In presenting mental connections as causally binding for his characters, the author manifests a critical yet understanding attitude that is essential to his world view (*Linguistics and Literary History*, pp. 11–13).

Both stylistics of *la langue* and stylistics of *parole* vary in the linguistic descriptions they employ—from the notions of secondary school grammar to the technical formulations of mathematical linguistics. Thus, the advent of transformational-generative grammar gave rise to new possibilities of stylistic description: the "deep structure" of a sentence, as it was defined at one point, could be treated as an underlying proposition, and style could be defined as the transformations that lead from the deep structure to the actual surface structure (for further discussion, see Sec. 3).

Any mode of linguistic description can give rise to a corresponding version of stylistics. What is likely to remain unchanged is the project of correlating linguistic features with literary effects and, for stylistics of *parole*, with an author's imaginative vision. Stylistics has been sharply attacked for its failure to give any rigorous content to the notion of correlation between linguistic forms and literary meanings (see Smith, *On the Margins of Discourse*). Often one finds only the claim that a particular form has occurred in the vicinity of a particular effect.

How to remedy this problem is the dilemma of stylistics. Attempts to introduce quantitative techniques have not solved it, for the more stylistics concentrates on "objective" and countable linguistic features, the further it removes itself from literary effects and the more its correlations of connections between linguistic forms and literary meanings seem either trivial or tenuous. One can, for example, calculate the average number of words per sentence in a text. If the figure is higher for Thomas Mann than for Franz Kafka, this would be a trivial confirmation of an effect we have experienced. But to try to infer something from the comparative figures for, say, Honoré de Balzac and Gustave Flaubert would be highly dubious. If, instead, stylistics concentrates on features of undeniable literary importance (often difficult to define in linguistic terms), then it will have less chance of demonstrating the relevance of linguistics to literature, for it will be open to the accusation, often leveled at Spitzer, that literary intuition, not linguistic analysis, has identified the features discussed and determined how they are treated.

Stylistics has not solved the problem of the relation between linguistics and literature, doubtless because it encompasses two opposed conceptions of the relation. One view values linguistic analysis for its independence and objectivity: it can be carried out without concern for literary effects and it shows what is truly there in the text, after which critics can quarrel about the relevance or meaning of the features or patterns discovered. Another view claims that the discovery of linguistic patterns is in principle an unending activity so that in fact it is always governed by some notion of relevance or importance. If the analysis is to have any value, it must be governed by a true understanding of literary significance. These opposing theories yield different practical results.

3. Russian and Czech Formalism

A most important and effective interpenetration of literary and linguistic studies occurred at the beginning of this century in the work of a group known as the Russian formalists — work continued by the Prague School in the years between the First and Second World Wars. Among the Russian formalists, Roman Jakobson, who later moved to Prague and then to the United States, was the most eminent linguist, and he has always been committed to the study of literary language. Taking as their primary object not the themes of literary works but their "literariness," Jakobson and his colleagues concentrated on a variety of literary devices, producing systematic analyses of sound patterns, rhythmic structures, narrative devices, and processes of literary evolution. More ambitious and more concerned with synthesis than the proponents of stylistics, they sought to produce comprehensive theories of literary techniques and structures and had no hesitation in proposing the integration of linguistics and literature (see Erlich, *Russian Formalism*).

The orientation of the Prague School was similar. Jan Mukarovsky sought the integration of linguistics and literature by defining the aesthetic function of language as the foregrounding of the utterance itself (whereas other functions of language emphasize, for example, the speaker, the propositional content, or the hearer's relation to the utterance). His work on poetic language concentrated on the means and effects of this foregrounding. Jakobson himself produced in later years many controversial analyses of the patterns formed within poems by the symmetrical and asymmetrical distribution of linguistic elements. While granting the importance of patterning in the foregrounding of the utterance, his critics have found Jakobson's quantitative symmetry unconvincing, particularly since he discovers the same patterns in poems from disparate periods and languages. Even his critics, however, would not deny the importance of the formalists' pioneering work.

4. Structuralism and Semiotics

The movement that arose in France in the 1960s under the name of structuralism and became an international phenomenon in the 1970s under the name of semiotics is heir to the work of the Russian and Prague formalists, even though it claims as its founders the Swiss linguist Ferdinand de Saussure, whose *Cours de linguistique générale* (1917) was crucial to the development of modern linguistics, and Charles Sanders Peirce (1839–1914), an American philosopher whose work on the theory of signs became widely known only after the advent of semiotics. Structuralism took its methods and concepts from structural linguistics and sought to study other kinds of signifying phenomena, including literature, as linguistics studies language. Structuralist critics analyzed literary works as the product of two kinds of relations defined by linguistics: syntagmatic relations (relations determining the appropriateness or inappropriateness of combining items to form larger units) and paradigmatic relations (relations of contrast between items that can occupy the same position with different meanings). In taking linguistics as a methodological model, structuralism sought to develop a poetics that would stand to literature as linguistics stands to language, describing the systems of conventions that enable works to have the forms and meanings they do. This led to a variety of specific projects, including attempts to develop a "grammar" of plot structure and a comprehensive account of the system of narrative possibilities (for discussion see my *Structuralist Poetics*). Meanwhile, there arose in Germany and Holland attempts to develop "text grammars," or *Textlinguistik*, that, after the fashion of transformational generative grammar, would formulate the rules for the generation of complete texts and thus account for linguistic relations beyond the sentence (see Van Dijk, *Some Aspects of Text Grammars*, and Ihwe, *Linguistik in der Literaturwissenschaft*).

Both these movements can be brought under the general heading of semiotics, the science of signs. Semiotics seeks to analyze all communicative and signifying phenomena in terms of systems of signs but, unlike structuralism, it does not necessarily assume that other systems of signs will be based on the same principles as those of natural languages. However, since many signifying practices are, like literature, inextricably dependent on language, linguistics necessarily occupies an important place in semiotic analysis. There are many strains of semiotics; one of the most active is the attempt in Russia to develop a comprehensive theory of the structure of literary works and their conditions of coherence (see Lotman, *Analiz poeticheskogo teksta* and Zholkovskij and Shcheglov, *K opisaniyu smysla svyaznogo teksta*). Semiotics is not a method of interpretation but an attempt to describe systematically the processes of signification. It necessarily posits a close and vital relation between linguistics and literature.

5. Pragmatics

Whatever else it is, a literary work is a speech act of some kind and thus deserves the attention of a branch of linguistics neglected until recent years: pragmatics, the study of language in use or language as action. There is considerable disagreement about whether literary works should be seen as imitating various speech acts (a lyric as an imitation of an attempt to seduce or persuade, for example) or whether they perform special literary speech acts and, if so, how these should be characterized (see Pratt, *Toward a Speech Act Theory of Literary Discourse*). Discussions of the conventions of speech acts will doubtless prove relevant to literature, which already contains many of the most acute and subtle discussions of language-events we possess. The danger is that linguists and philosophers of language who work in the field of pragmatics will continue to set literature aside, as a special case that need not be taken into account when dealing with speech acts but a special case that is wholly dependent on or derivative from other speech acts and that therefore requires no separate analysis. This view would both prevent linguists and philosophers of language from learning anything from literature and make it unlikely that their theories would be sufficiently rich and complex to benefit literary studies.

III

We have noted that linguistics can contribute to systematic accounts of an aspect of literary language and that for particular works it may often help to elucidate effects that would otherwise remain mysterious. A convenient way to classify linguistically based discussions of literature is according to the level of linguistic analysis involved. This classification has the disadvantage of slighting projects that are primarily concerned with the relations between levels — for example, the interaction of phonology and grammar — but if presented with each sort of analysis, readers can doubtless imagine how the levels might be related. We will therefore group our examples, under the headings of prosody, phonology, syntax, and semantics, omitting morphology as less important and pragmatics as relatively undeveloped.

1. Prosody

The traditional meaning of *prosody* is "rules relating to metrics," but linguistics studies, under the heading of prosody, elements of sound such as pitch, intensity (or accent), and duration (or quantity). The role of these features varies from language to language, and there is a close relation between the prosodic system of a language and its metrical conventions, so linguistic analysis of the prosodic features of a language is essential to systematic accounts of versification. There has been much confusion in English metrical theory because in English duration plays little role, but prosodic notions such as long and short syllables were imported from classical languages where quantity or duration is important (*līber* 'free' is distinguished from *liber* 'book' by its long *i*).

Meter is a pattern of regularity that can rest on three linguistic phenomena: the syllable, the accent, and quantity. Sanskrit, Greek, and Latin meters are generally quantitative. The Latin hexameter, for example, consists of six feet of certain types, each type a particular combination of long and short syllables.

Ārmă vĭr|ūmquĕ că|nō, Trōi|āē quī | prīmŭs ăb | ōrīs   (Vergil)
("Arms and the man I sing, the first who from Troy's shores")

The Romance languages and Japanese tend to use syllabic meters because accent and duration are less important in these languages. Thus the Japanese haiku consists of seventeen syllables; the most important meter in Italian poetry, the hendecasyllable, consists of eleven syllables:

Nel mezzo del cammin di nostra vita   (Dante Alighieri)
("In the middle of the journey of our life")

and the French alexandrine is essentially a meter of twelve syllables, with certain rules concerning stress and juncture:

Le navire glissant sur les gouffres amers   (Charles Baudelaire)
("The ship sliding over the bitter abysses")

Old English verse was accentual, often with stress reinforced by alliteration, a feature preserved in this Middle English example:

In a śomer śeson whan śoft was the śonne,
I śhope me in śhroudes as Í a śhepe were   (*Piers Plowman*)

But most later English meters have combined a syllable count with a prescribed number of stresses.

Linguistics and prosody are closely connected because the phonological system of a language conditions its verse forms. English theorists and poets have often championed classical, quantitative meters, but it is difficult to sustain a quantitative meter and make it perceptible in a language as strongly accentual as English, whereas an accentual pattern is perceptible even when the number of syllables per line varies:

Lády of sílences
Cálm and distréssed
Tórn and most whóle
Róse of mémory
Róse of forgétfulness   (T. S. Eliot)

The metrical effects that are possible in a language will depend on the interaction of various features of the language. Modern metrical theory in English owes much to the theory of stress and in particular to discussions of the number of levels of stress in English. Morris Halle and S. J. Keyser, who have developed a metrical theory indebted to transformational grammar, note that "a theory of prosody based, at least in part, upon stress placement, necessarily presupposes a theory of stress placement," and they attempt to provide such a theory. Instead of defining a meter such as iambic pentameter in terms that leave many lines of the best poets metrically deviant, Halle and Keyser have worked on the assumption that most if not all the verse of a poet such as Chaucer is metrically well-formed and that one must attempt to write the metrical rules that make these lines possible. (See Halle and Keyser, *English Stress*.)

It is important to emphasize that the role of linguistics is not to help one determine the meter of a particular poem. It may help to explain why one sequence is more effective than another. I. A. Richards was asked at a conference why the title of a poem of his, "Harvard Yard in April/April in Harvard Yard," was so much superior to its converse. Richards, the critic, faltered, but the linguist Jakobson stepped into the breach:

What is repulsive in the suggested inversion "April in Harvard Yard/ Harvard Yard in April"? The title of Richards' poem displays a clearcut metrical integrity: it begins and ends with a word stress and consists of two hexasyllabic parts, each with an initial and two further stresses. All six stressed syllables of the title are separated from each other, in four instances by a single unstressed syllable and in one case by two. The whole is both opened and closed by the same leading phrase "Harvard Yard." An inverted order of the two sentences would abolish their rhythmic continuity by a clash of two stressed syllables ". . . Yard/ Harvard . . .": such an inversion would destroy the symmetry between the stressed onset and end of the title and its penult stress would discord with the final stress in all subsequent lines of the poem. (Sebeok, *Style in Language,* p. 24)

In general, however, linguistics is important because one cannot develop an adequate theory of prosody without an understanding of the prosodic features of a language that are available for interaction in metrical composition. Theorists disagree about how to describe meter, but they cannot ignore linguistics.

2. Phonology

Traditional rhetoric defined sound patterns such as alliteration, assonance, and rhyme of various sorts, all of which involve the repetition of classes of individual sounds, or phonemes. Modern linguistics has analyzed the phonological system of languages in terms of minimal features that distinguish phonemes from one another, and it thus offers the critic the possibility of a more subtle and detailed description of sound in poetry, including the identification of patterns involving the repetition of particular features or combinations of features as well as individual phonemes. For example, the opening of Alfred Tennyson's "Oenone"

There lies a vale in Ida, lovelier
Than all the valleys of Ionian hills

involves intensive repetition of *l* and the *i* of *lies*, but this pattern does not suffice to explain the impression of a placid, almost featureless beauty, which doubtless owes much to the fact that all the consonants are voiced rather than voiceless (contrast the voiced *v* with the hiss of the corresponding voiceless consonant *f*). Moreover, with the exception of the *d* of *Ida*, already softened by its position between vowels, none of the consonants is a plosive (or, in another terminology, a stop), with the sharp release of breath that this feature marks (e.g., in *b, k, g, p, d, t*). (See Leech, *A Linguistic Guide to English Poetry*, p. 98.)

Contrast this pattern with that in Wallace Stevens' "Bantams in Pine Woods":

Chieftain Iffucan of Azcan in caftan
Of tan with henna hackles, halt.

The primary pattern is, of course, the repetition of *tan, can, can, tan, tan*; but the effect of repetition is intensified because both *t* and the *c* of *can* are voiceless plosives. They are very similar, distinguished only by the feature that Jakobson calls saturated versus dilute, so that *can* is very nearly a repetition of *tan*.

The application of phonological terminology to the sound patterns of poetry has been a common use of linguistics in literary studies, and it permits the identification of complicated relations. Analyzing Baudelaire's line,

Le navire glissant sur les gouffres amers

Nicolas Ruwet notes a phonological chiasmus in which *navire* is linked with *amers* and *glissant* with *gouffres*. In *navire/zamer* (the final *s* of *gouffres* is pronounced as an initial consonant of *amers*, whose own final *s* is not pronounced), the first vowel (*a*) and the last consonant (*r*) are identical. The second vowels (*i* and *e*) differ only by a single feature (compact versus diffuse), and the remaining consonants form a pattern in which $n : m : : z : v$. *N* and *m* are both nasals; *z* and *v* are voiced (or lax) and continuous, and in each case the first is acute and the second grave.[5]

A similar pattern of correspondences can be worked out for *glissant/gouffres*. This kind of analysis, however, is not without its problems. It often proceeds as if the more repetitions or the more elaborate patterns one can find, the better — a position difficult to justify. Moreover, it is seldom able to offer a convincing account of how a poem would be affected if the pattern were different (if, for example, in place of *gouffres* there were a word sharing more features with *navire* than with *glissant*). Discussion of phonological patterns in poetry requires a theory that would deal with the potential effects of patterns and thus give critics a sense of what sorts of patterns are likely to be worth noting.

A fascinating area of linguistic research that would contribute to a theory of sound patterns is investigation of the inherent or relative value of particular sounds and sound features. Critics have usually assumed that a pattern in *l* would not have the same effect as a pattern in *k*, but they have been suspicious of attempts to assign a value to each phoneme of the language. Experiments show surprising agreement, however, about the relative values of various sounds. Sapir reports that if people are asked to label three tables of different size *la*, *law*, and *lee*, nearly one hundred percent use *lee* for the small, *la* for the medium, and *law* for the large.[6] Given the nonsense words *skuk*, *mune*, *tade*, and *twonk*, and asked to match them with the characteristics "funny," "ugly," "beautiful," and "ordinary," speakers of English show remarkable agreement, even to the point where those who wish to dissent will say that, while they know *mune* is supposed to be beautiful and *tade* ordinary, they personally think *tade* is more beautiful. Other interesting experiments are reported by Fónagy (*Die Metaphern in der Phonetik*). Asked to compare /i/ and /u/ with respect to various qualities, eighty to ninety percent of the respondents found /i/ quicker, smaller, prettier, friendlier and /u/ thicker, hollower, darker, sadder, blunter, bitterer, and stronger.

Such research clearly has implications for literary studies, particularly if an explanation of these correlations can be found. Most proposals involve hypotheses about the psychological associations of articulatory movements and thus the breakdown of sounds into their minimal features. As Jakobson and Waugh suggest, "Most objections to the search for the inner significance of speech sounds arose because the latter were not dissected into their ultimate constituents."[7] The conclusions linguistics reaches will be essential to any theory of sound symbolism or the affective quality of sound in poetry, though it does seem that in literature there is a tendency to perceive and exploit values when they are appropriate and to ignore them when they are not. Stéphane Mallarmé complained about the perversity of the words *nuit* and *jour* because the sound of each better suits the meaning of the other; but despite this clash between sound and sense the two words figure prominently, and effectively, in French poetry.

3. Syntax

All discussions of literary language use some elementary syntactic categories — active and passive verbs, simple and complex sentences, subordinate clause, prepositional phrase — and in this way linguistics often has a role in literary studies; but the question at issue in debates about linguistics and literature is whether specialized knowledge of contemporary linguistics can contribute to literary studies. There seem to be three ways in which the linguistic analysis of syntax is used: to permit the discovery of patterns or common features in a text or group of texts, to help account for literary effects that otherwise might be difficult to explain, and to characterize special qualities of literary language.

At the level of syntax, as at the level of phonology, linguistics makes possible the perception of patterns by providing categories or terms with which to label the constituents of a text. For example, an analysis of transitivity in English that makes "goal" an important category enables Ruqaiya Hasan to note that the ten major clauses of William Butler Yeats's poem "The Old Men Admiring Themselves in the Water" have in common the absence of any item functioning as goal (see "Rime and Reason in Literature," in Chatman, *Literary Style*, pp. 299–326).

The use of transformational grammar to describe literary style, mentioned above, can also be placed under this heading. Richard Ohmann attempted to discover which transformations, among those identified by transformational grammar at a certain stage, are responsible for the distinctively Faulknerian style of a passage like the following:

> the desk and the shelf above it on which rested the ledgers in which McCaslin recorded the slow outward trickle of food and supplies and equipment which returned each fall as cotton made and ginned and sold (two threads frail as truth and impalpable as equators yet cable-strong to bind for life them who made the cotton to the land their sweat fell on), and the older ledgers clumsy and archaic in size and shape, on the yellowed pages of which were recorded in the faded hand of his father Theophilus and his uncle Amodeus during the two decades before the Civil War, the manumission in title at least of Carothers McCaslin's slave. . . .

Ohmann decides that three transformations that "are somewhat similar, both formally and semantically," are crucial to the effect of the passage: the relative clause transformation, the conjunction transformation, and the comparative transformation. If these three transformations are deleted from a paragraph by Ernest Hemingway, on the other hand, the passage "still sounds very much like Hemingway," as we can see:

> So his mother prayed for him. Then they stood up. Krebs kissed his mother. Krebs went out of the house. He had tried so to keep his life from being complicated. Still, none of it had touched him. He had felt sorry for his mother. She had made him lie. He would to go Kansas City. He would get a job. She would feel all right about it. There would be one more scene maybe before he got away. He would not go down to his father's office. He would miss that one. He wanted his life to go smoothly. It had just gotten going that way. Well, that was all over now, anyway. He would go over to the schoolyard. He would watch Helen play indoor baseball.

This experiment leads Ohmann to conclude that these three transformations do indeed play a role in creating a distinctively Faulknerian style ("Generative Grammars and the Concept of Literary Style," in Freeman, *Linguistics and Literary Style,* pp. 258-78). The account of transformations that Ohmann used has been superseded in transformational grammar, but his project shows how syntactic theory may help to reveal patterns characteristic of a text.

Syntactic categories can also be used to help explain effects that have been experienced by the reader or critic but that may remain mysterious without some pertinent linguistic information. Here linguistics is not so much a method of analysis as a reservoir of information about language, some of which may prove suggestive in a given case. Consider, for example, the problem of Yeats's "Leda and the Swan." Although the poem speaks of a violent event, it often strikes readers as distanced from the violence, as if it were describing a painting of the scene rather than the event itself:

A sudden blow: the great wings beating still
Above the staggering girl, her thighs caressed
By the dark webs, her nape caught in his bill,
He holds her helpless breast upon his breast.

How can those terrified vague fingers push
The feathered glory from her loosening thighs?
And how can body, laid in that white rush,
But feel the strange heart beating where it lies?

Linguistics can help in two ways to account for the effects of the passage (see Halliday, "Descriptive Linguistics in Literary Studies," in Freeman, *Linguistics and Literary Style*, pp. 57-72). First, it can note that definite articles in English enter three relations: anaphoric, where the context or preceding discourse indicates which entity is referred to (e.g., *the house,* where we already know what house); cataphoric, where a modifier or qualifier in the noun phrase distinguishes the object (*the red house,* as opposed to other houses); and homophoric, where we are dealing with the class identified by the noun (*The penguin* is a strange bird). In English when a noun with a definite article is accompanied by a qualifier or modifier, it is highly probable that *the* will be cataphoric, but in the stanzas from "Leda and the Swan" all five definite articles appear in phrases with modifiers or qualifiers and yet all are anaphoric rather than cataphoric. That is to say, "the great wings" does not pick out the *great* wings as opposed to the *small* wings. The definite articles all refer back to some antecedent; they take for granted a prior identification, a scene or situation already known, which their phrases help to characterize. It is as if they were saying, "the great wings in the picture." Halliday notes, "the only other type of writing I can call to mind in which this feature is found at such a high density is in tourist guides and, sometimes, exhibition catalogues."

Second, there is the matter of verbs. One way of describing many English sentences is to say that one or more propositions have been embedded in another, and when this happens the verbs of those embedded propositions either become verbs of subordinate clauses or else lose some of their verbal qualities as they are rankshifted into noun phrases ("the great wings *beating* still") or even made to function as adjectives in nominal groups ("the *staggering* girl," which can be seen as an embedded version of the proposition *the girl staggers*). In the first eight lines of "Leda and the Swan" there are three main verbs (*hold, push,* and *feel*) and then, on a scale of deverbalization, one finite verb in a subordinate clause (*lies*), five verbs shifted into noun phrases (*beating, caressed, caught, laid,* and *beating*), and finally two that function as adjectives in nominal groups (*staggering, loosening*).

What is striking here, says Halliday, is not just that so many verbs have been deverbalized but that the main verbs are those with least lexical power. An item is lexically powerful when its range of probable collocation is restricted — when it is associated with a small range of probable combinations (thus, *addled* is lexically powerful, since it is usually applied only to eggs and brains; *strangle* is lexically more powerful than *kill*). As Halliday says, in "Leda" "the more powerful of the verbal lexical items are items of violence, and it is precisely these that perform nominal rather than verbal roles." The main verb of the first stanza is *holds*, which gives us a static picture, with all the action shifted into noun phrases. The effect becomes more palpable if we consider an alternative version of the stanza, where these verbs are changed into unbound finite forms and *holds* is subordinated:

A sudden blow. The great wings beat above
The girl. She staggers. The dark webs caress
Her thighs. Holding her helpless breast upon
His breast, he catches her nape in his bill

One can certainly describe the differences between these two versions of the stanza without any linguistic training, but a critic unacquainted with linguistics might not have been led to reflect systematically on the deployment of verbs and definite articles in the poem or might have lacked the machinery to make such reflection productive.

The final use of syntactic analysis is in the attempt to describe the peculiarities of literary language. Here the goal is not to elucidate particular texts, although those working in this area will recognize forms or constructions that they might not otherwise have noticed in the works they read. One goal would be to produce a systematic description of the kinds of constructions that seem peculiar to narrative. In English there is an unusual first-person form, *I says*, and a present tense used with past adverbials: "Yesterday this guy comes into the bar, and I says to him. . . ." Other constructions, such as "over it went" or "down it came" also imply a context of storytelling (see Pratt, *Toward a Speech Act Theory . . .* , p. 50).

More attention has been devoted to constructions like the following, discussed by Käte Hamburger: "Aber am Vormittag hatte sie den Baum zu putzen. *Morgen war Weihnachten*" 'But in the morning she had to trim the tree. Tomorrow was Christmas.'[8] Narrative frequently combines certain past tenses with deictics that do not ordinarily designate a past. Deictics are orientational features of language that involve a reference to the moment or situation of enunciation (*I* means the person speaking, *tomorrow* is the day following the speech event, etc.). The linguist Emile Benveniste, working on French, distinguished elements belonging to the system of *histoire* (notably the *passé simple*), from those belonging to the system of *discours* (where there is always reference to a moment of enunciation).[9] Unusual combinations of elements from these systems seem to occur in narration and linguistics must describe and above all delimit these possibilities.

In *Morgen war Weihnachten* or *Tomorrow the axe would fall*, the past tense seems to locate the moment of enunciation invoked by the deictics in the past, when it becomes not so much a moment of enunciation as a moment of thought or consciousness. *Morgen war Weihnachten* suggests that at a time in the past someone was thinking that the next day, which for them is tomorrow, will be Christmas. Thus, this unusual combination of tense and deictic ought to be grouped with other odd syntactic combinations that imply a moment of consciousness different from the moment of enunciation. The following examples from Flaubert and Emile Zola seem similar in this respect, though only the first involves a temporal adverb: "De l'autre côté de la rue, sur le trottoir, un emballeur on manches de chemise clouait une caisse. *Maintenant* des fiacres passaient." ("Across the street, on the sidewalk, a packer in shirt sleeves was nailing a crate. Now carriages were passing.") "Catherine ne put que giffler son frère, la petite galopait déjà avec une bouteille. *Ces satanés* enfants finiraient au bagne." ("Catherine had to slap her brother; the little girl was already running around with a bottle. Those damned children would end up in jail.") Sentences like these, which imply that they are transmitting the thought or perception of a character, are usually called *style indirect libre* (also *erlebte Rede* or *free indirect speech*). The attempt to describe the linguistic features of *style indirect libre*, which has been fruitfully pursued by a number of linguists and critics, would also encompass the problem of past tenses and deictics and is best thought of as a systematic analysis of distinctive aspects of literary language.[10]

A final application of syntactic theory to literature has been the attempt to work out how to characterize certain highly ungrammatical literary sequences, such as e.e. cummings' "he danced his didn't, he danced his did." It is not enough to label such sentences ungrammatical, for when one encounters them in poems one gives them a grammatical structure and a meaning that results in part from that grammatical structure. There have been various theories about what that structure should be and how one should describe cummings' modification of the rules of grammar (see Thorne, "Stylistics and Generative Grammars," in Freeman, *Linguistics and Literary Style*, pp. 182–96), but unlike the problem of deictics, tenses, and *style indirect libre*, what we have here is an attempt to describe linguistically the particular deviations of a given author, not to produce a grammar of literary discourse.

4. *Semantics and Lexicon*

One important division of classical rhetoric was diction, to which the lexicological study of linguistic register is perhaps the closest modern analogue. Sensitivity to register is essential to anyone studying literature, which frequently comments on this aspect of language:

> Therefore, you clown, abandon — which is in the vulgar leave — the society — which in the boorish is company — of this female — which in the common is woman — which together is: abandon the society of this female; or clown, thou perishest; or to thy better understanding, diest; or to wit, I kill thee, make thee away, translate thy life into death. (*As You Like It* V.i.45–51)

A comprehensive and subtle description of register would clearly assist anyone trying to distinguish period styles or to characterize in systematic fashion the vocabulary of an author, but so far critics have generally not found reason to substitute the linguist's categories for their own.

Semantics, the study of meaning, is potentially of greater relevance, but the difficulties of semantics have so far proved resilient, and most semantic theories are too crude to assist in the description of subtle literary effects. Thus, an ambitious and perspicacious attempt by the linguist and critic Samuel Levin to develop an account of metaphor based on possible-world semantics may succeed for his preferred example, *the stone died*, but proves disappointing when applied to literature (Levin, *The Semantics of Metaphor*; see also Eco, *The Role of the Reader*).

An example of a different kind is A. J. Greimas's comprehensive semantic theory, which seeks to provide all the concepts necessary for describing the semantic structure of complete texts. These include a theory of semantic features organized according to basic oppositional structures (*le carré sémantique*); an account of the way in which the *isotopies* or levels of coherence established in a text lead to the selection of some semantic features and the suppression of others, thus guiding the establishment of signification; a semantically based scheme of six basic interrelated roles (*le modèle actantiel*) in terms of which sentences, episodes, and basic plot structures are said to be organized; and finally a set of *programmes narratifs* based on the fundamental ways of relating to the world that underlie the system of verbs. Much Greimasian semantic analysis of a text, however, is devoted to working out the semantic structures of its universe by articulating correlations and oppositions that appear in the work upon basic cultural ("axiological") structures. At one point, for example, Greimas compares a structure discovered in Guy de Maupassant with one discovered in Georges Bernanos.

In this diagram the four-way relation *vie* : *mort* :: *non-mort* : *non-vie* is an organization of values on the basic "semantic square": in each author various elements are differently associated with these values (Greimas, *Maupassant*, p. 141):

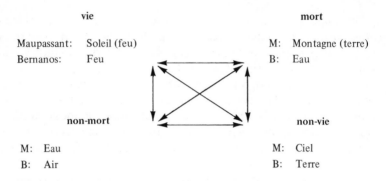

	vie		mort
Maupassant:	Soleil (feu)	M:	Montagne (terre)
Bernanos:	Feu	B:	Eau

	non-mort		non-vie
M:	Eau	M:	Ciel
B:	Air	B:	Terre

Though there are reasons to think that Greimas's semantics does not achieve all that he claims for it (see my *Structuralist Poetics*), it is certain that texts do have semantic structure and that accounting for this structure or structures is one of the tasks of semantic theory.

IV

The preceding examples, which are only indicative rather than representative, involve the direct application of linguistic description to the language of literature rather than the use of linguistics as a general methodological model for a poetics or a semiotics. If these examples demonstrate the possibility of a relation between linguistics and literature, they nevertheless leave us with a problem about the nature of that relation. Much of the attraction of linguistics for literary critics is that, while literary perceptions and judgments are frequently said to be subjective, linguistics seems to offer the possibility of objective description and analysis, independent of any literary judgments. The critic might hope that an objective linguistic analysis of a poem or a passage would offer a sound basis on which to erect literary interpretations.

This ideal seems difficult to attain. Insofar as linguistic description is carried out as an autonomous activity, without regard to judgments of literary importance, it courts irrelevance and excess. The detailed analysis of the sound patterns of a sonnet, for example, would be a massive undertaking if one tried to include every possible relation, each repetition of a distinctive feature. (Indeed, this is one of the criticisms leveled at Jakobson's analyses, that they could go on forever and cannot distinguish the important from the unimportant.) Yet insofar as one does make literary decisions about what to focus on or what relations are relevant, one compromises the scientific independence that made linguistics attractive in the first place. Thus a major virtue of linguistics seems inseparable from a major failing.

Moreover, it is not clear that linguistic analysis could in any case be separated from literary judgments or interpretations so as eventually to provide independent confirmation of them. Again and again one can argue that literary judgments or interpretations have been and must be made before linguistic analysis. It is the reader's sense of the literary effect of "Morgen war Weihnachten" that leads the linguist, first, to treat it as more than an ungrammatical sentence and, second, to group it with other sentences involving some sort of represented speech or thought. It is the literary judgment that most of Chaucer's verses should be regarded as metrically well-formed that leads Halle and Keyser to propose rules to achieve this result. Ohmann's stylistic analysis depends on the literary judgment that a particular passage is typically Faulknerian and that when certain transformations are deleted it is no longer Faulknerian.

It may be, then, that our examples illustrate an interaction between linguistic analysis and literary perception which, though fruitful, is disappointing to those wishing to claim that certain conclusions or interpretations are justified because they are based on independent linguistic analysis. The relevance and the significance of that analysis can always be challenged, especially when one attempts to enlist it in the service of interpretation. Indeed, one might conclude that linguistics is not primarily a tool for interpretation of literary works, much less a method of "objective interpretation," but a body of knowledge to be drawn on when attempting to develop a systematic account of the functioning of literary language — a theory of meter, of sound patterns, of narrative syntax, of semantic coherence.

Here the application of linguistics to literature joins forces with the indirect use of linguistics as a model for a structuralist poetics or a semiotics of literature. Linguistics attempts to describe the elements of a language and their rules of combination; it is in effect describing the linguistic competence that enables speakers of a language to produce and understand sentences. A poetics or semiotics of literature, modeled on linguistics, would be a similar attempt to describe the various constituents of literature and their modes of combination and thus to characterize the literary competence that readers deploy when they read and understand a literary work. Study of the "grammar" of plot, for example, involves working out the constituents of plot and the rules of plot formation, so as to account for readers' judgments that certain sequences of actions do form a complete plot whereas other sequences are incomplete. Linguistics may continue to be a stimulus in this sort of research. Moreover, if linguistics succeeds in moving beyond the sentence and characterizing in a systematic way the linguistic relations that produce coherent discourses or texts, the results will be of interest to the critic and particularly to the student of poetics; but they will not be a panacea. Here too the relevance of linguistic categories will be a matter of debate and will depend on precisely what sort of project the critic undertakes.

In concluding we should give some kind of answer to the question about the relation between linguistics and literary studies that we posed at the beginning. If, "above everything else, poetry is words," what follows? The fact that poems are "made" of language does not mean that readers require a knowledge of linguistics, but those who are interested in studying literature as a signifying practice will find linguistics useful, especially in assisting them to undertake those general and systematic projects that are the heart of any discipline.

Notes

[1] Roman Jakobson, "Linguistics and Poetics," in Sebeok, ed., *Style in Language*, p. 350. Subsequent references to works listed in the bibliography will be given in parentheses in the text.

[2] "Linguistics and Literature: A Reply by F. W. Bateson," in Roger Fowler et al., *The Languages of Literature* (New York: Barnes, 1971), p. 26.

[3] William G. Moulton, "Linguistics," in *The Aims and Methods of Scholarship in Modern Languages and Literatures*, ed. James Thorpe, 2nd ed. (New York: MLA, 1970), p. 26.

[4] Dionysius Thrax, quoted in R. H. Robins, *A Short History of Linguistics* (London: Longmans, 1967), p. 31.

[5] Nicolas Ruwet, *Langage, musique, poésie* (Paris: Seuil, 1972), pp. 204–05.

[6] Edward Sapir, "Language as a Form of Human Behavior," *English Journal*, 16 (1927), 429.

[7] Roman Jakobson and Linda Waugh, *The Sound Shape of Language* (Bloomington: Indiana Univ. Press, 1979), p. 182.

[8] Käte Hamburger, *The Logic of Literature*, trans. Marilynn J. Rose (Bloomington: Indiana Univ. Press, 1973), p. 72. See W. J. M. Bronzwaer, *Tense in the Novel* (Groningen: Wolters-Noordhoff, 1970).

[9] Emile Benveniste, *Problèmes de linguistique générale* (Paris: Gallimard, 1966), pp. 258–66.

[10] On *style indirect libre* see Ann Banfield, "Narrative Style and the Grammar of Direct and Indirect Speech," *Foundations of Language*, 10 (1973), 1–39.

Bibliography

Adam, Jean-Michel. *Linguistique et discours littéraire*. Paris: Larousse, 1976. Discusses and illustrates a range of theories, primarily French.

Bailey, Richard W., and Dolores M. Burton. *English Stylistics: A Bibliography*. Cambridge: MIT Press, 1968. A full critical bibliography.

Bally, Charles. *Traité de stylistique française*. 2 vols. 1905; rpt. Geneva: Georg, 1963. A pioneering work in stylistics.

Bronzwaer, W. J. M. *Tense in the Novel: An Investigation of Some Potentialities of Linguistic Criticism*. Groningen: Wolters-Noordhoff, 1970. A full discussion of time and tense in fiction.

Chatman, Seymour, ed. *Literary Style: A Symposium*. New York: Oxford Univ.

Press, 1971. An excellent anthology, the product of a symposium of linguists and literary critics.

————. *A Theory of Meter*. The Hague: Mouton, 1965. A theory based on work in linguistics.

————, and Samuel Levin, eds. *Essays on the Language of Literature*. Boston: Houghton, 1967. An important anthology, emphasizing sound texture, meter, and grammar.

Culler, Jonathan. *Structuralist Poetics: Structuralism, Linguistics, and the Study of Literature*. Ithaca, N.Y.: Cornell Univ. Press, 1975. A critical survey of the role of linguistics in the literary studies of the French structuralists.

Davie, Donald. *Articulate Energy: An Inquiry into the Syntax of English Poetry*. London: Routledge and Kegan Paul, 1955. Studies emphasizing the effects of different kinds of syntax in poetry.

Dubois, Jacques, et al. *Rhétorique générale*. Paris: Larousse, 1970. An attempt to redefine rhetorical figures in modern linguistic terms.

Ducrot, Oswald, and Tzvetan Todorov. *Dictionnaire encyclopédique des sciences du langage*. Paris: Seuil, 1972. English edition: *Encyclopedic Dictionary of the Sciences of Language*. Trans. Catherine Porter. Baltimore: Johns Hopkins Univ. Press, 1979. Includes authoritative articles on many aspects of this topic.

Eco, Umberto. *The Role of the Reader: Explorations in the Semiotics of Texts*. Bloomington: Indiana Univ. Press, 1979. Essays by an eminent semiotician.

Eikhenbaum, B. M. *Melodika russkogo liricheskogo stikha*. Petrograd: Opoiaz, 1922. Studies the role of intonation in verse organization.

Erlich, Victor. *Russian Formalism: History-Doctrine*. 3rd ed. The Hague: Mouton, 1969. The standard account of the work of this school.

Fónagy, Ivan. *Die Metaphern in der Phonetik*. The Hague: Mouton, 1963. Includes an important discussion of the bases of sound symbolism.

Fowler, Roger. *Linguistics and the Novel*. London: Methuen, 1977. An introductory essay using very little formal linguistics.

Freeman, Donald C., ed. *Linguistics and Literary Style*. New York: Holt, 1970. A well-chosen anthology.

Greimas, A. J. *Maupassant: La sémiotique du texte*. Paris: Seuil, 1976. Application of Greimas's semantic theory to the detailed analysis of a short story.

Halle, Morris, and Samuel J. Keyser. *English Stress: Its Form, Its Growth, and Its Role in Verse*. New York: Harper, 1971. Develops a theory of meter based on transformational-generative grammar.

Halliday, M. A. K. *Explorations in the Functions of Language*. London: Edward Arnold, 1973. Essays outline Halliday's functional theory of language and apply it to literature.

Ihwe, Jens. *Linguistik in der Literaturwissenschaft: Zur Entwicklung einer modernen Theorie der Literaturwissenschaft*. Munich: Bayerischer Schulbuch-Verlag, 1972. An attempt to work out a system of rules, comparable to those of a generative grammar, for the generation and analysis of literature.

Jakobson, Roman. *Questions de poétique*. Paris: Seuil, 1973. A collection of his linguistic analysis of literature.

Leech, Geoffrey N. *A Linguistic Guide to English Poetry*. London: Longman, 1969. An excellent introduction to linguistic devices in poetry.

Levin, Samuel. *Linguistic Structures in Poetry*. The Hague: Mouton, 1962. Describes a series of linguistic devices or techniques.

————. *The Semantics of Metaphor*. Baltimore: Johns Hopkins Univ. Press, 1977. Applies linguistics and work in the philosophy of language to the description of metaphor.

Lotman, Juri M. *Analiz poeticheskogo teksta: Struktura stikha.* Leningrad: Prosveshchenie, 1970. English edition: *Analysis of the Poetic Text.* Trans. and ed. D. Barton Johnson. Ann Arbor, Mich.: Ardis, 1976. A semiotic approach to poetry with specimen analyses.

Matejka, Ladislav, and Kristina Pomorska, eds. *Readings in Russian Poetics: Formalist and Structuralist Views.* Cambridge: MIT Press, 1971. An anthology of linguistically inspired work on literature.

Mukarovsky, Jan. *The Word and Verbal Art: Selected Essays.* Trans. and ed. John Burbank and Peter Steiner. New Haven: Yale Univ. Press, 1977. The most important essays on linguistics and literature by the leading member of the Prague School.

Pratt, Mary Louise. *Toward a Speech Act Theory of Literary Discourse.* Bloomington: Indiana Univ. Press, 1977. Uses the work of Austin, Searle, Grice, and Labov to describe literature.

Sebeok, Thomas A., ed. *Style in Language.* Cambridge: MIT Press, 1960. Papers from an important interdisciplinary conference.

Smith, Barbara Herrnstein. *On the Margins of Discourse: The Relation of Literature to Language.* Chicago: Univ. of Chicago Press, 1978. Criticizes applications of linguistics to literature and proposes a functional theory of literature.

Spitzer, Leo. *Linguistics and Literary History.* Princeton: Princeton Univ. Press, 1948. Influential essays in stylistics.

Tynianov, Jurij. *Problema stikhotvornogo jazyka.* Leningrad, 1924; rpt. The Hague: Mouton, 1963. On problems of poetic language.

Uitti, Karl. *Linguistics and Literary Theory.* Englewood Cliffs, N.J.: Prentice-Hall, 1969. A historical survey.

Ullmann, Stephen. *Language and Style.* Oxford: Blackwell, 1964. A judicious survey of stylistics.

Van Dijk, Teun A. *Some Aspects of Text Grammars: A Study in Theoretical Linguistics and Poetics.* The Hague: Mouton, 1972. A highly technical proposal for expanding grammars to encompass the generation of texts.

Zholkovskij, Alexandr K., and Jurij Shcheglov. *K opisaniyu smysla svyaznogo teksta*, I–VIII. Moscow: Institut russkogo jazyka AN, predvaritel'nye publikacii, 1971–78. English edition: I, "Towards 'Theme-(Expression Devices)-Text' Model of Literary Structure." In L. M. O'Toole and A. Shukman, eds. *Russian Poetics in Translation*, 1 (1975), 4–50. II, "The Poetic Structure of a Maxim by La Rochefoucauld: An Essay in *Theme-Text* Poetics," *PTL*, 3 (1978). 549–92. An attempt to describe systematically the processes by which themes are given poetically expressive linguistic form.

2

Literature and Philosophy

Thomas McFarland

"Philosophy," said Cicero in *De Officiis*, is "the study of wisdom." A "philosopher," he said in *De Oratore*, is one "who strives to know the significance, nature and causes of everything divine or human, and to master and follow out as a whole the theory of right living." Whether we accept these definitions as our base or prefer to supply others, it should be apparent that of all the cultural activities to which the study of literature, and literature itself, can relate, philosophy is perhaps the most important. The relation is also probably the most problematic and, in terms of clear and distinct formulation, historically the most encumbered of all those that arise from literary concerns. Declarations of a community of aims alternate with declarations of a separation of aims. "Do not all charms fly," asked the poet John Keats, "at the mere touch of cold philosophy?"; but the poet-philosopher Samuel Taylor Coleridge asserted unequivocally that "no man was ever yet a great poet without being at the same time a profound philosopher."

As with so many problems, the primary nexus here is to be found in Plato, and in truth almost all the subsequent permutations of this paradoxical relation can be seen—the phrase is Alfred North Whitehead's—as a series of footnotes to Plato. Plato not only evicted the mimetic poets from his ideal commonwealth (*Republic* 595A, et seq.) but provided the absolute formula of "a quarrel between philosophy and poetry" *(διαφορὰ φιλοσοφία τε καὶ ποιητικῇ* [607D]). In other places, however, notably in the *Ion* and the *Phaedrus*, Plato speaks of poetry's large possibilities and, in the latter dialogue, even says that a poet who conforms to certain criteria can be called by the name "philosopher" (278C–D); he says also that "all great arts demand discussion and high speculation about nature" (269E).

The paradox of Plato's attitude toward poetry and philosophy carries over into historical attitudes toward Plato himself. Thus Giovanni Boccaccio, in his *Genealogia Deorum Gentilium* (c. 1371), refuses to accept Plato's rejection of the poets. The authority of Plato, he says, does not license an attack on poets, for Plato has been misinterpreted: "I can only believe that great poets and their kind are to be rightly regarded not as merely citizens of

25

his state and all others, but as the princes and rulers thereof" (trans. Charles C. Osgood). Even more influentially, Sir Philip Sidney, in his *Defence of Poesie* (1595), says that "truly even *Plato* who so ever well considereth, shall finde that in the body of his worke though the inside & strength were Philosophie, the skin as it were and beautie, depended most of Poetrie." Sidney must concede, however, that Plato is also, at least on the surface, the chief opponent of poetry: "And lastly and chiefly, they cry out with open mouth as if they had overshot *Robinhood*, that *Plato* banished them out of his Commonwealth. Truly this is much, if there be much truth in it. . . . But now indeede my burthen is great, that *Plato* his name is laide uppon mee, whom I must confesse of all *Philosophers*, I have ever esteemed most worthie of reverence; and with good reason, since of all *Philosophers* hee is the most *Poeticall*." But, like Boccaccio, Sidney ultimately refuses to accept Plato's rejection of the poets: "*Plato* . . . in his Dialogue called *Ion*, giveth high, and rightly divine commendation unto *Poetrie*. So as *Plato* banishing the abuse, not the thing, not banishing it, but giving due honour to it, shall be our Patron, and not our adversarie." Elsewhere in the same essay, Sidney invokes the language of Aristotle to insist that poetry is "more serious and more philosophical" than history.

Leaving aside the possible answers to the question of why Plato was inimical to poetry,[1] we may see in the rubric itself, "Literature and Philosophy," the seeds of a paradox. First of all, the term "literature" is so large and inchoate that it sometimes needs to be focused as "poetry" — as we have done above — but in other contexts seems to be so small that it must be expanded, under the term "art," to include such things as painting and music.

Secondly, the term "philosophy" can imply different standpoints and different pertinences to different minds. Modern usages tend to limit the reference intended by "philosophy," and older ones tend to expand it. In our own century, the dominant traditions of philosophy have divided along a watershed consisting roughly of positivist/analytic conceptions, on the one hand, and phenomenological/existential conceptions, on the other. Of these two main categories only the second one has much relevance to literature. The positivists were interested in radically reducing, not expanding, the philosophical realm; and in the generation after the First World War this movement devoted much of its energy to a polemic against those evanescences and ambiguities of imagination and feeling with which literary art is characteristically engaged. The goals sought by the positivist cast of mind were rigor and scientific accuracy; "philosophy," summarized A. J. Ayer, "is a department of logic." So conceived, philosophy could have no very rich or urgent connection with literary art.

Still another consideration that maintains the "quarrel between philosophy and poetry" is the existence of psychological needs that work against the mingling of fields. "We have got the world divided into boxes," as José Ortega y Gasset laments, and one trend in modern cultural life is quite content to think of "literature" and "philosophy" as separate boxes. A revealing example of this tendency in a literary-critical mind of high distinction is F. R. Leavis' statement in *The Common Pursuit* (1952) of his understanding of his literary role: "If I profess myself so freely to be no philosopher it is because I feel that I can afford my modesty; it is because I have pretensions — pretensions to being a literary critic." He continues:

> Literary criticism and philosophy seem to me to be quite distinct and different kinds of discipline — at least, I think they ought to be (for while in my innocence I hope that philosophic writing commonly represents a serious discipline, I am quite sure that literary-critical writing commonly doesn't). This is not to suggest that a literary critic might not, as such, be the better for a philosophic training, but if he were, the advantage, I believe, would manifest itself partly in a surer realization that literary criticism is not philosophy.

If we take Leavis as a powerful representative of the systolic motion by which the concerns of literature are separated from those of philosophy, we could take Coleridge ("Coleridge's pre-eminence we all recognize," concedes Leavis) as a representative of the diastolic movement by which literature and philosophy tend to merge their interests. Thus Coleridge asks a correspondent in 1796, "Why so violent against *metaphysics* in poetry?" Coleridge's question suggests but hardly reveals how deeply he was committed to the mingling of the two areas of cultural activity. He reverenced Plato as "a poetic philosopher" and Shakespeare as "a philosophic poet," and he said that "from Shakespeare to Plato, from the philosophic poet to the poetic philosopher, the transition is easy." He sought always "that delightful harmony, which ever will be found where philosophy is united . . . with poetry." The true poetic "Whole" is one where "the Thinker and the Man of Learning appears as the Base of the Poet." A "great Poet must be, implicitè if not explicitè, a profound Metaphysician."

Coleridge was even more insistent on the reciprocal necessity of poetry and philosophy in his view of William Wordsworth. Wordsworth, he says, "is a Poet . . . he will hereafter be admitted as the first & greatest philosophical Poet — the only man who has effected a compleat and constant synthesis of Thought & Feeling and combined them with Poetic Forms." Of Wordsworth's unfinished poem *The Recluse*, Coleridge wrote that "I expected the Colors, Music, imaginative Life, and Passion of *Poetry* but the matter and arrangement of *Philosophy* — not doubting . . . that the Totality of a System was not only capable of being harmonized with, but even calculated to aid the unity of a *Poem*." "How shall he fully enjoy Wordsworth," asks Coleridge, "who has never meditated on the truths which Wordsworth has wedded to immortal verse?" Of a portrait of Wordsworth painted by William Hazlitt, Coleridge wrote Wordsworth:

> Sir G[eorge Beaumont] & his wife both say, that the Picture gives them an idea of you as a profound strong-minded Philosopher, not as a Poet — I answered (& I believe, truly —) that so it must needs do, if it

were a good Portrait — for that you were a great Poet by inspirations & in the Moments of revelation, but that you were a thinking feeling Philosopher habitually — that your Poetry was your Philosophy under the action of strong winds of Feeling — a sea rolling high.

It might be useful to follow this track a little further, because Wordsworth elicits the full range of paradox that inheres in the relation in whatever forms, theoretical or practical, that can occur. Thus, despite Coleridge's unequivocal endorsement of Wordsworth's work as a combining of philosophy and poetry, Matthew Arnold, in a consideration of the same materials, moves toward a separation of poetry and philosophy:

> The Wordsworthians are apt to praise him for the wrong things, and to lay far too much stress upon what they call his philosophy. His poetry is the reality, his philosophy . . . is the illusion. Perhaps we shall one day learn to make this proposition general, and to say: Poetry is the reality, philosophy the illusion. But in Wordworth's case, at any rate, we cannot do him justice until we dismiss his formal philosophy.[2]

In such contradictory assessments, however, we should not think of one attitude as being true in the sense that the other set is false. In fact the alternatives are not even characterized by the law of excluded middle, for A. C. Bradley in effect has it both ways, declaring that Wordsworth both is and is not a subject of philosophical as well as literary relevance. Almost in the same breath in which he rejects the contention that "Wordsworth was first and foremost a philosophical thinker . . . " and points out that though Wordsworth "reflected deeply and acutely, he was without philosophical training," Bradley asserts, "His poetry is immensely interesting as an imaginative expression of the same mind which, in his day, produced in Germany great philosophies. His poetic experience, his intuitions, his single thoughts, even his large views, correspond in a striking way, sometimes in a startling way, with ideas methodically developed by Kant, Schelling, Hegel, Schopenhauer."

These heterogeneous opinions, in all their variety, are legitimate views attendant on differences in cultural perspective. Such differences, each valid but each revealing different priorities for attention, point us to further truths about the relation of literature to philosophy. First of all, the schematizing of such differences shows us that the two areas of cultural concern, though not identical, are not fundamentally disparate either. Instead of forming two essentially incompatible areas of discourse, they make up, so to speak, a continuum; one can slide along the base of this continuum to the extreme limit of, say, mathematical logic or philosophy of science, and at this limit one is far removed from literary concerns. For if philosophy is contiguous to literature on one of its perimeters, it borders science on another. If thinking humans move back from the outer edge of logical science, however, they increasingly find the relevances of literature entering their ken; and, crossing the middle of the continuum, they begin to see, not the world of literature from the perspective of philosophy, but the world of philosophy from the perspective of literature. At the extreme limit going this other direction, literature seems far removed from philosophy, which can be discerned only faintly and sometimes not at all; at this boundary the hegemony of purely literary or artistic preoccupations emerges in such formulas as "l'art pour l'art," or, in the title of Bradley's inaugural lecture for the Chair of Poetry at Oxford in 1901, "Poetry for Poetry's Sake."

The continuum of poetry and philosophy as such is constituted by a common interest and an intensely human need: the understanding of life. "Ars est enim philosophia vitae" 'for philosophy is the art of life,' says Cicero (*De Finibus* III.ii). And the old adage, "primum vivere, deinde philosophari" 'first live, then philosophize,' certainly could hold true for literature as well as for philosophy. "Poetry is at bottom a criticism of life," says Arnold, and of Wordsworth he says that "he deals with *life*, because he deals with that in which life really consists." "Where then, is Wordsworth's superiority? It is here; he deals with more of *life* than they do; he deals with *life*, as a whole, more powerfully."

Though poetry and philosophy are different ways of attempting to understand the mystery of life (philosophy begins in wonder, say both Plato and Aristotle [*Theaetetus* 155D; *Metaphysics* 982^{b}10–20]), the fact that they are contiguous cultural areas allows for a certain realm of interpenetration, a borderland whose inhabitants speak both languages as native languages.

Coleridge was one of these inhabitants. But he was by no means the only one. Indeed, Ernst Cassirer has urged that "to poeticize philosophy and to philosophize poetry — such was the highest aim of all romantic thinkers." Among formal philosophers, none was more insistent than Friedrich Schelling on asserting the common interest of poetry and philosophy. Thus, in a memorable passage at the conclusion of his *System des transzendentalen Idealismus* (1800), he says that

> art is the only true and eternal organ and document of philosophy; it always and continually proclaims anew what philosophy cannot outwardly represent, namely, the unconscious in productive activity and its original identity with the conscious. Just for this reason art is for the philosopher the apex, because it reveals to him, as it were, the Holy of Holies, where in eternal and original union burns in one flame what in nature and history is sundered, and what in life and action, just as in thought, must eternally flee itself. . . .
>
> If, however, it is art alone that can succeed in making objective, with universal validity, that which the philosopher can represent only subjectively, then it is to be expected, as a corollary, that just as in the childhood of knowledge, philosophy (and also all those disciplines that

are brought to fulfillment through philosophy) was born from and nourished by poetry, so, after its maturity, it will flow back as so many individual streams into the universal ocean of poetry.

Many other figures of that era concurred in such attitudes. "The poetic philosopher, the philosophizing poet is a prophet," says Friedrich Schlegel. "That which can be done as long as philosophy and poetry are separated," he writes again, "is done and completed. Therefore the time has come to unite them both." And he hails Novalis: "Thou dost not hover on the border, but in thy spirit have poetry and philosophy inwardly mingled." For his part, Novalis says that "the transcendental poesy is compounded of philosophy and poetry." "The separation of poet and thinker is only apparent," he added, "and to the disadvantage of both." Such opinions were not confined to German literati. "Plato was essentially a poet," writes Percy Bysshe Shelley, ". . . Lord Bacon was a poet. . . . Shakespeare, Dante, and Milton (to confine ourselves to modern writers) are philosophers of the very loftiest power."

Though the Romantic era tended, in both theory and practice, to mingle poetry and philosophy (Alfred de Vigny, Alphonse de Lamartine, and Victor Hugo could be added as examples from French literature; Giacomo Leopardi, from Italian), such intermingling is not restricted to that epoch; the contiguity of the two realms of thought dictates that in every era there will be at least some who occupy their borderland. Thus, to take an instance virtually at random, Boccaccio, in the treatise quoted earlier, says that "one can never escape the conviction that great men, nursed with the milk of the muses, brought up in the very home of philosophy, and disciplined in sacred studies, have laid away the very deepest meaning in their poems." Of some lines in the *Aeneid* he says:

This is poetry from which the sap of philosophy runs pure. Then is any reader so muddled as not to see clearly that Virgil was a philosopher. . . . Again, let any man consider our own poet Dante as he often unties with amazingly skillful demonstration the hard knots of holy theology; will such a one be so insensible as not to perceive that Dante was a great theologian as well as philosopher?[3]

The way in which the interests of philosophy can combine with those of poetry (or, to broaden the term to include such forms as novels and dramas, of literature) is twofold. It can either be as a body of thought rendered in the language of a poem — Alexander Pope's *Essay on Man* or Leopardi's *Operette morali*, for instance — or it can be as a poetic or literary statement that engages questions of meaning and being. Here we might think of Wallace Stevens' *Sunday Morning*, or Rainer Maria Rilke's *Duineser Elegien*, or Marcel Proust's *A la recherche du temps perdu*, or Fedor Dostoevsky's *The Brothers Karamazov*, or Shakespeare's *Hamlet*. That examples of the second possibility flock so readily to mind indicates that the latter form of philosophical complication is the one most consonant with great literature; and it is the existence of this second kind of philosophical-literary relation that allows Leavis, and all those who wish to see literary activity defined independently of formal philosophical activity, to stand on solid ground. Perhaps as good a formulation of this second possibility as any is William Carlos Williams' pronouncement: "The poet thinks with his poem, in that lies his thought, and that in itself is the profundity."

Williams here enunciates an irrefragable truth. It is possible to be a literary artist, and a significant one, without an overt interest in the world of formal philosophy; and it is also possible to be a significant philosopher without an interest in literature. One can be a poet without a theory of poetry; one can even be a critic without a theory of literature. Theory, indeed, at least in a literary ambience, is at its best always retrospective, not prescriptive. Literary figures of the seventeenth and eighteenth centuries tried to generate forms of literature—the epic, for instance—out of a prescriptive theory of genre, but their efforts for the most part resulted in either the nugatory or the burlesque.

But if the most admired way of mingling philosophy and literature is to have perspectives on being arise from the work of art as such, it is nevertheless true that the way of mingling philosophy and literature in which a body of thought is clothed in literary form also stands on firm historical ground. Schelling at one time meditated the presentation of his philosophy in the form of a poem, and Coleridge proposed to convey his own thought in the shape of a vast poem to be called "The Brook" and at another time thought of incorporating it into a novel. That neither thinker carried through may show that such enterprise is not feasible, but cultural entities like Sir Richard Blackmore's *Creation: A Philosophical Poem* or Vigny's *Poèmes philosophiques* or Shelley's *Queen Mab: A Philosophical Poem* do exist. Plato's dialogues themselves are forms of dramatic art as well as treatises of philosophy. The *Bhagavadgita*, which is a dialogue between Arjuna and Krishna about the nature of reality and about the meaning of human action, is ineluctably a poem. Its body of thought, however, is separable and, on its own terms, occupies a major place in the history of philosophy. Similarly, the *Hymn to Zeus* of Cleanthes is a standard document in the history of Stoic philosophy, while the *De Rerum Natura* of Lucretius is avowedly a vehicle for the philosophy of Epicurus at the same time that it is a major poetic artifact of Latin literature.

A poetic-philosophical complex such as *De Rerum Natura* can illustrate a second truth about the relation of literature to philosophy. As George Santayana observes, in his *Three Philosophical Poets: Lucretius, Dante, Goethe* (1910):

The intellect of Lucretius rises, but rises comparatively empty; his vision sees things as a whole, and in their right places, but sees very little of them; he is quite deaf to their intricacy, to their birdlike multiform little souls. . . . .It is necessary to revert from Lucretius to Goethe to get at the volume of life.

The "volume of life": this is the peculiar apprehension of literature as distinguished from philosophy. "We live in a world," writes John Crowe Ransom in *The New Criticism* (1941), "which must be distinguished from the world, or the worlds, for there are many of them, which we treat in our scientific discourses. They are its reduced, emasculated, and docile versions. Poetry intends to recover the denser and more refractory original world which we know loosely through our perceptions and memories."

Some such understanding, though its language varies with its context, is reached by everyone who thinks deeply about the characteristics of literary art. What provides literature a different cultural anchorage from philosophy is, as it were, a distinctive preoccupation with the "earthiness" of the earth. "A Poet's *Heart & Intellect*," says Coleridge, "should be *combined, intimately* combined & *unified* with the great appearances of Nature." Poetry, says Wallace Stevens, provides "contact with reality as it impinges on us from outside, the sense that we can touch and feel a solid reality which does not dissolve itself into the conceptions of our own minds." Philosophy, by contrast, anchors itself in the abstract. "The power of thinking the *general*," summarizes Novalis, "is the philosophical power; the power of thinking the particular, the poetic."

The abstractly general and the concretely particular, however, are not absolute separations; rather they are universally available possibilities in the structure of human attention. Like philosophy and literature, their vehicles of cultural expression, they constitute a continuum with a graded spectrum of shadings in their intensities. Some art looks from the immediate and particular to the abstract (the paintings of Willem de Kooning or Piet Mondrian, for instance), while some philosophy looks from the abstract to the more particular (pragmatism, possibly, or certain aspects of "ordinary language" analysis, or Thomas Reid's philosophy of common sense). It remains true, however, that the abstract and the concretely particular are the characteristic or fundamental domains of philosophy and literature respectively. Thus, to pursue this important distinction somewhat further, we may quote Cassirer:

Language and science are abbreviations of reality; art is an intensification of reality. Language and science depend upon one and the same process of abstraction; art may be described as a continuous process of concretion.

The description holds good when "philosophy" is substituted for "language and science." Accordingly, Leavis, in a controversy that caused him to formulate his views as to the separation of philosophy and literature, says at one point that the reading demanded by poetry is of a different kind from that demanded by philosophy. I should not find it easy to define the difference satisfactorily. . . . Philosophy, we say, is "abstract". . . and poetry "concrete." Words in poetry invite us, not to "think about" and judge but to "feel into" or "become" — to realize a complex experience that is given in the words. They demand, not merely a fuller-bodied response, but a completer responsiveness — a kind of responsiveness that is incompatible with the judicial, one-eye-on-the-standard approach. . . . The critic — the reader of poetry — is indeed concerned with evaluation, but to figure him as measuring with a norm which he brings up to the object and applies from the outside is to misrepresent the process.

From another standpoint and in different language, Benedetto Croce in his *Estetica* invokes the same criteria as Leavis does:

Knowledge has two forms; it is either *intuitive* knowledge or *logical* knowledge; knowledge obtained through the *imagination* or knowledge obtained through the *intellect*; knowledge of the *individual* or knowledge of the *universal*; of *individual things* or the *relations* between them: it is, in fact, productive either of *images* or of *concepts*.

From this beginning, Croce goes on to say that a

work of art may be full of philosophical concepts; it may contain them in greater abundance and they may there be even more profound than in a philosophical dissertation, which in its turn may be rich to overflowing with descriptions and intuitions. But notwithstanding all these concepts the total effect of the work of art is an intuition; and notwithstanding all those intuitions, the total effect of the philosophical dissertation is a concept.

Even if Croce and Leavis agree in their insistence on the "intuitive" or the "concrete" as the peculiar domain of poetry or art, their assertions are grounded in different realms of discourse. Croce's work is a contribution to the theory of *aesthetics* and Leavis' to the theory of *criticism*. Although it was argued above that critics do not need "theory," the limiting case for such an assertion is that they do not need it only when they stay strictly within the precincts of the individual work of art as a given object of attention. The moment they seek to connect their immediate activity with other human knowledge, or adjudicate the value of the immediate object in terms of other kinds of awareness, theory arises. It would not be difficult to show that Leavis, despite his avowal of the concrete and the particular, actually is a theorist of formidable, and even, especially during the latter portion of his life, "philosophical" coherence. And when a great practicing artist like Leo Tolstoy wishes to ask the question "What is art?" this eternally legitimate query plunges him willy-nilly into theory, so much so that his specific answers involve him in a broad-gauge account of the whole history of European aesthetic theory. As often as theory is dismissed by the particular-minded, it is generated again.

So both the philosopher and the artist formulate theory, even if from different perspectives and for different ends. The two terms *aesthetics* and *critical theory* (or *theory of literature*) identify the two activities, the first looking from philosophy toward art, the second from art toward philosophy.

A theory of *aesthetics* is characteristically generated by the need to relate artistic activity to a general theory of cognition and/or value, and because of this tendency, aesthetics frequently has no direct relation to the particularity of any given work of art as such. Croce's great work on aesthetics has a first part called "Teoria"; but the second part is not, as the critic or poet might expect, an application of that theory. Rather it is "Storia," that is, a history of other aesthetic theories. A chief aim of the aesthetician is the relating of art to other areas of philosophical preoccupation.

The word "aesthetics" was first used to indicate the philosophical investigation of art by the philosopher Alexander Baumgarten, in his *Meditationes Philosophicae de Nonnullis ad Poema Pertinentibus* of 1735. Unlike many later cultivators of the aesthetic garden, Baumgarten says at the outset that "I wish to make it plain that philosophy and the knowledge of how to construct a poem, which are often held to be entirely antithetical, are linked together in the most amiable union." He emphasizes that the realm of the artistic is that of sense impression: Section 4 says that "by *sensate discourse* we mean discourse involving sensate representations," and Section 9 says that "by *poem* we mean a perfect sensate discourse." Indeed, Baumgarten broaches the term "aesthetics" specifically to indicate the relation of art to perceived reality:

> The Greek philosophers and the Church Fathers have already carefully distinguished between αἰσθητά [things perceived] and νοητά [things thought]. It is sufficiently apparent that they did not equate αἰσθητά solely with things of sense, since they honored with this name things also removed from sense (therefore, images). There are therefore νοητά, to be known by the superior faculty as the object of logic; αἰσθητά, to be known as the science of perception, or AESTHETICAE.

Among the many contributions to the theory of aesthetics since Baumgarten's time, perhaps the four most important are Immanuel Kant's *Kritik der ästhetischen Urteilskraft* (1790), G. W. F. Hegel's *Vorlesungen über die Ästhetik* (posthumously published in 1835), Croce's *Estetica come scienza dell'espressione e linguistica generale* (1902), and John Dewey's *Art as Experience* (1934). Among the profusion of contributions to critical theory or the theory of literature, perhaps four not unworthy to set alongside the four just named would be the writings of Coleridge, Arnold, Leavis, and William Empson.

Ideally, aesthetic theory, as in Baumgarten's initial hope, would be a bridge extended from the philosophical concern to the particularities of literary or other art; ideally, too, the critical formulation would arise from the literary particularity at hand and extend with undiminished power and pertinence to the realm of philosophical connections. In fact, however, neither ideal is ever entirely realized (Coleridge perhaps came as close as anyone ever has to bridging the channel between literary particularity and philosophical abstraction). The problem, to vary the metaphor, is one of focus: just as a photographer gains sharp definition in the foreground only at the cost of a certain blurring in the middle distance, and vice versa, so the philosopher and the critic do justice to one perspective at a certain cost to the other. The working hypotheses of those close to the artist's experience often tend to dangle inconclusively. Arnold's goal in reading poetry was to isolate "a sense of the best, the really excellent, and of the strength and joy to be drawn from it," but his "touchstones" for detecting such excellence depend on "tact," which begs the question somewhat. The limitations of such an offhand approach are apparent; and the critic's need for more precision and for an at least nominally philosophical elucidation of the notion of quality is embodied in the very title of Ransom's article, "Wanted: An Ontological Critic," which speaks of "the unsatisfactoriness of poetic theory" due to "the absence from it of philosophical generalities." A similar reaching from the critical standpoint toward a more philosophical texture can be seen in René Wellek's "The Mode of Existence of a Literary Work of Art," or in W. K. Wimsatt's "The Concrete Universal." Wimsatt, indeed, found it fruitful in a number of articles to collaborate with a practicing philosopher, Monroe Beardsley. Though literature and philosophy sometimes come together in mutual fecundation, they sometimes occlude one another; and at other times they move widely apart.

Such coming together and moving apart characterize also the relations of literature to the two great forms of twentieth-century philosophy. The positivist/analytic tradition stemming from Ernst Mach, from the Vienna Circle, and from Ludwig Wittgenstein, has its eye on the firmly knowable, and its models, especially for practitioners such as Rudolf Carnap and Hans Reichenbach, are strict logic and scientific precision.[4] Although philosophers of this cast of mind might well make statements or write articles about literature — some of them have done so — their faces are fundamentally turned to science and their backs to literature. W. V. Quine may be the most eminent American philosopher of the last half century, and perhaps Michael Dummett or Gilbert Ryle or J. L. Austin — possibly P. F. Strawson — the most eminent of those recently active in Britain; for none of them is literature an important tropism of thought. With whatever qualifications might be necessary, it is certainly the case that in the twentieth-century positivist/analytic tradition the "quarrel between philosophy and poetry" remains the dominant state of affairs.

The other great line of twentieth-century philosophical activity, however, the phenomenological/existential tradition stemming from Franz

Brentano and Edmund Husserl, presents an entirely different picture. Here the diastolic movement by which philosophy and literature intermingle once again asserts itself. Everywhere we find the phenomenological approach benign to literary interests. The most important French philosopher of this century, Jean-Paul Sartre, is also a literary critic, a literary dramatist, and a prolific novelist. Sartre was Husserl's follower, and his philosophical work grew out of Husserlian soil. The two most important German descendants of Husserl, Martin Heidegger and Karl Jaspers, are also oriented toward concerns important for literature. Jaspers, for instance, in his *Von der Wahrheit* formulates perhaps the most satisfying of all theories of tragedy, while Heidegger becomes increasingly involved with poetry as an uncovering of being, especially in the work of Friedrich Hölderlin.[5] Again, the present ferment in France, which has so excited literary theorists in America, is at bottom nothing other than the lessons of Husserl applied to a cultural potpourri of Rousseau, Marx, Freud, Heidegger, Saussure, Sartre, and Lévi-Strauss. Indeed, Jacques Derrida, Paul Ricoeur, and Emmanuel Levinas — to cite three figures significant in this ferment — have each written a treatise on Husserl. In Germany, a critic of Rilke like Otto Bollnow is also an academic philosopher of status. Still again, Roman Ingarden, whose book translated as *The Literary Work of Art: An Investigation on the Borderlines of Ontology, Logic, and Theory of Literature* is one of the best contemporary contributions to aesthetics, was a formal student of Husserl's.

As to why the phenomenological movement has proved so fertile for literature, the answer is not the expected one, that where positivism turns its back on literature in the quest for science, phenomenology rejects science in favor of literature. Quite the contrary. Phenomenology too looks toward the ideal of science. Husserl's own orientation was to mathematics and logic rather than to literature; and both he and lesser phenomenologists vigorously opposed positivism on the grounds that it was scientifically irresponsible.

The answer is rather that phenomenology's special kind of analysis provides favored status for purely mental constructs, and that thereby the imagination of the poet and the fictions of the novelist are not relegated to the background as they are in the positivist tradition. Briefly, phenomenology is a philosophy of subject-object relation in which the reality of the object is left out of consideration (its realness is not disputed, but rather "bracketed" [*eingeklammert*]). For instance, if I examine a chair from the phenomenological perspective (one recalls Austin's words about "the philosopher's professional addiction to furniture"), I neither contest its reality nor exercise myself about its "chairness"; I am interested in it solely as an *object of attention*. The chair as such is bracketed; the chair in the phenomenological *epoché* is a mental construct (*cogitatio* or *noema*), an object inseparable from the ideational perspective in which I cognize it. As Husserl was well aware, the chair taken in this way — and phenomenology contends that this is the only way in which the chair is ever available — is not necessarily different from a chair in the house of a family in a Charles Dickens novel. An absent friend, from the phenomenological perspective, is a *cogitatio*; so too is Hamlet. Your great-grandfather and King Lear are both available to consciousness in the same way. Phenomenology, which is a science of *formal* reality rather than *substantial* reality, is as much at home with fictional imaginings as with locally encountered actuality; for phenomenology, acts of mental attention in both cases "constitute" the world.

The matter is important enough to justify at least the rudiments of historical elucidation. Husserl may variously be held to be an epigone of Plato (his *Ideen* could hardly have been composed before the appearance of Paul Natorp's *Platos Ideenlehre*), of René Descartes, and of Kant. The common factor in all these possibilities is the primacy of the thinking mind. "A radical and universal continuation of Cartesian meditations," says Husserl in his *Cartesianische Meditationen*, "or (equivalently) a universal self-cognition, is philosophy itself and encompasses all self-accountable science. The Delphic motto, 'Know thyself,' has gained a new signification. Positivism is a science lost in the world. I must lose the world by *epoché*, in order to regain it by a universal self-examination. 'Noli foras ire,' says Augustine, 'in te redi, in interiore homine habitat veritas'" 'Do not seek to go out; go back into yourself; truth dwells in the inner man.'

Thus Husserl enormously augments the philosophical weight of the subject. As to how (and why) he arrived at his "bracketing" or "disconnecting" of external reality, the answer is to be found in the academic tradition of German philosophy in which he was steeped. That tradition had argued that philosophy must deal with three focal realities and their relations: the thinking mind, or ego — that is, the logical subject; the things that make up the external world, or nature — logically represented as the object; and the repository of all questions of origin and purpose arising from the primary relation of mind and nature — that is, God. As Christian Wolff said, in his *Discursus Praeliminaris de Philosophia in Genere* of 1728:

> The beings that we know are God, human souls, and bodies or material things. If we examine ourselves, we find that whenever we are conscious of things outside ourselves acting upon our sensory origin we are also conscious of ourselves. That in us that is conscious of itself is called the *soul*. Extended things, which differ from each other in figure and magnitude and which we intuit outside ourselves, are called *bodies*. Thus we admit a twofold genus of beings, namely, *bodies* and human *souls*. And as soon as we have seen that bodies and human souls are not independent beings, that is, they do not arise and persevere by their own power, we have also admitted an author of both bodies and souls, by whose power both of these genera of being were produced. This author of the things whose existence we know we call God. Therefore the beings that we know by examining ourselves before we philosophize are God, human souls, and bodies.

This is not the place to discuss the vicissitudes of the philosophical concept of God in the nineteenth and twentieth centuries, although it should be apparent that any historically comprehensive treatment of the topic "literature and philosophy" would actually have to treat three subjects, "literature, philosophy, and theology," with each subject triangulated by the other two. Wolff's "twofold genus of beings, namely, bodies and human souls," however, represents philosophical bedrock. Kant was trained in the school of Wolff, and he accepted Wolff's premises. His own philosophy—if we penetrate its technical surface—should be seen as an attempt to prevent the dissipation of the idea of "soul" or "personality,"[6] and thus to avoid a shattering insult to human self-esteem and the possibility of final meaning in human existence (we should here remind ourselves both of Friedrich Nietzsche's canny description of Kant's position as "subterranean Christianity" and of Arthur Schopenhauer's insistence that "the aim" of both Kant and Plato is "the same").[7] Like Plato (and Augustine and Descartes), Kant took his stand on the primacy of the thinking self. By so doing he reinforced "soul" at the expense of "body"; for body and its more general category "thing" threatened the ontological subsistence of soul.[8]

Kant's specific disposition of the subject-object relation was to displace the idea of thing as such—or thing in itself—into the realm of the unknowable. The thing as experienced he was thereby able to conceive as a mind-controlled form ("It must be possible for the 'I think' to accompany all my representations"). By retaining the thing as experienced, which he called "phenomenon," under the control of mind, and shoving "thing in itself" into the unknowable, Kant was able both to disarm lifeless materiality as an ontological threat to soul and to keep open an "empty space" for the idea of God (as he said in his *Reflexionen zur Metaphysik*, "The phenomenon of a thing is a product of our sensibility, God is the originator of things in themselves").

Yet Kant's thing in itself (*Ding an sich*), though necessary to his position, involved a logical inconsistency: if it is totally inaccessible to knowledge, how can we even know it is there at all? Friedrich Jacobi was the first to formulate this objection, and he was followed in a cumulatively withering historical crossfire by others, including Johann Fichte, Schelling, Hegel, Nietzsche, and in Husserl's own era, Hermann Cohen and Natorp.

Husserl was immersed in the philosophy of Kant.[9] Still, because of the logical vulnerability of the *Ding an sich*, he could not accept Kant's disposition of the subject-object relation. He retained its essence, however, by dismissing the *Ding an sich* (and thereby the objections it incurred) and substituting instead the concept of *Einklammerung*. The "thing," instead of being shoved outside into the unknowable, was accepted in its natural setting as really subsisting—but then it was bracketed and set aside; the phenomenon, however, was raised in importance by being taken inside, in conjunction with the mind's activity.

The logical modality by which Husserl accomplished this second step was supplied by Brentano's resuscitation of the medieval concept of "intentionality": that consciousness is defined only by its objects; that is, every act of consciousness is consciousness *of something* (I do not see, I see a chair; I do not smell, I smell a rose; I do not touch, I touch a hand). By this binding of consciousness to the *formal* (phenomenological) thing, Husserl was able to bracket the *real* thing.[10] Accordingly, though it was not his primary aim to do so, he valorized the imaginative and fictional things with which the artist is involved. The ghost in *Hamlet* is as valid an object of attention as the paperweight on the desk.

So much for the phenomenological movement, which is, of the traditions of philosophy current in the twentieth century, the one most favorable to the interests of literature. To conclude this brief conspectus, we may note a more recent mode of theorizing prevalent in our own era. This mode constitutes in effect a third form that stands between the theories of literary critics and those of philosophers. Or more precisely, it is not so much a genuine third form as an ambitious extension of critical theory. It is produced by literary critics rather than by philosophers, but in texture and aim it is quasi-philosophical.

Actually, it is in its volume rather than in its form that the currency of the quasi-philosophical mode consists. Its individual examples can be seen as utterances in an old tradition, one that has boasted such distinguished statements as Longinus' *Peri Hupsous* ("On the Sublime"), Sidney's *Defence of Poesie*, Friedrich Schiller's *Briefe über die ästhetische Erziehung des Menschen*, Friedrich Schlegel's *Gespräch über die Poesie*, Shelley's *Defence of Poetry*, Charles Baudelaire's *Salon de 1859*, André Gide's *Traité du Narcisse*, and T. E. Hulme's *Speculations: Essays on Humanism and the Philosophy of Art*. Its accelerated importance in recent intellectual history perhaps has something to do with the proliferation of academic critics. At any rate, where critics usually so described tend to refer ideationally to relatively self-contained terms — "irony," "paradox," "coherence," "intelligence," "excellence," and the like — the rise of the quasi-philosophical has given modern culture ambitiously extended works such as Erich Auerbach's *Mimesis: The Representation of Reality in Western Literature* (1946; English trans., 1953). We may note also Emil Staiger's *Grundbegriffe der Poetik* (1946), philosophical in direction though literary in origin; or, less successful perhaps, Wolfgang Kayser's *Das sprachliche Kunstwerk* (1948). Among works written in English, Northrop Frye's *Anatomy of Criticism* (1957) has been an influential representative of the mode.

While much of the contemporary ferment in France comes from writers trained as philosophers, in America, where the new mode is in the ascendant, writers trained in literature ever more frequently go beyond the traditional "critic's job of work" to produce abstract theory. For instance, Harold Bloom's series of volumes beginning with *The Anxiety of Influence:*

A Theory of Poetry (1973) have as they progressed involved themselves with configurations of rhetoric and psychoanalysis and reference to Kabbalistic and Gnostic complexes of thought. The so-called Yale School of criticism, in which Bloom is a central figure, has more and more taken an influential stand in this middle group between philosophy and literary criticism proper.

The efforts of the Yale School have aroused so much controversy and emulation that perhaps a notice of its nature and emphasis, as provided by one of its chief members, J. Hillis Miller, will be a useful way of rounding off this brief discussion of the quasi-philosophical mode: "The new turn in criticism involves an interrogation of the notion of the self-enclosed literary work and of the idea that any work has a fixed, identifiable meaning. The literary work is seen in various ways as open and unpredictably productive. The reading of a poem is part of the poem. It produces multiple interpretations, further language about the poem's language, in an interminable activity without necessary closure." Historically, the Yale School both represents a reaction against the New Criticism of Ransom, Cleanth Brooks, R. P. Blackmur, and other theorists of the preceding generation and shows the influence of contemporary French structuralist thought. Miller speaks of "a new group of critics gathered at Yale: Harold Bloom, Paul de Man, and Geoffrey Hartman." These critics, he continues, "are not tragic or Dionysian in the sense that their work is wildly orgiastic or irrational. No critic could be more rigorously sane . . . than Paul de Man. One feature of Derrida's criticism is a patient and minutely philological 'explication de texte.' Nevertheless, the thread of logic leads in both cases into regions which are alogical, absurd. . . . The work of these critics is in one way or another a labyrinthine attempt to escape from the labyrinth of words."

Central to the procedure of this group of critics is the concept of "deconstruction." "The deconstructive critic," says Miller, "seeks to find, by [the] process of retracing, the element in the system studied which is alogical, the thread in the text in question which will unravel it all, or the loose stone which will pull down the whole building. . . . Deconstruction is not a dismantling of the structure of a text but a demonstration that it has already dismantled itself."[11] The concept is so important that we may also avail ourselves of the more elaborate notice provided in Paul de Man's *Blindness and Insight: Essays in the Rhetoric of Contemporary Criticism* (1971):

> Derrida's considerable contribution to Rousseau studies consists in showing that Rousseau's own texts provide the strongest evidence against his alleged doctrine. . . . Rousseau's work would then reveal a pattern of duplicity . . . he "knew," in a sense, that his doctrine disguised his insight into something closely resembling its opposite, but he chose to remain blind to this knowledge. The blindness can then be diagnosed as a direct consequence of an ontology of unmediated presence. It remains for the commentator to undo, with some violence, the historically established pattern or, as Derrida puts it, the "orbit" of

significant misinterpretation—a pattern of which the first example is to be found in Rousseau's own writings—and thus, by a process of "deconstruction," to bring to light what had remained unperceived by the author and his followers.

The critics here invoked have of course each produced a distinctively individual oeuvre with idiosyncratic intellectual contours. Taken in their common emphases, however, they constitute the most notable contemporary resurgence of the quasi-philosophical mode. To "deconstruct" their joint efforts, indeed, it might seem that underlying their ostensible concern with a text at hand is a hope that their own writings will become equal partners with that text. Geoffrey Hartman's essay on Keats's "To Autumn," for instance, in his *The Fate of Reading* (1975), achieves a prose texture that makes it virtually an alternate poem to the one under investigation. A corollary of this underlying tendency is that by their hierophantic vocabularies, arbitrary selection of favored texts, and wide-ranging deconstructive license —together with their helpful notices of one another's work—the Yale writers are elevating their own cultural function: from scholars, they have become critics; from critics, they are attempting to become sages.

Notes

1 Of the numerous answers, perhaps the one most historically responsible is supplied by Eric Havelock, *Preface to Plato* (Cambridge: Harvard Univ. Press, 1963). For a more personal approach, see Iris Murdoch, *The Fire and the Sun: Why Plato Banished the Artists* (Oxford: Clarendon, 1977).

2 Arnold's attitude finds many echoes in modern assessments of Wordsworth. Critics like R. D. Havens, in his *The Mind of a Poet: A Study of Wordsworth's Thought* (Baltimore: Johns Hopkins Press, 1941), and John Jones, in *The Egotistical Sublime: A History of Wordsworth's Imagination* (London: Chatto and Windus, 1954), deny that Wordsworth should be considered a philosopher. But in the very teeth of such twentieth-century opinion, critics like E. D. Hirsch, in *Wordsworth and Schelling: A Typological Study of Romanticism* (New Haven: Yale Univ. Press, 1960), and Melvin Rader, in *Wordsworth: A Philosophical Approach* (Oxford: Clarendon, 1967), insist on the necessity of the philosophical perspective.

3 For further discussion of the mingling of poetic and philosophical interests in the early Renaissance, see, among others, Charles Trinkaus, *The Poet as Philosopher: Petrarch and the Formation of Renaissance Consciousness* (New Haven: Yale Univ. Press, 1979).

4 Hence the propriety of Schelling's essay "Über Dante in philosophischer Beziehung" ('On Dante in Philosophical Context'). See also Etienne Gilson, *Dante and Philosophy*, trans. David Moore (New York: Harper, 1973).

5 See, for example, Beda Allemann, *Hölderlin und Heidegger*, 2nd ed. (Zurich: Atlantis, 1954). See also David A. White, *Heidegger and the Language of Poetry* (Lincoln: Univ. of Nebraska Press, 1978), William V. Spanos, ed., *Martin Heidegger and the Question of Literature* (Bloomington: Indiana Univ. Press, 1979), and David Halliburton, *Poetic Thinking: An Approach to Heidegger* (Chicago: University of Chicago Press, 1981).

[6] Thus in his *Kritik der reinen Vernunft* Kant says that "the ultimate aim" of reason concerns three objects: "the freedom of the will, the immortality of the soul, and the existence of God" (A798/B826). The argument of the *Kritik* "taken as a whole" must "convince the reader" that metaphysics "must always continue to be a bulwark" of religion (A849/B877).

[7] Again, Richard Kroner says that "the Kantian philosophy, leaving aside all those contexts in which it relates to its immediate predecessors, can be regarded as a renewal of Platonic idealism from out of the German mind" (*Von Kant bis Hegel*, 2nd ed. [Tübingen: Mohr-Siebeck, 1961], I, 35). In this context, cf. Plato: " . . . the soul is the eldest of all things that are born, and is immortal and rules over all bodies" (*Laws* 967D).

[8] It is interesting in this regard to note that the positivist/analytic tradition, from Mach's *Analyse der Empfindungen* through Ryle's *The Concept of Mind*, aggressively dissipates and dismisses that very idea of soul, or what Kant called *pure apperception*: "The abiding and unchanging 'I.'"

[9] See, e.g., Iso Kern, *Husserl und Kant: Eine Untersuchung über Husserls Verhältnis zu Kant und zum Neukantianismus* (The Hague: Nijhoff, 1964).

[10] Both the primacy of the subject and the validity of the subject-object relation are maintained by the *universal necessity* of objectivity as defined by intentionality. The phenomenon actually gains in importance at the expense of the "real"; whereas in Kant importance was not vested in the phenomenon but remained with the unknowable *Ding an sich*. As a commentator almost poetically observes, "Intentionality thus signifies that man and the world are of the same family: the communication that it connotes founds itself on a community" (Mikel Dufrenne, *Esthétique et philosophie*, I, 61).

[11] Miller also points out that "the critics of the uncanny must be exceedingly nimble, as de Man, Hartman, Derrida, and Bloom in their different ways conspicuously are, in order to keep their insights from becoming pseudo-scientific machines for the unfolding (explication), or dismantling (deconstruction), of literary texts." See J. Hillis Miller, "Stevens' Rock and Criticism as Cure, II," *Georgia Review*, 30 (1976), 332, 333, 336, 341, 348.

Bibliography

The subject of the relation of literature to philosophy is so shifting, so variegated, and so vast that bibliographical comprehensiveness is neither feasible nor desirable. Even an extensive compendium of titles would tend more to obscure than to illuminate the topic. The aim here is instead to provide reference to a representative selection of both important work and less decisive statement and also to afford some sort of foothold to those who feel this a steep mountain to climb. In the interests of the latter aim, some standard anthologies are included. The total list has been limited to about fifty authors.

I. From Literature toward Philosophy

Adams, Hazard. *The Contexts of Poetry*. Boston: Little, 1963.

———. *The Interests of Criticism: An Introduction to Literary Theory*. New York: Harcourt, 1969.

———, ed. *Critical Theory since Plato*. New York: Harcourt, 1971.

Arnold, Matthew. *Essays in Criticism: First Series*. 1865: rpt. London: Macmillan, 1905. See especially "The Function of Criticism at the Present Time."

———. *Essays in Criticism: Second Series*. 1888; rpt. London: Macmillan, 1905. See especially "The Study of Poetry."

Atkins, J. W. H. *English Literary Criticism: The Medieval Phase.* New York: Macmillan, 1943.

————. *English Literary Criticism: The Renascence.* 2nd ed. London: Methuen, 1951.

————. *English Literary Criticism: Seventeenth and Eighteenth Centuries.* London: Methuen, 1951.

————. *Literary Criticism in Antiquity: A Sketch of Its Development.* 2 vols. Cambridge: Cambridge Univ. Press, 1934.

Bate, Walter Jackson. *The Burden of the Past and the English Poet.* Cambridge: Harvard Univ. Press, 1970.

————. *Coleridge.* New York: Macmillan, 1968.

————. *From Classic to Romantic: Premises of Taste in Eighteenth-Century England.* Cambridge: Harvard Univ. Press, 1946.

————, ed. *Criticism: The Major Texts.* Rev. ed. New York: Harcourt, 1970.

Bloom, Harold. *The Anxiety of Influence: A Theory of Poetry.* New York: Oxford Univ. Press, 1973.

————. *Kabbalah and Criticism.* New York: Seabury, 1975.

————. *A Map of Misreading.* New York: Oxford Univ. Press, 1975.

————. *Poetry and Repression: Revisionism from Blake to Stevens.* New Haven: Yale Univ. Press, 1976.

Burke, Kenneth. *Counter-Statement.* New York: Harcourt, 1931.

————. *A Grammar of Motives.* Englewood Cliffs, N.J.: Prentice-Hall, 1945.

————. *The Philosophy of Literary Form: Studies in Symbolic Action.* Baton Rouge: Louisiana State Univ. Press, 1941.

————. *A Rhetoric of Motives.* Englewood Cliffs, N.J.: Prentice-Hall, 1950.

Coleridge, Samuel Taylor. *Biographia Literaria* (1817). Ed. J. Shawcross. 2 vols. London: Oxford Univ. Press, 1907. Contains the important essays "On the Principles of Genial Criticism" and "On Poesy or Art."

Daiches, David. *Critical Approaches to Literature.* Englewood Cliffs, N.J.: Prentice-Hall, 1956.

Eliot, T. S. *On Poetry and Poets.* 1956; rpt. New York: Farrar, 1961.

————. *The Sacred Wood: Essays on Poetry and Criticism.* 2nd ed. 1928; rpt. London: Methuen, 1972.

————. *The Use of Poetry and the Use of Criticism: Studies in the Relation of Criticism to Poetry in England.* 1933; rpt. London: Faber, 1975.

Elledge, Scott, ed. *Eighteenth-Century Critical Essays.* 2 vols. Ithaca, N.Y.: Cornell Univ. Press, 1961.

————, and Donald Schier, eds. *The Continental Model: Selected French Critical Essays of the Seventeenth Century in English Translation.* Rev. ed. Ithaca, N.Y.: Cornell Univ. Press, 1970.

Empson, William. *Seven Types of Ambiguity.* 3rd ed. 1953; rpt. London: Chatto and Windus, 1970.

————. *Some Versions of Pastoral.* London: Chatto and Windus, 1935.

————. *The Structure of Complex Words.* London: Chatto and Windus, 1951.

Leavis, F. R. *The Common Pursuit.* London: Chatto and Windus, 1952.

————. *Letters in Criticism.* Ed. John Tasker. London: Chatto and Windus, 1974.

————. *Revaluation: Tradition and Development in English Poetry.* 1936; rpt. London: Chatto and Windus, 1969.

————. *Thought, Words, and Creativity: Art and Thought in Lawrence.* New York: Oxford Univ. Press, 1976.

Ransom, John Crowe. *The New Criticism.* Norfolk, Conn.: New Directions, 1941.

————. *The World's Body.* New York: Scribners, 1938.

Richards, I. A. *The Philosophy of Rhetoric.* New York: Oxford Univ. Press, 1936.

————. *Practical Criticism: A Study of Literary Judgment*. London: Kegan Paul, 1929.

————. *Principles of Literary Criticism*. 1924; rpt. London: Routledge and Kegan Paul, 1950.

Schorer, Mark, Josephine Miles, and Gordon McKenzie, eds. *Criticism: The Foundations of Modern Literary Judgment*. New York: Harcourt, 1948. Contains fifty-six selections from writers both ancient and modern, grouped under three headings: Source, Form, and End.

Smith, G. Gregory, ed. *Elizabethan Critical Essays*. 2 vols. London: Oxford Univ. Press, 1904.

Spingarn, Joel E. *Creative Criticism*. 2nd ed. New York: Columbia Univ. Press, 1925.

————. *A History of Literary Criticism in the Renaissance*. New York: Macmillan, 1899.

————, ed. *Critical Essays of the Seventeenth Century*. 3 vols. 1908; rpt. Bloomington: Indiana Univ. Press, 1957.

Staiger, Emil. *Grundbegriffe der Poetik*. 6th ed. 1946; rpt. Zurich: Atlantis, 1963.

Tolstoy, Leo. *What Is Art? [1898] and Essays on Art*. Trans. Aylmer Maude. London: Oxford Univ. Press, 1930.

Valéry, Paul. *The Art of Poetry*. Trans. Denise Folliot. New York: Pantheon, 1958.

Weinberg, Bernard. *A History of Literary Criticism in the Italian Renaissance*. 2 vols. Chicago: Univ. of Chicago Press, 1961.

————, ed. *Critical Prefaces of the French Renaissance*. Evanston, Ill.: Northwestern Univ. Press, 1950.

Wellek, René. *Concepts of Criticism*. Ed. Stephen G. Nichols, Jr. New Haven: Yale Univ. Press, 1963.

————. *Confrontations: Studies in the Intellectual and Literary Relations between Germany, England, and the United States during the Nineteenth Century*. Princeton: Princeton Univ. Press, 1965. Contains "Carlyle and the Philosophy of History," "The Minor Transcendentalists and German Philosophy," and "Emerson and German Philosophy."

————. *Discriminations: Further Concepts of Criticism*. New Haven: Yale Univ. Press, 1970. Contains "Immanuel Kant's Aesthetics and Criticism" and "The Literary Theory and Aesthetics of the Prague School."

————. *A History of Modern Literary Criticism, 1750–1950*. 4 vols. New Haven: Yale Univ. Press, 1955– .

————, and Austin Warren. *Theory of Literature*. 3rd ed. New York: Harcourt, 1962.

Wimsatt, W. K. *Day of the Leopards: Essays in Defense of Poems*. New Haven: Yale Univ. Press, 1976.

————. *Hateful Contraries: Studies in Literature and Criticism*. Lexington: Univ. of Kentucky Press, 1965.

————. *The Verbal Icon: Studies in the Meaning of Poetry*. Lexington: Univ. of Kentucky Press, 1954.

————, and Cleanth Brooks. *Literary Criticism: A Short History*. New York: Knopf, 1957.

Winters, Yvor. *Forms of Discovery*. Chicago: Swallow, 1967.

————. *The Function of Criticism*. Denver, Swallow, 1957.

————. *In Defense of Reason*. Denver: Swallow, 1947.

II. From Philosophy toward Literature

Aristotle. *The Poetics*. Bilingual ed. Trans. and ed. W. Hamilton Fyfe. Loeb Classical Library. 1960; rpt. Cambridge: Harvard Univ. Press, 1973. (Volume also contains Longinus' *On the Sublime* and Demetrius' *On Style*.) For analysis and historical orientation, see entries below for Cooper and Else.

Beardsley, Monroe C. *Aesthetics: Problems in the Philosophy of Criticism*. New York: Harcourt, 1958.

———. *Aesthetics from Classical Greece to the Present: A Short History*. New York: Macmillan, 1966.

———, ed. *Literature and Aesthetics*. Indianapolis: Bobbs-Merrill, 1968.

Bosanquet, Bernard. *A History of Aesthetic*. 1892; rpt. New York: Humanities Press, 1966.

———. *Three Lectures on Aesthetic*. London: Macmillan, 1915.

Buchler, Justus. *The Main of Light: On the Concept of Poetry*. New York: Oxford Univ. Press, 1974.

Carritt, E. F. *Philosophies of Beauty from Socrates to Robert Bridges*. New York: Oxford Univ. Press, 1941.

———. *The Theory of Beauty*. 3rd ed. London: Methuen, 1928.

———. *What is Beauty? A First Introduction to the Subject and to Modern Theories*. Oxford: Clarendon, 1932.

Collingwood, R. G. *The Principles of Art*. Oxford: Clarendon, 1938.

Cooper, Lane. *The Poetics of Aristotle: Its Meaning and Influence*. 1923; rpt. New York: Cooper Square, 1963.

Croce, Benedetto. *Aesthetic as Science of Expression and General Linguistic* (1902). Trans. Douglas Ainslie. 2nd ed. 1922; rpt. New York: Noonday, 1963.

———. "Aesthetics." *Encyclopaedia Brittanica*. 1929 ed. Rpt. in *Modern Literary Criticism, 1900–1970*. Ed. Lawrence I. Lipking and A. Walton Litz. New York: Atheneum, 1972.

Dewey, John. *Art as Experience*. New York: Minton, Balch, 1934.

Dufrenne, Mikel. *Esthétique et philosophie*. 2 vols. Paris: Klincksieck, 1967–76.

———. *The Phenomenology of Aesthetic Experience*. Trans. Edward S. Casey et al. Evanston, Ill.: Northwestern Univ. Press, 1973.

Else, Gerald F. *Aristotle's Poetics: The Argument*. Cambridge: Harvard Univ. Press, 1967.

Elton, William, ed. *Aesthetics and Language*. 1954; rpt. Oxford: Blackwell, 1967.

Gentile, Giovanni. *The Philosophy of Art* (1931). Trans. Giovanni Gullace. Ithaca, N.Y.: Cornell Univ. Press, 1972.

Hegel, G. W. F. *Aesthetics: Lectures on Fine Art* (1835). Trans. T. M. Knox. 2 vols. Oxford: Clarendon, 1975.

Ingarden, Roman. *The Cognition of the Literary Work of Art*. Trans. Ruth Ann Crowley and Kenneth R. Olson. Evanston, Ill.: Northwestern Univ. Press, 1973.

———. *The Literary Work of Art: An Investigation on the Borderlines of Ontology, Logic, and Theory of Literature*. Trans. George Grabowicz. Evanston, Ill.: Northwestern Univ. Press, 1973.

Kant, Immanuel. *Critique of Aesthetic Judgement* (1790). Trans. James Creed Meredith. Oxford: Clarendon, 1911.

Kennick, W. E., ed. *Art and Philosophy: Readings in Aesthetics*. New York: St. Martin's, 1964.

Langer, Susanne K. *Feeling and Form: A Theory of Art*. New York: Scribners, 1953.

———. *Mind: An Essay on Human Feeling*. Baltimore: Johns Hopkins Univ. Press, 1967.

———. *Problems of Art: Ten Philosophical Lectures*. New York: Scribners, 1957.

———. *Reflections on Art: A Source Book of Writings by Artists, Critics, and Philosophers*. Baltimore: Johns Hopkins Univ. Press, 1958.

Lipps, Theodor. *Ästhetik: Psychologie des Schönen und der Kunst.* 3rd ed. 2 vols. Leipzig: Voss, 1923.

Nahm, Milton C. *Aesthetic Experience and Its Presuppositions.* New York: Harper, 1946.

———. *The Artist as Creator: An Essay on Human Freedom.* Baltimore: Johns Hopkins Univ. Press, 1956.

Osborne, Harold. *Aesthetics and Art Theory: An Historical Introduction.* New York: Dutton, 1970.

———. *Aesthetics and Criticism.* London: Routledge, 1955.

———. *Theory of Beauty: An Introduction to Aesthetics.* London: Routledge, 1952.

———, ed. *Aesthetics.* London: Oxford Univ. Press, 1972. Contains essays by Valéry, Sartre, Ingarden, Merleau-Ponty, G. E. Moore, and others.

Pepper, Stephen C. *Aesthetic Quality: A Contextualistic Theory of Beauty.* New York: Scribners, 1938.

———. *The Basis of Criticism in the Arts.* Cambridge: Harvard Univ. Press, 1946.

———. *Principles of Art Appreciation.* New York: Harcourt, 1949.

———. *The Work of Art.* Bloomington: Indiana Univ. Press, 1955.

Prall, D. W. *Aesthetic Analysis.* New York: Crowell, 1936.

———. *Aesthetic Judgment.* New York: Crowell, 1929.

Schelling, F. W. J. von. *Philosophie der Kunst* (posth. 1859). Darmstadt: Wissenschaftliche Buchgesellschaft, 1960.

Sparshott, F. E. *The Concept of Criticism.* Oxford: Clarendon, 1967.

———. *The Structure of Aesthetics.* Toronto: Univ. of Toronto Press, 1963.

Taine, Hippolyte. *The Philosophy of Art.* Trans. John Durand. New York: Holt, 1873.

Urban, Wilbur Marshall. *Language and Reality: The Philosophy of Language and the Principles of Symbolism.* London: Allen and Unwin, 1939.

Weitz, Morris. *Hamlet and the Philosophy of Criticism.* Chicago: Univ. of Chicago Press, 1964.

———. *Philosophy in Literature: Shakespeare, Voltaire, Tolstoy, and Proust.* Detroit: Wayne State Univ. Press, 1963.

———. *Philosophy of the Arts.* Cambridge: Harvard Univ. Press, 1950.

———, ed. *Problems in Aesthetics: An Introductory Book of Readings.* 2nd ed. New York: Macmillian, 1970.

3

Literature and Religion

Giles Gunn

While literature's association with religion goes back to the very origins of literature, which took rise from sacred myth and found some of its earliest uses in religious rites, their relation remained intimate and intricate long after literature ceased being a medium of revealed truth or a component of religious ritual. Many literary genres and traditions, from medieval allegory and seventeenth-century metaphysical poetry to American transcendentalism, developed out of religious traditions, and forms of literature as various as Elizabethan tragedy, Romantic poetry, and the theater of the absurd continue to presuppose religious notions or to raise religious questions, even when they make no obvious reference to inherited traditions of religious belief. Modern literary historians and critics have been particularly sensitive to the ways that various literary conventions, from the heroic couplet of the eighteenth century to the unreliable narrator of modern fiction, draw on, and consequently need to be interpreted by, religious conceptions; and within the last several decades, literary scholars have utilized a variety of critical methods, from the New Criticism to deconstructionism, which either presuppose a theory of reality or are intended to yield insights that can be described as ontological as well as aesthetic. Thus while much contemporary literature exists at an intellectual and emotional remove from orthodox religious traditions and while most modern scholars have little interest in turning their criticism into a medium of theological discussion, religious concerns and issues remain at the center of much of the critical discussion today.

It is therefore all the more curious that in contemporary critical forums this area of study has so often been misunderstood or discounted, even by those who have contributed to it in important ways. Many of its strongest advocates, for example, have created the false impression that the critical importance of the study of the interrelations between literature and religion is confined largely to the modern period and that the most significant work in the field has been done almost exclusively by Anglo-American scholars drawing on the comparatively modest theological legacy of European existentialism. Many of its most severe critics have assumed just as falsely that

47

the study of literature and religion holds no real interest beyond the Jewish and Christian households of faith, where it exists primarily to allow the already committed either to vindicate their own beliefs or to censure the beliefs of others.

The difficulty on both sides has been provincialism. Those sympathetic to the study of literature and religion have often failed to realize that its scope extends far beyond the boundaries of apologetic theology to the theory of aesthetics and culture, on the one hand, and to literary history and the history of ideas, on the other. Those suspicious of this field of study have been largely insensitive to the intimate connection, though not always obvious, between the development of scholarly interest in the relations between literature and religion and the religious crisis of cultural modernism. Where proponents of the subject have lacked sophisticated understanding of those formal and structural properties of literature that legitimate its religious analysis in any age, skeptics of the subject have been insensible of those spiritual factors, at least since the Renaissance, that have lent particular urgency to the religious analysis of literature in the present age.

The nature of the relations between literature and religion thus tends to be more various and complex than is often imagined. Just as evidence of an interest in such relations can be found in almost every age of Western history, so the serious study of these relations has been pursued for a variety of motives and has taken a diverse set of forms. Literature has been viewed by some, from Sir Philip Sidney to Leo Tolstoy and T. S. Eliot, as a way of confirming, or at least of shoring up, belief. It has been viewed by others, from Alexander Pope and Jonathan Swift to Miguel de Unamuno and Jean-Paul Sartre, as a way of challenging, even disconfirming, belief. It has been conceived by still others, from Longinus to Percy Bysshe Shelley and Paul Valéry, as a way of preparing for or inducing belief. Literary classics as different as the *Gilgamesh* epic, *Beowulf*, *El Cid*, the classic tale from China known in English as *The Journey to the West*, Dante's *Divina commedia*, and the eighteenth-century Chinese novel *The Dream of the Red Chamber* by Tsao Hsueh-chin have been variously interpreted as legitimating religious notions, reconceptualizing them, repossessing them, relativizing them, demystifying them, confounding them, and even, whether intentionally or not, undermining them. And when one moves to texts whose cosmological and anthropological orientation is less overt but no less consequential, to Giovanni Boccaccio's *Decameron*, Lady Murasaki's *The Tale of Genji*, the *Chanson de Roland*, and Geoffrey Chaucer's *Troilus and Criseyde*, the relations between literature and belief become even more subtle and perplexed.

Equally as manifold as the conceptions of literature's relation to belief have been the conceptions of belief itself, and religion's general relation to culture. By belief some scholars have meant only those ultimate but more often subconscious commitments that find expression in individual works; still others have meant simply those largely unconscious or only half-conscious concerns that constitute the general world view or metaphysical frame of mind that particular texts, like whole traditions, seem to reflect. Most scholars have confined their understanding of belief to the body of insights contained in the great historic faiths, such as Judaism, Christianity, Islam, Buddhism, and Hinduism; but a sizable and influential minority have directed their attention instead to forms of belief that are theologically heterodox or metaphysically irregular, and not a few have been interested chiefly in modalities of belief that lack an assured name, that seem to originate from within those unspeakable experiences behind creed or conviction.

This diversity of conception and practice has raised numerous and still-unanswered questions about where the religious component is found in literature and how it is defined. Should the religious factor in literature be identified in terms of traditional doctrine or heretical desire? Should it be associated with specific ideas about God, man, and the cosmos expressed in works of literature or with generic actions like penance, adoration, or rebirth that are represented by works of literature? And how is the religious component accessible to critical scrutiny? Is it expressed in the themes of literature, dramatized in the motifs of literature, reflected in the structures of literature, inscribed in the forms of literature, or deposited in the languages of literature?

To these and other queries there are no certain or fully satisfactory anwers; there is only the elaboration of further issues, which leads to continued debate. But the debate, at least among those who do not view this subject as intellectually privileged, has by now produced a measure of consensus, not about those issues that have been resolved but about those issues that are worthy of more extensive discussion. These issues can be summarized as follows:

1. Literature and religion, at least at certain times and in certain ways, have been historically related in fact and conceptually related in theory. Thus, to deny or overlook the nature and significance of their relation would be to cut oneself off from a portion of the meaning of each. To put this more emphatically, it is as misguided to suppose that one can understand, say, the literary heritage of the West dissociated from the variety of religious assumptions, doubts, and aspirations that underlie it as it is to presume that one can comprehend the manifold variety of the Western religious experience without examining the literary as well as liturgical, doctrinal, and ecclesiastical forms in which that experience has been expressed.

2. While there is a certain propriety in raising theological questions about works of literature (so long as one does not assume that all works of literature provide answers to such questions or that all the questions works of literature raise are inherently theological), the discipline of theology does not provide any special methodological access to works of literature, and the religious meaning of works of literature cannot be reduced to a specific set of theological ideas.

3. If literature and religion belong to the same universe of meaning, they nonetheless constitute that universe and inhabit it in different ways. Literature employs meanings heuristically, to show where they lead and how they matter; religion employs meanings more parabolically, to suggest where they came from, the origin of their authority, by clarifying the order of significance, of mattering, they entail.

4. If literature and religion are thus made of the same cultural material — namely, meanings — and serve the same experiential function — namely, to help us understand and negotiate through symbols our relations with our environment, both spiritual and material — then the study of both in conjunction, as of each individually, is a form of cultural studies and one that offers no immunity from the methodological demands and constraints placed on all students of culture.

In the light of these several areas of agreement that furnish the basis of dispute among most scholars who explore religious approaches to literature, it seems fair to conclude that literature and religion exist not only because we need them — we can scarcely manage our relations with the otherness of our surroundings, of our circumstances, without them — but also because in a certain sense they need each other. Religion may be said to provide us with those basic paradigms by which we define the nature of that otherness of our circumstances and attempt to bring our lives into some measure of conformity with it. Works of literature explore hidden, and often potentially disturbing, dimensions of those paradigms by organizing them into an encompassing structure that, through the light it sheds on their existential nature, helps release us from anxiety about those paradigms by clarifying the alternative kinds of response we can imaginatively, if not actually, make to them.

The relation between literature and religion is therefore symbiotic and not merely complementary — literature is more than, as Charles Baudelaire said, a metaphysics made sensible to the heart and expressed in images — but its operation is more subtle than is generally supposed. Religious paradigms function in actual experience only as a kind of "court of last resort," a court that, while essential to the structure and well-being of the entire judicial system, is rarely called into session until all appeals to lower courts have been exhausted. We are therefore constantly in need of confirming their operational status and of determining their range of control over the constantly changing, often confusing field of ongoing experience. Representing what José Ortega y Gasset described as ideas that *we are* rather than ideas that *we have*, ideas so central to our existence that, while we can think in and with and through them, we can rarely think about them, religious paradigms remain masked or buried without some instrument, some technique, to reveal their hidden elements and to show us how far they reach into the uncharted regions of potential experience. This is one of the offices performed by works of art: their purpose is to help us know what we feel about these paradigms, and feel what we know, by illuminating the implications of what they conceal as well as disclose, what they disguise as well as express; and works of literature accomplish this end by casting these paradigms, these "ideas of order," as Wallace Stevens called them, into forms where they are addressed not only by the intellect but also by the senses, or by what an earlier age called the affections. The purpose of such strategies is to enable us not merely to see but, as the blind Gloucester reminds Lear on the heath, to see feelingly.

If we confine ourselves to the Western literary tradition, it is possible to argue that literature has been related to religion in at least three ways and that these three ways tend roughly to parallel major shifts in the spiritual history of Western literature. From classical antiquity to the Renaissance, literature in the West for the most part exhibited a complementary, often deeply supportive relation to inherited religious traditions. In some instances, such as medieval miracle plays, like *Mystère d'Adam* or the Chester and Wakefield cycles, which grew out of liturgical drama and dealt with biblical stories and motifs, or later morality plays, such as *The Castle of Perseverance* and *Everyman*, which dealt with personified abstractions of virtues and vices who contend for man's soul, literature served directly as an allegorical representation of religious ideas and feelings that were explicitly Christian in character. In other instances, ranging from classical epics like the *Iliad*, the *Odyssey*, and the *Aeneid* to medieval and Renaissance romances like *Sir Gawain and the Green Knight* and Edmund Spenser's *The Faerie Queene*, literature provided a form for the exploration, articulation, and revivification of religious conceptions and sentiments through their fusion with contemporary social, political, and aesthetic beliefs. In either case, however, and one could add examples ranging from Sophocles' *Oedipus at Colonus* through Sir Thomas Malory's Arthurian tales to late Renaissance works like John Bunyan's *Pilgrim's Progress* and John Milton's *Samson Agonistes,* literature served to valorize religious ideals and values, whether Christian or pagan, by replicating in its structures no less than in its themes both the premises of religious faith and the forms of religious experience.

Toward the end of the Renaissance, however, literature slowly began to develop a more adversative relation to traditional systems of faith and experience. One can see this shift as early as the late Middle Ages with the new emphasis on courtly love—the romances of the twelfth-century French writer Chrétien de Troyes epitomize the type—and the new spirit of humorous, secular impiety introduced into the literature of romance through the French tradition of the fabliau, which was so successfully exploited by Chaucer in *The Canterbury Tales*. But the new critical spirit toward conventional religious ideas and feelings also found its way into the mainstream of Western literature through such tributary routes as the tradition of Renaissance prose, in such works as Erasmus' *Encomium Moriae*, Sir Thomas More's *Utopia*,

Michel Eyquem de Montaigne's *Essais*, and Francis Bacon's *Advancement of Learning* and also through the Renaissance translations of such modern and ancient classics as Baldassare Castiglione's *Cortegiano*, Plutarch's *Lives*, and Livy's *Ab Urbe Condita Libri*. These influences, coupled with the expansion of knowledge precipitated by Renaissance voyages of exploration and discovery, were eventually to alter the relation between imaginative literature and traditional religious understanding, allowing some writers to conceive of literature as a criticism of inherited orthodoxies and paving the way for others to turn literature into an instrument for subverting them. Works that criticize forms of religious orthodoxy run from the comedies of Molière to the romances of Nathaniel Hawthorne, from Voltaire's *Candide* to Mark Twain's *The Adventures of Huckleberry Finn*. Works that intend to undermine conventional religious ideas and feelings include texts as different as Denis Diderot's *Le Neveu de Rameau* and Herman Melville's *The Confidence-Man*, Baudelaire's *Les Fleurs du mal* and the novels of Thomas Hardy.

Toward the end of the eighteenth century, another change began to occur in the relations between literature and religion. Whereas until then the relation between literature and religion had been either complementary or oppositional, the Romantic movement introduced the idea that literature might become an alternative to or substitute for religion. This view of the relation between literature and religion gained adherents throughout the nineteenth century among writers as different as Novalis and John Keats, or Shelley and Friedrich Nietzsche, but it was not until the end of the century, in the poetics of French symbolist writers like Stéphane Mallarmé and in the criticism of Victorians like Thomas Carlyle and Matthew Arnold, that the conception of literature as a kind of surrogate or displaced religion began to achieve public acceptance. This is the view that characterizes Gustave Flaubert's *Madame Bovary* no less than James Joyce's *Portrait of the Artist as a Young Man*, Rainer Maria Rilke's *Duineser Elegien* no less than Arthur Rimbaud's "Une Saison en enfer," Thomas Mann's *Doktor Faustus* no less than the later poetry of Wallace Stevens. The act of writing becomes the search for what Stevens calls "Supreme Fictions," which for the time being will suffice, and the satisfactions these fictions afford seem ironically to increase the more we are made aware of their purely imaginative as opposed to factual basis.

This spiritual modality has apparently reached its ultimate extension in the contemporary period by threatening to undermine the whole artistic enterprise. Much recent literature, far from attempting to displace or supplant religion, is in the process of displacing and supplanting itself. The writer has willy-nilly become a critic, and literary criticism has nearly replaced all other fictive forms as the only authentic literary mode, with writers like Thomas Pynchon, Jorge Luis Borges, and Roland Barthes now devoting more and more of their work to a parodistic contemplation of its own spiritual enervation.

The historical exceptions to this classificatory scheme are obvious and important. Certain strains of literature have exhibited an adversary relation to inherited religious traditions for at least as long as there have been modes like tragedy and comedy, and other strains of literature have sought to become a substitute for approved traditions of faith and sensibility ever since the advent of the courtly romance in the late Middle Ages and the reappearance of utopias in the early Renaissance. Just as works as different as Aeschylus' *Agamemnon*, Aristophanes' *The Frogs*, Jean Baptiste Racine's *Phèdre*, Pedro Calderón's *La vida es sueño*, Christopher Marlowe's *Tamburlaine*, Johann Wolfgang von Goethe's *Faust*, and Fedor Dostoevsky's *Crime and Punishment* all attest the sense of a gap, and very often a chasm, between the way life is supposed to be legitimated by a culture religiously and the way life is experienced by the individual existentially, so works of romance and fantasy as various as Ludovico Ariosto's *Orlando furioso*, Luís Vaz de Camões' *Os Lusíadas*, Francis Bacon's *The New Atlantis*, William Morris' *News from Nowhere*, and Aldous Huxley's *Brave New World* all presume to bridge that gap by formulating idealized alternatives to the historic relations between humankind and nature, society and civilization.

The more significant limitations of this typology, however, come about not because there are notable exceptions to its tripartite structure but because most literary texts of any religious complexity will incorporate several of these structural tendencies at once. The poetry of T. S. Eliot affords an excellent example. According to this schema, Eliot's poetry, at least in its most experimental modes, should exhibit a tendency to displace conventional religious notions with heterodox conceptions of its own devising. Yet as most of Eliot's more astute critics have argued, it seems to do just the opposite. Instead of subverting and displacing inherited religious beliefs, Eliot's poetry has found a way of repossessing them and thus of giving them a new valorization in the present. But one can also object that this view fails to account for the great power of religious disturbance in Eliot's verse and for the fact that the poetry is most disturbing religiously precisely where it is more, rather than less, dependent on traditional religious imagery. The explanation lies not in the nature of the traditional symbols Eliot uses, but in the untraditional uses to which he puts them. His verse can appear theologically conservative to some and theologically innovative to others because his interest is neither in reviving certain religious symbols nor in displacing them but in getting beneath and behind them, in evoking a sense of what they once signified in experience before the strangeness and disruptive energy of their initial meanings became domesticated through incorporation in an inherited mythological and theological framework.

But this complexity of religious structure is not restricted to modern works like the poetry of T. S. Eliot or W. B. Yeats; it can also be found in texts of more ancient vintage, like Cervantes' *Don Quijote*, that are assumed to be interpretively stable. In point of fact, however, Cervantes' great novel is not stable at all. To the eighteenth century, for example, the novel represented a critique of all religious and idealistic enthusiasms and a defense of the world of fact and reason. To the nineteenth century, it constituted a defense of imaginative and religious ideals and a criticism of the world of prosaic fact. And now the twentieth century reads the novel in both ways: as an attack on all human idealisms and also as an indictment of the mundane. But again something seems missing from these interpretations, namely, a satisfactory explanation for the strange and beautiful power of the novel's tensions, contradictions, and conflicts in all their combinatory force. Cervantes' genius, even his religious genius, seems to lie in his ability to hold in tension precisely what these various traditions of interpretation would split apart: a desire to valorize the place of religious and moral idealisms even as he ridicules the lengths to which they can be carried and a concern to challenge the claims of all vulgar materialism while upholding the sacred integrity of the actual and the ordinary. The result is a novel in which a new and unquestionably unorthodox meaning is given to the Christian understanding of incarnate life, and even to the Christian doctrine of the Logos, or Word made Flesh, but in a form that radically resists all theological and moral reductionisms.

Modern study of the interrelations between literature and religion has not emerged in a self-conscious, systematic fashion. The motives propelling such study, the forms it has assumed, the significance attributed to it — all have been too various to reveal much in the way of a consistent pattern of development. Any adequate historical survey would have to trace the subject's origins at least as far back as the second edition of Giambattista Vico's *Scienza nuova* (1744), where, for the first time, the imaginative, or what we would call the fictive, was conceived as a generic category of human consciousness, of which the ultimately true and the merely poetic were but species, and the way was paved for a sympathetic understanding of myth and fable as expressions of the lived experience of a people. It would need to account for the way Johann Gottfried von Herder, especially in *Ideen zur Philosophie der Geschichte der Menschheit*, took up this challenge by arguing that poetry is the essential language of humanity and poets the most representative authors of any nation. It would be obliged to trace the enlarged role of the aesthetic in human spiritual affairs from David Hume's "Of the Standards of Taste" and Immanuel Kant's *Kritik der Urteilskraft* to Friedrich Schiller's *Ueber die aesthetische Erziehung des Menschen*, Georg Hegel's *Phänomenologie des Geistes*, and Samuel Taylor Coleridge's *Biographia Literaria*. And it would necessarily have to come to terms with the way the intersections of the aesthetic and the religious took on new clarity and centrality in the major works of the great nineteenth-century historians from Jules Michelet and Alexis de Tocqueville to Jacob Burckhardt and Hippolyte Taine.

If we restrict our attention to the present century, we can discern some pattern in the rise and fall of various critical schools, emphases, and orientations. In the 1920s, for example, New Humanists like Irving Babbitt and Paul Elmer More encouraged an interest in the religious dimensions of literature that was decidedly ethical, even moralistic. A nonsectarian species of moralistic platonism provided the basis of all sound literature and culture, they assumed, and this ethical monism expressed itself for Babbitt in his stress on the importance of classical restraint, for More in his emphasis on the realization of human imperfection. Less than twenty years later the American New Critics, following one side of T. S. Eliot, shifted discussion of the religious elements of literature from the moral plane to the aesthetic. The literary work comes closest to religion, they argued, in formal terms, by re-enacting the Christian model of the Incarnation through the artist's sacrifice of him- or herself to the materials of his or her craft.

No more than ten years after, with the arrival of existential and phenomenological theories from the Continent, the religious dimensions of literature were being discussed in terms that were explicitly ontological rather than moral or aesthetic. Under the influence of Martin Heidegger, critics were talking about the work of art as a revelation—actually an unveiling—of Being itself, the artist becoming a kind of sacred visionary or intermediary for the divine. More recently, with the ascendance of structuralist and poststructuralist theories of art, the religious dimensions of literature have been reinterpreted in semantic or semiotic terms. The religious elements of individual works of literature, as of whole strains or traditions, are now to be found, if anywhere, either in the linguistic codes out of which all verbal statements are made or in relation to the larger system of signs that compose culture as a whole.

Where it has exhibited a modicum of critical self-awareness, modern study of the relations between literature and religion has developed in several overlapping stages, each expressing itself in a distinctive set of forms and each characterized by a set of methodological orientations. The first stage began in the late 1920s and reached its prominence just before World War II. Its achievements in the main were the work of clergy rather than academics, though the influence carried over from the cloister to the university and even to the wider provinces of literary life. During this initial stage, two kinds of concern dominated the study of literature's relation to religion. Where liberal theological tendencies predominated, the study of literature became important to religious understanding for pastoral or therapeutic reasons. Literature was examined for its diagnostic or educative merits, either to help Christians comprehend the existential dilemmas of the modern world or to save Christians from the soporifics of their own doctrines. Where conservative tendencies were more powerful, literary study was of religious use for dogmatic or prescriptive reasons. Literature was studied for its evaluative or apodictic merits, either to dramatize the problems of a life without faith or to serve as a propaedeutic for life within faith.

The second stage in the modern study of religion and literature developed shortly after World War II and continued unabated well into the mid-sixties. During this stage, owing in equal measure to the influence of existential philosophy on Protestant theology and the rediscovery or revival of older models of traditional, historical scholarship, critical study became dominated by concerns that were either broadly apologetic and correlative or essentially historicist. The apologists valued literature for its ability to give concrete and enduring expression to the great themes and motifs of Western religion and thereby to lend fresh theological relevance to aspects of the Judeo-Christian heritage. The historicists tended to value literature as a repository of the manifold religious inheritance of the West and therefore attempted to restore individual works to those concrete historical traditions that constitute a portion of their contemporary meaning. Thus while the apologists appreciated literature chiefly for the religion in it, the historicists appreciated religion chiefly for the literature of it.

The last, or third, stage began in the middle or late 1960s, when still newer philosophical currents — phenomenology, structuralism, hermeneutics — made themselves felt, first in Europe and then in America (English criticism still seems untouched by these movements). In this period study of the relations between literature and religion focused on issues that are either generic or, in the broad sense, anthropological. Among those concerned with generic issues, critical interest has centered on determining the nature of literature (and writing in general) as part of a larger system of meaning and thus on finding spiritual residues sedimented or inscribed in literature's being. Among those whose orientation is more anthropological, critical interest has centered on the nature of the human animal as that creature which not only makes the literature it needs but needs the literature it makes. Where the generic critic has operated as a kind of cryptographer whose business is to break down complex linguistic codes into their cultural components, the anthropological critic has functioned as a kind of ethnographer looking for traces of the human in the strange behavior of verbal forms.

Modern scholarship devoted to the relations between literature and religion has taken a variety of forms and employed a galaxy of methods. If one separates the methods somewhat artificially, it is apparent that until quite recently they were largely dictated by the forms scholarship took, and those forms have in considerable measure mirrored the historical patterns of literature's relation to religion. Hence one can loosely differentiate modern critical studies that treat literature as a valorization of religion, modern studies that view literature as a criticism of religion, and modern studies that interpret literature as an alternative to or substitute for religion.

Modern studies of literature as a valorization of religion have been for the most part historical and formal in orientation, focusing on literary traditions where religious themes, feelings, and assumptions have been valorized, or on literary techniques and structures that have made such valorization possible, or on writers for whom such valorization has been of paramount concern. Modern studies of literature as a criticism of religion have been predominantly philosophical or theological. Their focus has been either on epistemological and ontological factors responsible for literature's critical view of religion, or on ethical and theological issues that have been the target of such criticism, or on the consequences such criticism has for an understanding of religion and morality. Modern studies of literature as a displacement of religion have been either structural or broadly mythographic and metaphysical in orientation. Where structural interests have predominated, attention has been fixed on those new modes of expression in which such literary displacements or substitutions have occurred. Where mythographic or metaphysical interests have been stronger, emphasis has been placed on the deviant or irregular world views on which such displacements and substitutions have been based.

But again a caveat is in order. Describing the general critical orientation that characterizes these several ways of studying the relation between literature and religion in modern scholarship is not the same as isolating and defining the specific methods that modern scholars have used in analyzing the relation. Scholars working in this interdisciplinary area have included New Critics, Neo-Aristotelians, myth critics, Freudians, Marxists, Croceans, Burkeans, historicists, philologists, linguists, and all other modern schools, but their distinctive methodological commitments can perhaps best be delineated in relation to the theoretical coordinates of the mimetic, the expressive, the rhetorical, and the formal-semantic. Thus religious interpretations of literature that concentrate on the writer's vision of experience have drawn on expressive and mimetic critical theories and have accentuated those factors influencing the writer's beliefs, whether express or implied, that have enabled him or her to constitute the world according to certain specifiable metaphysical principles. Religious interpretations of literature that examine instead the meaning and import of individual works or of whole traditions have employed critical theories that are mimetic and rhetorical, seeking to draw out the implications of assertions made within the work or tradition either for the realm of personal belief and conduct or for the more public realm of social thought and action. Religious interpretations that probe literature's nature and function in human experience tend to fall back on rhetorical and formal-semantic critical theories, attempting to connect the sorts of things literature is purported to be—whether a kind of statement, gesture, or event—with the effects it is presumed to have, either on the psychoreligious makeup of individual readers or on the socio- and politicoreligious organization of particular reading publics. Finally, religious interpretations of literature that study the genetic lineage or generic identity of particular works or kinds of works have relied on critical theories that are both formal-semantic and mimetic and have tended either to situate literature within an anatomy of other, similar kinds of objects, forms, and techniques or to define the ontology of its linguistic and grammatical components.

In recent years these classic theoretical designations have given way to newer methodological orientations. The structuralist approach, whether of the Prague School associated with Roman Jakobson, Jan Mukarovsky, and N. S. Trubetzkoy, the Russian formalist school associated with Boris Eikhenbaum, Mikhail Bakhtin, and Victor Shklovsky, or the French school associated with Claude Lévi-Strauss, Roland Barthes, and Gérard Genette, among others, is now the new mode of the formal-semantic and mimetic orientation. The phenomenological approach, deriving from the philosophy of Edmund Husserl, Martin Heidegger, and Maurice Merleau-Ponty and associated with the work of Roman Ingarden, Georges Poulet, Jean Starobinski, and the early J. Hillis Miller, has become the new mode of the expressive and mimetic orientation. The hermeneutic approach and its subsequent development into the poetics of the imagination on the one side and the aesthetics of reception on the other, originating in the modern period in the work of Wilhelm Dilthey and Hans Georg Gadamer and now associated in the theory of interpretation with the work of philosophers like Paul Ricoeur and Mikel Dufrenne and in the theory of reception with Constance critics like Wolfgang Iser and Hans Robert Jauss, has replaced the mimetic and rhetorical orientation. And the poststructural, or deconstructive, approach, strongly associated with the Paris group loosely organized around Jacques Derrida, Michel Foucault, and Jacques Lacan and represented in this country by critics like Paul de Man, Joseph N. Riddel, and J. Hillis Miller, is the new conflation of the formal-semantic and mimetic orientation.

But what, in fact, have these newer methodological orientations produced in the way of fresh understanding of the possible relations between literature and religion, and how much promise do they hold for further study of these interrelations? The structuralist approach has made its most important contributions by challenging the distinction, long maintained by Anglo-American literary critics, between imaginative literature and other verbal forms. In doing so, it has made possible new understanding of the linkages among poetry, drama, and fiction and such protoreligious forms as myth, legend, and folktale. It has also promoted new interest in the ontology of specific literary subgenres, such as the fantastic, and specific literary structures, such as narrative. These accomplishments arise in considerable measure because structuralists are less interested in the meanings to be extrapolated from such forms and structures than in the way these forms and structures provide the conditions for meaning and thereby establish the conventions that make literature possible.

Phenomenology explores the way an author's consciousness composes and expresses itself in literary form. Like structuralism, with which it bears certain affinities, phenomenology has been instrumental in overcoming the gap between literary and nonliterary forms and has thus made accessible to literary analysis and interpretation many modes of verbal experience that had formerly been dismissed as artistically inconsequential or personally unexpressive. But where the structuralists have examined literary and nonliterary forms for their dichotomous patterns of form and content, for what they call "binary oppositions," phenomenologists have focused attention on the sense of life and manner of expressing it that makes out of any writer's total oeuvre a unified vision. Just as the structuralists have given us new insights into the cultural and linguistic constants of verbal forms, the phenomenologists have increased our perception of what is distinctive about the experienced life world, or *Lebenswelt*, of individual writers and whole traditions.

The hermeneutic approach can be contrasted with the phenomenological and structuralist just insofar as it pays greater attention to the interaction between text and reader, or between the horizon of assumptions expressed and projected by the work and the horizon of assumptions possessed by any one of its potential audiences. Textual understanding thus occurs only when these two horizons of assumption or meaning converge, or at least overlap, and this process of horizon convergence is taken to be reciprocal and potentially disruptive. What must eventually converge in the event of understanding are two inevitably different cultural and metaphysical mind-sets, and what is produced by this intersection of mind-sets is an existential situation in which both text and reader are altered as the identity of each is challenged, revised, and expanded through exposure to the strangeness of the other. According to the new hermeneuticists, there are no absolutely fixed interpretations of any text; there is only the incessant process of interrogation in which readers seek the question for which the text is purportedly an answer and texts seek to determine and constitute an answer for the questions presumably posed by their readers.

The poststructuralist, or deconstructionist, approach has achieved its greatest success in demonstrating the unreliability and instability of all statements made in verbal forms. Its representatives have not exempted criticism itself from this view; indeed, in such books as Paul de Man's *Blindness and Insight* and Roland Barthes's *S/Z*, they have made some of their shrewdest contributions to our understanding of the contextual bias of language. The attack on language and its assertive capacity has carried with it a skepticism about the religious claims made by works of literature, but their own methods, which depend on the ability to locate the linguistic center of any text and then to "decenter" it by showing how ultimately indeterminate and referentially ambiguous its linguistic axis is, are not without a religious premise. As expressed by the foremost philosopher of the approach, Jacques Derrida, deconstructionism is a response to the fallacious ontological assumption of our traditional theory of language, a theory that presupposes an inherent connection between words and the things they signify, between language and being. If this ontological assumption is false, as Derrida and others contend, then there is no necessary or integral relation between the meanings of a text and their referents. All meanings are instead perfectly arbitrary and hence, in the end, self-canceling. The most one can say about any text is that it is composed of a potentially infinite number of nonreferential and unrestricted meanings through whose endless play, as one learns to participate in it through acts of decentering or deconstruction, one may momentarily glimpse the indeterminateness and unreliability of all meaning. The chief motive behind all acts of interpretation, according to this theory, is prophylactic: to resist the seductions of texts and their meanings. All forms of verbal exchange are attempts to play false with experience by inscribing it in words with which it is presumed to bear an inherent relation. The only alternative to this radical epistemological skepticism is to nourish the hope that it is somehow possible to play "true" to experience by refusing all the consolations of linguistic certitude.

If the greatest problem confronting this field of study in the past was its susceptibility to subversion from within, its greatest challenge in the future may arise from its vulnerability to subversion from without. The danger in the past came from the theologization of criticism and the dogmatization of religion. Literary study was turned into a branch of theology and literary experience reduced to a dramatization of doctrines and rituals. At its worst the assumption that theology could provide the categories of literary interpretation and that religious dogmas could define the structures of literary experience produced a serious confusion of categories. Writers as self-consciously agnostic, even atheistic, as Samuel Beckett, Albert Camus, and Franz Kafka were turned into crypto-Christians, while writers as religiously unorthodox as Gerard Manley Hopkins, Ignazio Silone, or Nathaniel Hawthorne were converted into spokesmen for the church. Even at best this assumption created the false impression that the whole of literature's relation to the sacred could be comprehended in theological as opposed to ethical, aesthetic, or sociopolitical terms.

With this problem now widely acknowledged and generally overcome, the field is currently endangered by the reification of criticism itself into a new hierophantic mode. This affliction presents a serious threat to all the newer critical orientations, but it seems particularly infectious among those who want to couple criticism's new visionary status with a wholesale attack on the literary and cultural inheritance of the West. This eschatological mood in criticism has produced mixed results. In its most extreme form, it has reduced all writing to the level of a hostile act and turned criticism in general into a kind of higher pathology whose mission is to diagnose and, if possible, to eradicate the disease called literature. In more moderate form, however, it has encouraged scholars to become more self-conscious about the cultural and the metaphysical entanglements of their own methods and has raised essential and long-neglected questions about the nature and effect of literacy, that is, of our simultaneous infatuation with and dependence on scriptable forms.

To be more specific, the new critical dispensation to which all the recent methodological developments have contributed is expressive of a much-
needed attempt to probe beneath the prejudices and perspectives of methods
per se to the root principles on which the methods depend and from which
they spring. This metacritical impulse has had — or at least could have — the
effect of establishing better communication among specialists within all
branches of criticism by encouraging more systematic reflection on the
foundations of their particular disciplines and orientations. Such reflection
has made us aware as never before of the extent to which all our interactions
with the environment are controlled by linguistic protocols, are mediated by
symbolic actions and objects, and are governed by the cultural endowment.
The crucial question yet to be resolved is whether, as some of the advocates
of the new methodological orientations contend, all our relations with the
environment are determined by the cultural endowment, are confined to
symbolic exchanges, are imprisoned within linguistic warrants and prescriptions. For students of the relations between literature and religion, the key
issue has become whether literature can be said to challenge such conclusions by propelling us toward, perhaps even putting us in touch with, larger
and more inchoate, though just as real, fields of experience that we can
never subjugate to the forms of our speech, that we can never subsume within the conventions of language, that we can never domesticate or control
through symbolic intervention.

The adequate formulation of an answer to this question will determine
much of the critical relevance of work in this field for years to come and will
necessitate theoretical advances on a number of fronts. Chief among them,
perhaps, is greater clarity about the religious assumptions and moral implications of various critical perspectives. Just as all critical orientations afford
a certain epistemological privilege, they also mask an ideological prejudice.
By what techniques, then, are we to determine their range of analytic control and assess their measure of interpretive utility and interest? How are we
to guard against making any critical method absolute without making all
methods relative? Are there any criteria by which we can balance the truth
methods refract against the bias they project?

Increased sensitivity to the respective increments of perception and
distortion in individual critical theories will depend in no small part on the
development and utilization of more sophisticated models of religion and
morality in the interpretation of literature and on a more refined understanding of the bearing of such related fields of study as literature and
myth, literature and folklore, literature and philosophy, literature and politics, and literature and popular culture. In this regard, conceptual advances
in the humanities have not kept pace with — indeed, in certain instances have
fallen woefully behind — developments in the social and behavioral sciences.
Thus while the structuralists and their semantic predecessors have taught us
something about the processes of linguistic encoding in cultural forms, we
know comparatively little about what, for example, Durkheimian sociology

could illumine concerning literature's hieratic role in the constitution and maintenance of various cultural minorities and elites. We still have much to learn from Weberian sociology about the functions played by literary symbols in the process of cultural world formation and individual self-governance. We have just begun to sense what semiotics can teach us about the relations between particular levels and kinds of experience that are integrated within cultural and religious sign systems. And we lack sufficient awareness of post-Freudian psychology's insights, into the relations among the cognitive, the agentic, and the affective in human experience and also into the role of sublimation, transference, and repression in the realm of the aesthetic.

Still another issue awaiting full address is the place and play of theological formulations in religious and cultural traditions. Do theological conceptions operate on any other level of cultural and religious life than systematic discourse? Are they influenced by cultural frames of reference even as they insinuate themselves into and help alter those frames? Do they refer only to a certain species of ideas, or may they also refer to a distinctive range of questions? Does theology function in various traditions to verify the existence of certain objects with which its propositions are supposed to correspond, or is it instead an instrument for determining the implications that certain propositions have for the reorganization and enhancement of human experience?

Few of these issues can be addressed in the abstract. Their further exploration depends on new historical discoveries by scholars and critics alike. In the future, however, because of what we have learned about the nature of both literature and religion, the historical study of their interrelations is not likely to remain intracultural and diachronic but will become more cross-cultural and synchronic, as evidenced in most of the seminal studies in the area, from Albert Béguin's *L'Ame romantique et le rêve* and E. R. Curtius' *European Literature and the Latin Middle Ages* to Erich Auerbach's *Mimesis*, M. H. Abrams' *Natural Supernaturalism*, and Hans Robert Jauss's *Alterität und Modernität der mittelalterlichen Literature*. In addition to the insights yielded by their comparative approach, such works also suggest that advances in this area are not likely to occur in a wholly logical or incremental fashion, with each new discovery building on those previous and all slowly adding to the sum of our knowledge, but are certain to be more haphazard and revisionary, with new discoveries often challenging the whole store of accumulated wisdom and thus requiring at least a partial reconstruction of the entire tradition of interpretation. But the goal of research in the humanities has always been deepened understanding as well as increased knowledge, and for this aim fresh starts and new beginnings are often as instructive as final accountings.

To sum up, then, as this intellectual interest has moved from the far edges of theology, history, and criticism into the mainstream of literary scholarship, it has brought with it problems and concerns that are no different from those that confront scholars in any field of interdisciplinary literary study. What are the forms in which this relation has occurred in history? How have these forms expressed or reflected the experience of individuals as well as communities? What causes these forms to emerge at certain moments of history, undergo revision at others, and disappear at still others? What does our contemporary interest in the evolution, anatomy, and effect of such forms reveal about our own cultural and religious situation? And how may we rescue such forms from historical forgetfulness and reclaim them as a permanent component of the human endowment?

Underlying each of these questions is an issue that now sits squarely at the center of critical debate both in Europe and in the United States. That issue has to do with the complex grammar of motives that compel what someone has whimsically called our "rage to interpret." Do we interpret to demythologize or to remythologize, to decipher or to reinscribe, to inter or to resurrect? Do we interpret for the purpose of determining the limits of literacy or to absorb the lessons of literary experience?

The usual modern answer to this question, as formulated by Karl Marx, Sigmund Freud, and Friedrich Nietzsche, is that we interpret in order not to be deceived. The alternative possibility, as stated more recently by Martin Heidegger, Gabriel Marcel, Hans Georg Gadamer, and Paul Ricoeur, is that we interpret in order to be replenished. Where the first has been described as a hermeneutics of suspicion, the second has been called a hermeneutics of restoration. While the former is chiefly concerned with complicating our methods of reading, the latter is more interested in refining our understanding of what is read and of how it can be applied. At the present moment it would appear that we need to supplement — I do not say replace — the diagnostic emphasis of the hermeneutics of suspicion with the heuristic emphasis of the hermeneutics of restoration. What we need, and what a new hermeneutics of restoration would provide, is a study of such collective expressions of meaning as literature and religion in terms of the ecology rather than the pathology of their relations, that is, in the light of that cultural experience in relation to which they were originally construed, and can still be construed, to make sense, even to seem true.

Bibliography

I. *Works of Theoretical Interest*

Abrams, M. H. *The Mirror and the Lamp: Romantic Theory and the Critical Tradition.* New York: Oxford Univ. Press, 1953. A study of the metaphysical as well as aesthetic implications of the development of expressive theories of art in the Romantic period.

Detweiler, Robert. *Story, Sign, and Self: Structuralism and Phenomenology as Literary-Critical Methods.* Philadelphia: Fortress; Missoula, Mont.: Scholars,

1978. An assessment and comparison of phenomenology and structuralism in relation to their application to biblical as well as literary studies.

Gadamer, Hans Georg. *Truth and Method*. New York: Seabury, 1975. The most important work in religious hermeneutics since the time of Friedrich Schleiermacher.

Gardner, Helen. *Religion and Literature*. London: Faber, 1971. A collection of two sets of lectures, the first treating religion and tragedy, the second exploring the nature of religious poetry.

Gunn, Giles. *The Interpretation of Otherness: Literature, Religion, and the American Imagination*. New York: Oxford Univ. Press, 1979. An examination of the study of literature and religion that focuses on their interrelations in the American tradition.

Hart, Ray L. *Unfinished Man and the Imagination*. New York: Herder, 1968. A theological study of the interpretive role of the imagination and its place in a religious anthropology.

Heidegger, Martin. *Poetry, Language, Thought*. Trans. Albert Hofstadter. New York: Harper, 1971. Seven essays drawn from various works that develop a phenomenological theory of the relation of thought, poetry, and language to Being.

Ingarden, Roman. *The Literary Work of Art*. Trans. George G. Grabowicz. Evanston, Ill.: Northwestern Univ. Press, 1973. A classic phenomenological study of the ontology of literary artworks.

Leeuw, Gerardus van der. *Sacred and Profane Beauty: The Holy in Art*. Trans. David E. Green. New York: Hold, 1963. A theological aesthetics of poetry, drama, dance, painting, music, and sculpture.

Maritain, Jacques. *Creative Intuition in Art and Poetry*. New York: Pantheon, 1953. A major neo-Scholastic theory of the integration of artistic creativity and aesthetic expression.

Ong, Walter J. *The Barbarian Within*. New York: Macmillan, 1962. Critical explorations of literature, religion, and contemporary culture that focus on the aural dimensions of aesthetic experience.

Ricoeur, Paul. *The Conflict of Interpretations: Essays in Hermeneutics*. Ed. Don Ihde. Evanston, Ill.: Northwestern Univ. Press, 1974. Twenty-one theoretical essays on hermeneutics and structuralism, hermeneutics and psychoanalysis, hermeneutics and phenomenology, the symbolism of evil, and religion and faith.

Schneidau, Herbert. *Sacred Discontent: The Bible and Western Literature*. Berkeley: Univ. of California Press, 1976. A theoretical study of the forms of biblical influence on the Western literary inheritance.

Wheelwright, Philip. *The Burning Fountain: A Study in the Language of Symbolism*. Bloomington: Indiana Univ. Press, 1962. A philosophical analysis of the interrelations among mythic, poetic, and religious speech.

II. Works of Practical Interest

Abrams, M. H. *Natural Supernaturalism: Tradition and Revolution in Romantic Literature*. New York: Norton, 1971. A classic study of German and English Romanticism as stages in the process of Western religious secularization.

Auerbach, Erich. *Mimesis: The Representation of Reality in Western Literature*. Trans. Willard R. Trask. Princeton: Princeton Univ. Press, 1953. A definitive study of the stylistic forms of religious and historical realism from classical antiquity to the modern period.

Béguin, Albert. *L'Ame romantique et le rêve: Essai sur le romantisme allemand et la poésie française*. Paris: Corti, 1939. A study of the visionary Romantic soul that dominates German Romanticism and modern French poetry.

Bercovitch, Sacvan. *The Puritan Origins of the American Self*. New Haven: Yale Univ. Press. 1975. An examination of the evolution of Puritan hermeneutics into a distinctive symbolic mode expressive of the American identity.

Buckley, Vincent. *Poetry and the Sacred*. London: Chatto and Windus, 1968. The application of modern theories of religion to the analysis of writers as spiritually diverse as Wyatt, Donne, Blake, Melville, Yeats, and Eliot.

Cochrane, Charles Norris. *Christianity and Classical Culture: A Study of Thought and Action from Augustus to Augustine*. New York: Oxford Univ. Press. 1940. An examination of the impact of Christianity on life and letters in the Greco-Roman world from Augustus and Vergil to Theodosius and Augustine.

Driver, Tom F. *Romantic Quest and Modern Query: A History of the Modern Theatre*. New York: Delacorte, 1970. A study of spiritual motifs in modern drama from Ibsen and Chekhov to Brecht and Genet.

Fairchild, Hoxie Neale. *Religious Trends in English Poetry*. 6 vols. New York: Columbia Univ. Press, 1939–1968. A history of religious thought and feeling in English poetry from 1700 to 1965.

Heller, Erich. *The Disinherited Mind: Essays in Modern German Literature and Thought*. 4th ed. New York: Harcourt, 1975. A study of spiritual deracination and recovery in German writing from Goethe and Schiller to Rilke and Karl Kraus.

Hoffman, Frederick J. *The Mortal No: Death and the Modern Imagination*. Princeton: Princeton Univ. Press, 1964. A study of the relation between violence and self-reconstruction in modern literature, with special focus on sacred and secular interpretations of time and death.

Jaeger, Werner. *Paideia: The Ideals of Greek Culture*. Trans. Gilbert Highet. New York: Oxford Univ. Press, 1945. A philosophical study of the interaction between the historical process by which the character of Greek civilization was formed and the intellectual process by which it constructed a set of ideal images of man.

Jauss, Hans Robert. *Alterität und Modernität der mittelalterlichen Literatur*. Munich: Fink, 1977. A hermeneutics of the otherness and modernity of literature in the European Middle Ages.

Lovejoy, A. O. *The Great Chain of Being: A Study of the History of an Idea*. Cambridge: Harvard Univ. Press, 1936. A definitive examination of one of the root philosophical and religious ideas of Western culture.

Martz, Louis L. *The Poetry of Meditation: A Study in English Religious Literature of the Seventeenth Century*. 2nd ed. New Haven: Yale Univ. Press, 1962. A reinterpretation of English metaphysical poetry that relates its distinctive literary qualities to contemporary methods of spiritual meditation.

Miller, J. Hillis. *Poets of Reality: Six Twentieth-Century Writers*. Cambridge: Harvard Univ. Press, 1965. Individual studies of Conrad, Yeats, Stevens, Eliot, Williams, and Dylan Thomas that trace their efforts to establish a new spiritual relation with the real.

Murdock, Kenneth B. *Literature and Theology in Colonial New England*. Cambridge: Harvard Univ. Press, 1949. An examination of the forms of religious literature in seventeenth-century New England, together with an important chapter on the Puritan strain in American literature.

Nicolson, Marjorie Hope. *Mountain Gloom and Mountain Glory*. Ithaca, N.Y.: Cornell Univ. Press, 1959. A study of the religious aesthetics of mountain landscape art and literature from the Renaissance to the Romantic period.

Pearce, Roy Harvey. *The Continuity of American Poetry*. Princeton: Princeton Univ. Press, 1961. A study of antinomian or Adamic impulses in American poetry and their eventual contrast with what the author calls the mythic mode in the modern period.

Poulet, Georges. *The Metamorphoses of the Circle*. Trans. Carley Dawson and Elliot Coleman. Baltimore: Johns Hopkins Univ. Press, 1966. A phenomenological analysis of the circle as a structural principle of consciousness in a variety of thinkers and writers from the Renaissance to the modern period.

Raymond, Marcel. *From Baudelaire to Surrealism*. New York: Wittenborn, Schutz, 1950. The quest for transcendence and visionary modes of expression in French literature of the later nineteenth and early twentieth century.

Scott, Nathan A., Jr. *The Wild Prayer of Longing: Poetry and the Sacred*. New Haven: Yale Univ. Press, 1971. A study of the death of the figural imagination and the development of the sacramental imagination in modern literature.

Spitzer, Leo. *Classical and Christian Ideas of World Harmony*. Ed. Anna G. Hatcher. Baltimore: Johns Hopkins Univ. Press, 1963. An exercise in historical semantics, or the placement of the history of words within a general history of thought, directed at understanding ancient and Christian notions of the unity of experience.

Wilder, Amos. *The New Voice: Religion, Literature, Hermeneutics*. New York: Herder, 1969. A theoretical study of religious rhetorics in biblical as well as modern literary texts.

Ziolkowski, Theodore. *Fictional Transfigurations of Jesus*. Princeton: Princeton Univ. Press, 1972. A critical study of twenty modern novels that center around a modern hero whose life is modeled on that of the historical Jesus of the Gospel accounts.

III. Critical Anthologies of General Interest

Gunn, Giles, ed. *Literature and Religion*. New York: Harper, 1971. Critical essays on the forms and purposes of the study of religion and literature.

Hopper, Stanley Romaine, ed. *Spiritual Problems in Contemporary Literature*. New York: Harper, 1952. An important early anthology on religion in relation to the artist's situation, the artist's means, and the artist's beliefs.

Scott, Nathan A., Jr., ed. *The New Orpheus: Essays toward a Christian Poetic*. New York: Sheed and Ward, 1964. Essays on Christian aesthetics and the theological character of the modern imagination.

Tennyson, G. B., and Edward E. Ericson, Jr., eds. *Religion and Modern Literature: Essays in Theory and Criticism*. Grand Rapids, Mich.: Eerdmans, 1975. Essays on the nature of religious criticism and the religious meaning of modern literature.

4

Literature and Myth

JOHN B. VICKERY

I

The history of literature everywhere attests to the closeness and complexity of the relation between literature and myth. The tragedians of classical Greece; the epic, lyric, and dramatic poets of the Renaissance; the representatives of English and German Romanticism in particular; and many of Europe's and America's finest modern novelists and poets all show us not only the impact of myth on literature but also the formal and functional resemblances between them. And what is true of Europe and America seems to hold good for Asia and Africa as well. In Asia, traditional literary modes such as the No drama are rooted in ancestral legends and rites, while in Africa artists such as Amos Tutuola deliberately reach back to the myths of their region in order to give form and continuity to their explorations of the novel as a genre. In short, the world's literature and its myths are so entwined that it is virtually impossible to give full consideration to the one without at least a significant measure of attention to the other.

But what is the nature of this relation? The question is simple. Unfortunately, the answer is not, for a variety of complex reasons. It is possible, nevertheless, to single out four aspects of the interrelation of myth and literature. These, needless to say, are by no means mutually exclusive. The most obvious is that which can be called the formal one. Here we are struck by the myriad ways in which myths resemble works of literature. Reading of, say, Prometheus' experiences and exploits in Hesiod or in Apollodorus resembles reading a macro-plot summary of the plays of Aeschylus and Percy Bysshe Shelley. One does not confuse the two, but one sees the similarities. The images of Prometheus nailed to Mount Caucasus and of Oedipus blinding himself, for instance, reverberate in myth as in literature just as the sacrificial and judgmental nature of both events is inherent in the renderings of mythographers as well as dramatists. In effect, then, myth and literature are interrelated because of their shared traits of narrative, character, image, and theme. This relation, however, is one of similarity and not of identity. In the main, the formal traits mentioned above occur in myth in a less developed, explicit, and sustained fashion than they do in literature. Actions are more arbitrary, motivation more simple and also enigmatic, and continuity and form more a matter of the perfunctory and ruptured than of design and resolution. This difference can be likened to that existing between certain biblical tales, such as that of Samson, and the developed genre of the short story.

When two things as vital as myth and literature are seen to bear markedly similar elements, it is inevitable to wonder whether one is responsible for the other's existence, and, if so, which occasions which, or whether there is no causal connection but merely isolated and accidental resemblances. This issue makes up the second aspect of the relation of myth to literature. Since the roots of myth and the earlier forms of oral literature are lost in prehistory, any answer is speculative. Nevertheless, both the number and degree of similarities between particular myths and specific works of literature make it highly improbable that they can all be ascribed to accident or coincidence. In effect, the question of origins becomes central here, for the answers, no matter how tenuous, will shape our critical attitudes. One view of the relation would stress the logical and temporal priority of myth over literature. According to this view, myth's formal properties are simple, elementary forms that naturally become more complex and diverse as society develops and changes and as authors become more aware of the possibilities and significances of myth. Such a view sees myth as culture's earliest mode of responding to its world. Literature together with religion, science, history, and philosophy are later developments from it. It is as if myth were a group of undifferentiated iron filings that in time were sorted out into various different patterns through the introduction of a number of magnets. To the extent that this view has a "causal" dimension, it might be described as a kind of pluralistic teleology.

Another view argues that the relation is a matter not so much of myth's priority to literature as of myth and literature's temporal or logical coincidence. Such a position derives much of its weight from a close study of the oral stage of human culture. Since much if not all of oral poetry originates in ritual functions and purposes, and since ritual is essentially a physical rendering or equivalent of myth, it follows that these earliest forms of poetry often deal with the same subjects as myth—the nature of the gods, the origin of the world, human beings, society, law, and the sundry interrelations of these. In short, the oral culture possesses in its myths, legends, and folktales what is tantamount to a literature save only for the lack of a written text. Needless to say, the differences between an oral and a written literature are considerable, but they do not obliterate the similarities or continuities of form. As a result, the relation between myth and literature that emerges in this view is less one of cause and effect or of generic evolution than one of differing social roles. That is to say, myth and literature differ in that one is sacred (at least so long as the culture at large believes in it) and the other secular or profane in the original sense. The role of the one is to encourage actual worship, that of the other to provide entertainment of an order that does not rule out moral reinforcement, social responsibility, and religious piety. The two come together in the concept of celebration, which weds work and play, activities later separated by literate cultures.

A third aspect of the connection between literature and myth concerns the historical and the specific. One cannot read much of either myth or literature without discovering that the former often serves as source, influence, and model for the latter. The most notable and sustained illustration of this role, of course, is the extent to which Western European literature resonates with classical, particularly Greek, mythology. Edmund Spenser, Christopher Marlowe, George Chapman, and Shakespeare, for example, show us how fraught with myth is the literature of the English Renaissance. Similarly, Pierre Corneille and Jean Baptiste Racine, like Vittorio Alfieri later, in works such as *Médée, Polyeucte, Andromaque*, and *Phèdre*, reveal the diffusion of those mythic figures from their native literature to that of France and the Continent. Later John Keats and Shelley use figures like Endymion and Prometheus even as Heinrich von Kleist and Ernst Theodor Amadeus Hoffmann do. What is the most striking about these and the multitude of other instances available is not only their number but the variety of forms that the relation is capable of taking. The same, of course, is true of nonclassical materials, such as the Bible, medieval figures like Faust and Tristan and Don Juan, and the Celtic tales of Cuchulain, Ossian, Finn, and Taliesin.

Literature uses mythological materials as direct source for events and characters in which transcription is the relation, but it also draws on myth for stimulus to original conceptions and formulations. A prime instance is the transformation wrought in the medieval and Renaissance legend of Faust by Johann Wolfgang von Goethe, who made of a knave a hero of human aspirations. And mediating these two renderings is that of Thomas Mann, who made of the same mythic protagonist a much more enigmatic and morally ambiguous figure. The function of influence need not necessarily be a positive or affirmative one. Alexander Pope, for instance, uses classical myths and allusions for incidental yet incisive contributions to his overarching satiric design. Before him Aristophanes did the same in such works as *The Thesmophoriazusae* and *Plutus*. Even more detached treatment of mythic materials appears in André Gide's *Prométhée mal enchaîné* and *Thésée* and in Jean Cocteau's *Orphée* and *La Machine infernale*. They range from moral satire of ancient but enduring modes of thought to witty yet haunting demonstrations of the modernity of myth and on to coolly ironic interrogations of the nature and functions of myth itself. Thus, the role of myth as model for literature may be as much iconoclastic as iconographic.

Another striking feature of this historical relation is the range of the diffusion of myth throughout its own culture and into that of other cultures. Mythic figures such as Ulysses, Prometheus, Hercules, Cain and Abel, and Orpheus have been traced in their literary apparitions throughout much of Europe, particularly in German, French, and English literature. And there is no single direction or migratory pattern to this diffusion. Writers are drawn to their own culture's myths, as Heinrich Heine, C. P. Cavafy, and Nelly Sachs demonstrate. But they are also fascinated with the structural, thematic, and narrative possibilities in myths quite alien to their immediate culture. The nineteenth-century American Herman Melville and the twentieth-century German Thomas Mann utilize the Egyptian deity and culture figure Osiris. The British novelist David Stacton goes to the Hindu god Shiva for a fictional locus, while the American John Berry seizes on Krishna. The German novelists Hans Jahnn and Guido Bachmann plunge back to the Babylonian epic hero Gilgamesh for their protagonist. And the Japanese novelist Kobo Abe invokes the Greek figure of Sisyphus, as did the French writer Albert Camus before him, in order to dramatize the existential ordeal and dilemma. Even more inclusive in his response to myth is the American poet Charles Olson, who finds poetic models in classical, Babylonian, Mexican, and Mayan mythology.

At the same time, it is important to recognize that the whole relation does not come down simply to a random plundering of myth by writers. In some cultures, the relation between myth and literature, whether oral or written, is direct and intimate, a fact apparent both in ancient Greek and contemporary African literature. But in other cultures, such as English and French, a body of literature (e.g., Greek or Roman) often serves as an intermediary between the dominant, classical myths and the native literatures. In still other cultures, we find some of the relations between myth and literature proving to be arbitrary and largely self- or group-determined. An obvious example is the recurring fascination with Eastern myths that American writers from Ralph Waldo Emerson, Henry David Thoreau, and Walt Whitman to Allen Ginsberg and Gary Snyder evince at the same time as they struggle furiously to embody the intrinsic myths of their native land. In sum, then, the historical relation obtains even in those writers, such as William Blake, J. R. R. Tolkien, Mervyn Peake, or E. R. Eddison, who seek to articulate their own personal or self-created mythologies.

The final relation between myth and literature is psychological insofar as it concerns itself with the dynamics of the two activities. Three issues stand out. The first is the attitude toward the production of myths and works of literature. Linguistically, both differ from activities such as science or commonsense empirical statements of descriptive or predictive fact. Neither Apollodorus' "Pluto fell in love with Persephone and with the help of Zeus carried her off secretly" nor T. S. Eliot's "Apeneck Sweeney spreads his knees / Letting his arms hang down to laugh" are read as records of historically actual events. Yet both are taken seriously, that is, held to possess meaning or significance or, in Bertrand Russell's words, to consist of "an idea or image combined with a yes-feeling." Belief or something similar to belief seems to be involved in both cases, yet not in the way of accuracy or truth of report-making utterances. Even members of a culture holding or revering a particular myth are not always prepared to assert its absolute truth even when convinced of its importance as a model of past or future events. And to persons outside of that culture its myths appear either undeniably false, as John Milton viewed classical myth, or fictional, tales capable of reinforcing social or religious convictions, stimulating the imagination, or broadening human sympathies. And as such, they are of substantially the same order as works of literature. The existence of both drives us to recognize that these fictions are essential, that we need to define and classify their functions and to face (or evade) the possibility that fiction making is the central activity of the human mind.

A closely connected issue in the relation of myth and literature is the activity of storytelling, because often, for the serious student, the fact of literature's existence outweighs the question of why literature does exist. Here myth's relation to the narrative dimension of literature is enlightening. Because of the bizarre and puzzling nature of many mythical stories and because of our cultural detachment and distance from many of them, we are more likely to ask ourselves about the rationale for their existence. Why should an individual or a series of individuals tell about persons having fifty heads and a hundred hands, or about children cutting off parents' genitals, or about shape-changing, thieving, promiscuous deities? Why should a number of writers recount the exploits of a crippled child who acts violently toward a parent, rises to high office through his sagacity, discovers a terrible secret concerning himself and his parentage, leaves his homeland after destroying his vision, and dies in exile? And why for that matter should anyone ever tell any story at all?

The answer to all these questions would appear to be that the story form is the basic way we structure our awareness of the world. Because time figures in experience, all verbal efforts to render it seem to fall into or to derive from the story form. As levels of abstraction increase, the story form is less explicit, as one can see from the social and natural sciences. But for myth and literature the narrative activity remains paramount. Consequently, they direct attention to the fact that the human world is a story-shaped one and that the human being lives surrounded by fictions. Faced with a world and with experiences that give rise to everything from wonder to tedium, the human mind turns to story in order both to explore and to escape, to celebrate and to query, those feelings. In short, both myth and literature are the meeting point of minds warmed and bedeviled by their perceptions of the world; they are the means by which active and passive responses to experience are fused, for in the writing-reading activity, the mood of idleness, as Keats saw, is one with the mood of energy.

While the nature of the relation between myth and literature is important in its own right, perhaps of even greater significance is the value it possesses for the student of literature. Like the relation, that value is multiple and diverse. Essentially it engages several basic questions and provides a di-

versity of perspectives on them. The first of these questions concerns literature's source, where it came from logically and temporally. No ultimate answer is possible. But in approximate terms, one can say that literature comes
from the tradition of oral narrative and nonnarrative performance. In this
tradition myth and ritual occur both as subject and as form or event. Whether
myth ever existed historically anterior to the oral tradition is impossible to
say. But since thought is logically prior to speech or writing and since beliefs
precede their assertion, we can say this: myth—here regarded as the conviction or convictions, explained in various ways by the actions of beings superior in kind and degree to humans, that provide a rationale for existing patterns of belief and behavior—constitutes the religiosocial matrix from which
literature emerges as an endlessly self-complicating phenomenon.

A more immediate question confronting thoughtful readers is why
literature affects us as it does. Here again the relation with myth affords a
possible answer or line of investigation. Historically this question has had a
variety of responses—moral, religious, social, imaginative, historical, and
psychological. But it is difficult today not to feel that some form of the affective and the constructive powers of the individual psyche is the root of
explanation. That is, literature affects us through its capacity to construct
persons, scenes, and even worlds that arouse responses uncircumscribable
by rational knowledge or empirical description. The same is true of myth,
which, however socially vital, still leaves us with the tantalizing mystery and
puzzle as to its ultimate or real meaning. Myth's roots in religious ritual,
however, suggest that one of its central functions is to provide contact with
that transrational but empirical power called variously mana, orenda, or the
numinous. Even though the bulk of literature is secular, literature clearly
shares in the spiritual or emotional core of myth's power. Its role is to perpetuate and focus the significance of that awe, wonder, and above all vitality
that is the human response to the experiential that lies both within and without the individual. To that extent, not only the forms of literature but also
its functions can be seen as displacements from those of myth.

In addition to the historical and psychological dimensions of these two
basic questions, there is a third, formalistic, value in the interrelation of
myth and literature. It is not enough to probe the origins and affective power
of literature; we also seek to appreciate or understand literature, to convey
to ourselves and others how we feel about it and what values we place on its
instances. Yet one of the most persistent features of this activity is our inclination to be parochial, provincial, or conventional in our judgments. The
artist's rage for disorder seems perennially to be countered by the reader's
passion for the familiar. Expectations and preconceptions about narrative,
subject matter, plausibility, tone, form, and related issues threaten appreciation and understanding. Though it may be neither a necessary nor a sufficient condition for the appreciation of literature, myth here too may exercise a positive value on the relation. Essentially, it can encourage readers to

move beyond limitations of place, time, and cultural perspective. Myth provides clues to the variability of literary forms and the defensibility of new ones. In so doing it renews or encourages catholicity of response. The adventures of the Argonauts, the grotesque appearance of Typhon, the familial violence of Cronus, the helter-skelter sexuality of Zeus, the rampages of Hercules, the amoral incitements of Dionysus, even the tedious genealogies and arbitrary conclusions such as "so much for that subject" all serve to alert us to the range of possibilities inherent in the act and art of storytelling. They also serve to point up the intricate relations, both congruent and incongruent, obtainable between form and content. And out of the interaction of these two avenues of suggestion, myth further bears in on the reader of literature the full and reverberant implications of both forms being a matter not only of what is said but of what is not said, a matter not only of declaration but also of interpretation.

II

Because of the antiquity and persistence of myth, its interrelations with literature are protean, and the perspectives from which they are viewed are multiform. Any historical overview has to recognize that the explicit interest of literary critics in myth is of recent vintage, scarcely more than a matter of late nineteenth- and twentieth-century concern. In other areas the interest is of an older order going back as far as the Stoics and Neoplatonists in philosophy. But for our purposes, the prevailing current extraliterary perspectives on myth are anthropological, psychological, sociological, and philosophical. Each has several distinctive emphases or points of view.

The anthropological perspective has at least three different groupings. The first and earliest of these is the Cambridge School, consisting of Sir James G. Frazer, Jane Harrison, and F. M. Cornford, which derived from the classical evolutionary views of E. B. Tylor and Andrew Lang. This group concentrates largely on Greek mythology, though in Frazer's *The Golden Bough* and elsewhere it casts a comparative net over a larger but looser body of materials. The central contention of its members lies in the ritual character of myth; they feel that ritual expresses in action an emotion or complex of emotions that in myth is expressed in words. In their eyes, since actions, such as ritual dances and gestures, may be developed more readily than is possible for the public or communal narratives of myth, ritual carries a measure of logical priority. They are also convinced that ritual is comparatively permanent in form whereas myth possesses a shifting and manifold character. For them, myth is not originally etiological but may become so when the emotions giving rise to the ritual lose their immediacy. At this point, the myths purport to explain the existence and origin of the rituals.

A quite different approach is found in those anthropologists who worked with, and developed within the general intellectual frame of reference of, Franz Boas with his concern with the factual, his skeptical and even negative view of generalization and speculation, and his emphasis on specific cultural context. For one thing, his insistence on fieldwork and the collecting of data led, in his studies of North American Indians such as the Bella Coola and Tshimian and in Ruth Benedict's of the Zuñi, to copious records of what those cultures themselves considered their myths to be. This led to the view that the genesis of myth was communal and cultural rather than individual and psychological. Their studies concluded that a single genealogical explanation of the origin and development of myth was not possible.

A third anthropological perspective on myth is that associated with structuralism and preeminently with Claude Lévi-Strauss, though others, such as Marcel Detienne, Harald Weinrich, and Georges Dumézil, are also involved. This view rejects both the evolutionary emphasis and the avoidance of generalization. Its shaping influences are three. One is Karl Marx's functional analysis of society as a global unit. Another comes from the structural linguists—notably Ferdinand de Saussure, Roman Jakobson, and Nikolay Trubetskoy—and their differentiation of synchronic and diachronic together with their stress on the primacy of the relational. And finally it reflects the Freudian or psychoanalytic emphasis on latent meanings and the techniques for discovering them. As a result, Lévi-Strauss regards myth as a particular kind of language possessing properties or features that are more complex than those of language. Myth is the antithesis of poetry in that its value and meaning persist throughout all translations.

Because of its linguistic nature, myth is composed of constituent units, but unlike the rest of language it possesses units unique to it. Such units are bundles of relations rather than isolated relations because mythological time is both synchronic and diachronic. That is to say, a given subject in a myth has different functions at different times within the narrative. As a result, the subject's meaning consists of all the relations obtaining between all the functions. Therefore, the meaning of a myth consists of all such relations of all the identifiable subjects it possesses. Analysis of these relations, the structuralist argues, reveals that any myth—construed as all the existing versions including interpretations of it—consists of polar and contradictory assertions or implications. These are progressively mediated by other conceptual formulations until the original contradiction is in a sense resolved. The language of myth expands the context of the original logical or metaphysical problem until it is translatable into issues of a social and moral order. Since these issues have socially structured solutions embedded in the culture, their equation with the logically insoluble problem enables the society and its members to continue to function.

Myth, then, is a conservative force dedicated to perpetuating social and mental existence by absorbing a culture's metaphysical and cosmological contradictions into its societal convictions and customs. Underlying this activity of myth is a logic, it is claimed, that differs from that of contemporary science only in its subject matter and not in its methodology or rigor. Such a logic, however, is not apparent from myth's manifest or surface narrative, which is full of discontinuity, arbitrariness, and repetitiveness. At the same time, myth exhibits, says Lévi-Strauss, an enormous measure of similarity in its manifestations from widely disparate geographical regions and cultures. It can do so only because these manifestations possess an underlying structural pattern that is both synchronic and diachronic. One of the chief indexes of this pattern is the pronounced tendency of myth to multiply similar narrative sequences, characters, and attributes. In sum, what the structural approach to myth stresses is that myths cohere in a kind of system. Their latent structure is as vital as their manifest content and they function on various levels — social, psychological, economic, cosmological, to mention only the most frequently adduced — but in the same basic way. They also underscore the polarities and antitheses of human experience, of which the most notable appears to be that between nature and culture. At the same time myths embody in their narratives balanced adjustments of emphasis and attitude that gradually approximate to a viable resolution of the initial dichotomy.

The second major intellectual perspective on myth is the psychological and in the main consists of the ideas of Sigmund Freud and Carl Jung and their followers and successors. For the early analysts myth was regarded as the dream of the race, which functioned in a cultural, social, public fashion much as the dreams of an individual did. Both myth and dream were symbolically constructed messages from the unconscious testifying to its problems, needs, and goals. Closer examination of actual myths in relation to actual dreams showed a significant structural difference in degree if not in kind. Condensation, displacement, and splitting dominate the dream mechanism. Myths reveal a narrative order, a selection of material or content, a temporal sequence, even a choice of symbol that betray a greater measure of conscious ordering. As a result, the psychoanalytic view came to ally myth less with dream per se and more with the daydream. In the latter the mechanisms of the unconscious still obtain but are modified by some impact of external reality.

All analysts from Freud, Otto Rank, Karl Abraham, and Sandor Ferenczi to Géza Róheim, Theodor Reik, and Erich Fromm agree that myth is preoccupied with the basic elements of human existence. Its topics, either manifestly or latently, are those of the child ego that in some measure may persist into adulthood. These include the hatred or the resentment of the father; the incestuous desire for the mother; infantile curiosity about sexuality as it manifests itself both in the parents and in the child's own developing behavior; the anxiety aroused by apprehensions and fantasies concerning physical and psychological acceptance and rejection; the terrors of being left alone in a strange and alien world that culminate in the fear of destruction represented most powerfully in the threat of castration; the network of personal rivalries both generational, as with siblings, and intergenerational, as with parents and children; and the longing for acceptance into a secure and independent state of existence identified with the adult world.

Natural events such as urination, defecation, copulation, masturbation, and menstruation, together with the feelings of aggression, anxiety, disgust, pride, and so on, that they arouse, are projected into fantasy form so as to reject or sublimate individual sexuality. To the extent that myths' projections entail reversals of real or actual interpersonal relations, as, it is claimed, happens in the Oedipal myth, myths are called paranoid, at least by early theorists such as Rank. Later analysts, especially those influenced by ego psychology, are more inclined to see myth and folklore generally as providing individuals and groups with fantasy escapes from socially imposed repressions such as taboos on incest or polygamy as well as from blockages of drives other than those of sex.

In contrast to the Freudian approach to myth, which sees it as deriving from other basic aspects of existence, Jung views myth as an inherent function of the human mind. Freud and Jung are related by their concern with the genesis and the forms of myth. Though their answers diverge significantly, each seeks to explain the production of myth by the human psyche and the meaning of its symbols, images, and narrative patterns. Jung's answers reflect his divergence from Freud in three key particulars. First, he shifts the genetic motive for myth from the libidinal impulse to a more encompassing concept of psychic maturation based on a recurring pattern of challenge and response. Second, Jung regards the unconscious as an irreducible symbolic structure, at least part of which is common to all individuals. That is, it is a reality that is untranslatable not because linguistic versions are not possible but precisely because they are possible and are limited to the status of versions. And finally, rather than postulating a psyche structurally given and largely determined in its response capacities during infancy, Jung proposes one that is the product of its own continuous development throughout time.

The Jungian psyche generates archetypal images that belong to the possibilities of imaginal representation inherited from the evolving totality of the human race's experience. Such images appear both in the individual's dreams—though not all dreams or all aspects of dreams are archetypal—and in the myths of the world. They do so in order to pose both the recurring threats of regression and the traditional modes of coping with those threats that human beings have experienced since they first began to struggle toward and into a consciousness of the world and of themselves. These polarities of regression and progression, self and world, inner and outer are represented in myth in the figures of mother and father. The ambivalence of reaction toward them, especially toward the former, testifies to the dangers as well as the benefits inhering in each pole. Facing, and coping with, these polarities—on the parts of the protagonist within the myth, the individual or group audience outside the myth, and the creator or narrator mediating between myth and respondents—yield those psychic transformations that not only symbolize but bring about the emergence of the truly individual person who is simultaneously creative and morally and culturally responsible.

The foremost sociological perspective on myth is the functionalist one advanced by Bronislaw Malinowski, who was influenced to some degree both by the Cambridge School and by the French school of sociology associated with Emile Durkheim. Durkheim saw myth as a significant aspect of the religious system operative in a society, being to language what ritual was to action. Perhaps because of his anthropological field experience in Melanesia, Malinowski minimizes the symbolizing role of myth. Instead he stresses the intimate connection between a tribe's sacred tales and its social organization, including such practical activities as agriculture and economics.

What myth does in his eyes is to provide the institutions and beliefs of a society with a charter, a justification capable of resolving conflicting claims whether of empirical fact or of rational argument. Because the realities of history, geography, politics, and economics are frequently inconsistent, a society needs and so creates a means of resolving the competing claims in a manner that seeks to ensure the persistence of the society itself. Myth does this by recounting events from a remote past about ancestors whose racial continuity with the tribe is balanced frequently by traits, powers, and relationships discontinuous with those of the tribe. In so doing, myths exert a justificatory force — sanctioning certain beliefs and actions and rejecting others — on the day-to-day life of their society. This role, argues Malinowski, rather than that of explaining or symbolically representing spiritual states or natural phenomena, constitutes the function of myth.

To determine precisely what any particular myth actually sanctions is far from simple. To see that sacred tales about flying witches or earliest ancestors emerging from holes in the earth are charters for certain clan or territorial rights is almost as incredible as the psychoanalytic identification of gold with feces or eyes with testicles in myths. Instead of taking the manifest content of myths at face value, one defines their meaning in cultural terms that take into account the society's view of the creatures and objects and actions referred to in the myths. To understand this view, one must grasp such things as the prevailing system of marriage and kinship, criteria of citizenship or tribal membership, and customary rights to territory such as hunting and fishing grounds.

Another aspect of Malinowski's functionalism, and one that follows from his field sources, is his discrimination among the prevailing narrative forms of a society. Not all stories are myths in the Trobriand Islands, only those regarded as true and of extreme age and sacred. Distinguished from myths are both legends and folktales. Legends are thought to be both true and factual, at least in part, but they possess no magical properties or efficacy and have no prescribed manner of telling. Folktales are fictional so far as belief is concerned, recounted dramatically, and identified with a particular teller or family. The crucial point of this differentiation is that Malinowski took these categories from the culture itself and from its members. In addition, he valued the total immediate, as well as mediate, context of myth. Thus, of equal importance are such factors as the occasion and location of myths' recital, the nature of the teller and the audience as well as the teller's devices and the audience's degree of participation, and the tribal attitude toward these narrative classifications.

The final perspective on myth is that of philosophy, where the principal names are those of the Neo-Kantian Ernst Cassirer and his American supporter Susanne Langer, though Philip Wheelwright has made significant contributions to the semantics, meaning, and symbolic function of myth in relation to literature. Even more recently there is the work of Roland Barthes, A. J. Greimas, and other semiologists, which radically alters the notion of myth. Barthes treats myth as both a system of signs and a system of beliefs. Society develops a system of beliefs in order to preserve its sense of its significance. The system of signs is based on the system of language and functions connotatively in such a way as to covertly produce meaning that appears to be natural or ultimate or "given" when in fact it is manufactured. Such an approach tends to concentrate on the range of sign-producing activities and on their contemporary forms rather than on the mythologies of prehistory and ancient times.

Historically, philosophy has had a good deal to say about myth, from the allegorical approach of the Sophists and Neoplatonists as well as Francis Bacon and the euhemeristic view of the Epicureans to the fusion of the two in Giambattista Vico's *La Scienza nuova*, the rationalistic treatment of Bernard le Bovier de Fontenelle, Voltaire, and the Encyclopedists, and the subsequent idealistic reaction of German Romanticism in the works of such thinkers as Johann Gottfried von Herder, Friedrich Schlegel, Friedrich Schelling, and Friedrich Nietzsche. But the directions philosophy has taken more recently with the analytic school, existentialism, pragmatism, and phenomenology have, in general, precluded its attending in any sustained fashion to myth.

Cassirer focuses on two topics or issues: the cultural role of myth as one of the symbolic forms by which human beings creatively apprehend existence, including their own, and the nature of mythical thinking or mythopoeic consciousness. Like Schelling, Cassirer regards myth as an independent expression of the human spirit that cannot be explained or reduced to any other cultural form such as language, art, or science. It does, however, have a significant relation to these and other symbolic forms, for all constitute progressive differences of consciousness. Human thought and, perhaps, language begin in an undifferentiated state in which image and entity, the ideal and the real coexist. With the gradual development of the human spirit and consciousness, the symbolic and significatory split off from the original matrix until they become separate and distinct modes aware of their individuality. Art, for instance, knows itself as art and also as not science or religion or myth. Each of these is essentially a human disposition to a particular mode of expression that gradually crystallizes into self-awareness and objective differentiation. Thus, as his study *The Myth of the State* reveals, Cassirer treats myth as a basic and ineradicable activity of human consciousness.

This activity of mythopoeic consciousness differs from that of philosophy or science in being neither rational nor intellectual. Its perceptions are not a matter of dispassionately registering objective entities. Instead, it is a question of concentratedly possessing in all its immediacy an aspect of external reality that includes the perceiver's vital emotions aroused by both the act and object of perception. Mythic perceptions, in short, are affect-saturated. As a result, one is capable of sensing real but nonexistent entities such as spirits, demons, divinities, or even ominous or benign shapes and locations. In whatever form mythic images present themselves to consciousness they do so with an aura of preternatural significance and power.

With such a mode of consciousness, not only the object but its causal connections are of a unique and dynamic order. The perceptual process disregards consistency, predictability, and even possibility in its contents and in its affects, while at the same time it stresses both the recurrent and the singular character of the awareness. In short, myth is, for Cassirer, a mode of consciousness that symbolically structures the world and a record of the mind's processes projected on to the external world. Its symbolizing activity, therefore, contributes to the human creation of a meaningful and so-called objective world. By so objectifying human emotions in image and symbol, myth serves the socially pragmatic function of generating a shared feeling and conviction of social and natural unity.

III

There are a number of other theories and approaches to myth, especially in the areas of comparative religion, the classics, comparative mythology, and folklore. The foregoing, however, represent not only the major recent influences but also a conspectus of the most common ways of viewing myth. With the possible exception of the Boasian approach, all are reflected in the approaches of literary critics. These approaches, in turn, represent not so much clearly defined methodologies as differing intellectual influences and personal predilections.

Earlier myth critics, such as Colin Still, G. R. Levy, William Troy, H. H. Watts, Francis Fergusson, Philip Wheelwright, and perhaps Alan Watts, stood fairly close to the Cambridge myth-and-ritual school, partly because it seemed to support their formalist preoccupations with the autonomy of the text. In some instances, an additional motivating factor was the longing, frequently subliminal, for a cultural surrogate — found in art — for the sanctions and solace of religion. Other critics were less concerned with the timeless pattern than with personal responses, especially of the author, sublimated into mythic narratives and images. Harry Slochower, Morton Seiden, Honor Matthews, and Claire Rosenfield exemplify this focus as well as the distinctive emphases of the Freudian and Jungian perspectives.

Though these approaches have not disappeared, they have been significantly modified by the appearance of other, more socially oriented focuses. Literary works, like tribal myths and rituals, have also been perceived as reflections — no matter how dim, oblique, and ambiguous — of their cultural setting and social dynamic, as in the works on American literature of Henry Nash Smith, Daniel Hoffman, R. W. B. Lewis, and Richard Slotkin. Concepts and images such as the "New Adam" and the "land as virgin" are seen as permeating a culture during certain historical epochs in much the same way as the myths of a tribal culture provide a sanction for its traditions and customs. Midway between these formal and social approaches are critics who share with Malinowski, A. Irving Hallowell, William R. Bascom, and other cultural anthropologists the emphasis on functionalism, but adapted to the nature and interpretive boundaries of the literary text. Critics such as Herbert Weisinger, Patricia Merivale, C. L. Barber, H. Bruce Franklin, and this author maintain a historical stance toward their subject, as seen by their concern with influence, derivation, and periodicity. At the same time, they concentrate on the myriad functions of myth as a factor in the text and in the interpretation. In short, they are probably concerned more with the particular ways in which myth merges with literary texts than with the fact or identification of its presence. Of the same general emphasis, though giving more attention to the formal aspects of the question, are recent studies by Lillian Feder and J. J. White.

One cannot emphasize too strongly that none of the foregoing groups of critics constitutes anything resembling a school. The unity among these critics, such as it is, comes from their shared interest in myth as a narrative, symbolic, and structural phenomenon that materially impinges on literature. Most myth critics, however, would probably subscribe to the following general principles. First, the creating of myths, the mythopoeic faculty, is inherent in the thinking process, and it answers a basic human need. Second, myth forms the matrix out of which literature emerges both historically and psychologically. Consequently, literary plots, characters, themes, and images are complications and displacements of similar elements in myths and folktales. How myth got into literature is variously explained by the Jungian racial memory, historical diffusion, or the essential similarity of the human mind everywhere. Third, myth not only can stimulate the creative artist, but it also provides concepts and patterns that the critic may use to interpret specific works of literature. Knowing the grammar of myth gives a greater precision and form to our reading of the language of literature. In recognizing that mythic features reside beneath as well as on the surface of a work, myth criticism differs substantially from earlier treatments of the mythological in literature. Fourth and last, the ability of literature to move us profoundly is due to its mythic quality, to its possession of mana, the numinous, or the mystery in the face of which we feel an awed delight or terror at the world. The real function of literature in human affairs is to continue myth's ancient and basic endeavor to create a meaningful place for human beings in a world oblivious of their presence.

The question of what the relation of literature and myth is leads logically to what the relation can contribute to our understanding of literature. Foremost is the capacity, shared with all good criticism, to sharpen our perception of theme, structure, imagery, and character in a specific work and their continuities and development throughout an author's canon. Through the relation we are able to reveal the transmogrifications of a single motif or figure such as Orpheus, Oedipus, or Ulysses in a period or several periods and to underline the ways a genre in a particular historical period, such as modern Continental drama, utilizes the materials of myth. We are also able to interpret a period or group of writers like those of the American renaissance as embodying a dominant myth or concatenation of myths. Finally, the relation can even lead, as we see preeminently from Northrop Frye, to an inclusive theory of literature. Recognition of the pattern of *sparagmos* ("the tearing apart of the sacrificial body") in *Tender Is the Night*, the rites of passage of the protagonist in *The Plumed Serpent*, or the role of divine king and scapegoat in James Joyce's HCE in *Finnegans Wake* uncovers significant aspects of these works that other forms of criticism slight. An awareness of myth enables the critic to isolate latent elements, which, like those of dreams, possess the force that vitalizes the manifest pattern. Shakespeare's tragic heroes, like Spenser's Garden of Adonis, Goethe's Walpurgis Night, Hermann Broch's meditations on Vergil, and Mann's bloody ritual temple dismemberment (in *Der Zauberberg*) resonate with primordial affect because individual genius was receptive to sources with mythic content.

Myths and rituals may also help gauge the unique features of literary works. For instance, identifying William Faulkner's Joe Christmas, Euripides' Pentheus, Henrik Ibsen's Dr. Stockmann, Fedor Dostoevsky's Prince Myshkin, or August Strindberg's Libotz as sacrifical scapegoats is but the first step. In terms of the myth model of the scapegoat, one is driven to ask of the texts a number of functionally specific questions, including why these characters were chosen, what differing kinds of communal sins they are to remove, what forms — physical, psychological, or social — the expulsion takes, and what view of the myth is implicit in the creative interaction of author and text. In the process the reader comes to a concrete and precise apprehension of how individual and cultural dynamics shape the character's fulfillment of his mythic role. Almost inevitably this approach leads to a comparative method that uses myth and archetype as the ground for thematic and dramatic comparison and differentiation. It follows the arc of the Promethean myth from Aeschylus to Shelley to Saul Bellow or that of the Oedipal myth from Sophocles to Alberto Moravia and Alain Robbe-Grillet or the permutations of the trickster from the classics through tribal tales to Goethe's *Reinecke Fuchs*, Melville's *The Confidence-Man*, and Mann's *Bekenntnisse des Hochstaplers Felix Krull*, not to mention Ted Hughes's *Crow*. In so doing it enriches our understanding of artist and age alike.

Such a concern for the emotional patterning in myth is peculiarly appropriate to the twentieth century's struggle to achieve a viable mode of psychic and cultural order. Writers as diverse as Nelly Sachs, George Seferis, C. P. Cavafy, and Federico García Lorca show us this connection unmistakably. Their immersion in the reality and unreality of the present in no way precludes their reaching out to the mythological figures and events of their cultures for the powers to endure. They may elect to see poetry and myth as converging on an intuitive knowledge that surpasses rational understanding, as Hermann Broch, Rainer Maria Rilke, William Blake, and perhaps Boris Pasternak do. Or they may, like Gide, Jean-Paul Sartre, Bertolt Brecht, Eugène Ionesco, and the contemporary American novelist John Barth, find in myth the relentlessly human wisdom resident in the bracing ironies of the narrative act, which for them exist both within and without the text. But whatever the stance toward, and the uses of, myth, literature draws on, perpetuates, and re-creates myth as vigorously today as in the past.

An equally important facet of this perspective is that it affords a unifying point of view that more nearly than any other derives from literature itself. Its key terms—myth and ritual—encompass that from which literature emerged; therefore, it is aligned with literature essentially, not accidentally, and in a way that social, political, philosophical, and religious concepts are not. Its terminology, perspective, and values are inherently and radically literary; to this extent, myth criticism is nonideological. Thus, whatever anthropologists may say about the meaning of the word "myth," critics legitimately extend or alter its sense to the needs of their own discipline. For instance, one speaks of the myth in Franz Kafka's work and refers to a projection of the author's psychoses. Used of *Ulysses*, say, myth means a formal extrapolation of, or structural parallel to, an ancient story. In some of D. H. Lawrence's short stories and short novels as well as in Ionesco's drama, myth may function as a satiric device offering both a contrast and a sense of continuity between the forms of life lived by ancient and contemporary humanity. Or myth may refer essentially to a new version of an old story, as in Robert Graves's *King Jesus*, Mann's *Joseph* series, Gide's *Thésée*, Faulkner's *Light in August*, and William Golding's *Lord of the Flies*. Here it describes what has been called the writer's "mythistoria," that is, "the circumambient atmosphere of his place and time."

In short, the multiplex relation of myth and literature demonstrates that the term may refer to the author, to his work, or to the society that attends to both. Accordingly, it acquires manifold dimensions: psychological, rhetorical, semantic, ideological, or sociological. What is essential is not reduction to a single definition but skill in discriminating the meaning relevant to the occasion. Through extended and sensitive development of these various dimensions — as Frye's *Anatomy of Criticism* shows us — myth criticism may help close the gap between formal analysis, whether semantic, rhetorical, or archetypal, and the functional, genetic concerns of the literary historian, biographer, and psychoanalyst.

While myth criticism endorses the autonomy and study of literature, it does not consign the critics to the vacuum-sealed containers of their own brains. Instead it links them to other disciplines, notably anthropology and psychology, and so broadens their approaches to, and their modes of experiencing, reality. It thus aspires to reverse the practical achievement of the New Criticism, which was to cut off the critic from direct access to the resources of science, sociology, and philosophy. By espousing the necessity of extraliterary knowledge for the critic while reserving the right to adapt that knowledge in accordance with the needs of literary study, myth criticism serves as a reminder of the dangers of concentrating too narrowly on limited areas and approaches. To avoid its own form of narrowness without resorting to a fuzzy ad hoc eclecticism is one of the premier and abiding challenges confronting this approach to literature.

IV

From the foregoing one might think a critical millennium is at hand. But as Gilbert Ryle once observed, intelligent theory always holds out the possibility of unintelligent practices. What concerns us here are the major general issues inherent in the subject. Though considerable simplification and some distortion may be inevitable, nevertheless we can perhaps distinguish four such issues, which carry, it is hoped, as much relevance as rhyme. They are the problems of definition, limitation, relation, and "inflation."

The first revolves around the question of whether in literature figures such as the dying god or scapegoat and actions such as rites of passage or quest journeys are actually myths and rituals of the sort recorded in a culture's sacred works (or its oral equivalents). That is to say, is the work itself a myth? This question, rightly perhaps, troubles anthropologists and comparative religionists more than literary scholars. The former groups are concerned with the possible confusions attendant on the multiplication of meanings for terms such as myth. For them, the term should be reserved for societal, communal narratives of a sacred or largely sacred order that sanction and reflect the existing cultural order and that either have at one time generated, or continue to generate, large-scale beliefs concerning either the actuality or meaningfulness of the narratives. But so long as one retains a firm grip on the mimetic character of literature and the modal concept of displacement, there should be little difficulty over such a use, for these notions will effectively preclude attributing to texts the sociocultural and spiritual functions of communal myths. Further, it is quite possible to envisage certain texts attaining for certain readers and writers the status of myth and ritual but operating on a personal level in which the factors of obsession and projection are prominent.

More important in general is the matter of definitional range. That is to say, may the term "myth" be applied to scholarly patterns such as Frazer's dying and reviving god; Mircea Eliade's eternal return; the several syncretistic formations of the hero by Joseph Campbell, Otto Rank, and Lord Raglan; Cassirer's notion of the state; and even more encompassing notions such as Frye's myths of detachment and concern or Jacques Ellul's of history and science? At what point, in short, does the definitional power of myth cease and that of other terms, such as concept, construct, and fiction begin? Might useful discriminations be made through the development and refinement of such terms as "para-myth," "meta-myth," and "proto-myth" for use in those areas outside the anthropological and sociological study of actual peoples' sacred narratives? An important related matter is the issue of allusion and its acceptable extensional range from explicit through oblique to implicit. Calling a character or scene mythic poses relatively little problem when names, titles, and undisplaced events or descriptions from classical, Celtic, Scandinavian, or some other mythology occur. But the situation is quite different when demands such as that of verisimilitude and other literary conventions intrude. In many ways the problem underlying this issue of allusion, and indeed the whole question of definition, is whether all or only some literature may be linked with myth or called mythic. And as with so many deceptively simple questions, there is much to be said on both sides.

Even more critical, at least in terms of what we say about the relations of myth to specific texts, is the problem of limitation. It raises, in its own way, the most vital and certainly the most enduring question of literary criticism, namely, whether patterns and interpretive significances are in a given instance discovered or created. The issue is one of, among other things, plausibility, the nature of the critical copula, and by extension the problems of value and identity. It is in the light of these issues that we have to examine specific assertions concerning the relation of literature to myth. Is, for instance, Faulkner's Dewey Dell an inverted Persephone, as has been claimed, or is the narrative form of *The Great Gatsby* that of the Grail quest?

At one time critics argued for the identity of myth and literature and the value of the myth in the context of the literature. Now critics are increasingly probing the relation in terms of the character and functions of not only analogy but also homology, in part because of the growing recognition that the awareness and use of myth in understanding literature need not be inimical to historical criticism, even though much myth criticism has been more heavily weighted toward formal and structural concerns. To the extent that this possibility is developed, it is likely that more myth studies devoted to single authors in their milieus or to limited historical periods will appear. If so, clearly specific cultural issues will gain greater prominence, not only in the act of textual interpretation but also in critical theory.

As soon as history and theory loom in the discussion, the general problem of relation between myth and literature moves to the fore. Apart from the question of whether a myth occurs in a particular work, there is the problem of how to construe the general relation. It is a function of meaning or significance rather than simply of sociohistorical existence. One way of construing the relation is the loosely psychological and religious or spiritual approach. It views myth as a series of latent, oblique, or untranslatable symbols recurring in literature because of their human centrality and power. Another view is that of Northrop Frye, who sees myth as constituting the structural principles or meaning of literature. Myth in its earliest manifestations is protoliterature insofar as its narrative sequences, recurring images, and dramatic actions are of the same order as those of oral and written literature, however much refined and shaped by history and culture. The language in which early myth is cast is the principal differentiating factor from other kinds of mental response to experience. With time, however, this language begins to function beyond what traditionally or originally was regarded as myth; it operates also in religion, philosophy, and expressions of social concern.

A third view gives a slightly different perspective on the relation of myth and literature by placing the emphasis for the meaning of myth on literature. Essentially the argument is that, from the literary standpoint, myth, viewed as an imaginative construct rather than a verbal formulation, has no meaning, though from other standpoints, such as the anthropological, it has. From this view, that of the literary critic, literature then functions as a commentary on myth, assigning to it values or significance that it does not in itself possess. To the extent that myth has a relatively determined written or oral form — a text, if you will — it is protoliterature and so a partial commentary on itself. Literature thus becomes the provider of specific meanings for particular myths so that the historical sequence of literary works involving a myth constitutes the open-ended totality of that myth's literary meaning.

The diversity of these views underscores the inventiveness of the human mind in seeing a single relation from differing perspectives. It also shows that the historical plurality of the relation is a result of the shifting cultural relevance and hence mode and content of myth. Myth has been successively located in the areas of religion, psychology, sociology, and now semiotics and popular culture. That fact surely must condition the particular features of the relation between literature and myth in a given culture or historical period. Classical literature is what it is, at least in part, because myth impinges on it from the region of religion. Neoclassical literature in Europe, by contrast, is dominated more by myths emanating from the realms of society and politics. Where the dynamic and viable forces of myth are located in modern national literatures is one of the tantalizing questions facing the contemporary student of the relation of myth and literature.

The problem of "inflation" has more revolutionary implications. It consists of two major issues, one of which stems from the logical aspects of the relation and the other from the relation's historical development. The first issue involves the matter of genre and the phenomenon of writing. Myth clearly has close and unmistakable relations to the major genres of poetry, drama, and the novel and these genres can be studied in terms of these relations. What is not clear is whether other genres of literature, say, autobiography and the personal essay, are also informed by myth. If they are not, why they are not becomes a matter of some moment if for nothing more than purposes of definition and classification. Is literature one unified verbal continuum or does it consist of at least two distinct subsets, one mythic and the other nonmythic? The subjective, afactually shaped features of autobiography and the essay are too well known to need arguing, so that it is difficult to see how, at least theoretically, these genres are not also related to myth. And if they are, what are we to say of adjacent genres such as biography and literary criticism itself? Still further beyond lies the question of the relation of myth to essentially nonliterary forms such as history, philosophy, the social sciences, and perhaps even the biological and physical sciences. For if, as we are told, there is only *écriture* in which the distinction between literary and nonliterary modes no longer obtains, how are we to adjudge the conflicting claims of traditionally and recognizably differentiable species of writing? Are facticity and truth values to be taken as convenient fictions, conceptual myths whose nature is completely heuristic? If so, what criteria and decision procedures will enable us to select among them those that are truly viable?

The historical dimension of the problem leads to a similar perplexity. The modern literary concern with myth was initially associated with the early representatives of modernism — William Butler Yeats, T. S. Eliot, Joyce, Rilke — then with the exponents of neoromanticism, surrealism, and religious conviction until by degrees it came, on the contemporary scene, to be represented by parodists, ironists, and black humorists from Jorge Luis Borges and Barth to Ionesco, Nabokov, Walker Percy, Günter Grass, John Updike, and John Hawkes. With them myth is not invoked as an ordering principle or as a vade mecum to spiritual power. Instead it is an essentially comic invitation to the infinite varieties of narrative proliferation and interpretive possibility. And this quality of parody and burlesque is not confined to literature's handling of myth. When we turn, for instance, to Lévi-Strauss's Bororo myths (notably M_1 and M_5) in *Mythologiques*, we find more than a touch of absurdist humor playing around the scenes and details, which is not to say that the Bororo do. And when one comes to comment critically on and to study seriously these instances of literature and myth, our traditional modes of treatment — sober in organization, cautious with evidence, dedicated to interpretive knowledge — themselves seem unable to capture the perceived and felt realities of the narratives, and by this failure they stand forth as almost parodies in themselves. Can it be — and there are already more than a few signs on the horizon — that criticism, like literature and myth, will increasingly become deliberately parodic as it endeavors to attest meaningfully to the age's dominant forms and perceptions of myth and literature?

Bibliography

This bibliography is intended to introduce the nonspecialist to some representative theories of myth and to studies of general or specific relations between myth and literature.

Albouy, Pierre. *Mythes et mythologies dans la littérature française*. Paris: Colin, 1969. An examination of the forms in which certain classical myths have been developed in French literature.

Aler, Jan, ed. *De Myth in de Literatuur*. The Hague: Mouton, 1964. Essays by Dutch scholars assessing the recurrence of ancient myths in modern literature.

Barber, C. L. *Shakespeare's Festive Comedy: A Study of Dramatic Form and Its Relation to Social Customs*. Princeton: Princeton Univ. Press, 1959. A seminal assessment of Shakespearean comedy in the light of the work of the Cambridge school.

Barksdale, E. C. *The Dacha and the Duchess: An Application of Lévi-Strauss's Theory of Myth in Human Creativity to Nineteenth-Century Russian Novelists*. New York: Philosophical Library, 1974.

Barthes, Roland. *Mythologies*. Paris: Seuil, 1957. English version, trans. and ed. Annette Lavers. New York: Hill and Wang, 1972. Semiological analyses of the myths of French daily life. Included is "Mythology Today," a useful introduction to his approach.

Bush, Douglas. *Mythology and the Renaissance Tradition in English Poetry*. Rev. ed. New York: Norton, 1963. A standard historical treatment of the subject.

Campbell, Joseph. *The Hero with a Thousand Faces*. 2nd ed. Princeton: Princeton Univ. Press, 1968. Develops a loosely Jungian "monomyth' of the hero's ritual quest in legend and literature.

Cassirer, Ernst. *The Philosophy of Symbolic Forms*. 3 vols. Trans. Ralph Manheim. New Haven: Yale Univ. Press, 1955. Volumes I and III treat, respectively, language and the phenomenology of knowledge; Volume II, subtitled *Mythical Thought*, is devoted to a Neo-Kantian treatment of the role and nature of myth.

Chase, Richard. *Quest for Myth*. Baton Rouge: Louisiana State Univ. Press, 1949. A survey of modern anthropological and psychological views of myth, with some indications of their applicability to literature.

Feder, Lillian. *Ancient Myth in Modern Poetry*. Princeton: Princeton Univ. Press, 1971. An examination of poets' thematic responses to myth, which the author sees as structuring the unconscious experience.

Fergusson, Francis. *The Idea of Theater*. Princeton: Princeton Univ. Press, 1949. Explores plays from Sophocles to Shakespeare as ritual expressions. Influenced by the Cambridge School and Malinowski.

Frye, Northrop. *Fables of Identity: Studies in Poetic Mythology*. New York: Harcourt, 1963. Essays based on the view that myth is literature's basic structural principle.

Hamburger, Käte. *From Sophocles to Sartre: Figures from Greek Tragedy, Classical and Modern*. Trans. Helen Sebba. New York: Ungar, 1969. A study of recurring character figurations from classical to modern drama.

Hays, Peter L. *The Limping Hero: Grotesques in Literature*. New York: New York Univ. Press. 1971. A study of the maimed character as a mythic archetype in literature.

Hoffman, Daniel G. *Form and Fable in American Fiction*. New York: Oxford Univ. Press, 1961. Treats mythic sources and forms in classical American novels and short stories.

Jung, Carl G., and Karl Kerényi. *Essays on a Science of Mythology: The Myth of the Divine Child and the Mysteries of Eleusis*. Trans. R. F. C. Hull. Princeton: Princeton Univ. Press, 1949. Depth psychology and the classics brought to bear on selected mythic patterns.

Kirk, G. S. *Myth: Its Meaning and Functions in Ancient and Other Cultures*. Berkeley: Univ. of California Press, 1970. A critical examination of the theories of Lévi-Strauss, Cassirer, Freud, and Jung by a classicist.

Lévi-Strauss, Claude. *Mythologiques*. 4 vols. Paris: Plon, 1964–71. Detailed illustration of the structuralist method of myth analysis.

Levy, Getrude R. *The Sword from the Rock*. London: Faber, 1953. Traces the hero's development and the beginnings of epic literature.

Maranda, Pierre, ed. *Mythology: Selected Readings*. Harmondsworth, Eng.: Penguin, 1972. Essays and selections representative of current thinking, particularly in a Continental context.

McCune, Marjorie W., et al., eds. *The Binding of Proteus: Perspectives on Myth and the Literary Process*. Lewisburg, Pa.: Bucknell Univ. Press, 1980. Essays on aspects of myth and literature from the medieval to the modern period.

Murray, Henry A., ed. *Myth and Myth-Making*. New York: Braziller, 1960. Essays from the standpoint of the anthropologist, psychologist, historian, Orientalist, literary critic, and creative writer.

Richardson, Robert D., Jr. *Myth and Literature in the American Renaissance*. Bloomington: Indiana Univ. Press, 1978. Studies the deliberate use of myth by writers to resolve antithetical traditional attitudes in their works.

Righter, William. *Myth and Literature*. London: Routledge and Kegan Paul, 1975. Brief critique of current theories and practice, with some suggestions for further lines of investigation.

Rougemont, Denis de. *Love in the Western World*. Trans. Montgomery Belgion. Rev. ed. New York: Pantheon, 1956. Influential and provocative study of the Tristan legend in relation to literature.

Ruthven, K. K. *Myth*. London: Methuen, 1976. Brief introduction to the various historical attitudes toward myth, with a consideration of contemporary problems in connection with literature.

Sebeok, Thomas A., ed. *Myth: A Symposium*. 1955; rpt. Bloomington: Indiana Univ. Press, 1958. Essays by anthropologists, folklorists, philosophers, and literary critics, reflecting the views of their disciplines.

Slote, Bernice, ed. *Myth and Symbol: Critical Approaches and Applications*. Lincoln: Univ. of Nebraska Press, 1963. Essays on the interrelation of myth, literature, and symbol in various historical periods.

Vickery, John B., ed. *Myth and Literature: Contemporary Theory and Practice*. Lincoln: Univ. of Nebraska Press, 1966. Representative essays on theories of myth, their relation to literature, and specific authors and texts.

Vries, Jan de. *Heroic Song and Heroic Legend*. Trans. B. J. Timmer. London: Oxford Univ. Press, 1963. Treats the thematic relation between myth and epic and saga literature, as evidenced in a number of traditions.

Weisinger, Herbert. *The Agony and the Triumph: Papers on the Use and Abuse of Myth*. East Lansing: Michigan State Univ. Press, 1964. Essays on contemporary applications of mythic patterns to literature.

Wheelwright, Philip. *The Burning Fountain: A Study in the Language of Symbolism*. Bloomington: Indiana Univ. Press, 1954. A philosopher's approach to myth, meaning, and symbolism in literary texts from the classics to the moderns.

White, John J. *Mythology in the Modern Novel: A Study of Prefigurative Techniques*. Princeton: Princeton Univ. Press, 1971. A methodology for myth in American, German, and English fiction.

5

Literature and Folklore

BRUCE A. ROSENBERG

Folklore is often understood to be all those aspects of culture — customs, beliefs, rituals, superstitions, crafts, costumes, foods, many forms of verbal expression, and so on — that are transmitted orally or by custom. Folklorists study the way chairs are made in the Nile Delta, the function of maypoles in Bavaria, the significance of pre-Lenten carnivals in Latin America, or the cooking practices of the Pennsylvania Dutch. And they treat the function, usage, and persistence of riddles and proverbs in speech, legends, sagas, miracles and saints' stories, and fairy tales. Recently, folklorists' interests have expanded to include personal-experience stories.

But folklore study has come to encompass more than those "items" just mentioned, which are the products of the folkloric process: the finished chair, the usable plow, the cooked meal, the erected barn, the "text" of the recited or performed folktale. Folklorists want to know about the context in which the item is produced and the medium of production and transmission. The context of folklore — the situation in which the folkloric event occurs — has been to date of lesser interest to literary scholars, whereas context or situation is a more important element in folkloric production and transmission. In the latter case the worker will want to study the informant in relation to his or her audience, the circumstances surrounding the folkloric event, the purpose of the event, the attitudes expressed toward the item, and so forth.

The medium of nearly all folklore, orality, also has its special problems and hence its special methodologies for analysis. To identify just one among many differences, the literary work is embodied in a fixed text that readers may examine at their own speeds and on which they may reflect. The reader can turn back the pages. Not so with the oral performance: the event (usually) proceeds at the performer's pace, though the performer may make some adjustments to accommodate his or her audience, having an instant feedback unavailable to the writer of literature. The folklorist also wants to study the ways in which the medium per se affects oral transmission.

Because folklore, thus understood, is so pervasive and so universal, it is bound to appear in any literature that is descriptive of culture. Writers mature within a culture; they learn their skills and their craft within that culture; and so they inevitably reflect some aspect of that culture in their writing. Unless the written narrative be about animals or some rarefied aristocracy or something of the sort, some aspect of folklore will appear. The question may then be asked, by folklorist and literary critic alike, if folk materials are so widespread, how may they be identified and of what value, once made, is that identification?

What is the significance of Charlemagne's gesture in the *Chanson de Roland* when he strokes his beard or of the Cid's when he tweaks the beards of others? The interpretation of the gesture tells us something about the mood and attitude of the Frank and of the Spaniard's relation to certain other persons. Folklore is involved in literature when one of D. H. Lawrence's characters, in *The Plumed Serpent*, calls for a return of Mexico's ancient gods; when Robert Graves alludes to or dedicates one of his poems to the "White Goddess"; or when Federico García Lorca incorporates local beliefs and rituals in a dramatic narrative, such as *Bodas de sangre*. And literary critics or historians will want to know the oral or folkloric backgrounds when they study one of the *Canterbury Tales* that Chaucer has taken from a story he heard, or a *Decameron* tale that Giovanni Boccaccio has experienced in the same way, or an oral story embedded in Ludovico Ariosto's *Orlando furioso*, or the Icelandic *Grettissaga*, or the full tradition—oral as well as written—of the Faust legend. In all these works and many thousands more, students of literature will want to know something about gestures, comparative religion and religious belief, the nature and life history of folktales—and much else, depending on the literature and the nature of the lore within it—in order to enrich their understanding of that literature.

Who the folk are from whom this lore comes is at least as controversial among folklorists as is the definition of folklore itself. Sufficient for our purposes here will be the broadest concept workable, that since folklore is any aspect of culture transmitted orally, we all participate in the process. We are the folk, whether we live in urban areas rather than rural, whether we are learned or illiterate. Folk society, as anthropologist George Foster has conceived it, is an intimate part of the larger society to which it belongs.[1] The relation between folk and so-called high culture is inextricable and symbiotic. Prokofiev's *Love for Three Oranges* is based on a folktale, as is the more obvious *Hänsel und Gretel* of Humperdinck, or Tschaikovsky's ballet *Sleeping Beauty*. Shakespeare was once popular and is now elite. And many of the Middle English romances have entered an oral, folk tradition, primarily as ballads. The flow of cultural goods between these strata of society is circular and continuous, each steadily contributing to the other, though in varying degrees.

While folklorists who are primarily interested in the medium and context of folk literature, especially oral narrative, study transmission as well as the text, literary critics are concerned primarily with the latter aspect—namely, product. How the item is transmitted, particularly the interpersonal dynamics of the situation, is of greater interest to the folklorist. Mary Ellen Lewis has shown, for instance, how novels can capture the story-telling situation more effectively than the folklorist's indexes and taxonomies can, because in (well-written) narrative we are given more detail about the actants and their interrelations; the indexes simply list and cross-index items. The intent of the transmission, its reception, the setting—all these things that permit us to understand that aspects of culture orally transmitted occur in a live, organic milieu, may be lost unless the folklorist is exceedingly thorough and as sensitive and expressively able as the writer of fiction.[2] Lewis has shown how Chinua Achebe vividly portrays the dissemination of a legend (in *Arrow of God*)[3] and how Mark Twain, with equal vitality, places Huck Finn's superstitions within the entire fabric of Huck's beliefs ("Why Study Folklore and Literature?").

The matter of medium—ostensibly either written or oral—is not a clearly defined distinction. While it was once thought that such a phenomenon as the "oral style" existed, distinctive and easily isolatable from written narrative, recent fieldwork has assembled data that tend to question whether the two modes of transmission are entirely separate. However, for those narratives that appear to derive from an oral tradition that is not far removed in time from the received text—for example, the Homeric epics, *Beowulf*, *Gilgamesh*, or *Digenis Akritas*—the mode of previous transmission and composition (ostensibly oral) and the social situation of the works' transmission have had an effect on the printed products. The style is said to reflect the oral, improvisational technique though the matter is still controversial. Nevertheless, the main pedagogical point—that when medium and situation are known, the literary critic or historian can benefit—remains an important one.

The relation of oral to written literature is a complicated one. Oral literature is always fluid, always in flux, and that characterization holds not only for the obvious aspects of performance, such as the reciter's facial expression, gestures, eye contact, and vocal intonation, but for the "text" itself. But the text in written literature is fixed; it does not change, and the only variation is in our changing perceptions of the work. In the aspect of literature just discussed—performance—the most obvious differences emerge. But in other aspects, composition and transmission, the differences are less clearly distinguishable.

For instance, not all oral literatures are composed without the assistance of writing. The poets of some cultures do not compose spontaneously during the moment of performance, as was suggested in the past few decades by advocates of oral formulaic theory. In some cases the process of composition is performed in darkened rooms, as it was by the bards of medieval Ireland; in others, the poets discuss their works with others in the community and do not perform until they get everything "right." And in still others, they may make notes to themselves concerning their forthcoming compositions. Transmission is even more mutually dependent. We know that much oral literature is transmitted in writing, that many folk informants read tales and, if they like them, recite them as part of their repertoire.

Writing does something "unnatural" to the life of an authentic oral lyric or narrative: it concretizes it, removes it from the living stream of its existence. For one thing, literature in print deprives the performer of all the histrionic skills of performance, while it also proscribes the possibility of change in the text, as an oral reciter might well make minor adjustments in his or her material depending on his or her inclinations and those of the audience. An older woman, for instance, might tell a certain tale involving a sexual encounter one way to her friends, another way to the village priest, and still quite another to her grandchild. The author does not have this audience-centered flexibility.

The relation of folklore to literature is important to the critic in other ways as well. A session held at the Modern Language Association's convention and then published in the *Journal of American Folklore* in 1957 presented differing views on folklore and literature that point up not only the interrelation of the two but the variant aims and perspectives of scholars in the field. Folklorist Richard Dorson, in setting out the means by which we can identify authentic folklore in literature, used the example of T. B. Thorpe's "The Big Bear of Arkansas." But Dorson's conclusion was negative; while the character in the story tells a tale to his fascinated audience, coincidentally describing the storytelling event as it may well have happened, the tale itself is not a folktale. The "Big Bear" of the title is the creation of a literary imagination and so, for the folklorist, of little value.[4]

But literary scholars on the panel held different views. One felt that folkloric classification procedures had enabled us to recognize the similarities between Thorpe's "Bear," Herman Melville's *Moby-Dick*, and William Faulkner's "The Bear." Celticist Gwyn Jones's *Kings, Beasts and Heroes* quite independently extends the list to include the hunting of Twrch Trwyth in *Culhwch and Olwen*, even tracking the Calydonian Boar in Book VIII of the *Metamorphoses*. Once having made this identification, we can see how this plot structure — folk or otherwise — has fascinated millions of listeners and readers for centuries and may lead us to inquire into those aspects of commonality that the centuries have found of interest and aesthetic profit. Literary critic and historian Daniel G. Hoffman found that the theme of the "Great Hunt" — to remain with this one example — transcended the "minor work" in which it was contained. Hoffman found in Thorpe's "Bear" a characteristic American attitude toward nature: in the tenacity of the hunter, the ferocious strength and cunning of the animal, and the final domination of nature by the hunter. If these ideas are characteristically American, we will have to account for their occurrence in the literatures of Wales, and perhaps other places as well.

One of the uses of literature for the folklorist is as a source of ethnographic data, particularly during those eras when no one recognized folklore as data to be collected. Serious folklore study is mainly a phenomenon of this century. We have seen how literature often provides a rich context by describing both folklore as it is lived and, again in the instance of "The Big Bear," the storytelling event. The student or scholar of literature will have other purposes entirely. Some writers "use" folklore to impart verisimilitude to their representation of a regional setting, as Ivan Turgenev does in some of the stories in *Fathers and Sons*, as Chaucer does when he gives his reeve a Kentish dialect or, for ironic effect, when he has John the Carpenter (in The Miller's Tale) mouth several ludicrous superstitions in order to show how credulous and gullible he is and thus how easily he will be duped. Among such writers we can also include D. H. Lawrence, John Steinbeck, and Gustave Flaubert, authors whose knowledge of folklore derived mainly from their reading. Chaim Potok and Isaac Bashevis Singer portray the lush texture of their own ethnic heritages through the use of the folklore that included their customs, beliefs, and stories—lore that is a part of their lives. Still other writers—Joel Chandler Harris is an obvious example—have intentionally recorded the lore of other cultures (or subcultures) and have never pretended that it was anything else.

A second use of folklore by literary narrators has been to absorb the entire plot of an oral tale and rewrite it. "The Celebrated Jumping Frog of Calaveras County" of Mark Twain is a folktale rewritten. Gottfried von Strassburg uses some version of "The Dragon Slayer" folktale in his *Tristan*; in *Parzival* Wolfram von Eschenbach seems to incorporate some version of "The Literal Fool" and "What Should I Have Done or Said?"; Chrétien de Troyes bases the structure and major episodes of *Yvain* on the folktale "The Man on a Quest for His Lost Bride," with its episode of "The Forgotten Fiancé"; and *Culhwch and Olwen* appears to be closely related to the popular tale "Six Go through the Whole World."[5]

A third literary usage of folkloric materials is symbolic. Citing an often-read essay by Q. D. Leavis,[6] Daniel Hoffman gives as an example of folklore as literary symbol Hawthorne's "The Maypole of Merry Mount," in which pagan rituals are contrasted with austere Puritan attitudes to set off the ethos of two cultures. The New Englanders are criticized at the same time as they are shown to have attained a state at once more difficult but more worthy than Eden.

For more than a decade in the United States, folklore studies have moved away from an interest in literature toward the traditional concerns of anthropologists. But for many decades in this country and throughout most of the nineteenth century in Europe, the relation of literature to folklore was important. We are indebted to the Finns for the development of that methodology facilitating folktale comparison and the description of the narrative's growth and development. It developed, though distantly, out of their nationalistic fascination with their national epic, the *Kalevala*. During the first half of the nineteenth century, the folklorist and poet Elias Lönnrot collected a great many short epic poems, or *runot*, mainly from Karelia, and himself assembled them to be comprised in what he felt had once existed in oral tradition, the epic the *Kalevala*. The attempt to trace the *runot* and to place them within the framework of folk narrative of the world was for many years the chief interest of Finnish folklorists.

The historical-geographic, or Finnish, method involves the collection and comparison of as many known variants of particular tales as the workers can locate. They then isolate those versions with traits characteristic of a particular region or subculture and attempt to reconstruct the outline of the earliest versions of the tales. To identify origins precisely is an impossible task, and many folklorists have given up the attempt, discouraged in part by the failure of the Finns to be more than vague about the "archetype." The regional variants, or oicotypes, are of greater interest because the region in question will most likely still be in existence and can thus be studied in the present; also, because of their nature, limited geographical regions offer realizable challenges to the folklorist, whereas global problems are usually overwhelming in their scope.

The Finnish method developed under the influence of Darwinian positivism, and in folklore study it was understood to mean that each folktale ought to be studied both individually and as part of an international matrix. Literary incorporations of folktales were examined with particular thoroughness because they almost assuredly had more influence on other versions than any one oral tale. The circulation and geographic spread made possible by print almost guarantees this influence. Thus, nineteenth-century folklore scholars throughout Europe informed themselves about literature, especially that which was derivative of oral materials.

The Finns assumed that oral narratives of the complexity of the folktale never developed independently but spread only through diffusion. Working on this assumption, the Finns compiled indexes of both small units of narrative occurring in oral circulation (called "motifs") and the folktales of which they were the constituent parts. As other countries and regions began to do the same, it became possible to make international and cross-cultural comparisons. One of the first major analyses of a literary work — or at least one that has survived only in manuscript — was that done by the German scholar Friedrich Panzer, comparing over two hundred versions of a folktale that he thought was related to *Beowulf*. If Finnish ideas and methodologies did not actually make his study possible, they certainly facilitated the kind of comparative study Panzer undertook. And the archives, which several Baltic countries had by then begun to compile, were Panzer's sine qua non. Earlier and subsequent analyses of the Homeric epics, of the *Nibelungenlied*, of Shakespeare's plays, and so forth, with varying degrees of success and value, have identified individual customs, beliefs, and episodes in those literary works that appear to have their origins in oral folk traditions.

If Panzer had not developed his methodology from direct contact with the Finns, he might have wished for the extensive, multivolume annotation of the folktales collected and edited by the Grimm brothers that the European scholars Johannes Bolte and Georg Polívka produced. Much more thorough and informative than the word "annotation" suggests, this work is in effect an encyclopedia of not only folktales but also literary fiction, drama, opera, and the like that are related to each of the Grimms' tales. Now outdated, the Bolte-Polívka was in the early twentieth century an invaluable resource for folklore comparative studies; it is still useful for the student of literature who is interested in discovering folktale analogues in high-culture narratives in any of several media.

Meanwhile, ballad scholarship was progressing along a track roughly parallel. The early collections, including the famous and important one by Bishop Thomas Percy, had not been "scientific" works in the Finnish sense but had been by and large unclassified anthologies. Sir Walter Scott, loving the folklore of his native Scotland — a deep interest in the folk and their lore was an aspect of Romanticism in many countries in Europe — collected ballads of the Scottish borderland. But literary man as he was, he could not refrain from editing and revising some of his materials to "improve" them, at least by his literary standards.

Ballad scholarship was promoted in a more precise and organized way when, between 1882 and 1898, Harvard's James Child compiled specimens of what he then thought was the entire corpus of English and Scottish ballads. Though one of Child's aims was completeness, several problems have since arisen regarding many aspects of this index. Yet it remains one of the important monuments of ballad scholarship, and it did for the ballad and literature, to some extent, what Bolte and Polívka were to do for the folktale.

Both works, but particularly the Bolte-Polívka, parallel the indexes of motifs and tale types that the Finns were then developing. The indexes were to classify all oral narrative material from a wide range of genres and from the folklore archives of the world by the quality of the episode, rather than by Grimm tale or Child ballad. This change in approach allowed for the future inclusion of material and even categories of material not known at the moment of publication, a substantial improvement on the earlier works, which were restricted to a limited body of material. In so expanding their range, the Finnish indexes further enhanced the possibility of comparative studies of folklore and literature. The Finnish scholar Antti Aarne was the editor of the first *Verzeichnis der Märchentypen*. The translation and enlargement of this milestone by the American Stith Thompson (published as part of the monograph series Folk Fellows Communications) contains hundreds of references to literary works related to the folktales in question. And Thompson's survey of the folktales of the world, appropriately entitled *The Folktale*, also has numerous references to related literary works.

The major theoretical publication relating folklore to literature in the past fifty years has been *The Singer of Tales*. Its author, Albert Lord, and his mentor at Harvard, Milman Parry, collected the heroic songs of a group of Yugoslavian folk singers (the *guslari*) in the expectation that they could learn about the compositional techniques of Homer, whom they assumed also to have been an "oral poet." Parry died shortly after the first field trips to the Balkans, and Lord continued the work, though he did not publish his book-length study until 1960. The Parry-Lord thesis is a complicated one that does not lend itself easily to condensation, but basically the two men gleaned texts of *guslar* songs for stylistic characteristics — notably repetitive phrases, especially the "heroic" epithets — which same qualities are also found in Homer. Since Parry and Lord theorized that these stylistic features characterized the "oral style," distinct from the literary, they reasoned that the features, if found elsewhere, would be evidence of oral composition and performance.

Their research led to a wide range of stylistic examinations of narratives that have come down to us only in writing but that appear to contain the same features that Parry and Lord found in the Balkans. Old English scholars were among the first to apply the thesis to their material, particularly *Beowulf*. Jean Rychner made the application to the *Chanson de Roland*, while others have made claims for the oral style in the *Nibelungenlied*, in a number of the medieval romances, and in the Greek *Digenis Akritas*. Literally hundreds of essays, monographs, and books have followed in the wake of *The Singer of Tales*, many of them challenging both the original thesis and its applications; but one of the results has been an increased awareness on the part of scholars of the symbiotic relation of verbal and written narrative, of folklore and literature. Whatever else *The Singer of Tales* has accomplished — and one thing was to change the critical focus of many scholars from the audience to the problems of the performer — it has heightened the literary critic's awareness of oral, folk traditions.

In very recent years, however, the interests of most American folklorists have shifted toward the traditional concerns of anthropologists. Their attention has turned away from texts to the act of performance. The folklorist now tends to be uninterested in literature except in those few cases where the writer can provide otherwise unavailable data. As a result, a steadily widening gulf has developed between the practitioners of these two disciplines and little research has been done to bridge it; what is being performed in each area seems to have small bearing on the interests of the other. Consequently, the student or scholar of literature and folklore relies heavily on the research, theory, and methodologies of the past.

Richard Dorson's recommendations for the demonstration of folklore in literature are those of the folklorist seeking ethnographic data. But they are useful to the literary scholar who is interested in determining a methodology for the identification of authentic folklore. First, we will want to show, through our knowledge of the author's life, that he or she has been exposed to the folklore that seems to appear in his or her writing. William Butler Yeats had collected folklore in the field and had discussed Irish traditions with Lady Gregory and other interested friends before he used such materials in his poems and plays. And the legendary quality of "Rip Van Winkle" can be shown to be one of the results of Washington Irving's contact with Germanic traditions.

Second, the folklorist or literary historian or critic will want to examine the work itself for evidence of the author's knowledge of lore. Dorson cites the authenticity of Irving's detail in "The Legend of Sleepy Hollow," but knowledge of folklore often comes only through his or her reading. We know from supporting biographical data that T. S. Eliot's use of Arthurian materials in *The Waste Land* reflected his reading of Jessie Weston, Sir James Frazer, and others. Federico García Lorca's use of gypsy folklore concerning blood beliefs is both obvious, since as a Spaniard he was often among gypsies, and problematic, since he does not appear to have been intimate in their affairs. Truman Capote's *Other Voices, Other Rooms*, Bernard Malamud's *The Natural*, and Thomas Pynchon's *Gravity's Rainbow* all seem, in varying degrees, to have borrowed from the legends of King Arthur — mainly those about the Grail quest — but that borrowing is often so subtly performed, and the biographical evidence so vague, that we cannot be certain.

In addition to biographical and internal (textual) evidence, the researcher will seek for corroborative evidence, which means for Dorson that the folkloric item under examination (narrative, proverb, ritual, etc.) has an independent existence in oral tradition. Unlike the other two elements of proof, this one concerns itself with the nature of the folkloric material and not with the author's knowledge. An independent existence in oral tradition is a moot issue in several of Robert Graves's poems or in the Ossian epic, for which so much was claimed at the time of its publication. Folkloric antecedents have usually been claimed for the Russian *Song of Igor's Campaign* (as the title is sometimes translated), but the folkloric elements have so far only been assumed; data from oral tradition have been scarce.

Two of the major aids in establishing the existence of an oral tradition are works of Stith Thompson, the *Motif-Index of Folk Literature* and *The Types of the Folktale*. These indexes classify known motifs and folktale types from contributing archives. Though they are far from complete and are often complicated and confusing to use (especially for the beginner), they are nevertheless invaluable for establishing the existence of narratives in an authentic oral tradition, and they provide a reasonably reliable means of identifying the analogues and components of tales. In addition to the Child collection, the ballad scholar has recourse to G. Malcolm Laws's *American Ballads from British Broadsides: A Guide for Students and Collectors of Traditional Song.* Archer Taylor has compiled an extensive list of proverbs and a separate volume on riddles in literature, classified by subject, but the nature of the genre works against organizing the material the way folktales have been organized. For other genres — such as beliefs, superstitions, charms, gestures, and the like — no international, precisely organized lexicon is available, and the researcher must consult regional collections, many of them assembled with little taxonomic rationale.

We have discussed some of the difficulties in demonstrating that a given author had access to, and did in fact use, lore from an authentic tradition. In those eras in which biographical evidence is scanty, if at all extant, and in which there is no knowledge or even understanding of the folklore, the researcher is faced with yet other problems. For instance, many narratives from classical times, the Middle Ages, and the Renaissance bear a close resemblance to the overall structure of folktales; how can that identification be made convincingly? Organized folklore collection is a feature of the last 150 years; we do not have any material earlier than the nineteenth century (and little during that period) that contemporaries labeled folklore — by whatever name. And we are not certain how previous centuries would have considered such material. Was the appearance of the ghost in *Hamlet*, for example, considered by Shakespeare's contemporaries a questionable superstition — or learned orthodoxy?

In the identification of analogous narratives — folktale and literary tale — the procedure involves a three-step demonstration. First, the scholar will attempt to identify the episodes or actions in the manuscript as versions of those that have been collected in an oral tradition. This identification can most easily be done with the aid of the *Motif-Index.* Since a great many brief narratives are simple enough and imitative enough of life to have been thought of independently, the researcher will look for several of them, not merely one or two.

Second, the sequence of the episodes (motifs) is important in establishing a literary-oral relation. The episodes from oral tales are not taken over by a writer randomly; stories have specific sequences of episodes, with only slight variations, and it is this sequence that establishes the structure of the narrative. Thus, reading in a story that a young man, after some significant accomplishment is given as reward a bride whom he only later discovers is his mother, we would be motivated to look in the *Motif-Index* for "Mother-Son Incest" (Motif No. T 412). But that single motif does not constitute a complete narrative, and so we would next want to see whether, in *The Types of the Folktale*, Tale Type No. 931, "Oedipus," matches the narrative in question in other particulars as well. If other motifs — "Parricide Prophecy," "Exposure of Child to Prevent Fulfillment of Parricide Prophecy," "Exposed Infant Reared at Strange King's Court," and so on — are present in our manuscript, in the order in which they appear in oral tradition, then the relation may be postulated.

Finally, we will want to know, if possible, whether our author has had access to the folktales we believe we have found in his or her work. This procedure is the vaguest of all, first, because of our ignorance of folklore in the past and, second, because the only records we have of the lore of the past will probably be in literature, and authors tend to alter their oral sources according to their own lights. We can be sure that, when the Oedipus story appears in the fourteenth-century *Sir Degaré*, the author has probably had access to tales of this unfortunate Greek king, though whether in written or oral form is not certain. But when, for example, one of the tales in *Decameron* has no known European analogues, other — and possibly insoluble — problems come up.

While we would like to be able to demonstrate that our hypothetical folktale source was in fact historically available to our author, the evidence may not be present. Less satisfactory, but by no means irresponsible, would be an invocation of the folklorist's principle of monogenesis, which holds that it is so unlikely that two or more complex narratives would ever be composed independently that the possibility is no longer seriously considered in any reconstruction of a folktale's development. If this is true of folktales, why not written narrative? If a sequence of episodes as complicated as that occurring in "The Dragon Slayer" (Tale Type No. 300) also occurs in several of the Tristan romances, a folklorist would be inclined to suspect a direct relation. Whether that relation is between the manuscript and a folktale or another written source brings up a new set of problems.

One other methodological problem concerning the identification of folktales analogous to written narratives needs to be examined here. It involves a matter already touched on, that of the random compilation of similar motifs in the attempt to link folktale and literature, a frequent practice in the first few decades of this century that still occurs occasionally. In brief, although the worldwide distribution of a motif may be known, many of the versions may be, by reason of distance, of no relevance. If one wishes to find the source for Boccaccio's *Il Filocolo* (of the same type as Chaucer's Franklin's Tale), the listing of central Asian analogues serves no useful purpose unless the same tale can be found in intervening areas. We know that neither Boccaccio nor Chaucer traveled in Asia; the story was transmitted to them in Europe by means not known to us, but the absence of analogues in both England and Italy suggests that either by mischance the story has not been collected or else it had no currency in these countries.

One of the criticisms of Panzer's study of *Beowulf* and related folktales concerns the scholar's use of analogues from quite distant places. The folklorist's recent preference for discovering oicotypes and working with relatively small areas has been mentioned. The same principle must be applied to folktale and literature comparisons. Materials from distant continents must be used with great caution, because they are not likely to be similar enough to the text being examined to make the comparison valid. Through time and over space, tales are altered somewhat, occasionally radically. When Panzer studied Tale Type No. 301, therefore, he would have been on firmer methodological ground had he limited his comparisons to those tales in the Baltic, versions close to the one the poet probably heard. When folktales several hundred or even thousands of miles away are used, the analysis is likely to be confused by the consideration of narrative elements that the author would never have had any experience with. As oicotyping is useful to the folklorist, so it should be to the literary historian and critic.

So far, the attempt has been made to outline the procedures by which the materials of folklore and literature may be analyzed. A number of issues remain for which there may be no satisfactory answer or methodology. For instance, an item may be authentic—that is, it may have been honestly taken from a living oral tradition—but unless it has been collected and is available to other researchers, the demonstration of its authenticity will be very difficult.

The matter of dating items of folklore is an equally important and equally difficult problem. Literary scholars prefer to deal with texts, printed (or written) and datable; folklorists, given the bias of their training, rarely work with materials that are fixed in print in the course of transmission. And the difference in the basic nature of the material each studies has often become a source of misunderstanding and suspicion, especially when the literary historian is confronted with texts of stories that "evaporated" immediately after they were told, leaving no record except in human memory—with all its faults.

A narrative in print of, say, one of the lais of Marie de France, may well have been in circulation for decades, even centuries, before being recorded in writing, either by a scribe or by Marie herself. But the literary historian or folklorist must also consider the possibility that she was the inventor of the narratives we associate with her name, that the oral tradition comes after—not before—her writing, and that recently collected versions are the reflexes of the survivals, and not the antecedents, of her fiction. Since dating materials in oral tradition, particularly in eras when no collecting was done, is nearly impossible, deciding which came first, folktale or literary tale, is an uncertain matter. The distribution of the tale (or of any folkloric trait, for that matter) is not a reliable guide to the tale's age. For while a widely distributed tale most likely has considerable antiquity, narrowness of distribution does not prove a tale's youth. Several reasons may explain its limited spread: it may have been very popular a long time ago even though restricted now; or it may have enjoyed favor since antiquity, but only in a relatively small area because of historical or cultural features not apparent during a brief examination.

Nevertheless, despite the difficulties in deciding whether a literary or an oral tale had precedence, some attempt at solving this problem can be made through a close textual comparison such as a critic would make between two texts. If enough oral versions of the type analogous to the literary rendering in question can be found to enable the researcher to reconstruct a hypothetical analogue, that reconstruction is used in the comparison. This method is basically what Panzer used in his analysis of *Beowulf*. Comment has already been made on his failure to give proper weight to the Scandinavian oicotypes; but even so, Baltic versions of Tale Type No. 301 have no counterpart to the epic's character Unferth, the surly member of Hrothgar's court (whence Beowulf has traveled to rescue the land from a monster) who challenges the hero's credentials when Beowulf first appears. Now, if the epic had chronological precedence, we would expect nearly all the folktales to include a character like Unferth, or at least one performing his function. That so many tale-tellers would hear the court version of the epic, complete with Unferth, and then omit him — "get it wrong" — seems very unlikely. It is far more likely that the folktales of the time did not include an Unferth, as they do not now, and that for various reasons related to the conventions of Germanic epic, the *Beowulf* poet added him to his narrative.

That the literary historian can use modern folkloric fieldwork techniques to advantage has been demonstrated by Parry and Lord. Though they intended to learn about the compositional techniques of Homer and to understand certain stylistic features of the text, they also illuminated our understanding of the situation and medium of oral narrative performances, particularly the ways in which the mode of delivery — oral, of seemingly improvised renditions of traditional stories — leaves a mark on the text, in fact gives the text its shape.

The reservations about this research have centered mainly on the claims by some of the Parry-Lord extenders that simply because a text exhibits qualities similar to those found in the *guslar* songs, it must be oral. But in what way can a text be oral? The orality of narratives is no simple matter; we can speak of orality in composition, in transmission, and in performance. The fact that *Beowulf*, or the *Chanson de Roland*, or one of the Russian *byliny* of Vladimir, survives in manuscript is strong evidence against the most obvious aspect of orality, the performance. But are the manuscripts written records of oral performances? If so, how were they copied down at the fast-paced recitation, and by whom? If recited at the poet's ease and not during live performance, and so copied down with care, how was the text affected by this change in situation? Scholars who consider such matters must also consider the literate poets who, brought up and trained in societies in which oral poetry and oral narratives are the predominant forms, write in styles that approximate orality, styles best known to them and to their audiences.

These issues have not been resolved to everyone's satisfaction; they are still among the important matters to be dealt with by the worker who seeks to understand nearly all narrative before 1600 and some that is current.

The value of folklore to literary research should not be diminished by limiting one's study to those texts in which an authentic tradition can be positively demonstrated. By doing so, one is restricted to examining only local colorists and regional writers, whose works may well incorporate interesting ethnological data, but whose merit as artists is often slight. Such writers may be of interest to the folklorist, of course. But the folklorist who has gone to the trouble of identifying the genuine tradition from which an author is said to have borrowed has probably already made as much of an identification of folklore as would be necessary for his or her purposes.

The greater value of the interrelation of these two disciplines has been argued throughout this essay. If the relation of an oral tale to one written can be established, the critic has a useful means of evaluating the literary product. Albert Friedman has argued that, in the *Nibelungenlied*, when Siegfried (in disguise as Gunther, Brunhild's bridegroom) assists the husband on the first night of marriage, his taking her maiden belt has a significance best elucidated through folklore. Later, Siegfried's wife Kriemhild taunts Brunhild by claiming that her own husband, and not Gunther, "enjoyed your beautiful body" on that night, and she produces the maiden belt as proof. The original story, as the *Nibelungenlied* poet received it, probably made Siegfried the actual seducer. The use of the maiden belt (*Borte*) thus avoids mentioning an actual seduction, which would have put Siegfried in a bad light with the later courtly audience but also suggests it strongly enough to Brunhild to begin the ensuing disaster. The belt is a folkloric symbol of chastity, taken by bridegrooms as a sign of sexual union. In the *Nibelungenlied* its use enables the poet to present the conflict that will lead to disaster without discrediting Siegfried to his audience, which (we assume) would not have accepted him as readily if his actions had been described as in earlier versions of the story.[7]

Similar analyses have been done with the folktale analogues of Chaucer's Miller's Tale, suggesting that the character of Absolon, not present in the oral versions, was added by Chaucer. If so, the critic has then an important means of evaluating Chaucer's intentions in creating such a character and his plan for the tale as a whole: not only the tale's structure and the motivation of the characters but how Chaucer uses Absolon in his redaction of a traditional story in which the character is not present at all. Thus, all the other characters must originally have had somewhat different relations to each other.

Brunhild's belt is a nonnarrative aspect of the folklore-and-literature relation, yet it provides hints of the author's intentions. To return to Charlemagne's beard stroking: although the context and what we know of the emperor's behavior will be fairly good clues to the meaning of this gesture, if we can identify the gesture more positively and specifically by recourse to its use in society generally, we may have an important insight into Charlemagne's character and intentions—or that of anyone who strokes his beard in any literary situation.

Finally, other folkloric methodologies enable literary scholars to evaluate the traditional qualities of the language in which the work of literature is expressed. This interest has at least three aspects. We know that in the performance of traditional literature, the audience has expectations of plot or theme, of the style of performance, and of language. When such performances are rendered in literature, critics may want to understand the preconceptions the audience brings to such performances so that they can see how the artist responds, making the work conform (however slightly) to the taste of the listeners or readers. And, perhaps most importantly, the student of text literature may want to know how the language of poetry and formalized narrative differs from that of ordinary speech. That concern, of course, extends beyond the interrelation of folklore and literature, having been the concern of many literary critics, particularly the Prague School, for more than half a century.

In nearly all phases of the creative process in literature, from composition to finished text, the folklorist's methods—or the literary critic's understanding of folkloric theory and methodology—will enable the critic to make a distinctive explication of the text. In general, the knowledge of folklore is quite valuable to an understanding of literature; in many specific cases, it is invaluable.

Notes

[1] George Foster, "What Is Folk Culture?" *American Anthropologist*, 55 (1953), 159–73.
[2] Mary Ellen B. Lewis, "Why Study Folklore and Literature?" *Folklore Forum*, 11 (1978), 163–75.
[3] Lewis, "Beyond Context in the Analysis of Folklore in Literature," pp. 44–52.
[4] Dorson, "The Identification of Folklore in American Literature," pp. 1–8.
[5] Utley, "Arthurian Romance and International Folktale Method," pp. 596–607.
[6] Q. D. Leavis, "Hawthorne as Poet," *Sewanee Review*, 59 (1951), 179–205.
[7] Albert B. Friedman, "Folklore and Medieval Literature," Folklore and Literature, Special Session, MLA Convention, New York, 27 Dec. 1976.

Bibliography

Bolte, Johannes, and Georg Polívka. *Anmerkungen zu den Kinder- und Hausmärchen der Brüder Grimm.* 5 vols. Leipzig: Dieterich'sche Verlagsbuchhandlung, 1913–32. Encyclopedic, though now somewhat outdated, compilation of high-culture works related to the Grimms's fairy tales. Vol. V contains a large bibliography.

Braun, Maximilian. *Das serbokroatische Heldenlied*. Göttingen: Vandenhoeck and Ruprecht, 1961. A conventional survey of Yugoslavian heroic songs that does not stress oral performance.

Chadwick, H. Monro, and N. K. Chadwick. *The Growth of Literature*. 3 vols. Cambridge: Cambridge Univ. Press, 1932–40. Learned, thorough survey of the "development" of literature, taking cognizance of oral traditions.

Child, Francis James, ed. *The English and Scottish Popular Ballads*. 5 vols. Boston: Houghton, 1882–98. Frequently modified and appended, this was the first attempt in English at a complete taxonomy of the English and Scottish ballad; annotations are extensive. Still a basic work.

Dorson, Richard. "The Identification of Folklore in American Literature." *Journal of American Folklore*, 70 (1957), 1–8. Sets forth a rigorous methodology applicable to the literature of many countries.

Eisner, Sigmund. *The Tristan Legend: A Study in Sources*. Evanston, Ill.: Northwestern Univ. Press, 1969. A detailed folklore analysis of the legend, mainly as it occurs in manuscript, attempting to locate its origins and to trace its development.

Friedman, Albert B. *The Ballad Revival*. Chicago: Univ. of Chicago Press, 1961. A historical survey of the ballad, its cultural and intellectual settings, and its relations to literary forms.

Goody, Jack, ed. *Literacy in Traditional Societies*. Cambridge: Cambridge Univ. Press, 1968. Several excellent essays by different authors anthropologically oriented. A useful bibliography is included.

Haavio, Martti Henrikki. *Kirjokansi: Suomen Kansen Kertomarunoutta*. Porvoo: Söderström, 1952. Excellent study of Finnish folk narrative and the *Kalevala*. A useful bibliography is included.

Havelock, Eric Alfred. *Preface to Plato*. Cambridge: Harvard Univ. Press, 1963. Perceptive post-Parry-Lord analysis of oral traditions in Plato's world.

Hoffman, Daniel G. *Form and Fable in American Fiction*. New York: Oxford Univ. Press, 1961. Probably the most perceptive analysis of folk forms in American literature.

Jackson, Kenneth Hurlstone. *The International Popular Tale and Early Welsh Tradition*. Cardiff: Univ. of Wales Press, 1961. Introductory in tone, though several important insights into the sources and traditions of much Welsh narrative are presented clearly. An important interdisciplinary work.

Jones, Gwyn. *Kings, Beasts and Heroes*. Oxford: Oxford Univ. Press, 1972. Literature, primarily medieval, is analyzed with an international perspective in comparison with folktales and literary works: superbly well written and lucid.

Kirk, Geoffrey Stephen. *Homer and the Oral Tradition*. New York: Cambridge Univ. Press, 1976. An intelligent, learned study of the subject by a classicist who knows a great deal about the oral tradition.

Lewis, Mary Ellen. "Beyond Context in the Analysis of Folklore in Literature: Chinua Achebe's *Arrow of God*." *Research in African Literatures*, 7 (1976), 44–52. An argument for broadening perspectives when examining folklore in literature to include modes of transmission as well as social contexts of narrative performances.

Loomis, Roger Sherman. "Arthurian Tradition and Folklore." *Folklore*, 69 (1958), 1–25. This famous scholar's renunciation of folklore approaches to Arthurian literature.

Lord, Albert B. *The Singer of Tales*. Cambridge: Harvard Univ. Press, 1960. The classic study, now much modified after extensive controversy, of oral narrative performance and its relation to several literary compositions.

Panzer, Friedrich Wilhelm. *Studien zur germanischen Sagengeschichte.* 2 vols. Munich: Beck, 1910–12. The first systematic analysis of *Beowulf* and related folktales, it is still, despite its flaws, a useful study. A companion volume examines Siegfried.

Raglan, Fitz Roy Richard Somerset. *The Hero: A Study in Tradition, Myth and Drama.* London, 1937; rpt. New York: Vintage, 1956. Much criticized by folklorists of late, Raglan's comparison of several culture heroes is still stimulating and provocative.

Rosenberg, Bruce A. *Custer and the Epic of Defeat.* University Park: Pennsylvania State Univ. Press, 1975. A study of how historical events become both folklore and literature, and an attempt to determine the common elements in both.

———. "Folklore Methodology and Medieval Literary Criticism." *Journal of the Folklore Institute,* 13 (1976), 311–25. Identifies and describes those folklore methodologies useful to the literary critic of medieval literature.

Taylor, Archer. "Folklore and the Student of Literature." In *The Study of Folklore.* Ed. Alan Dundes. Englewood Cliffs, N.J.: Prentice Hall, 1965, pp. 34–42. Discusses in general terms the several perspectives the student of folklore can bring to literary analysis.

———. *The Literary Riddle before 1600.* Berkeley: Univ. of California Press, 1948. A valuable survey of riddles in literature before Shakespeare.

Thompson, Stith. *The Folktale.* New York: Dryden, 1946. A comprehensive survey of the most popular folktales, how the genre is studied, and their histories in brief, with frequent reference to literary usage.

———. *Motif-Index of Folk Literature.* Rev. ed. 6 vols. Bloomington: Indiana Univ. Press, 1955–58. The basic research tool for classifying motifs.

———, and Antti Aarne. *The Types of the Folktale: A Classification and Bibliography.* Folk Fellows Communications, 184. Helsinki: Suomalainen Tiedeakatmia, 1961. The basic research tool for classifying folktales.

Utley, Francis Lee. "Arthurian Romance and International Folktale Method." *Romance Philology,* 17 (1964), 596–607. Surveys several medieval romances and their development from folktales; contains an important methodological discussion.

———. "Oral Genres as a Bridge to Written Literature." In *Folklore Genres.* Ed. Dan Ben-Amos. Austin: Univ. of Texas Press, 1975, pp. 3–16. Claims that oral narratives should be studied for the light they may shed on more "serious" literature.

———. "Some Implications of Chaucer's Folktales." *Laographia,* 22(1965), 588–99. A reevaluation of the sources of many of the stories in *The Canterbury Tales,* stressing the likelihood of their derivation from oral narratives.

Vries, Jan de. *Heroic Song and Heroic Legend.* Trans. B. J. Timmer. London: Oxford Univ. Press, 1963. An excellent analytic survey of the major epics of the world, perceptively discussing their development in oral as well as written modes.

Winner, Thomas G. *The Oral Art and Literature of the Kazakhs of Russian Central Asia.* Durham, N.C.: Duke Univ. Press, 1958. A survey of the major collected poems from central Asia, with a thoughtful analysis of their content.

6

Literature and Sociology*

PRISCILLA B. P. CLARK

I

Whatever else it may be, literature is a social discourse, shaped by the many and complex relations it entertains with the societies that write and read, discuss and define literary works. As students of literature we attend to these social relations of literature because they not only deepen our understanding of particular texts and authors but also give us a sense of the many and varied phenomena that those works and authors address and express. However amorphous as an intellectual enterprise, the sociology of literature nonetheless recognizes the significance — the literary significance — of the social contexts that define literature, contexts that literature in turn defines. This dialectic between text and context recommends the sociology of literature to the literary critic.

If all literature attends to the social in one way or another, some works do so more patently than others, and it is to these that the sociology of literature has turned most often. Its obvious concern with working out a modus vivendi for the individual in society and its realistic mode of presentation do much to explain the attraction of sociological studies to the nineteenth-century novel and the disinclination to confront the modernist and avant-garde. But all literature draws on social relations and expresses social experience. Every work of literature fuses the observed and the imagined; every work perceives the social in terms of the aesthetic. The social relations of literature are not extraliterary but are literature itself.

Infusion of the literary and the social does not mean reduction of the one to the other. It would be as absurd to confine literature to its social components as to ignore them altogether. If literary works necessarily make social statements, sometimes even blatant ones, they never do that only. Thus utopian novels, no matter how programmatic they may seem, give us visions of another life, not blueprints for social reform. *Gulliver's Travels*, *Candide*, *Rasselas* imagine better worlds. They do not indicate how or even if these worlds might be realized.

This imbrication of the literary and the social explains why the sociology of literature draws on literary studies and social sciences alike. Sociological analyses do not supplant, they supplement more familiar kinds of literary inquiry. For although the two modes may seem incompatible, they are in reality complementary. To be sure, the generalizing mode of social science runs counter to the individualistic bias of most literary criticism. Where literary studies seek what is singular about a text or an author, the social sciences typically look beyond the individual for the patterns that order social life. Still, a sociological perspective does not deny singularity so much as it links the individual person, act, or work to collective phenomena, to social groups, institutions, and forces. The excitement of the sociology of literature derives in large measure from these differences, which provoke the unexpected comparisons that lead to discovery.

The many combinations of literary and sociological perspectives have produced many diverse studies, which one is hard put to place under a single rubric. Sociology of literature or literary sociology? The terminology itself points to a fundamental division. The *sociology of literature* most often designates the study of literary institutions and the social organization of literary life: discussions of publishers, publics, critics, writers' circles, journalists. An especially empiricist version of this sociology of literature (often dubbed "positivistic") concerns itself with gathering as many data as possible about literary life, preferably those data most amenable to aggregation: books written, published, sold, bought, reviewed, read, remaindered, forgotten. On the assumption that literature is above all an act — or several acts — of communication, such studies focus on the circuit of institutions that makes communication possible.

Those closer to literary criticism are more likely to favor *literary sociology* for readings of literary texts from one or another sociologically informed point of view. The distinction between literary institution and literary text is not absolute since almost any sociologically oriented study makes some sort of accommodation between the two. The student of literature will return to the literary work; the more sociologically disposed will revert to social phenomena. But each will have moved away from the point of origin before returning to it. The most provocative studies move in just this way from text to context, or the reverse, and back again, because whether one speaks of the *sociology of literature*, as I do, or of *literary sociology*, the subject is not an entity or a product but relations.

In view of the misconceptions that abound on the subject, one ought to say something about what the sociology of literature is not before attempting to say what it is. To begin with, the sociology of literature is neither deterministic nor reductionist. No one, no study can derive a formula whereby social class X plus economic condition Y yields author Z and work Z^l. Although they perhaps seem more alien to literature, the social forces on which any sociology of literature depends are no more reductionist than the categories applied to literature by any number of disciplines, from psychoanalysis to semiotics. Nor is the sociology of literature irremediably divorced from aesthetic questions. As a general rule, the more empiricist a study and the more it relies on quantification, the less pertinent aesthetic considerations will be. Nevertheless, most work, even if it does not explicitly raise aesthetic issues, assumes their sociological significance. Whether the relation is taken as positive or negative, it is taken as important.

A negative connection between aesthetic quality and sociological significance is most evident in the deliberate selection of minor works, of "popular," or what German criticism calls "trivial," literature. Anyone who sees literature as an act of communication will prefer to study works with which a definite public can be identified. The choice of popular literature further supposes a community of interest between writer and vast numbers of readers. The response to these works, clearly measurable in sales, justifies the assumption that they reveal something important about the society in question. Sociological resonance may equally well be a function of aesthetic vision and interpretive power. The legitimate interest in popular literature does not restrict the sociology of literature to works of little aesthetic interest. On the contrary, critics who consider literature a unique creation will avoid the more conventional works and turn instead to major works and authors precisely because of their power and complexity.

Correlations between aesthetic quality and sociological significance are more often implied than defended. The significance of Marxist aesthetics lies in the theoretical justification it elaborates for the equation of the aesthetic and the social. The numerous permutations of Marxist literary criticism derive from a common theoretical foundation that posits art as an amalgamation of the aesthetic and the social, as a means, first, of expressing ("reflection" is the usual Marxist terminology) the forces at work in any society and, second, of transforming that society. In Marxist terms art can be conservative as well as revolutionary, conservative insofar as it depicts what is, revolutionary to the extent that it provokes consciousness of the imperfection of society and incites the individual to action. More than any other approach, Marxism insists on the dual nature of literature, which registers the effects of social forces and redefines them at the same time.

II

Like so much else having to do with literary studies, a sociological perspective on literature can be traced to Plato and to Aristotle. Assuming an important and direct effect of what is read on the reader and ultimately on society, Plato banished poets from his ideal republic on the grounds that these dealers in illusion sapped the moral health of the individual and, hence, of the state. Concerned primarily with the preservation of society, subsequent censors have followed Plato both in denying the autonomy of literature and in investing literature with considerable power for perversion. The actual influence often remains a matter of conjecture. The medieval romances read by Don Quixote, like the romantic novels read by Emma Bovary, acted on the favorable terrain of active fantasy lives; literature alone cannot be held responsible for such aberrations.

Plato conceded that literature could have a positive effect and that patriotic hymns might reinforce the public virtues undermined by lyric effusions. The conservative defense of literature has continued to emphasize the beneficent influence of literature in its distinctive combination of what Horace called *utile et dulce*, the useful and the sweet, which makes the educational importance of a literary work a direct function of its beauty. For all his skepticism about literature Rousseau traced his exalted conception of civic virtue to his childhood reading of Plutarch's *Lives* (*Confessions*, Bk. I), while Horatio Alger's poor-but-honest-boy-makes-good series in late nineteenth-century America was intended to instill virtuous conduct, thus serving as a modern version of traditional fairy tales and children's stories.

Plato stands at the head of a long line of critics who define literature as the explicans, that which explains, and society as the explicandum, that which is to be explained. Aristotle redresses the balance in favor of literary criticism since, at least by implication, he reversed the order of explanation by making literature the end, the explicandum, and society the means, the explicans. The rules for literature elaborated by Aristotle in the *Poetics* were founded on the correspondence of literary and social hierarchies, which made tragedy the domain of noble situations and personages and defined comedy by its ignoble situations and plebeian characters.

Despite the prestigious antecedents of Plato, Aristotle, and Horace, a specifically socioliterary perspective did not emerge until the eighteenth century, when history came to be viewed not as the effect of a divine cause but as the record of human actions directed by a great many, and potentially contrary, purposes. What was eventually termed "cultural history" (*Kulturgeschichte*) gloried in the varieties of historical experience that included literature and the arts along with wars and politics, and it is to a historian that we owe the first extended examination of literature in terms we can call sociological. In *Principi di una scienza nuova* (1725) Giambattista Vico sought to explain the patent differences between the *Iliad* and the *Odyssey* by positing not one but two Homers, two authors writing at different times in Greek history whose different societies marked the two works.

Vico had few readers among his contemporaries. His cues were not heeded until the nineteenth century, when a series of intellectual changes concurred to favor new perspectives on literature: intense interest in national identity; concern for the radical dislocations effected by political revolution, urbanization, and nascent industrialization; and finally, philosophical inquiry into the nature of knowledge and its relation to historical development. A classicism that stressed the continuity of literary traditions yielded to a romanticism that stressed discontinuities. Germaine Necker de Staël raised many of these questions, notably in *Sur la littérature considérée dans ses rapports avec les institutions sociales* (1800). Applying to literature Charles de Secondat, baron de Montesquieu's theory of the influence of climate and Johann Gottfried von Herder's stress on *Volk*, she contrasted the melancholy "romantic" tradition of the foggy northern countries (England, Germany, Scandinavia) and the "classical" works indigenous to the sunny south (Greece, Rome, Spain, seventeenth-century France). Though inclined to overstatement, Mme de Staël is wonderfully exciting as she explores the social relations of literature and attacks the premises of classical aesthetics.

Hippolyte Taine's *Histoire de la littérature anglaise* (1863) was more focused and more rigid. Taine was the first to formulate his argument in terms of causes and effects, and, inevitably, his theory did not serve him well. The infamous trio of race, milieu, and historical moment, which he invoked to explain literary works, did not turn out to be the social equation hoped for. The concepts remain fuzzy, and the reasoning often moves in circles of deduction and induction. Yet Taine well repays reading. The extended comparison of Becky Sharp in *Vanity Fair* and Valerie Marneffe in *La Cousine Bette* makes a strong case for an unbridgeable gulf between Victoria's England and Louis Philippe's France and has nothing to do with the theory.

Where the French examined national traditions in the spirit of historical positivism, seeking answers in specific social institutions and traditions, English critics like Samuel Taylor Coleridge, Thomas Carlyle, John Henry Cardinal Newman, and Matthew Arnold confronted the cultural crisis precipitated by the advancing industrialization, urbanization, and democratization of society and were especially concerned with the social roles of the artist, and of art, what they were and what they should be—concerns that continue to animate contemporary debate over the meaning and the effects of mass culture.

In contrast to the French, who concentrated on the mechanisms of the social relations of particular literatures, and to the English, who pondered the state of culture, the more philosophically inclined Germans speculated on the nature of aesthetics and of art. Opposing Immanuel Kant, who had considered aesthetic judgment (taste) entirely subjective, Georg Hegel proposed art as a source of knowledge that could be studied systematically. This he proceeded to do in a vast survey of art from the Greeks to the Romantics in which he subjected art and society alike to the laws of historical development. But it was not Kant or Hegel, any more than the English or the French, who gave the single greatest impetus to the sociological study of literature. Karl Marx's influence on literary criticism rests wholly on the theory of knowledge that insists on the interdependence of ideas and the organization of society. Because knowledge is ultimately conditioned by economic structures, literature can be said to "reflect" or hold a mirror to society. The Marxian theory of knowledge does more than specify the social and especially economic locus of literature; it insists on the vital role these ideas play in creating society. The mind and the artistic imagination join to articulate, to codify, and thereby to impel historical change.

The problems posed by Marx have variously inspired and haunted Marxists (and almost everyone else) ever since. Responses vary greatly from strict application of Marxian categories to literary studies where "reflection" is little more than a metaphor. Most literary critics find it impossible to accept the determinism of literature by social forces. If all intellectual activity is determined by economic forces, what does the artist contribute? The rigidity of certain of Marx's epigones gave Marxism a bad name in some literary circles as did a rather indiscriminate reliance on "reflection" — a critic of sufficient ingenuity can find reflections of virtually anything almost anywhere. Notwithstanding these theoretical inadequacies, Marx succeeded where others failed in imposing a framework for a sociological conception of literature. In some sense every sociology of literature today can be traced to Marx, who combated the Romantics' almost extraterrestrial conception of genius by firmly rooting literary works and their authors in those same social forces that touch the rest of society.

III

Like every other intellectual activity, the sociology of literature is defined by the decisions it makes, by the subjects it selects, the objectives it pursues, and the problems it poses. Perhaps the most immediately striking limitation is the choice of modern subjects. If there is no reason why a sociological perspective cannot be adopted for any literature, it is nonetheless true that post-Renaissance Western literatures account for the majority of subjects discussed, and within those literatures the nineteenth-century novel stands out as the most favored genre. The traditionally realistic conventions of these novels make their sociological relevance obvious. After all, novels often deal quite explicitly with the sorts of social phenomena that define sociology — society at large, social groups, marriage and the family, careers, revolutions. The inclination toward the modern is reinforced by the relative dearth of information about premodern societies. Since literature supplies much of what we know, or surmise, about many societies, we cannot use that same information to understand those literary works. Finally, the very concept of literature is a product of late eighteenth-century Europe. To talk of ancient Greek or Roman or early Chinese literature seriously misstates the situation because it implies, even when it does not actually impose, a conceptual framework alien to the topic. Marxist thought in particular has oriented even non-Marxist work to modern society and its literatures. However useful, indeed necessary, such anachronisms may be, it is only to be expected that the sociology of literature will favor those subjects most appropriate to the concepts at hand.

Every study that looks to literature and society or literature in society must come to terms with the different levels of generality of literature and society. Social phenomena do not act on literary works directly so much as they work through specific intellectual and cultural factors. Abstractions like the novel or the bourgeoisie depend on specific novels or particular bourgeoisies and on the cultural, economic, and social context of each. The modern English novel developed in the eighteenth century as an interpretation no less than a product of a complex of social factors: the economic prosperity and consequent leisure of an emergent middle class, and especially of women; urbanization, which encouraged geographical and social mobility and blurred traditional social hierarchies; secularization, which turned writers and readers alike from religious works like *Pilgrim's Progress* toward the more worldly novels of Daniel Defoe, Samuel Richardson, and Henry Fielding. In different ways *Robinson Crusoe, Pamela*, and *Tom Jones* were signs of a modernizing novel and a modernizing society (see Watt, *The Rise of the Novel*).

The fundamental choice is the object of inquiry. What does one want to know? Which, of literature or society, is to be the explicans, which the explicandum? Is literature the means or the end? A text or an institution? The principal contribution a sociological perspective has to make is the sense that literature is more than works and their authors. It is a system of relations, of individuals and institutions, of functions and roles, which join to define literature and to give it a social presence. What we call "literature" covers all those creations and products, individuals and institutions defined by their relations to those works designated by society as "literary." For an idea of these many literary relations and of the interrelations with which the sociology of literature must deal, it is useful to consider a model of literature as the sum of these relations. The literary system thus conceived comprehends the basic stages in the life of literature — creation, production, diffusion, reception[1] — each of which performs characteristic functions and is associated with particular institutions, roles, and products. Each stage is essential to our understanding because each forges new and different bonds between literature and society.

The literary system assumes a basically modern phenomenon, the institutionalization of literature and the identification of specifically literary activities and roles. By the nineteenth century in Europe, literary activities acquired a measure of autonomy and the institutions to maintain it. The increase in the numbers and kinds of readers, writers, and works, the development of the market, technological advances (roller presses, cheap paper, etc.) concurred to endow literary activities with an independent momentum very different from the economic, social, and cultural dependence characteristic of the literary system supported by aristocratic or royal patronage.

If literary works are not all the literary system, they are surely its raison d'être, which explains why the sociology of literature, like literary studies, has been conspicuously interested in the manifestations, conditions, and associations of creativity. Textual analysis is the more usual interest of literary studies and supplies the closest point of contact with the sociology of literature. Sociological readings of literary works differ from other readings in the kinds of connections they seek to establish with the extraliterary world. Where others tie literature to myth, to linguistic structures, or to psychological constructs, sociological readings view literature as either a document of social phenomena or a product of those same phenomena. One may read from society into a text or one may reverse the procedure. Popular literature aimed at an increasingly broad, or "mass," audience signals prevailing norms, values, attitudes, and behavior and at the same time responds to those values and norms. Since that response also carries an interpretation, literary works can never be taken as a direct reflection of society, although the interpretation itself will vary from reliance on conventional formulations in stock mass-periodical fare to the originality of highly individualistic works.

That the artist is the more or less active reproducer of social meaning, a maker as well as a product of social influences, is a view current in much modern sociological criticism. It is the defining principle of the approach to textual analysis known as sociocriticism, which represents something of a reaction to the stress of much Marxist criticism on the social conditioning of literature and on the historical development of capitalism and its literary parallels (see Duchet, *Sociocriticism*). The relatively crude equivalencies of some Marxist criticism reinforced the prejudices of those who refuse connections of text and context. Yet Marxist criticism can be as sophisticated as any other. It can argue, for instance, that the French Revolution did not create the historical novel directly but that the two are tied through a common transformation in conceptions of history (see Lukács, *Studies in European Realism*). Or again that the administrative and judiciary nobility (*noblesse de robe*) did not create the works of Blaise Pascal and Jean Baptiste Racine but was linked to those works through the common structure of Jansenist religious belief by which both authors were influenced (see Goldmann, *The Hidden God*). The basic category of social class is not discarded but is rather extended and redefined by the particular context to which it is applied.

Creation concerns writers as well as texts. Although writers have attracted critical attention at least since Samuel Johnson's *Lives of the Poets*, a sociological perspective departs from a more traditional focus in its use of biography to establish broader patterns of literary life and to chart the effects of social and economic factors on that life. The fundamental patterns of contemporary literary life were set by, and evolved as a reaction to, the expansion of the market and the decline of aristocratic and royal patronage. In the late eighteenth and early nineteenth centuries, writing became an occupation rather than merely a preoccupation; it became, in sociological parlance, a social status in its own right. Whence the importance of the literary groups (*cénacles*, *académies*, and such) that mitigated the effects of the market and supported that social status (see Clark, "Literary Culture in France and the United States").

Social conditions affect not only how and what one writes but the very decision to write. By excluding some definitions of literature and some kinds of writers while favoring others, characteristics such as sex, race, education, occupation, and social milieu shape literary careers and, more broadly, the definitions of literature we hold. Recent feminist criticism has reminded us of the ways women writers and their writings have been and are defined by their sex, both positively and negatively. Traditionally, a woman of certain social standing had at her disposal certain resources that favored the writing of literature: leisure and little need to earn a living, some education and familiarity with certain kinds of literature (a "woman's domain"). Yet there were limitations in these advantages: few women had the psychological or even physical room of their own that Virginia Woolf long ago deemed essential to independence; their education tied them to private, domestic literature like the novel and kept them away from a public genre like drama; prevailing values and norms dictated the use of a pseudonym or anonymous publication; and even so the (male) literary establishment controlled journals and publishing houses. Legally, women were seldom empowered to act on their own; psychologically, they were not often prepared to do so. For all the diversity of women writers one is justified in associating them with a subculture within the broader literary culture whose mark one can distinguish in writers as contrary as Margaret Fuller and Louisa May Alcott, Colette and Simone de Beauvoir, Doris Lessing and Nathalie Sarraute.

Such marginality within a literary culture is a permanent source of a tension that can be extraordinarily creative. The most casual observer is struck by the literary works, especially of modern times, that express a sense of being on the periphery of society rather than securely at its center. As it does for women writers, marginality may derive from social status: race for black Americans but also for Africans writing in the language of former colonial powers. One can also choose the periphery, and numerous writers have done so: political exiles like Voltaire in England and later in Geneva, the Russian Alexander Solzhenitsyn in Switzerland and the United States, the Czech Milan Kundera in France, the Guinean Camara Laye in Senegal. What may be termed cultural exile is no less important a means of making sensibilities more acute (see in particular Orr, *Tragic Realism and Modern Society*), hence of raising one's cultural and literary consciousness. One thinks of such exiles as Ivan Turgenev in France; Americans in England and France, from Henry James to James Baldwin via Getrude Stein, Ernest Hemingway, and F. Scott Fitzgerald; the Colombian Gabriel García Márquez in Spain. An even greater cultural dislocation is assumed by writers who choose the exile of another language, like the Pole Joseph Conrad, who wrote in English, or the contemporary Jewish writer Elie Wiesel, who is an American citizen but a French writer. Or the most stunning example of all, Vladimir Nabokov, who had written a good deal in Russian before he turned to French and then definitively to English.

The effects of such profound cultural and even linguistic marginality are significant for the work that gives it expression and also for the literary cultures by and against which minority literature is defined. However creative the sense of alienation may prove to be, the fact of marginality is one more obstacle between writer and public. To the extent that the dominant literary culture weighs on the production and the diffusion of literature, it will tend to filter out works and writers that counter prevailing conceptions of what is literary. Spectacular advances in technology in the early nineteenth century transformed literature from a vehicle of elite society into a general medium of communication, and technological developments thereafter realized and extended the Gutenberg Galaxy. The Enlightenment in eighteenth-century Europe was an intellectual enterprise; it was also one very much involved in and dependent on a commercial enterprise. Production, or publication, provides one more means of defining literature and of establishing its place in society.

The diffusion and reception of literature are important because they complete the literary circuit, making the connection between writer and reader. In philosophical terms, literature may arguably exist without readers; from a sociological perspective, a public is essential for literature to live beyond its creator and thus to acquire a presence and meaning in society. Literature is continually redefined by its publics, whose various readings all inhere in its social definition. What reception aesthetics posits for the individual work, the sociology of literature proposes for literature: as the individual reader reconstructs each text encountered, so too literary institutions of every sort define literature. Works we call masterpieces have evoked response in the most diverse publics over time and place and have found institutional support.

Closing the literary circuit requires intermediaries — reviewers of books in magazines and newspapers, authors of articles in scholarly journals, teachers of literature from primary to graduate school, advertisers, television broadcasters — engaged in diffusing literary works and, alternatively, neglecting the prodigious number of works that then all but disappear. For every work canonized a classic by the educational system, for every work translated into another or several languages, for every work purchased in quantity year after year, thousands are remaindered or consigned to the shredder's oblivion. The astronomical attrition rate concerns literature itself still more than individual works. Even the "classics" soon cease to be part of the active literary vocabulary, left to survive through the schools and the scholarship of specialists. The range of literary reference of book reviews in a sample of Swedish journals in the late nineteenth century and mid-twentieth century was limited and oriented toward the present. The works most mentioned in the earlier period, even those recognized as classic works, were barely noticed sixty years later (see Rosengren, *Sociological Aspects of the Literary System*). And though book reviews are not the only agent of diffusion or the sole indicator of the state of literature, such evidence makes one reflect on the consequences of a literary system that greatly overexposes a very few works (by advertising campaigns or television appearances of the authors) while leaving the vast majority to languish.

Diffusion is more than transmitting literary works. A process of defining literature, it is an instance of criticism. The usual focus on individual critics and the judgments of specific works obscures the broad social significance of criticism, which in sociological terms is as essential to literature as creation. Every reader engages in criticism. Criticism conveys the individual's response to, hence definition of, the text. Through this reaction, every reader contributes to the collective definition of literature, to the life of literature in society, and to its death. Nathalie Sarraute's novel *Les Fruits d'or* dramatizes just this life of a literary work in the conversation it prompts, the criticism it provokes, and eventually, when conversation and criticism cease, the silence that is death.

The sociology of literature takes this process of definition and redefinition as one of its subjects. What are its causes, its functions, its effects, the institutions by which it is realized? What defines popular literature as popular? Surely numbers provide only a partial response, since not all "popular" fiction is equally popular. Some detective novels, westerns, science fiction, gothic romances, and so on, attract a wide readership; others do not. The fragmentation of modern reading publics makes it all but impossible for any given work to reach more than a fraction of its potential readers. What then defines that same popular literature as literature? Is *Les Misérables* "literature" or "popular literature"? To what extent does criticism attract or discourage readers? Surely criticism is important, but just as surely many works gain great popularity with scarcely any critical notice. J. R. R. Tolkien's *Lord of the Rings* was an underground best-seller in the 1960s, notably on American college campuses, and when critics finally took notice, it was often to ask the sociological question posed above: why? Publishers and critics are notoriously defective in predictive powers, and publishers conduct little market research. The literary game becomes one of chance, for writers, who may be read and then again may not be, and for readers, who may happen on a marvelous work but may well not. Unlike classics, imposed by the educational system, contemporary literature is subject to the vagaries of distribution, of connections between journals and newspapers, of critics' whims and convictions, as well as of chance. The congruence of values, expectations, even mood does much to explain why various literary works evoke responses where and when they do, why some are read for centuries and others disappear within weeks of publication.

IV

The task of any sociology of literature is to make clear the literary significance of the social contexts of literature, to make us aware of the infinite complexity and endless fascination of these social relations. Which social factors are linked how and when to what sorts of literature and what literary differences do these connections make? With careful attention to particular texts and contexts, the sociology of literature perpetually questions the concepts on which it relies: "the writer," "the public," "genre," "literature" are notions redefined by the context in which they occur. Thus the connection between the novel and the bourgeoisie, already a commonplace in the nineteenth century when Marxist thought gave questions of social class new urgency, is both banal and vague. Since neither bourgeois society nor the novel is a simple affair, equation between the two cannot be simple. Which aspects of bourgeois society affected which elements of the novel; how was that influence transmitted? The eighteenth-century English novels studied by Watt illustrate one set of interrelations between middle-class society and a genre linked to the middle class. To what extent does the relation obtain for the modern French novel, which developed almost a century later? What about the novel in socialist countries, where the bourgeoisie is not supposed to exist? How is the self-reflexive, convoluted work of a Jorge Luis Borges or the fantastic epic of a Gabriel García Márquez tied to contemporary Latin America? Do their visions of society apply elsewhere?

If we elaborate the connection between genre and society, we see that the critic could move from eighteenth-century England to nineteenth-century France to consider how broad social changes were translated into literary terms. The social, economic, and political dislocations of the French Revolution were mostly mediated by the institutions of the literary system. The market most emphatically but also writers' groups, journals, critics, and publics affected the writer, who, freed from patronage, became tied to the market; technological advances in publishing permitted expanded production; innovations in the marketing of books and the rise of journalism aggravated the commercialization of literature; and new publics, literate but lacking a classical education, turned to the novel for a good, easy "read." As the elements of bourgeois society must be distinguished, so, too, must the kinds and types of novels. The novel and the novelist are composites of many and often very different styles, attitudes, works, and authors.

Comparisons across literatures and across societies, across the arts and intellectual activities lay the foundation for any sociological approach to literature. Without comparisons we cannot distinguish between the general and the particular, between that which is characteristic of a given society or literature and that which is shared by many societies and several literatures, between the specifically literary and the broadly aesthetic, intellectual, or cultural. Socioeconomic systems like feudalism or capitalism, processes like modernization, secularization, democratization, or the division of labor exercise their effects in and through specific literary and cultural traditions. Industrialization, for example, had quite distinct literary results in England and in France. Literary critics would agree in calling the social novel of George Sand, Eugène Sue, or Honoré de Balzac very French and that associated with Benjamin Disraeli, Mrs. Gaskell, or Charles Dickens very English. The resemblances — acute consciousness of social change, interest in social problems — are instructive, the differences no less so. The social context reveals a good deal about what separates the two responses to similar phenomena.

Where the example of comparative literature directs us to the contrast of literary traditions, that of literary history enjoins the sociology of literature to make comparisons within a single literary tradition. These traditions may be diversely defined, by a national literature (English literature) and also by a linguistic community (Anglophone literature) or again by a particular style, conception, or "school" of literature (Romanticism, realism, modernism). Again one is struck by the affinities between a sociological approach and certain subjects: like the traditional novel with which it is often associated, realism has attracted considerable attention. But there are realisms other than the social realism of Defoe and Richardson; of Balzac, Stendhal, and Zola; of Walter Scott and the historical novel. There is the psychological realism of the eighteenth-century French novel, from Abbé Prévost to Denis Diderot, and there is the tragic realism of a Joseph Conrad or a Fedor Dostoevsky, each of which also illuminates a unique constellation of social forces.

In taking the social territories of literature for its subject, their relations as its object, the sociology of literature partakes of both literary and intellectual history, of linguistic and semiotic analysis; it points to institutions and to individuals, to ideas, to styles, to languages and discourse. Like literary criticism, the sociology of literature extends our understanding of literature, and it does so through its sense of literature as a social phenomenon in a continuous process of definition rather than as a product fixed in time and space. Again like literary criticism, the sociology of literature is concerned with the production and effect of meaning. Some of those who adopt a sociological approach to literature will prefer to explore the social factors that affect, even effect, meaning. Others will focus on the functions of literature for the writer, for the reader, for society. Some critics will attend more to the text, others the context. The sociology of literature encompasses all these orientations, and in that diversity it is, like literature itself, a literary no less than a social enterprise.

Notes

*For their comments and criticisms, I should like to thank Arnold Foster, S. Clark Hulse, Robert Leighninger, Thelma McCormack, Laura Oswald-Koenigsknecht, Sandy Petrey, and Jeffrey Sammons.

[1] Despite the objection that the very term "creation" unduly emphasizes the individual author, I retain the traditional term "creation" to distinguish the work of the (usually) individual author, who produces a text, from the collective product of the publisher, who produces the physical book.

Bibliography

I. History of, and General Statements on, Literature and Sociology

Clark, Priscilla P. "The Sociology of Literature: An Historical Introduction." *Research in Sociology of Knowledge, Sciences, and Arts,* 1 (1978), 237–58. The intellectual roots of the sociology of literature; emphasis on French and German traditions.

Duncan, Hugh D. *Language and Literature in Society: A Sociological Essay on Theory and Method in the Interpretation of Linguistic Symbols.* 1953; rpt. Totowa, N.J.: Bedminster, 1961. Primarily for extensive bibliography of traditional philosophical and historical material.

Eagleton, Terry. *Marxism and Literary Criticism.* Berkeley: Univ. of California Press, 1976. Succinct introduction to the major questions of Marxist literary criticism.

Lowenthal, Leo. "Literature and Sociology." In *Relations of Literary Study.* Ed. James Thorpe. New York: MLA, 1967, pp. 89–110. Perspectives of a European sociologist well versed in literature; considers especially the place and functions of literary activities in the social system; extensive bibliography.

Strelka, Joseph P., ed. *Literary Criticism and Sociology.* Yearbook of Comparative Criticism, 5. University Park: Pennsylvania State Univ. Press, 1973. See especially the articles on trends of literary sociology in German, Russian, and British and American criticism.

II. Anthologies

Albrecht, Milton C., James H. Burnett, and Mason Griff. *The Sociology of Art and Literature: A Reader.* New York: Praeger, 1970. The opening article by Albrecht, "Art as Institution," reviews various sociological conceptions of art, art's functions and roles; other articles treat style, artists, distribution and reward systems, tastemakers and publics, methodology, history, and theory.

Burger, Peter, ed. *Seminar: Literatur- und Kunstsoziologie.* Frankfurt: Suhrkamp, 1978. Similar to Albrecht et al., but with greater emphasis on German work.

Burns, Elizabeth, and Tom Burns, eds. *Sociology of Literature and Drama.* Harmondsworth, Eng.: Penguin, 1973. Especially good selection from French critical theory and practice.

Duchet, Claude, ed. *Sociocriticism.* Special issue of *Sub-stance,* 15 (1976).

Lang, Berel, and Forrest Williams, eds. *Marxism and Art: Writings in Aesthetics and Criticism.* New York: McKay, 1972. Articles include theoretical writings from Marx to Mao Tse-tung as well as studies of particular problems (methodology, theoretical concepts) and works (e.g., Brecht on *Coriolanus*); a judicious introduction.

Rosenberg, Bernard, and David M. White, eds. *Mass Culture: The Popular Arts in America*. Glencoe, Ill.: Free Press, 1957. Articles by literary critics and social scientists taking positions for and against mass culture, analyzing its products (e.g., comic strips, radio, popular novels).

Routh, Jane, and Janet Wolff, eds. *The Sociology of Literature: Theoretical Approaches*. Sociological Review Monograph, 25. Totowa, N.J.: Rowman and Littlefield, 1977. A selection of mostly British studies, several illustrating Marxist perspectives.

Solomon, Maynard, ed. *Marxism and Art*. New York: Knopf, 1973. The most substantial anthology of Marxist aesthetics, including critical readings of works as well as more theoretical statements; excellent introductions place each section and author in the development of Marxist thought and socialist politics.

III. Individual Studies

Altick, Richard. *The English Common Reader: A Social History of the Mass Reading Public, 1800–1900*. Chicago: Univ. of Chicago Press, 1975. A classic study of popular literature, its readers, writers, and publishers.

Auerbach, Erich. "La Cour et la ville." In *Scenes from the Drama of European Literature: Six Essays*. New York: Meridian, 1959. The public of the seventeenth-century French theater, its evaluation and values; notable for cultural integration of a socially disparate public (see also entry for Harbage).

Charvat, William. *The Profession of Authorship in America, 1800–1870*. Columbus: Ohio State Univ. Press, 1968. Pioneering studies of the business of literature.

Clark, Priscilla P. "Literary Culture in France and the United States." *American Journal of Sociology*, 84 (1979), 1057–77. Treats the interaction of literary tradition and social change in the creation and maintenance of distinct cultural traditions.

Dubois, Jacques. *L'Institution de la littérature: Introduction à une sociologie*. Brussels: Editions Labor, 1978. Analyzes concept of literature as semiautonomous institution in society, with its own system of values, stratification, functions, and so forth; readings of texts as well as analysis of social groups and institutions; oriented to work in various French traditions.

Ferguson, Robert A. "Longfellow's Political Fears: Civic Authority and the Role of the Artist in *Hiawatha* and *Miles Standish*." *American Literature*, 50 (1978), 187–215. Projection onto a historical setting of ideological conflicts occasioned by the Civil War.

Goldmann, Lucien. *The Hidden God: A Study of Tragic Vision in the* Pensées *of Pascal and the Tragedies of Racine*. Trans. Philip Thody. New York: Humanities Press, 1964. An extensive examination of the interrelation of social, intellectual, and literary structures; traces structure of the works of Pascal and Racine to the "world vision" of the *noblesse de robe* in seventeenth-century France as mediated through the religious vision of Jansenism.

Green, Martin. *The Problem of Boston: Some Readings in Cultural History*. New York: Norton, 1966. Provocative study of a particular milieu and of integration into the community as both support and obstacle to creativity.

Harbage, Alfred. *Shakespeare's Audience*. New York: Columbia Univ. Press, 1941. A model for the use of historical evidence to delineate a theater public.

Lukács, György. *Studies in European Realism: A Sociological Survey of the Writings of Balzac, Stendhal, Zola, Tolstoy, Gorki, and Others*. Trans. Edith Bone. 1950; rpt. New York: Grosset, 1964. Readings on Zola dogmatic, but very perceptive on Balzac and Stendhal; socially informed literary criticism from a generally flexible Marxist perspective.

Orr, John. *Tragic Realism and Modern Society: Studies in the Sociology of the Modern Novel.* Pittsburgh: Univ. of Pittsburgh Press, 1977. Reviews conceptions of realism (Lukács, Auerbach, and others) and illustrates his own definition of tragic realism (through Dostoevsky, Conrad, and several others).

Rosengren, Karl Erik. *Sociological Aspects of the Literary System.* Stockholm: Natur och Kultur, 1968. Important study of the writers referred to in journalistic book reviews in the 1880s and 1950s; the striking lack of continuity signals the extreme selectivity of literary life and the overwhelming fact of oblivion.

Sammons, Jeffrey L. *Literary Sociology and Practical Criticism: An Inquiry.* Bloomington: Indiana Univ. Press, 1977. Extensive current bibliography; critical examination of concepts used in current Marxist and Neo-Marxist literary criticism; stress on Marxist-inspired work, especially of German origin.

Thomson, George. *Aeschylus and Athens: A Study in the Social Origins of Drama.* 3rd ed. 1966; rpt. New York: Haskell House, 1967. Striking exception to the modernity of sociological studies of literature.

Watt, Ian. *The Rise of the Novel.* 1957; rpt. Berkeley: Univ. of California Press, 1962. A model for the interaction of social, religious, and economic factors affecting the writer and the public of novels in eighteenth-century England.

7

Literature and Politics

Matei Calinescu

I

Since the dawn of Romanticism, the relation between politics and literature has been one of the most sensitive and controversial issues that modern aesthetic consciousness has had to face. Clearly, students of the interaction between literature and politics are embarking on a difficult and intellectually dangerous enterprise: the cultural landscape that they set out to explore is enormously complex and undermined by contradictions, paradoxes, and clichés. After almost two centuries, the debate about literature and politics is far from being resolved.

Many critics today would agree that the interpretation of literature should not avoid dealing, when necessary, with political questions. Even some of those who see the ultimate goal of criticism as the recovery of the "intrinsic" meaning of literary works may recognize that certain auxiliary "extrinsic" approaches (historical, sociological, or political) can have a limited usefulness. But there are still many critics who dislike the notion that literature could or should have any direct connection with politics. From their point of view, whether the literary work is seen (rather old-fashionedly) as a pure aesthetic construct, or as an embodiment of "literariness," or as a skillful use of devices for purposes of aesthetic surprise, or (more fashionably) as the realization of a "deconstructive" project, the experience of art not only is autonomous but somehow enjoys a primacy over other types of experience. As Oscar Wilde would have it, "Life imitates art far more than art imitates life."[1] The politically self-contradictory character of the "autonomist" position has been noticed for some time: the opinion that art has nothing to do with utilitarian values in general, and with politics in particular, is itself a political attitude. Serious aestheticists will not deny this view; they argue that the politics of antipolitics is the right politics in artistic matters, and perhaps in all other matters as well (in the latter case, they are likely to be anarchists; I might add that, historically, most of the representatives of aestheticism, Oscar Wilde among them, have been close, if not to the doctrines, to the spirit of anarchism). Oddly, the defender of "art for art's sake" (including "antiart for antiart's sake," which is the avant-gardist version of the same principle) turns out to be a proponent, if not of a new kind of political art, of a definite politics of art.

In reaction to the "autonomist" view, politically minded critics not only have stressed the "heteronomy" of art but have made politics or ideology its central element. But if all art is political, the epithet "political" becomes so general as to lose any useful function. And worse, the political criterion itself ceases to be relevant if the most serious theorists of political art, from Friedrich Engels to György Lukács, are as right as they seem to be when they admit that bad politics can result in good art and, conversely, that good politics often leads to inferior art. When Engels describes Honoré de Balzac's *La Comédie humaine* as a triumph of "realism" over Balzac's own deep-rooted reactionary ideas, he is unwittingly paying tribute to the mystical notion of genius and its power to see through the deceptive veil of ideology.[2] That one of the founders of the ideological theory of art can so serenely dismiss the significance of a great writer's opinions and political allegiance is one of the most intriguing occurrences in the history of literary sociology.

The mere possibility of such inconsistencies and self-contradictions on the part of the representatives of such extreme positions as aestheticism and sociologism indicates the intricate nature of the relation between literature and politics. The origins of the split between the defenders of the "autonomist" concept of art and the defenders of the "ideological" concept of art go back to the first half of the nineteenth century and to the dispute between the proponents of "militant" or "tendentious" or "committed" art and the representatives of "art for art's sake." The appearance of these two trends marks the beginning of a new phase in the history of the relations between politics and literature. This essay is concerned mostly with problems and authors characteristic of this new phase. I do not rule out the possibility of literature-and-politics approaches to poets of earlier times. The farther we go into the past, however, the more we are bound to deal with literature and history, literature and society, or literature and philosophy (including political philosophy), rather than with the more limited questions of literature and politics. There are two reasons why my chronologically circumscribed view of the subject seems preferable to others that, in principle, are equally justified.

1. The bulk of critical material treating explicitly and specifically the issues of literature and politics is confined to the last two centuries.[3] Even within this limited but vast corpus of criticism, there is a noticeable shift, as the authors under scrutiny come closer to us in time, from more "conventional" historical and aesthetic critical strategies to a more direct stress on politics as such, and to a higher degree of ideological/anti-ideological polarization of critical opinion.

2. If we agree that a central problem of literature and politics is the problem of commitment and of the various theories of literary discourse that are implicit in this notion, we would look in vain for examples of politi-

cally committed, or self-consciously uncommitted, writers before the beginning of the nineteenth century. It was not until then that the slow erosion of religious beliefs witnessed by the previous century had, insofar as literature and the arts are concerned, two diametrically opposed but equally significant consequences: the appearance of committed art (displaying most of the signs of a displaced religious fervor) and the rise of "art for art's sake" (offering a totally aestheticized version of the sacred). Although writers of earlier periods expressed political ideas for which they were sometimes persecuted, jailed, tortured, exiled, or even put to death, the dawn of modernity, with its characteristic demise of traditional views of the sacred, brought about radically new relations between literature and politics.

II

Political thinkers with large-scale utopian projects have traditionally entertained serious doubts about artists and their role in society. In most ideal cities there is little or no room for artists, perhaps because these cities themselves are total and perfect works of art. From the totalizing (and totalitarian) point of view of most utopias, the poet is an unruly being, dominated by irrational drives, and, as such, an enemy of order and a potentially dangerous troublemaker. In Plato's eyes, poetry as mimesis is from the outset going in the wrong direction, since the things that it attempts to "imitate" are nothing but approximate and corrupt copies of the transcendent, perfect, and unchanging Ideas. And the treacherous character of the poet's activity is compounded by the fact that poetic works are the result not of calm reflection but of passion, of "inspiration," of that kind of temporary madness brought about by demons who take possession of the poet's soul. Born from irrational forces beyond the control of reason, poetry tends to kindle the passions and stir the most obscure impulses of the public.

Plato's condemnation of poetry, in the name of a metaphysical moral code that can be convincingly reduced to "a code of collectivist or political utilitarianism,"[4] provides a paradigm of almost all future utopian (religious or, more recently, revolutionary) condemnations of the aesthetic as such. The fundamental arguments for the corrupting influence of art are surprisingly similar, whether they invoke the ultimate authority of God or whether, more recently, they speak in the name of the revolution.

Plato's stern antiaestheticism, justified as a form of what Karl Popper has called "political hygiene," has no parallels in the world of the ancient Greeks. The more typical attitudes of Greek antiquity concerning the poet and the role of the arts are seen in Aristotle's reaction to Plato's strictures against art. Opposing the notion that the poet is a fundamentally irrational being, Aristotle stresses the philosophical (rational) component of the poet's mimetic activity when he establishes his famous distinction between history and poetry: "for poetry tends to express the universal, history the particular"

(*Poetics*, IX.iii). Furthermore, if poetry does not have any direct utilitarian value, far from being as harmful as Plato thought, it can exert a generally beneficial influence, through such psychological effects as those achieved by tragedy, whose spectators are faced with representations of powerful passions and emotions and led, through the experience of pity and fear, to the "proper purgation of these emotions," or *katharsis* (VI.ii). Seeing the arts as having their origin in certain universal instincts (the instinct of "imitation," the instinct for "harmony" and "rhythm"), Aristotle believes that by being true to their nature they can, beyond giving pleasure, have positive (if not directly utilitarian) effects on the communities in which they are cultivated.

With the exception of Plato, the critics of both Greek and Roman antiquity concur with Aristotle's positive appraisal of the role of art, although, unlike him, many assign art broadly defined moral-didactic tasks (a line of thought summarized by Horace's well-known principle of *utile dulci* in his *Ars Poetica*). Actually, no one in antiquity (not even the later Neoplatonic philosophers, including Plotinus) seems to have shared Plato's view of art as "ontologically" corrupt and, inherently, "politically" subversive. In short, antiquity did not see the poet as either a political threat or a political asset. Individual poets did reflect on political matters, had political views and biases, "imitated" actions and emotions with political significance, and chastised political and other vices, but they saw their real business as both larger and narrower than that: to produce poetry, whose sources of inspiration are more diverse than political thoughts and passions and whose aims are more modest than the *eudaimonia* or general "felicity" that, according to Aristotle, constitutes the end of politics.

Leaving aside the relations of literature and politics (more precisely, the politics of religion) during the long and complex history of Christianity, we may say that, from the Renaissance's rediscovery of antiquity through the various neoclassical movements that flourished in Europe in the seventeenth and eighteenth centuries, the relation between literary writing and politics was not substantially different from what it had been in antiquity. But toward the end of the eighteenth century the signs of a dramatic change appeared. With the Romantics, political radicalism (itself not free from certain "literary" influences) became incorporated into literature and aesthetics, where it took a variety of forms, some of them easily recognizable (such as the application to literature of such military-political labels as "avant-garde" or "militancy"), some less obvious but not less significant.

Many paradoxes accompany this major shift in cultural consciousness. Here are a few particularly striking ones: the Enlightenment critique of (religious) fanaticism, instead of leading to toleration, turned into a new critical fanaticism of the "ruthless negation of everything existing" (Karl Marx) or of demystification; the doctrine of gradual progress was replaced by revolutionary messianisms, catastrophic theories of the universe and history, and widespread intimations of a new apocalypse, based on the belief that any real change can only be sudden and can only involve the total destruction of the old order (we recall Mikhail Bakunin's anarchistic dictum, "To destroy is to create"); the politics of reason developed into what, in his important essay *L'Homme révolté*, Albert Camus called "rational terror," and then, by way of reaction to the terrorism of reason, into the various irrationalisms and anti-intellectual attitudes that characterize important aspects of Romanticism and aesthetic modernity; and, finally, the secularist legacy of the *siècle des lumières*, in its radicalized revolutionary versions, prevented the Romantic and post-Romantic resurgence of religious feeling from reviving traditional forms and thus contributed to the appearance of such new and odd phenomena as the "religion of politics" and the "religion of art."

III

Contrary to the expectation of one who is familiar with the notion of "committed" or "aligned" literature on the Left, the first advocates of the idea that writers should commit themselves politically and use the aesthetic means at their disposal for the achievement of a political goal were the representatives of reaction in the period that followed the French Revolution of 1789, as André Reszler has convincingly demonstrated.[5]. The fact that the first explicit plea for writers to commit themselves politically came from such embattled defenders of the "divine right" of the monarch and of strict religious orthodoxy as Joseph de Maistre and Louis de Bonald points to the direct link between religious commitment and political commitment, the latter being a natural extension of the former. It also shows how politically important the *homme de lettres* had become. In a sense, the failure to recognize his importance, as Alexis de Tocqueville was to point out a few decades later, had been one of the causes of the downfall of the ancien régime.[6] Nothing could illustrate this better than the tardy, rather pathetic appeals directed at the "man of letters" by the two most articulate spokesmen for the ancien régime, at a time when its restoration was plainly impossible.

The question of political commitment raises a number of thorny issues. To attempt to sort them out, we must keep in mind that political commitment is premised on the existence of competing ideologies. Although their ultimate purpose is to "mobilize" the writer to "serve," ideologies appeal in the first place to the writer's moral sense (often through the subtle method of making the artist feel guilty about being "uncommitted"). When these same ideologies come to power, their method changes, the question now being to assuage the guilt feelings that a writer may experience for being a supporter of the "official" line. The writer's reluctance to endorse an ideology that speaks from a position of power is an interesting modern phenomenon. Its origins must be sought in the rich traditions of critical thought and dissent of the intelligentsia, a group in which writers have always occupied a prominent place. If literature is a "criticism of life" (Matthew Arnold), modern literature can be said to have been—at least in one of its major directions, and more pointedly and self-consciously so than ever before—a criticism of life in history, as shaped by social conditions, institutions, and conflicts. During the last two centuries or so, many writers, irrespective of their aesthetic creed, have come to see nonconformity or dissent as both one of their highest rights and one of their highest duties. When an ideology that has stimulated a writer's critical imagination as long as it had opposed the existing system becomes itself the justification of a new system, the writer is clearly in an uncomfortable position. The triumphant ideology will doubtless call on the writer to remain "committed," even at the price of giving up the right to dissent; and to ensure this result, the ideology will not hesitate to use whatever means are in its power. Jean Starobinski's remarks on the question of "engagement" are clarifying:

> Today we have enough experience to know that intellectuals are mobilizable in two ways: through bad conscience, when they join movements of rebellion; through privileges and (occasionally) terror, when they rally themselves to the powers that be. Sartre is an excellent example of commitment for escaping bad conscience. . . . The Resistance was the typical situation that made such bad conscience legitimate. Then the time came when bad conscience became the object of untold "manipulations." But independently of any "manipulation," one must be aware today, in our [Western democratic] countries at least, of the domination of a diffuse atmosphere of *accusatory thought* (*pensée accusatrice*) and of the fact that, among its accusations, the one that declares us guilty of "not-doing-anything-for" is powerful enough to make itself heeded by many of us.[7]

All this does not mean that the ideologue, while trying to gain the writer's support, is unaware of the latter's cherished independence of mind. The theory of commitment illustrates the ambivalence of ideology toward literature: the more importance an ideology attaches to the writer's role, the more it attempts to make sure that the writer "represents" its positions with fidelity. Nowhere is this need for control seen better than in the original formulations of the idea of a cultural avant-garde, which occur in the writings of the French utopian socialists of the early nineteenth century. In *De l'organisation sociale* (1825), Claude Henri de Saint-Simon sees the artists as initiating the triumphant march of mankind toward its glorious socialist future: ". . . In this great undertaking," he writes, "the artists, the men of imagination, will open the march. . . . And for the attainment of their goal they will use all the means of the arts, eloquence, poetry, painting, music; in a word, they will develop the poetic aspect of the new system." And one of Saint-Simon's closest disciples, Olinde Rodrigues, writes in his dialogue "L'Artiste, le savant et l'industrialiste" (1825): "It is we, artists, that will serve as your avant-garde. . . . We address ourselves to the imagination and feelings of people, we are therefore supposed to achieve the most vivid and decisive kind of action; and if today we seem to play no role or at best a very secondary one, that has been the result of the arts' lacking a common drive and a general idea, which are so essential to their energy and success."[8] The "general idea" that the arts had been lacking will be, of course, that of the Saint-Simonian centralized type of socialism. The paradox involved in this kind of reasoning is not difficult to perceive: on the one hand, artists, previously marginal figures, are granted a honorific place in the forefront of the movement toward utopia; on the other hand, they lose their intellectual freedom, being given a complete and detailed program to fulfill.

It did not take the radical Left long to realize that the notion of committed art, although first advanced by the reactionaries, was more useful to its own purposes: it was not only easier to defend within the context of its revolutionary theories (why after all had the artists been such marginal figures in the past?) but more appealing to a number of artists who, influenced by the general climate of rebelliousness brought about by Romanticism, were more interested in the adventure of novelty and the future than in restoration of the past. Percy Bysshe Shelley summarizes a widespread Romantic view when he makes his famous statement about the poet as "unacknowledged legislator of the world" (in his *Defence of Poetry*, written in 1821, just a few years before the Saint-Simonians launched their politicized concept of the artistic avant-garde). For Shelley, the poet's mind is a mirror not of a reality that is already there (the known, the past) but of a reality in the making, a reality that the poet prophetically anticipates and renders possible: this is the sense in which Shelley's dictum that poets are "mirrors of futurity" should be taken.

We find in Shelley's *Defence of Poetry* some of the ideas stressed in the writings of Saint-Simon and his disciples. First, the view of the poet (or the creative artist in general) as primarily a "man of imagination." Then, the conception of the poet as the herald of a utopian future. Both Saint-Simon and Shelley emphasize the "progressive" role of the poet, although Saint-Simon sees this role as a new development, while for Shelley the poet has always been the true, albeit unacknowledged, "legislator of the world." The essential contrast between the ideologue and the poet consists in Saint-Simon's prescribing a clearly defined political program for the poetic imagination to carry out (imagination having no real power without a guiding "general idea"), while Shelley has unlimited confidence in imagination per se, free of any external constraints, and to be regarded, both intellectually and morally, as the highest human quality. Thus, although Shelley's political ideas resembled those of the utopian socialists of his time, he was committed only to the "politics of imagination" and not to any specific ideology.

From the point of view of the politician, well represented by the Saint-Simonian approach to the cultural avant-garde (and we should not forget that this approach contains the main ingredients of more recent doctrines of political aesthetics, such as the Leninist theory of "party literature" or the Stalinist-Zhdanovist theory of "socialist realism"), the problem is to control the poet's imagination; but poets, even when they embrace political creeds with unreserved enthusiasm, wish to preserve their freedom of imagination without which they feel that their very raison d'être as poets would be lost. This is the source of a conflict of which we find a direct and convincing illustration in the relations between Marx and the early Communist poet Ferdinand Freiligrath, "the first writer," as Peter Demetz points out, "who voluntarily subordinated himself to a modern Communist organization, and accepted its dictates in artistic matters, only to come, after a period of years, to the painful insight that the 'party' that had written the slogan of freedom on its banner was in reality a 'cage,' from which the instinct for self-preservation of the imagination demanded an escape."[9] After years of a close collaboration that had started before the revolutionary events of 1848, Marx wrote of Freiligrath in a letter (16 Jan. 1852) to Joseph Weydemeyer, requesting Weydemeyer to send a "friendly" and even "flattering" letter to the poet: "... All poets are, *plus ou moins*, even the best of them, *des courtisanes, et il faut les cajoler pour les faire chanter.*"[10] But apparently cajoling was not sufficient to keep Freiligrath from worrying about certain moral-aesthetic matters that poets cannot dismiss if they wish to remain true to themselves as poets. Here is how Freiligrath explains his estrangement from the Party, whose cause he continued, however, to support:

> Although I have always remained true to the banner of the *classe la plus laborieuse et la plus misérable* and always will . . . for these seven years [1853–1860] I have stood far from the Party, I have not attended its meetings, I have been unaware of its decisions and acts. . . . The Party, too, is a cage, and one can "sing" better, even *for* the Party, outside than in. . . . I was a poet of the proletariat long before I was a member of the *Bund.* . . . So I will continue to stand on my own feet; I will hearken only to myself, and I will answer for myself. . . . [11]

A history of the notion of commitment must take into account both the positive pronouncements on commitment and the negative ones. Art that is *engagé* and art that is *dégagé* (disengaged, pure, gratuitous) are as inseparable as the two terms of an antithesis. Both "political art" and "art for art's sake" tend toward a new form of the "sacred," and their ultimate achievement coincides, paradoxically, with their own abolition; ideally, political poets sacrifice poetry to absolute political goals, trying to purify their diction of any trace of its connection with the "corrupt," because unjust, forms of beauty of the past (in the name of a future, unspeakable utopian beauty), whereas "pure poets," in their solitary quests for total beauty, and in their implicit efforts to free their words from utilitarian associations, will be led to the Mallarméan poetics of nonexpression, absence, and silence.

Both attitudes share certain elements.[12] Both revolutionary art and "art for art's sake" are opposed to the civilization of modern capitalism, and their paradigmatic enemy is the type of the bourgeois (a semantic study of the negative connotations that the word "bourgeois" acquired in French during the nineteenth century will show that those responsible for this culturally symptomatic process were almost exclusively the representatives of aestheticism, from Théophile Gautier, through Charles Baudelaire and Gustave Flaubert, to the fin-de-siècle *décadents* and *symbolistes*). One also must not forget that the aestheticists, whose art was consciously and deliberately unpopular, were naturally attracted to unpopular political ideas that in some cases were radically conservative but in many others were radically leftist, socialist-anarchist. Accordingly, we should not be surprised to find that a doctrinaire of pure poetry like Stéphane Mallarmé not only had anarchist friends (like Félix Fénéon) and read with interest various anarchist publications but chose to describe the modern poet as being, in keeping with the great anarchist myth of the "millennial" strike, "en grève devant la société" 'on strike against society'. In the same interview with Jules Huret, published in the latter's *Sur l'évolution littéraire* (1891), Mallarmé speaks of the volatility of the contemporary social situation and of its direct effects on literary consciousness, which give legitimacy to an openly "experimentalist" concept of art based on irreducibly individualistic values (we recall that it is the cult of individualism that distinguishes anarchism from other, more collectivist, and hence more authoritarian versions of socialism): "In a society without stability, without unity, no stable or definitive art can be created. This unfinished social organization, which explains the disquietude of our minds, is at the same time the originator of the unexplained need for individuality, of which the present-day literary manifestations are a direct reflection."[13]

Another example of the same phenomenon is Oscar Wilde, whose decadent aestheticism extended into an advocacy of a libertarian kind of socialism, with many elements of anarchism. Wilde's essay "The Soul of Man under Socialism" (1891), openly and self-consciously utopian, summarizes a tradition of socioaesthetic thought, whose major representatives in England were John Ruskin, the Pre-Raphaelites, and William Morris, whose *News from Nowhere* and lectures on art and socialism present many similarities with Wilde's views. In a more general sense, it may be said (although this idea is not so obvious) that all modern utopian systems have an ultimately aesthetic goal. In spite of the noisy quarrels about the best political, economic, and social means by which the perfect society could be achieved, the modern nonreligious utopist cannot help but offer an aesthetic model of the future. In announcing the death of God and in rejecting any transcendent justification of human suffering, the utopian thinker postulates the possibility of "paradise" here on earth and in a not-too-distant future, and this paradise (no matter how reluctant the utopist might be in admitting it) can only be conceived along aesthetic lines, as a final transformation of economics and politics into aesthetics.

A complete study of the relation between aesthetics and politics should include, besides the obvious question of the influence of politics on aesthetics, the equally significant question of the influence of aesthetics on political thought. The nature of this essay prevents me from discussing in detail the connections between aestheticism and modern political radicalism, both on the Right (where they are more evident and more spectacular)[14] and on the Left. I shall limit myself to a suggestion of the potential fruitfulness of such an approach, as illustrated by Marxism and particularly by the Marxist theory of communism as transformation of labor, once class society is abolished, into free, creative, autotelic, that is, aesthetic, activity.

In the Judeo-Christian tradition labor had not only a religious explanation (punishment of original disobedience and a direct consequence of the Fall) but also a purifying and ultimately redeeming value (of which the Protestant work ethic is only one of the more recent formulations). In the secular world of modernity labor loses its "ecstatic" significance and becomes a mere reflection of unequal and unjust social relations in which the powerful exploit the weak. With the advent of the industrial revolution, labor also becomes increasingly (technologically) mediated and fragmented, less skilled and more mechanical. All these factors account for the modern socialist view of labor in any class society, and particularly in capitalism, as alienation and self-alienation of the worker.

The "model" of any kind of work in which effort and pleasure condition each other, and are in a sense inseparable, is the work of the artist who creates according to the Kantian principle of "purposiveness without purpose." I think that in his utopian theory of communism, Marx owes more to the autonomistic view of art expounded in Immanuel Kant's *Kritik der Urteilskraft* (1790) than many scholars of Marxism are prepared to recognize. Robert C. Tucker is among the students of Marx who have not ignored the aesthetic dimension of Marxist humanism:

> Human self realization means much more to Marx than the return of man to himself out of his alienated labor. . . . The ending of economic alienation will mean the end of the state, the family, law, morality, etc., as subordinate spheres of alienation. . . . What will remain is the life of art and science in a special and vastly enlarged sense of these two terms. Marx's conception of ultimate communism is fundamentally aesthetic in character. . . . The acquisitive and therefore alienated man of history is to be succeeded by the post-historical aesthetic man. . . . The alienated world will give way to the aesthetic world. Accordingly, Marx's discussion in the manuscript on communism is largely taken up with aesthetic questions.[15]

But what kind of aesthetics is implicit in Marx's prophecy of communism, as well as in his numerous but scattered remarks on literature and the arts? Or, to focus on a specific passage, what concept of beauty is Marx using when he writes that "An animal forms things in accordance with the measure and the needs of the species to which it belongs, while man knows how to produce in accordance with the measure of every species and knows how to apply everywhere the inherent measure to the object. Man, therefore, also forms things in accordance with the laws of beauty"?[16] Or, again, to take another example, one that Tucker also brings up, what does Marx mean by "beauty" when he refers to a dealer in minerals who can see only their market value and not their "beauty," the dealer's perceptive faculties being dulled by his acquisitive "sense of having" (*Sinn des Habens*)?

The paradoxical answer to such questions is that Marx's implicit aesthetics (which becomes occasionally explicit, as when he says that Greek art, although born in an undeveloped society, has set an aesthetic "standard and model beyond attainment")[17] is more compatible with late eighteenth- and early nineteenth-century German neohumanism and with the Kantian notion of art's fundamental disinterestedness or, derived from this, with the Schillerian concept of art as play than with Marx's own deterministic theory of ideology. The fact that Marx, wittingly or not, paid tribute to a concept of art apparently so alien to the major tenets of his historical and dialectical materialism is a confirmation that utopian perfection can be conceived, in a desacralized world, in a world that postulates the lack of any transcendency, only in terms of aesthetic immanence.[18]

There is little disagreement between the proponents of "art for art's sake" (if we take this phrase as meaning more than a mere passing fashion) and the most dedicated theorists of revolution in regard to the ultimate goal, the aestheticization of the world. With this realization in mind, we can understand better some of the paradoxes linked to the idea of political commitment. One of them is the willingness of certain modernist artists, and more particularly of representatives of the aesthetic avant-garde, to commit themselves to causes promoted by tightly knit organizations that openly expect them to surrender their intellectual freedom and to submit themselves to the most rigid kind of ideological control (some of the rebellious dadaists, like Tristan Tzara, or some of the surrealists, like Paul Eluard and Louis Aragon, became disciplined members of the staunchly "orthodox" French Communist Party). This is an extreme and rare case of sacrificing art "for art's sake."

The aesthetic component of utopian thought (from the point of view of which any utopia is of necessity both a "eutopia" and a "callotopia") can have another unexpected and more interesting consequence: it can lead, and has led, to the notion that art in and by itself is a revolutionary force (hence, politics should imitate art and not vice versa). This idea is contained, in a more or less implicit or diffuse fashion, in many Romantic statements concerning the "mission" of the artist, statements that cover the whole range between what we may term "progressive attitudes" (such as Shelley's) and "regressive attitudes" (such as those espoused by many of the German Romantics who, to use a phrase coined by Novalis, were intent on "romanticizing the world," no less intent than the surrealists were, a century later, on rendering the world "surreal," by setting free the boundless oneiric imagination). The belief in the intrinsic revolutionary power of art is not only more clear-cut when, toward the end of the nineteenth century, the artistic avant-garde becomes self-consciously and proudly different from the political avant-garde but also directly responsible for the split between the two avant-gardes. If art is by itself revolutionary, then obviously there is no need for artists to commit themselves to the orders of political leaders or organizations, orders that are bound to be narrow-minded and detrimental to the fulfillment of true art's spontaneously revolutionary vocation. From this standpoint, artists involved in the great work of imaginative "deconstruction" and reconstruction of the world, are called on to resist appeals to commitment. André Breton's view that "true art is unable not to be revolutionary" (beyond and even against any specific ideological commitment),[19] was shared, in the post–World War II period, by many of the representatives of the New Left, from Herbert Marcuse to Gilles Deleuze and Jean-François Lyotard. For the last of these, artists, engaged in their ever-renewed work of deconstruction, are, in right and in deed, politicians of desire, the only politicians that are acceptable from the point of view of the revolutionary force represented by universal desire or libido.[20]

As we have seen, the idea of commitment, conveyed by a number of more or less close synonymous phrases, is older than Jean-Paul Sartre's existentialist theory of "engagement." In addition to the general views on the question that I have referred to, the nineteenth century produced, mostly as a reaction against "art for art's sake," a type of literature, known variously as "tendentious literature" (*Tendenzliteratur*) or "thesis literature" (*littérature à thèse*), that could be compared to Sartre's concept of "littérature engagée." The phrase "tendency literature" is often used, in a restrictive historical sense, to mean the kind of propagandist literature written mostly between the 1830s or 1840s and the early decades of the twentieth century, a literature that was striving to bring to the attention of public opinion social, political, or legal problems in need of reform. Thus limited in scope and significance, "tendency literature" has, at least on the surface, almost nothing to do with Sartre's notion of "committed literature," as T. W. Adorno notes in his essay "Commitment" (1962), one of the most enlightening critiques of Sartre's position:

> In aesthetic theory commitment should be distinguished from "tendency." Committed art in the proper sense is not intended to generate ameliorative measures, legislative acts or practical institutions—like earlier propagandist (tendency) plays against syphilis, abortion laws or borstals—but to work at the level of fundamental attitudes. For Sartre, its task is to awaken the free choice of the agent, that makes authentic existence possible at all, as opposed to the neutrality of the

spectator. But what gives commitment its aesthetic advantage over tendentiousness also renders the content to which the artist commits himself inherently ambiguous. In Sartre, the notion of choice—originally a Kierkegaardian category—is heir to the Christian doctrine "He who is not with me is against me," but now voided of any theological content.[21]

If we look carefully at the aesthetic and political problems raised by "tendentiousness" and "commitment," they are not as heterogeneous as Adorno seems to believe. Certainly, Sartre's new stress on the moral dramatism of choice and responsibility, linked to his theory of freedom (with its strong tragic component, since the human being is "a useless passion," and, without any assistance or excuse in this Godless world, "condemned forever to be free"), has rendered the term "engagement" more attractive to modern writers than the older "tendentiousness," with its more direct and narrow political connotations. But in the long run Sartrean commitment is no less narrow than *Tendenz*, although it sets the political element in a larger and more nebulously dialectical perspective. This accounts for the curious fact that Sartre's commitment, transformed into a rallying cry, was adopted by many people (such as most of the representatives of the English New Left)[22] who do not seem to have read his *Qu'est-ce que la littérature?* (1948) or his more intricate philosophical writings.

Beyond its widespread success, what makes Sartre's theory of commitment relevant to our discussion is its insistence that choice in today's world can be only political. The range of choices is thus drastically limited. Even if none of the alternatives available is entirely morally justifiable, the desire to keep one's hands "clean" is less justifiable than any kind of action. Literature (with the exception of poetry, which Sartre defines as a noncommunicative, self-referential, and self-objectifying use of language) has no excuse for not choosing, with a full awareness of all the tragic paradoxes involved in any specific act of choice.

Sartrean commitment, then, is the fulfillment of an ethical and religious obligation in terms of a political choice; the fulfillment of an absolute duty in terms of a relative, fluid, and ambiguous situation of conflicting partisanships, shifting alliances, and often (Sartre does not address this question) self-righteous and self-congratulatory opportunisms. But what if, to use Adorno's phrase, "the politics of autonomous art" (as represented in our century by Franz Kafka or Samuel Beckett) is a better politics for the writer than commitment to an ideology or to a combination of ideologies and the writing of works that "all too readily credit themselves with every noble value" (Adorno, p. 317)? What if the "uncommitted" Kafka turns out to be one of the greatest political writers of our time—political in the sense that he offers us an opportunity to participate in a meditation on the "political condition" of man, with all the perplexities that it involves? Nowhere better than in the cruelly humorous world of Kafka can one see the close and disturbing relation between religion and politics as modes of approaching and attempts at answering the questions of power. The fact that the haunting bureaucratic nightmares, so realistically presented in *Der Prozess* and *Das Schloss*, have been persistently interpreted as religious allegories is significant. If we accept the view according to which the "fantastic" in fiction arises from the possibility of double interpretation, we can say that Kafka has discovered a new variety of the fantastic, the "political fantastic." No wonder, then, that the more obviously politically minded writers of dystopias (from Yevgeniy Zamyatin to George Orwell) can be said to describe certain typically Kafkian situations, even though uninfluenced by Kafka.

But the major limitation of Sartre's view of commitment is best illustrated by his own uneasy relation with French and international communism, and with Marxism in a general sense. This relation indicates that his choices of *prises de position* were restricted to endorsing certain political actions or to denouncing others, or, even worse, to qualifying or revoking previous endorsements. Commitment, insofar as it is a matter of praxis, that is, the fulfillment of a pledge to serve a definite political cause (even from outside), is little more than a commitment to change one's mind when the party line changes: with the party (which even born conformists may at times find a difficult and repulsive thing to do) or against the party (with or without impunity, depending on the party's policy toward dissenters and, more importantly, on whether the party is in power). There is irony in the fact that Sartrean commitment, with all its soul-searching moral seriousness and its formidable philosophical justifications, ends up being politically so naïve.

Although Sartre's concept of *littérature engagée* has been criticized for its idealistic and individualistic component by orthodox Marxist critics (even by the more sophisticated and less dogmatic representatives of this line, such as György Lukács), the Sartrean theory of commitment shares a basic element with the orthodox Marxist view of literature: they are both content-oriented. The aesthetic avant-garde, when it has not flatly rejected commitment, has adopted an entirely different strategy, consistent with its belief in the primary importance of form. If art has a revolutionary function, the avant-garde argument goes, this function can be fruitfully performed only on the level of form, by dislocating, disrupting, and unmasking old forms and by creating, if not new revolutionary forms, at least the conditions of possibility for the appearance of such forms. The formalist dialectic of literary change, as elaborated by the Russian formalists of the 1920s (Victor Shklovsky, Roman Jakobson, Boris Tomashevsky, Boris Eikhenbaum) or by the Prague School structuralists of the 1930s, is based on such notions as "defamiliarization," "violation of the norm," or "foregrounding of the device," all of which can be interpreted politically (in spite of the fact that the formalist critics themselves did not go in that direction). Actually, the formalist approach, which is largely a critical assessment of the iconoclastic manifestations of the artistic avant-garde (the Russian formalists were very close to the cubo-futurists, Velimir Khlebnikov, Vladimir Mayakovsky, etc.) can be said to consist of the application of a formal political model to the question of literary development. The aesthetic avant-garde in general has adopted, for its own artistic purposes, various revolutionary political models and has introduced radical political behavior in art (even in "art for art's sake"). All this indicates the possibility of a type of form-oriented commitment, which is both theoretically and practically more interesting than the kind advocated by Sartre. A good example of political commitment consistent with the polemical formalism of the avant-garde is Bertolt Brecht. An expressionist in his youth, Brecht became a committed Marxist writer without giving up his allegiance to the idea of formal novelty, in which he saw a powerful revolutionary weapon. Significantly, Brecht arrived independently at some of the cardinal notions of the Russian formalists, offering directly politicized versions of "defamiliarization" (his famous *Verfremdungseffekt*), of "violation of the norm" (taken in a more general sense as a rejection of mimesis, of the Aristotelian rules of imitation and empathy), or of the "foregrounding of the device" (art should openly recognize its "conventional" character; it should not conceal its nature behind a veil of "realistic" illusions). Even Brecht's well-known didacticism profits from its inclusion in a polemical-formal context, where it can be seen as an element in the larger pattern of foregrounding. In this case, content, without sacrificing any of its distinctive qualities, becomes artistically more effective by being overtly and unexpectedly treated as a device among other devices and counterdevices in the formal strategy of the work. But clearly this is not a recipe for effective committed art. When, through repetition, the unexpectedness of such didactic foregrounding is lost, the political "message" becomes boring (as it does even in Brecht when his plays are merely "Brechtian" plays). The possibilities and implication of formally oriented committed literature are richer and more diverse than I have been able to indicate in this discussion. They have rarely been investigated, but they have all the prerequisites for becoming one of the most exciting areas of the study of literature and politics.

IV

If commitment is perceived, and not only by those who watch it from afar, as an experience comparable to religious conversion, one can imagine the painfulness and indeed the tragic character of writers' discovery that their new God, to whom they had been ready to sacrifice everything, was but another false God. *The God That Failed*, edited by Richard Crossman, collects testimonies of six Western writers (Arthur Koestler, Ignazio Silone, Richard Wright, André Gide, Louis Fischer, and Stephen Spender), most of whom had joined the communist movement during the 1930s only to realize after several years in or near the Party that they had been victims of both deception and self-deception. Crossman's book provides a good working model of the typical moral-intellectual phenomenon of our age that, for lack of a better word, I would call "deconversion" (a phenomenon more intense and complex than mere disillusionment or disenchantment). Since I do not know of any significant case of a repentant fascist intellectual, it occurs to me that this situation might offer an interesting criterion for distinguishing between fascist and Marxist movements, which are so often lumped together (in the first place, by "deconverted" leftists, who do not seem to notice that their own central experience of loss of faith has few parallels on the extreme right).

In 1935, at the peak of his infatuation with communism, Gide declared: "I consider that on account of its compromises Christianity is bankrupt. I have written, and I believe firmly, that if Christianity had really prevailed and if it had really fulfilled the teaching of Christ, there would today be no question of Communism, there would indeed be no social problem at all" (Crossman, p. 169). That is why, for Gide and for many others, the bankruptcy of communism itself was perceived as a tragic event, as the betrayal of an authentic religious hope. I cannot discern the slightest signs of such a hope in the supporters of the doctrines of fascism. Fascism certainly had its intellectual sympathizers (I do not know of any significant one writing today), and their statements and attitudes have formed the object of numerous studies, among which I would cite John R. Harrison's *The Reactionaries*, Conor Cruise O'Brien's "Passion and Cunning: The Politics of W. B. Yeats" (in White and Newman), or William Chace's *The Political Identities of Ezra Pound and T. S. Eliot*. Harrison's "reactionaries" include several outstanding representatives of modernism — William Butler Yeats, Wyndham Lewis, Ezra Pound, T. S. Eliot, and D. H. Lawrence — and his book is symptomatic of a widespread tendency in recent Anglo-American criticism to see one of the defining characteristics of modernism (as opposed to postmodernism) in its preference for conservative, elitist, cryptofascist, or overtly fascist politics. What strikes me when I see the reactionary pronouncements of these authors, besides their irrelevance to the artistic substance of their authors' work, is that they do not carry the weight (ineffable but recognizable) of true commitment. These writers did not even attempt to commit themselves, either as writers or as men (with the notable exception of Pound), to the cause of fascism. They never considered (as so many leftists did in their religious fervor) sacrificing their art to their political creed, but on the contrary (and quite wrongly) they saw in the politics that they advocated an opportunity for the materialization of their artistic dreams of a new Renaissance, a triumph of what Wyndham Lewis called the "party of genius." They were attracted by the immediately recognizable aestheticist component of fascist rhetoric, which Walter Benjamin had in mind when he equated fascism with *l'art pour l'art* and when he saw in the fascist aestheticization of politics the triumph of the principle of *Fiat ars — pereat mundus.*[23] Stephen Spender is right when he says in direct reference to Harrison's book: "The most important thing common to the reactionaries was that they had a kind of shared vision of the greatness of the European past which implied hatred and contempt for the present.... On the secondary level of their attempts to carry forward the vision into action and propaganda there is a good deal of peripheral mess, resulting from their search for political approximations to their love of past intellect, art, discipline, and order. Often their politics only shows that they care less for politics than for literature" ("Writers and Politics," p. 373). Even Pound, who came closest to political activism, cared more for his art than for his fascism. There seems to be an element of cranky irresponsibility about the politics of such writers, which may come from their inability to take politics seriously, in spite of the apparent stubbornness with which some of them defended their political ideas. But stubbornness and commitment are different things. Although both attitudes can lead to incalculably dangerous and sometimes tragic consequences, the stubborn crank will never face the problem of personal responsibility with the same radical intensity as the person who sees the ideals for which he or she had been prepared to sacrifice everything betrayed and who realizes his or her (unwitting but not unblamable) participation in that betrayal.

V

Even though they may be uncommitted (in the strong, quasi-religious sense of the word "commitment" that has been stressed in this essay), readers of literature are likely to have political convictions, however confused or contradictory these may be. Even political neutrality, it has often been said, is a political attitude. One might argue that to reject all ideologies leads to one of the worst kinds of ideology, totally un-self-conscious and, therefore, exemplifying the Marxian equation between "ideology" and "false consciousness." The problem remains: How should readers or critics, with their own political backgrounds, approach works of literature that are directly or indirectly political? How should they deal with the political aspects of the works in relation to the literary aspects, as well as in relation to their own beliefs? In other words, what approaches qualify as legitimate and literarily relevant, given the reader-critic's love of literature, which must be theoretically assumed? The answer to such questions is not easy. Maybe the most convenient way to try to find an answer is to limit our discussion to the literary form that has been most directly and most interestingly affected by politics, the novel.

The modern novel, I would say, is almost constitutively political, in the sense that it comes into being, to quote Mark Schorer, "at a point where we can recognize the intersection of the stream of social history and the stream of the soul. This intersection gives the form its dialectical field, provides the source of those generic tensions that make it possible at all."[24] But even in the most easily recognizable political novels, writers will try (and readers should follow) to go beyond politics and to articulate a larger, moral-aesthetic vision. This movement is typical of any good political novel, which needs organically what Irving Howe calls the "apolitical" or even the "pastoral" element, for "providing it with polarity and tension." Howe also points to the demanding and uneasy relation in which political novelists and their readers ideally find themselves. His words offer a general answer to the questions posed at the beginning of this section:

> For both the writer and the reader, the political novel provides a particularly severe test. . . . For the writer, the great test is, how much truth can he force through the sieve of his opinions? For the reader, the great test is, how much of that truth can he accept though it jostle his opinions? . . . It is not surprising that the political novelist, even as he remains fascinated by politics, urges his claim for a moral order beyond ideology; nor that the receptive reader, even as he preserves his own commitment, assents to the novelist's order.[25]

But readers may change their commitments, or may render them more conscious and, therefore, more tolerant of other views. A dramatic change of commitment, for instance, was caused in the early 1970s by the impact in the West, and particularly in France, of the works of perhaps the most significant political writer that postrevolutionary Russia has produced, Alexander Solzhenitsyn, as well as by the personal and fictional testimonies of other Soviet and East European dissidents, such as Andrey Sinyavski, Lev Kopelev, Alexander Zinoviev, a group of extremely talented Czech authors connected with the Prague Spring of 1968 (Milan Kundera, Václav Havel, Pavel Kohout, Ludvík Vaculík), the Hungarian György Konrad, the Romanian Paul Goma, and others. The influence exerted by the dissidents from the "other Europe" was not chiefly literary, although literature (autobiographical accounts, "documentaries," "literary investigations" of the type of *The Gulag Archipelago*, and novels) has been their main means of expression; nor was it primarily ideological or political; it was rather a moral and philosophical influence, whose importance can be measured by the fact that it touched so many of the most fanatically committed French intellectuals who had been actively involved in the Paris revolutionary events of May 1968 (from philosophers like André Glucksmann or Bernard Henri Lévy to avant-garde writers like Philippe Sollers). What amounts to the most complete, passionate, and subtle critique of totalitarianism to be accomplished in our century was bound to have more than a merely literary or political-ideological effect. We are, I think, entitled to speak of a new movement of consciousness that, even though still in the beginning phase, promises to become one of the key developments in the intellectual history of our age.

There is nothing in the relation between the reader and the political novel to make it qualitatively different from the more general relation between the reader and any piece of literature. However, certain elements that may remain latent and almost invisible in the latter relation assert themselves more dramatically in the confrontation between the reader and the political novel, revealing the dialogic nature and the ultimate dialogic goal of any authentic reading. Reading, in fact, is largely an extension of live dialogue and is meant to fulfill all the basic functions that live dialogue can have. The old topos that books are our friends (but also, potentially, our enemies) is both metaphorically and literally true.

Participants in a dialogue are involved in hypothetical thinking, that is, the exploration of the realm of possibilities, and the testing of these possibilities by submitting them to various kinds of arguments which, in the long run, become "specialized" — philosophical, logical, scientific, or literary. Literature in the broadest sense presents us with images of possible worlds. Even realistic fiction is the expression of the same "possibilistic imagination" that manifests itself in "utopian fiction," as well as its opposite, "negative utopian" or "dystopian," fiction; and this is so because the "real" world is incomprehensible unless we see it within the context of possible worlds, of which it is a part.[26] Insofar as literary worlds are translations into more directly evocative language of the worlds made up by the prevailing religions or philosophies or political systems, they confront us with what it would be like to live under the laws of this or that religion or philosophy or political system.

Exploring possibilities, close or remote, positive or negative, personal or impersonal, normative or counternormative, relating to content or relating to form (diction, narrative syntaxes, compositional patterns, etc.), and constructing frames of reference for the intuitive understanding and assessment of such possibilities is what literature is all about. With the advent of modernity, traditional mythical and religious possibilities do not disappear, but they lose their old privileged status. They have to compete with other possibilities and to establish their credibility and desirability within an open political contest in which, ideally, the principle of persuasion should prevail against any form of direct or indirect coercion. In a period that has constantly denied any transcendent justification of authority (that is, the very condition of possibility of authority's persuasiveness), literature is one of the few activities in which the principle of persuasiveness is still alive. The politics of literature is (when it does not prostitute itself to become mere propaganda) a politics of imaginative persuasion and, implicitly, a critique of any politics based on coercion. The connection with the larger notion of dialogue is obvious (the basic rule of dialogue being that the settling of conflicting opinions should be achieved only through persuasion).[27] Good political literature is the most immediate confirmation of this rule. It is therefore not fortuitous that the first comprehensive formulation of the literary aspects of dialogue, as we find it in the criticism of Mikhail Bakhtin, originated from a commentary on the works of perhaps the greatest of political novelists, Fedor Dostoevsky. Dostoevsky makes his writing a space of dialogue, Bakhtin contends in *Problems of Dostoevsky's Poetics* (1929; 2nd ed., 1963), a space in which widely divergent opinions are fully and forcefully articulated by Dostoevsky's various characters, the novelist himself, with his own opinions, being just one of the voices heard in the complex polyphony of his novels; this polyphony could not exist if the voices that make it up were treated unequally, if any one of them were denied its fundamental dialogic freedom. That is why Dostoevsky's characters are truly independent fictional beings and not simply lifelike puppets manipulated by the author. The deep force of Dostoevsky's writings derives neither from the realist gift of the author nor from his strong theological-political opinions but from the dialogic compulsion of his imagination to invent convincing opponents of his opinions and give them opportunities to express themselves as fully as possible.

If there is any commitment in Dostoevsky, it is a commitment to the spirit of dialogue and to its rules — equality of treatment of all opinions and, from the point of view of the individual participant, always trying to argue against the strongest case. This intellectual drama of an on-going and unending dialogue among possibilities makes good political literature transcend the limitations of any particular ideology. Of course the political passions of the writer or the reader are not necessarily appeased or abandoned; if anything, by being confronted with a wide and sharply differentiated spectrum of possibilities, these passions are forced to become more lucid, more self-conscious and, therefore, to attain a higher degree of articulation.

Notes

[1] Oscar Wilde, *Intentions and the Soul of Man*, ed. Robert Ross (London: Dawsons, 1969), p. 33. And Wilde goes on to say, in the same "Decay of Lying," that art is not symbolic of any age but, on the contrary, "it is ages that are her symbols" (p. 35). Wilde's idea ceases to be paradoxical and becomes almost common sense if we integrate it in the framework of the modern trend to stress the imaginative or creative element in art.

[2] The reference is to Engels' letter to Margaret Harkness (April 1888), in which he writes: "The realism I allude to may crop out even in spite of the author's opinions. Let me refer to an example. Balzac whom I consider a far greater master of realism than all the Zolas . . . in *La Comédie humaine* gives us a most wonderfully realistic history of French society . . . from 1816 to 1848. . . . Well, Balzac was politically a Legitimist; . . . his sympathies are all with the class doomed to extinction. . . . That Balzac thus was compelled to go against his own class sympathies and political prejudices, that he *saw* the necessity of the downfall of his favorite nobles, and described them as people deserving no better fate . . . — that I consider one of the greatest triumphs of Realism, and one of the grandest features of old Balzac" (Marx and Engels, ed. Baxandall and Morawski, pp. 115-16). So the conscious ideological sympathies of the great writer become essentially irrelevant.

[3] This view is borne out by a majority of literary critics and by political scientists with an interest in literature. Anthologies such as *Politics through Literature*, ed.

Holland, or *The Political Imagination in Literature*, ed. Green and Walzer, which are meant to give the student of political theory concrete literary illustrations of political abstractions, present texts mostly from the nineteenth and twentieth centuries.

[4] See Karl Popper, *The Open Society and Its Enemies*, 5th ed., 2 vols. (Princeton: Princeton Univ. Press, 1966). In his detailed polemical analysis of "Plato's Political Program." Popper argues that the author of *The Republic* proposes a full-fledged theory of the totalitarian state and totalitarian justice, based on the recognition of "only one ultimate standard, the interest of the state." Thus, "Morality is nothing but political hygiene" (I, 106).

[5] See André Reszler, *L'Intellectuel contre l'Europe*, pp. 117–41; also "Prométhée engagé?" *Cadmos*, 1, No. 1 (1978), 5–16.

[6] In his *The Old Regime and the French Revolution* (1856), trans. Stuart Gilbert (Garden City, N.Y.: Doubleday, 1955), Alexis de Tocqueville discusses at length the political influence of the eighteenth-century *hommes de lettres* and maintains that the French Revolution resulted, among other things, from the extension of "literature" into direct politics: "Our men of letters did not merely impart their revolutionary ideas to the French nation; they also shaped the national temperament and outlook on life. . . . The result was that our writers ended up by giving the Frenchman the instincts, the turn of mind, the taste and even the eccentricities characteristic of literary man. And when the time came for action, these literary propensities were imported into the political arena."

[7] "Remarques," *Cadmos*, 1, No. 1 (1978), 104.

[8] For the sources of the quotations from Saint-Simon and Rodrigues, as well as for a more detailed discussion of their implications, in the larger context of the development of the concept of the avant-garde, see my *Faces of Modernity*, pp. 95–140.

[9] Peter Demetz, *Marx, Engels, and the Poets*, p. 101.

[10] Marx and Engels, ed. Baxandall and Morawski, p. 120.

[11] Letter to Marx, 28 Feb. 1860, in Marx and Engels, ed. Baxandall and Morawski, pp. 121–22.

[12] In the first place, an awareness of the importance of politics in the modern world. This idea receives a suggestive formulation in George Woodcock, *The Writer and Politics*: "The ivory tower is as much a symptom of inescapable social problems as the air raid shelter is of the inescapable evils of war" (p. 10).

[13] Stéphane Mallarmé, *Œuvres complètes*, ed. Henri Mondor and G. Jean Aubry (Paris: Gallimard, 1970), p. 866. Like many younger symbolists (Stuart Merrill, Francis Vielé-Griffin, Laurent Tailhade), Mallarmé was attracted, if not to the politics of anarchism as such, to the larger philosophical implications of the anarchist attitude. At the Trial of the Thirty in 1894, called as a witness on behalf of his younger anarchist friend Félix Fénéon, Mallarmé described him as "a fine spirit, curious about everything that is new." After quoting the revealing remark made by Mallarmé in his testimony, George Woodcock goes on to say in his *Anarchism: A History of Libertarian Ideas and Movements* (1962; rpt. New York: New American Library, 1974): "It was the anarchist cultivation of independence of mind and of freedom of action and experience for its own sake that appealed to artists and intellectuals" (p. 306).

[14] In the final part of "The Work of Art in the Age of Mechanical Reproduction," Walter Benjamin writes: *"Fiat ars—pereat mundus*, says Fascism. . . . This is evidently the consummation of '*l'art pour l'art*.' . . . Fascism is rendering [politics] aesthetic. Communism responds by politicizing art" (Benjamin, *Illuminations*, p. 242). But communism itself is not free from a different, but equally fundamental, version of aestheticism. In a broader sense, as Karl Popper remarks in

his discussion of what he calls Plato's "utopian engineering," all political radicalism is ultimately an "aesthetic radicalism" (see Popper, I, 162-63).

[15] Robert C. Tucker, *Philosophy and Myth in Karl Marx*, 2nd ed. (Cambridge: Cambridge Univ. Press, 1972), pp. 157-58.

[16] Marx and Engels, ed. Baxandall and Morawski, p. 51.

[17] Marx and Engels, ed. Baxandall and Morawski, p. 135. For a discussion of the contradiction between Marx's view of Greek art as unsurpassable and his deterministic theory of the "superstructure" (of which art is a part), see James P. Scanlen, "The Impossibility of a Uniquely Authentic Marxist Aesthetics," in *British Journal of Aesthetics*, 16 (1976), 128-36.

[18] For a more recent reconfirmation, from the point of view of the New Left, see Herbert Marcuse, *The Aesthetic Dimension*, who states quite unequivocally that "art represents the ultimate goal of all revolutions: the freedom and happiness of the individual" (p. 69).

[19] Breton's idea dates back to the 1930s, and its implications become clear if we see it within the context of the split between surrealism (as represented by himself and his followers) and the Stalinist-dominated Communist movement. Breton was joined in his "proclamation" of art's inherently revolutionary vocation by Leon Trotsky, who thus reversed his previously stated position (in *Literature and Revolution* [1924]) in favor of party control of literature. In the "Manifesto for an Independent Revolutionary Art" (1938), written by Breton in collaboration with Trotsky, we read: ". . . True art is unable not to be revolutionary. . . . In the realm of artistic creation, the imagination must escape from all constraint and must under no pretext allow itself to be placed under bonds. . . . To develop intellectual creation an *anarchist regime of individual liberty should from the first be established*. No authority, no dictation, not the least trace of orders from above" (italics added; see André Breton, *What Is Surrealism?* ed. and introd. Franklin Rosemont [New York: Monad, 1978], pp. 184-85).

[20] Jean-François Lyotard expresses this idea in several essays included in his *Dérive à partir de Marx et de Freud* (Paris: Union Générale d'Editions, 1973) and particularly in "Notes sur la fonction critique de l'œuvre," where he states: "I do not believe that the function of art is to keep desire awake in order that it may become revolutionary; the function of art *is immediately* revolutionary" (p. 235).

[21] *The Essential Frankfurt School Reader*, ed. Arato and Gerhardt, pp. 303-04.

[22] If we are to believe John Mander, who in his *The Writer and Commitment* declares pointedly that "we [he speaks in the name of the British New Left] adopted Sartre's term, and largely ignored its theoretical basis" (p. 11).

[23] *Illuminations*, p. 242.

[24] *Society and Self in the Novel* (New York: Columbia Univ. Press, 1956), p. ix.

[25] Howe, *Politics and the Novel*, pp. 25-26.

[26] That utopian imagination is always implicit in realistic fiction (and all the more so in what Marxist critics call "critical realism") is obvious. As Albert Guérard writes in the chapter "Art for the Sake of Propaganda," in *Art for Art's Sake* (New York: Lothrop, Lee, and Shepard, 1936): "If it were not for what might be, it would be futile to condemn that which is." That is why "Utopias, although in bulk and value they occupy but a minor place in literature," are quite important to study (p. 203).

[27] For a broad definition of dialogic consciousness, see Mikhail Bakhtin, *Problems of Dostoevsky's Poetics*, trans. R. W. Rotsel (Ann Arbor, Mich.: Ardis, 1973), Ch. iv and especially 87-113.

Bibliography

This bibliography is meant as an introductory reading list for the student of literature and politics. Authors and titles discussed or mentioned in the text or notes are listed without annotations, and works by foreign authors that are available in English translation are listed only under their English titles. The annotations of single items by the same author have usually been grouped in the annotation of the last relevant entry. An asterisk appears next to works that contain useful bibliographic information.

*Aaron, Daniel. *Writers on the Left: Episodes in American Literary Communism.* New York: Harcourt, 1961.

*Adereth, Maxwell. *Commitment in Modern French Literature.* London: Gollancz, 1967. "Littérature engagée" in Péguy, Aragon, and Sartre. A humanist-Marxist approach.

Adorno, Theodor W. *Noten zur Literatur.* 4 vols. Frankfurt: Suhrkamp, 1958-74.

———. *Prisms: Cultural Criticism and Society.* Trans. Samuel and Shierry Weber. London: Spearman, 1967. Brilliant, incisive, provocative essays by one of the leaders of the Frankfurt School.

*Arato, Andrew, and Eike Gerhardt, eds. *The Essential Frankfurt School Reader.* New York: Urizen, 1978. Anthology of writings by Adorno, Benjamin, Horkheimer, Lowenthal, etc. See esp. Pt. II, "Esthetic Theory and Cultural Criticism," pp. 185-368. Thorough presentations, ample bibliographical notes.

Arvon, Henri. *Marxist Esthetics.* Trans. Helen R. Lane. Ithaca, N.Y.: Cornell Univ. Press, 1973. Focuses almost exclusively (not uncritically) on the orthodox (Soviet) approach to Marxist aesthetics.

Barthes, Roland. *Mythologies.* Ed. and trans. Annette Lavers. New York: Hill and Wang, 1972.

———. *Writing Degree Zero.* Trans. Annette Lavers and Colin Smith. Pref. Susan Sontag. New Hork: Hill and Wang, 1968. Early but significant works by Barthes, in which his critique of ideology (as manifested in the myths of popular culture and in literary "writing," or *écriture*) is articulated from a position that is somewhere between the Marxist view of ideology as "false consciousness" and Barthes's own later structuralist and poststructuralist approaches.

Baxandall, Lee, ed. *Radical Perspectives in the Arts.* Baltimore: Penguin, 1972. Selections from Marcuse, Lukács, Carlos Fuentes, Jorge Semprun, Roger Garaudy, John Berger, Sartre, Ernst Fischer, Hans Mayer, and others. No bibliography, no index.

Benjamin, Walter. *Charles Baudelaire: A Lyric Poet in the Era of High Capitalism.* Trans. Harry Zohn. London: NLB, 1973.

———. *Illuminations.* Ed. and introd. Hannah Arendt. Trans. Harry Zohn. New York: Harcourt, 1969.

———. *Reflections: Essays, Aphorisms, Autobiographical Writings.* Ed. and introd. Peter Demetz. Trans. Edmund Jephcott. New York: Harcourt, 1978. Influenced by Jewish mystical thought (and particularly by the messianic component of Judaism) and at the same time by Marxism (especially by the millennialist implications of the doctrine of revolution), Benjamin is one of the most original critics of this century, with brilliant insights into the triple interrelation of art, politics, and religion.

Bloch, Ernst. *Das Prinzip Hoffnung.* Frankfurt: Suhrkamp, 1959.

———. *Man on His Own: Essays in the Philosophy of Religion.* Trans. E. B. Ashton. New York: Herder and Herder, 1970. Bloch's philosophy of hope has a crucial aesthetic dimension; moreover, to support or illustrate his ideas Bloch uses numerous literary and artistic examples.

———, et al. *Aesthetics and Politics*. Ed. and trans. Ronald Taylor. London: NLB, 1977.

*Blotner, Joseph. *The Modern American Political Novel, 1900–1960*. Austin: Univ. of Texas Press, 1966.

———. *The Political Novel*. Garden City, N.Y.: Doubleday, 1955.

Bowra, C. M. *Poetry and Politics, 1900–1960*. Cambridge: Cambridge Univ. Press, 1966. Essays on Trakl, Blok, Mayakovsky, T. S. Eliot, Dylan Thomas, based on a "thematic" definition of political poetry.

*Brantlinger, Patrick. *The Spirit of Reform: British Literature and Politics, 1832–1867*. Cambridge: Harvard Univ. Press, 1977. An incisively written, learned, and perceptive study.

Brecht, Bertolt. *Brecht on Theatre*. Ed. and trans. John Willett. New York: Hill and Wang, 1964.

Brinton, Crane. *The Political Ideas of the English Romanticists*. 1926; rpt. New York: Russell, 1962.

*Butt, John. *Writers and Politics in Modern Spain*. London: Hodder and Stoughton, 1978. Useful survey.

*Calinescu, Matei. *Faces of Modernity: Avant-Garde, Decadence, Kitsch*. Bloomington: Indiana Univ. Press, 1977.

———, and André Reszler. "Literature and the Social Sciences." *Yearbook of Comparative and General Literature*, 24 (1975), 43–50.

Camus, Albert. *The Rebel: An Essay on Man in Revolt*. Trans. Anthony Bower. New York: Random, 1956. Important philosophical-political statement by a prominent writer associated with existentialism.

Caudwell, Christopher. *Illusion and Reality: A Study in the Sources of Poetry*. 1937; rpt. New York: International, 1963.

———. *Studies and Further Studies in a Dying Culture*. Introd. Sol Yurick. New York: Monthly Review, 1971. Caudwell was essentially a "cultural Stalinist" with, occasionally, original and interesting insights.

*Caute, David. *Communism and the French Intellectuals, 1914–1960*. New York: Macmillan, 1964.

———. *The Illusion: An Essay on Politics, Theatre, and the Novel*. New York: Harper, 1972.

*Chace, William M. *The Political Identities of Ezra Pound and T. S. Eliot*. Stanford: Stanford Univ. Press, 1973.

Craig, David. *Marxists on Literature: An Anthology*. Baltimore: Penguin, 1975. Texts by Marx, Engels, Lenin, Trotsky, Plekhanov, George Thompson, A. Kettle, etc. An anthology by a British communist. Rudimentary bibliographical notes, no index.

———. *The Real Foundations: Literature and Social Change*. New York: Oxford Univ. Press, 1974.

Crossman, Richard, ed. *The God That Failed*. New York: Harper, 1950.

*Demetz, Peter. *Marx, Engels, and the Poets: Origins of Marxist Literary Criticism*. Trans. Jeffrey L. Sammons. Chicago: Univ. of Chicago Press, 1967.

*Egbert, Donald Drew. *Social Radicalism and the Arts: Western Europe: A Cultural History from the French Revolution to 1968*. New York: Knopf, 1970. A major book on the relation between politics and the arts. More useful to the student of literature than many similar studies focusing primarily on literary issues.

Fischer, Ernst. *Art against Ideology*. Trans. Anna Bostock. New York: Braziller, 1969.

————. *The Necessity of Art: A Marxist Approach.* Trans. Anna Bostock. Baltimore: Penguin, 1963. Formerly a cultural Stalinist, Fischer became one of the distinguished representatives of the humanist-Marxist position in aesthetics in the late 1950s and the 1960s.

*Flottes, Pierre. *Histoire de la poésie politique et sociale en France de 1815 à 1939.* Paris: La Pensée Universelle, 1976. Old-fashioned historical positivism, solid documentation; in short, a typical thesis for the French *doctorat d'état.*

*Flower, J. E., J. A. Morris, and E. E. Williams. *Writers and Politics in Modern Britain, France, and Germany.* New York: Holmes and Meier, 1977. Useful surveys.

*Gatt-Rutter, John. *Writers and Politics in Modern Italy.* New York: Holmes and Meier, 1978. Useful survey.

*Gilbert, James Burkhart. *Writers and Partisans: A History of Literary Radicalism in America.* New York: Wiley, 1968.

*Glicksberg, Charles I. *The Literature of Commitment.* Lewisburg, Pa.: Bucknell Univ. Press, 1976.

Goldmann, Lucien. *Cultural Creation in Modern Society.* Trans. Bart Grahl. St. Louis: Telos, 1976.

————. *Towards a Sociology of the Novel.* Trans. Alan Sheridan. London: Tavistock, 1975. A Lukácsian Marxist influenced by structuralism (he called his method "genetic structuralism"), Goldmann is one of the most highly respected representatives of literary sociology.

Gramsci, Antonio. *Gli intelletuali e l'organizzazione della cultura.* Turin: Einaudi, 1949.

————. *Letteratura e vita nazionale.* Turin: Einaudi, 1966.

————. *History, Philosophy and Culture in the Young Gramsci.* Ed. Pedro Cavalcanti and Paul Piccone. Trans. Pierluigi Molajoni et al. St. Louis: Telos, 1975. Gramsci is important as a Marxist philosopher of culture particularly for his theory of cultural "hegemony" (for a brief but enlightening discussion see Raymond Williams' *Marxism and Literature*).

Green, Philip, and Michael Walzer, eds. *The Political Imagination in Literature: A Reader.* New York: Free Press, 1969.

Hamilton, Alastair. *The Appeal of Fascism: A Study of Intellectuals and Fascism, 1919–1945.* London: Blond, 1971. Perhaps the best of the studies of modern writers and Fascism in Italy, Germany, France, and England.

Harrison, John R. *The Reactionaries: A Study of the Anti-Democratic Intelligentsia.* New York: Shocken, 1967.

Holland, Henry M., Jr., ed. *Politics through Literature.* Englewood Cliffs, N.J.: Prentice-Hall, 1968.

Howe, Irving. *Politics and the Novel.* 1957; rpt. New York: Avon, 1970.

Jameson, Fredric. *Fables of Aggression: Wyndham Lewis, the Modernist as Fascist.* Berkeley: Univ. of California Press, 1979.

*Jay, Martin. *The Dialectical Imagination: A History of the Frankfurt School and the Institute of Social Research.* Boston: Little, 1973. A comprehensive history of the Frankfurt School. See in particular Ch. vi, "Aesthetic Theory and the Critique of Mass Culture," pp. 173–218.

Lang, Berel, and Forrest Williams, eds. *Marxism and Art: Writings in Aesthetics and Criticism.* New York: McKay, 1972. Texts by Marx, Engels, Lenin, Trotsky, Plekhanov, Bukharin, Stalin, Mao, E. Fischer, Galvano della Volpe, Brecht, Lukács, Benjamin, Arnold Hauser, Lucien Goldmann, et al. Rudimentary presentations, no bibliography, no index.

Leenhardt, Jacques. *Lecture politique du roman: "La Jalousie" d'Alain Robbe-Grillet.* Paris: Editions de Minuit, 1973.

Liehm, Antonín. *The Politics of Culture.* Trans. Peter Kussi. Includes "The Socialism That Came In from the Cold," by Jean-Paul Sartre. New York: Grove, 1972. Interviews with writers associated with the Prague Spring of 1968.

Lukács, György. *Ästhetik.* Neuwied, West Germany: Luchterhand, 1972.

———. *Realism in Our Time: Literature and the Class Struggle.* Trans. John and Necke Mander. Introd. George Steiner. New York: Harper, 1964.

———. *Solzhenitsyn.* Trans. William D. Graf. London: Merlin, 1970.

———. *Writer and Critic.* Trans. Arthur D. Kahn. New York: Grosset and Dunlap, 1974.

Mander, John. *The Writer and Commitment.* London: Secker and Warburg, 1961.

Marcuse, Herbert. *The Aesthetic Dimension: Toward a Critique of Marxist Aesthetics.* Boston: Beacon, 1978.

Marx, Karl, and Friedrich Engels. *Marx and Engels on Literature and Art.* Ed. Lee Baxandall and Stefan Morawski. St. Louis: Telos, 1973.

———. *Über Kunst und Literatur.* Ed. Manfred Kliem. 2 vols. Berlin: Dietz, 1967–68.

O'Brien, Conor Cruise. *Writers and Politics.* New York: Pantheon, 1965.

Orwell, George. *The Collected Essays, Journalism, and Letters of George Orwell.* 4 vols. Ed. Sonia Orwell and Ian Angus. New York: Harcourt, 1968.

*Panichas, George, ed. *The Politics of Twentieth-Century Novelists.* New York: Crowell, 1974. Useful collection of essays on H. G. Wells, E. M. Forster, D. H. Lawrence, Wyndham Lewis, Huxley, Orwell, Graham Greene, C. P. Snow, Bernanos, Malraux, Camus, Solzhenitsyn, Günter Grass, Dreiser, William Styron, etc. Ample footnotes, index.

*Reszler, André. *L'Esthétique anarchiste.* Paris: Presses Universitaires de France, 1973.

———. *L'Intellectuel contre l'Europe.* Paris: Presses Universitaires de France, 1977.

———, and T. G. Sauer, eds. *Politics and Literature: Papers Presented at the Conference on Politics and Literature Held at Indiana University, October 5–7, 1972.* Special issue of *Yearbook of Comparative and General Literature,* 22 (1973).

*Rothberg, Abraham. *The Heirs of Stalin: Dissidence and the Soviet Regime.* Ithaca, N.Y.: Cornell Univ. Press, 1972.

*Rühle, Jürgen. *Literature and Revolution.* Trans. Jean Steinberg. New York: Praeger, 1969. Comprehensive study of the writer and communism in our century.

*Sammons, Jeffrey L. *Literary Sociology and Practical Criticism: An Inquiry.* Bloomington: Indiana Univ. Press, 1977.

Sanders, Scott. *D. H. Lawrence: The World of the Five Major Novels.* New York: Viking, 1973. A lucid sociopolitical reading of D. H. Lawrence by a pupil of Raymond Williams.

Sartre, Jean-Paul. *What Is Literature?* Trans. Bernard Frechtman. New York: Philosophical Library, 1949.

———. *Politics and Literature.* Trans. J. A. Underwood and John Calder. London: Calder and Boyers, 1973.

*Sérant, Paul. *Le Romantisme fasciste.* Paris: Fasquelle, 1960. On Brasillach, Céline, Drieu La Rochelle, and Lucien Rebatet, among others. Comprehensive bibliographies.

*Solomon, Maynard, ed. *Marxism and Art.* New York: Vintage, 1974. The best anthology of Marxist aesthetics and criticism in the English language. Comprehensive bibliographies, index.

Sontag, Susan. *Against Interpretation.* New York: Farrar, 1966.

——. *Styles of Radical Will.* New York: Farrar, 1969. Fine, provoking essays in cultural criticism by one of the most sophisticated representatives of the New Left.

Spender, Stephen. *The Destructive Element: A Study of Modern Writers and Beliefs.* Boston: Houghton, 1938.

——. *The Thirties and After: Poetry, Politics, People, 1933–1970.* New York: Random, 1978.

——. "Writers and Politics." *Partisan Review*, 34 (1967), 359–81.

Sperber, Murray. *Literature and Politics.* Rochelle Park, N.J.: Hayden, 1979. Good college textbook.

*Stein, Peter, ed. *Theorie der politischen Dichtung.* Munich: Nymphenburger, 1973. Useful selection of documents and literary sources bearing on the poetics of political literature.

Steiner, George. *Extraterritorial: Papers on Literature and the Language Revolution.* New York: Atheneum, 1971.

——. *Language and Silence: Essays on Language, Literature, and the Inhuman.* New York: Atheneum, 1967. Important essays on modern culture, some (such as those on the significance of the Nazi holocaust, antisemitism and literature, Marxist criticism, and others) directly relevant to literature and politics.

*Swayze, Harold. *Political Control of Literature in the U.S.S.R., 1946–1959.* Cambridge: Harvard Univ. Press, 1962.

Trotsky, Leon. *Literature and Revolution.* Trans. Rose Strunsky. 1925; rpt. Ann Arbor: Univ. of Michigan Press, 1970.

White, George A., and Charles Newman, eds. *Literature in Revolution.* New York: Holt, 1972. Originally a *Tri-Quarterly* issue. Essays by Noam Chomsky, Frederick Crews, Carl Oglesby (on Melville), Conor Cruise O'Brien (on the politics of Yeats), Aileen Ward (Blake and the idea of revolution), Harry Levin, Raymond Williams (on Solzhenitsyn), G. A. White, Sol Yurick ("The Politics of the Imagination"), Leo Marx (on Susan Sontag), and several others. No bibliographies, no index.

Williams, Raymond. *Culture and Society, 1780–1950.* New York: Columbia Univ. Press, 1958.

——. *Marxism and Literature.* Oxford: Oxford Univ. Press, 1977. Lucid discussion of the basic concepts and problems of Marxist aesthetics and criticism. A major contribution to Marxist literary theory.

*Winegarten, Renée. *Writers and Revolution: The Fatal Lure of Action.* New York: New Viewpoint-Watts, 1974. Survey of the relation between literature and the idea of revolution from "the apocalyptic vision of William Blake" to such modern writers as Victor Serge, A. Gide, Malraux, Drieu La Rochelle, Sartre, Camus, and Orwell. Notes, index.

Woodcock, George. *The Writer and Politics.* London: Porcupine, 1948. One of the rare books of literary criticism written from a philosophically anarchistic point of view. Very stimulating.

*Woodring, Carl. *Politics in the Poetry of Coleridge.* Madison: Univ. of Wisconsin Press, 1961.

——. *Politics in English Romantic Poetry.* Cambridge: Harvard Univ. Press, 1970. A sequel to the earlier Coleridge book, this is a comprehensive scholarly study of the politics in the poetry of Wordsworth, Byron, and Shelley.

8

Literature and Law

RICHARD WEISBERG AND JEAN-PIERRE BARRICELLI

Few fields related to the literary disciplines hold as much promise as the law
for interdisciplinary inquiry. Law, associated with literature from its incep-
tion as a formalized attempt to structure reality through language, retains
its literary essence today. But while all interdisciplinary approaches to literature must respond to the skepticism of traditionalists, law-and-literature
elicits a special measure of resistance. Law, after all, is a profession, literature an art. Lawyers practice a functional craft; writers and literary critics
contribute to a body of intellectual discourse. Distrust exists on both sides
of the table; yet, remarkably enough, the field gains in definition and theoretical focus every year. The two seemingly disparate pursuits invite comparison through their common fascination with problems of language: structure,
rhetoric, ambiguity, interpretation, and the quest for meaning through linguistic signs. Both law and literature, moreover, depend on abstract formulations and on patterns of associative thinking to attain humanistic judgment.
Thus the expressive and the conceptual processes of both resemble each
other, and the two fields form a natural and mutually sustaining partnership.

Any approach to the relation directed to students of literature begins,
quite naturally, with the fictional text itself. Literature's millennial infatuation with things legal (formalisms, lawyers, trials, investigations, procedures, precedents, codes, and laws) must remain, methodologically, the
starting point of our inquiry. We cannot speak yet of the field's historical
evolution, but we may follow the lead of a recent pioneer, Ephraim London,
by dividing the subject into two parts, "the law in literature" and "the law as
literature," and by identifying the universality of the former as an introduction to an understanding of the latter.

I

If, to begin, we look at the law in literature, we note that among scholars, legal or literary, the distinguished law professor John H. Wigmore, in
his *A List of Legal Novels* (1908), was the first to identify the ways in which

fiction uses legal themes. More recently, we have recast Wigmore's model into the following four categories:

A. Works in which a full legal procedure is depicted, sometimes exclusively a "trial scene," but just as frequently the preliminary investigations leading to the trial

B. Works in which, even in the absence of a formal legal process, a lawyer is a central figure in the plot or story, frequently but not always the protagonist

C. Works in which a specific body of laws, often a single statute or system of procedures, becomes an organizing structural principle

D. Works in which, in an otherwise nonlegal framework, the relation of law, justice, and the individual becomes a central theme

By allowing for dramas and epics, this scheme elaborates on Wigmore's exclusive concern with novels, and it aids a preliminary inquiry into literature's perception of the law. The immediate question is: how may we effectively read together a variety of literary works that exhibit no other similarities except an identifiable approach to the legal thematic?

For example, category A contains such disparate masterpieces as *The Merchant of Venice*, *The Brothers Karamazov*, and *L'Etranger*. In the first, Shakespeare's trial scene dramatically embodies at once the personal conflict between Shylock and the Venetian Christians (represented in court by Portia), the social conflict between the alienated individual and society, and the philosophical conflict between strict earthly justice and the "quality of mercy." Without the courtroom scene, and the subtly interconnected casket subplot of Act II, none of these tensions appears resolvable within the comic medium of the play. Portia's legal trick allows her in self-interest to use Shylock's insistence on the letter of the law and hence to bring to a happy end the fates of Antonio, Bassanio, and "true Venice" as a whole.

The fact that, despite generic exigencies, the courtroom scene leaves many modern viewers uncertain where to direct their sympathies derives as much from historical developments as from the complex nature of the scene. But for almost a century now, legally trained analysts of the play have been in the forefront of a new critical sensitivity to the aesthetic and legal merits of Shylock's position against Portia. "Mercy," whose lovely name has been invoked in the service of brutal attacks on "outsiders," appears to have no ascendancy over the more rigorous but eminently fairer concept of earthly justice.

In *The Brothers Karamazov*, too, a lengthy trial scene fully articulates a dominant theme of the work. Like several other major European novelists, however, Fedor Dostoevsky follows a fascinating aspect of Continental criminal procedure by first depicting in great detail a preliminary investigation. Employing, like Albert Camus in *L'Etranger*, a three-leveled structure to communicate the criminal act to the reader (narrative exposition, preliminary investigation, and trial), Dostoevsky sacrifices the dramatic force of the single trial scene and painstakingly reveals the subtle, falsifying tendencies of the complete criminal process.

Indeed, lawyers in many works of fiction contrive to use their verbal gifts to transform an anterior and hitherto unformulated reality into an enduring, and largely fictive, narrative frame. Their task, therefore, duplicates that of the novelist who has created them. And if so many novelistic criminal procedures end in error — another example is the trial of Goodwin in William Faulkner's *Sanctuary* — it may well be because the writer employs the law as a metaphor to articulate a troubling self-criticism. Literary artists, like eloquent attorneys, may unwittingly lead their audiences down a well-crafted path that loses sight of the vital and noncapturable essence of human reality.

While all works in category A necessarily introduce several important legal characters, works in our category B involve such characters in their out-of-court dealings with reality. For example, in Camus's *La Chute* and Herman Melville's "Bartleby the Scrivener," the protagonist and/or narrator is a lawyer. Robert Louis Stevenson's *Weir of Hermiston* is about a judge. Far from being coincidental, the character's professional training is made an implicit or explicit background to the events and the relations in the literary work. Similar use of lawyers is made in many works of Honoré de Balzac (Popinot in *L'Interdiction* or Derville in *Gobseck*) and Charles Dickens (Mr. Jaggers in *Great Expectations*, Sidney Carton in *A Tale of Two Cities*, or Eugene Wrayburn, the briefless barrister of *Our Mutual Friend*); Dickens' *Bleak House* is a novel about the law, as is in many ways Balzac's *Colonel Chabert*.

Turning now to category C, we find that some literary texts have dealt with a specific body of laws, while at the same time not necessarily depicting any particular adjudication based on those laws. Such works may have nothing else in common, but they can be read together profitably because of this single, unifying characteristic. Hence, in Sophocles' *Antigone* the protagonist must confront a royal edict that ultimately violates her own, and the community's, sense of justice; in *Njáls saga*, the thirteenth-century epic hero is subject to the strict formalisms of legal pleadings; the comic plot of Shakespeare's *Measure for Measure* is intricately woven and happily unraveled within the structure of a rarely used Viennese statute against fornication; the title heroine of Balzac's *Ursule Mirouët* is victimized by those who abuse the French law of property and inheritance; Victor Hugo's *Les Misérables* pits the zealous adherence to the demand for legal order against a compassionate necessity for human justice (the letter versus the spirit); and the characters in Alexander Solzhenitsyn's *The First Circle* live through their experiences with the dreaded Article 58 of the Soviet Criminal Code. In each case, the creative mind behind the text has chosen to devote to a law or set of laws a sizable amount of dramatic time or narrative space, even though the characters' problems are essentially nonlegal.

We may include Melville's *Billy Budd, Sailor* in this category, despite the story's fully drawn legal procedure culminating in a trial (category A). It is worth noting, especially in light of excellent recent scholarship on the matter by lawyers and literary critics alike, that Captain Vere conducts Billy's trial under the provisions, not always accurately followed, of the Articles of War as well as of the wholly inapposite Mutiny Act (inapplicable because it applied only to land forces, not to the Navy). Since Melville appears to have had some knowledge of these statutes, and of the law in general, Vere's highly ambiguous actions during the trial can be partially understood through an awareness of the military codes mentioned in the story.

As a final category, D contains a number of less patently "legal" works that nonetheless evoke the problems raised by the relation of the law to the individual or the society it seeks to serve. Katherine Anne Porter's provocative "Noon Wine" (which contains a trial) raises even more significantly than most of the works mentioned under category A the issue of the relative ability of legal procedures to dispose of human problems. In this story, a legal finding of nonculpability for murder fails to satisfy the defendant, who feels compelled to travel from house to house justifying his action against his lingering doubts, as well as those of his neighbors and his wife.

The narrative situation in "Noon Wine" can be compared and contrasted to that in Franz Kafka's *Der Prozess*, where the protagonist throws himself into a legal "procedure" following his arrest for an unstated crime, allowing his personal sense of guilt or innocence to be ruled by the innuendoes emanating from the agents of the never identified "court." And both modern stories can be juxtaposed to the situation in Sophocles' *Oedipus Rex*, in which the protagonist insists on investigating his own legal guilt or innocence, sensing that the law alone will uncover the full answer to his personal and royal dilemma.

In Porter's story, the protagonist fails to derive any personal comfort from the judicial finding of innocence and prepares to shoot himself. In Kafka's novel, Joseph K bestows an inverse overconfidence on the institution that finds him guilty; his fascination with the court's personalities and procedures, instead of its substantive jurisdictional qualities (a fascination that may be his only transgression), destroys him. He is executed, no wiser a man at death than he was when the story began. Precisely opposed to both these protagonists, Oedipus achieves personal growth and fulfillment through the law, even though it finds him guilty and strips him of his power and possessions. The reader of these three works (and one might add *King Lear* as an intermediary case) is left to ponder the development in the Western literary artist's vision from the Greek protagonist, in whom justice and personal well-being were synonymous, to the modern protagonist, for whom justice has become a frighteningly complex phenomenon, rather to be avoided than embraced.

Category D also subsumes several less known works that explore similar problems in a modern context. Anthony Burgess' *A Clockwork Orange* (which might be read in conjunction with *Crime and Punishment*) gives voice to the emerging technology of the criminal justice system; E. L. Doctorow's *The Book of Daniel* (not without interest juxtaposed to *Der Prozess*) articulates the dilemma produced by the confrontation of a mammoth system of procedures with relatively passive and powerless people; and Richard Wright's *Native Son* (which has much in common with *L'Etranger*) presents the difficulties experienced by a black man whose actions displace him from the protected area of institutional benignity. This category must also subsume a work like Mateo Alemán's *Guzmán de Alfarache*, centered on a preoccupation with justice and disgust at how society carries it out. And finally, we must not fail to mention Dante Alighieri's *La Divina commedia*, which, with its powerful messages (even outside of *Paradiso* XVIII–XX) concerning the implications of divine and human law for all, stands out as a major example of a literary work centrally concerned with individual and social justice.

Few of us will lack a favorite work to insert in each of the four categories. From pre-Socratic and biblical times to the present, the examples of the artistic-legal partnership are numerous. Indeed, it often appears difficult to distinguish between the artist and the lawyer. In a rapid, historical overview, we cannot fail to note that one of the earliest of Greek tragedies known, Aeschylus' *Oresteia*, settles the generational curse on the House of Atreus in court and through trial by jury. The last part of the triptych, the *Eumenides*, is a courtroom scene whose arguments might fit a brief or a treatise more easily than a play. Rome produced one of the greatest lawyers–men of letters, Cicero, whose adaptation of Greek learning and culture to Roman thought and institutions remains valuable both as jurisprudence and as literature. The *Manilian Law*, the *Republic*, the *Laws*, the *Offices* constitute but a few of his most influential writings, to which must be added his *Letters* as well as his *Defense of Archias*, in which he rests his client's case on a eulogy of literature. Law and literature also combined in Francis Bacon, who uniquely derived a literary essay from one of his own legal writings ("Of Usury," drafted as a bill for James I and then printed in the 1625 edition of the *Essays*). The list could be expanded, particularly in the modern period from Heinrich von Kleist (*Michael Kohlhaas*) to Ugo Betti (*Corruzione al Palazzo di Giustizia* or *Frana allo scalo nord*). And these serious demonstrations, of course, leave out the comic side of the coin: the medieval French *La Farce de Maître Pathelin*, the caricatured lawyers of Molière (e.g., M. Bonnefoy in *Le Malade imaginaire*) and the Avocatori of Ben Jonson (*Volpone*), Miguel de Cervantes' adjudicating governor Sancho Panza (*Don Quijote*, Pt. II), François Rabelais's burlesqued judge Bridoye (*Gargantua et Pantagruel*, Bk. III), Dickens' comic duo Dodson and Fogg (*Pickwick Papers*), and Alessandro Manzoni's crooked, parasitic, and cowardly attorney Azzeccagarbugli (*I promessi sposi*), to mention but a handful. Literature has always found fertile soil on the lawyer's home ground.

Why? If we proceed from empiricism to phenomenology, we must again recognize that literature's extraordinary fascination with the law derives from similarities between the disciplines. Artists, sensitive to these similarities, integrate lawyers, legal themes, and legal structures into their creations, and as a result we discern what centuries of artists have already perceived: the compatible, even congenial, identity of two seemingly distinct intellectual enterprises.

Perhaps the ideal literary text around which to frame a discussion of literature's use of the law is *The Brothers Karamazov*. Dostoevsky's masterpiece stands as paradigmatic because four typical elements are present: (1) a detailed and structurally integrated depiction of a full legal process (reminiscent of epic and medieval uses of the law as in the trials of the *Chanson de Roland* and the *Poema del Cid*); (2) legal events or portraits of lawyers for reasons not only of caricature but also of metaphor (as in Geoffrey Chaucer's Man of Law's Tale of the *Canterbury Tales* or the mock trial in Ludvig Holberg's *Jeppe paa Bierget*); (3) analogies drawn between a secular investigation and metaphysical, religious, and literary inquiries into the nature of reality (e.g., Nathaniel Hawthorne's *The Scarlet Letter* or Friedrich Dürrenmatt's *Die Panne*); (4) authorial knowledge of, and fascination with, historical and national developments in the law (as in Manzoni's *Storia della colonna infame* or Hugo's *Le Dernier Jour d'un condamné*).

On its own terms, *The Brothers Karamazov* cannot be fully understood without integrating its detailed legal aspects into the larger novelistic framework. Like such modern novelists as Faulkner, Camus, Solzhenitsyn, Cesare Pavese, Dickens, and Kafka, Dostoevsky took the time to learn the small as well as the large areas of the law that so compellingly held his interest.

During the years separating the publication of *Crime and Punishment* from *The Brothers Karamazov*, the recently instituted czarist legal reforms were of general interest in lay and legal circles. But in Dostoevsky, who actively participated in the famous Kroneberg Case of 1876, the courtroom and the procedures that culminate in a criminal trial appeared to generate a particularly fervent response. Thus it is no surprise that almost a fourth of *The Brothers Karamazov* concerns a single criminal procedure: the investigation of the role of Dimitry Karamazov (Mitya) in the death of his father.

Mitya's hatred of his father almost led him to commit parricide. But the narrative breaks off at precisely the moment when the grotesque old Karamazov lustfully peers out of the family window to await Grushenka, the woman whom Mitya, too, passionately desires.

The reader thus does not know, as the legal inquiry commences, who killed the old man shortly after Mitya stared at him with such malevolence.

Was it Mitya? All we know at this stage is that he has fled the Karamazov house and later indulged in an evening of blissful passion at the Mokroe inn with Grushenka. Here lawyers and the police confront and arrest him. Now begins the brilliant interplay of lawyer and suspect, reminiscent of Porfiry Petrovitch's investigation of Raskolnikov in *Crime and Punishment*. Mitya, like Raskolnikov, must participate in three inquisitorial "ordeals," although for him the three occur within a few hours instead of weeks. Book IX of the novel, called "The Preliminary Inquiry," deals with these events (Chs. iii–v). We gradually learn that Mitya's despair in the face of the legal inquiry stems from the converse of Raskolnikov's in the same situation; while the latter is tortured by Porfiry's increasingly intimate insights into his personality, Mitya is terrorized by his inquisitors' consistent incomprehension of his soul.

Someone like Mitya also senses the full humiliation of a procedural situation theoretically impossible under American law but to this day quite proper in Europe. He finds himself, prior to arrest, seated at a table, the center of interest of several interrogators who note his every gesture. Later, like a novelist, these lawyers will recast the event into a lengthy narrative, admissible in court. While his interrogators inform him on several occasions of his right to refuse to answer any question, Mitya nonetheless has during this first interview no right to the advice of an attorney as to when silence itself might be prejudicial.

Nor is Nikolay Nelyudov, the inquisitor (or examining magistrate), despite his inferiority to Dostoevsky's earlier lawyer, an easy interrogator. During the intense questioning around the table at Mokroe, Mitya learns that the inquisitor is "a skillful lawyer," reasonably competent in the art of psychology. Among the tactics common to Nikolay and Porfiry (and typical of lawyers' relation to protagonists in many literary texts) is the establishment of a calm and friendly tone, alternated cleverly with insinuating verbal mannerisms (Porfiry's giggle, Nikolay's prattling lisp) and disconcerting suggestions. The latter ploy finds expression in Nikolay's insistence — a slight and probably justified exaggeration of his powers of search and seizure — that Mitya fully undress in the presence of several peasant onlookers. Since Nikolay has observed that the suspect's clothes are covered with blood, his order is reasonable as an effort to procure evidence, but disrobing in front of others humiliates Mitya and makes him feel "almost guilty." Embarrassed especially by his feet ("All his life he had thought both his big toes hideous"), Mitya compares his predicament to "flogging" and later calls the lawyers his "torturers."

The theme of law as inquisition and torture is revived in Kafka and other twentieth-century writers. But on the level of legal detail, so dear to Dostoevsky, the incident reveals fully the immense powers and the medieval origins of the Continental legal inquisitor's office. Like Camus's Meursault, when faced with the crucifix-brandishing inquisitor in *L'Etranger*, Mitya almost capitulates to the clever tactics of European law.

Dostoevsky's fine knowledge of czarist criminal procedure reveals itself in the small, as well as the grandiose, actions of Nikolay during the preliminary investigation. But the full significance of the legal process finds expression more in the trial lawyers (and "The Grand Inquisitor") than in the preliminary inquisitor. This significance lies in the lawyers' passionate aim to eliminate from consideration in the case any spontaneous, emotional, and idiosyncratic factor failing to harmonize with their own narrative perspective on the situation.

No lawyer involved in Mitya's case grants credence to what they call his "romanticheskiy" 'literary,' or 'romantic' account of the matter. Conversely, when the prosecuting attorney Ippolit Kirillovich propounds his own "reasonable" theory of the case (Mitya killed his father out of jealousy over Grushenka, stole three thousand rubles from the victim's bedside, and spent the money at Mokroe), Mitya says he is "joking" and call him "base."

The dichotomy in Dostoevsky is not between romanticism and reason. Rather, it takes place on the level of two opposing value systems, one spontaneous and the other formulaic, each insisting passionately on its own supremacy. The law, for Dostoevsky as well as for most artists interested in the subject, displays subtly its own insistent standards, and it will have its way even, occasionally, by falsely fitting the individual suspect into a preordained pattern of behavior.

Hence, the preliminary inquisitor, the prosecutor, and even Mitya's defense lawyer have an interest in establishing a motive that will explain the crime in a manner conducive to ordered rearticulation. This interest spirals into a resentful campaign in the figure of Ippolit Kirillovich, whose seeming objectivity masks a personal dislike for the defendant. Not only has Mitya attracted Ippolit's wife, but the defendant's outgoing, forceful nature marks him as an object of Ippolit's fascination and negativism. The entire thrust of the legal procedure, and the task for which "artistic legality" is eminently suited, is to recreate verbally, and thus to devalue, the existence of the spontaneous, vital, and basically nonverbal individual who stands accused. Like some novelists, the lawyer employs his verbal gift to produce negative portraits of positive heroes. The personal problems of the novel's lawyers become institutionalized in the seemingly rational procedures of the criminal law.

Creative legality is expertly depicted by Dostoevsky, as later by Melville in *Billy Budd, Sailor* and Camus in *L'Etranger* and *La Chute*, with a careful eye for detail that suggests a certain amount of authorial self-identification. By the time the imaginative, articulate lawyer comes to formulate the official portrait of the defendant at the trial, his analysis has undergone a series of fateful—if tiny—errors produced by the overall narrowness of his vision.

Thus, when at the preliminary inquiry Mitya insists that the money he spent at Mokroe came from half of the three thousand rubles he had received from Katerina Ivanovna and not from his dead father's room, the following dialogue occurs, masking three testimonial mistakes (numbered in the text below) that only the perceptive reader, willing to arrest briefly his voyage into the novel, will discover:

". . . I brought [Grushenka] here to Mokroe [in an earlier visit], and in two days squandered half of that damned three thousand. But the other half I kept to me. Well, I kept that other half, that fifteen hundred like a locket around my neck. But yesterday I undid it, and spent it."

"Excuse me. How's that? Why, when you were here a month ago you spent three thousand, not fifteen hundred. Everybody knows that." (1)

. . . .

"Why, you told everyone yourself that you'd spent exactly three thousand." (2)

"It's true, I did. I told the whole town that. . . . But I didn't spend three thousand, only fifteen hundred. And the other fifteen hundred I sewed into a little bag. That's how it was, gentlemen. That's where I got that money yesterday."

"This is almost unbelievable," murmured Nikolai Nelyudov.

"Let me ask," observed the prosecutor at last. "Have you informed anyone of this circumstance before?"

. . . .

"Absolutely no one. No one and nobody." (3)

"What was your reason for this? What was your motive for making such a secret of it? . . ."

The prosecutor stopped speaking. He was provoked. He did not conceal his irritation, his resentful reaction, and he gave vent to all his accumulated spleen, without choosing words, disconnectedly and incoherently.

"It's not the fifteen hundred that's a disgrace, but that I put it apart from the rest of the three thousand," said Dmitri firmly. . . . "I squandered it, but I didn't steal it. . . . So in that case, I would be a scoundrel, but not a thief. Not a thief! . . ."

"I admit that there is a certain distinction," said the prosecutor, with a cold smile. "But it's strange that you see such a vital difference."
(Bk. IX, Ch. vii)

The first error, revealed several hundred pages earlier, indicates that at least one person, Alyosha, could have surmised that Mitya had spent only fifteen hundred of Katya's rubles, and then preserved in a little bag around his neck the other fifteen hundred, which he finally spent on Grushenka just prior to being arrested. Alyosha eventually does recall the earlier conversations when he testifies during the trial, but the tardiness of his recollection renders the testimony too weak to impede the convincing flow of the law's narrative version of the case.

The second error is more explicit. The lawyers have not discovered that Mitya told the innkeeper Plastunov that he had "spent more than a thousand [not three thousand] roubles the last time he was there," and that he had "come to do the same again." These remarks, if correctly ascertained by the lawyers, would have exonerated Mitya, since they indicate that he probably did not spend three thousand newly found rubles on the second spree at Mokroe. But, as just one inaccurate witness among many, Plastunov has lied about this issue at the preliminary inquiry, stating with great certainty that Mitya "told him" he brought three thousand rubles with him both times.

Small falsehoods such as these, ironically reiterated by Mitya himself (the third error), allow the lawyers to write an encompassing narrative exposition of Mitya's motives and actions. Thus, at the end of the trial, Ippolit Kirillovich, in the midst of the lengthiest verbal declaration in the novel since Ivan's narration of "The Grand Inquisitor," rewrites Mitya's personality by stating:

> This frantic but weak man, who could not resist the temptation of accepting the three thousand roubles [from Katerina Ivanovna] at the price of such disgrace, this very man suddenly develops the most stoical firmness, and carries about fifteen hundred roubles without daring to touch them. Does that fit in at all with the character we have analyzed? No, and I will venture to tell you how the real Dmitri Karamazov would have behaved in such circumstances, if he really had put away the money. . . . Before the end of the month he would have taken the last note but one, feeling that if he took back only a hundred it would answer the purpose, for a thief would have stolen it all. And then he would have looked at this last note, and have said to himself: "It's really not worth while to give back one hundred; let's spend that too!" *That's how the real Dmitri Karamazov, as we know him, would have behaved.* One cannot imagine anything more incongruous than this story of the little bag. Nothing could be more inconceivable.
>
> (Bk. XII, Ch. vi)

Through the legal theme, Dostoevsky submits that the person who attempts to formulate life verbally will succeed only in producing a witty and artistically convincing, but essentially unjust and inaccurate, portrait of reality. No juror apprehends the motives and errors of the artistic lawyers who reorganize the original reality of the crime; the deliberately falsified or unconsciously distorted testimony of witnesses such as Grigory and Katerina Ivanovna, both of whom harbor a form of Ippolit-Ivan's bitter resentment against Mitya, buttresses the unbreachable wall of prosecutorial language. Mitya stands convicted.

Not a single but a double level of legal judgment is posited within *The Brothers Karamazov*. Although the temporal level fills nearly ten times as much space as the metaphysical, and although its two full sections pertain more centrally to the "plot" of the novel, the latter level in "The Grand Inquisitor" permeates most critical reactions to the whole text. And yet the two areas, placed by the author into a single structure, invite observations that stress their complementary nature. Relating detailed legal depiction to overall literary structure and meaning within this text may remind the careful reader of similar effects in other fiction. The secular legal inquiry into Mitya's guilt is associated with the larger inquiry into Ivan Karamazov's legal and moral guilt; and through Ivan, the novelist extends the legal procedure's meaning to himself, to his reader, and to modern European culture generally.

The finest creative emanation of Ivan Karamazov's narrative abilities bears the name of one of its principals, "The Grand Inquisitor." In Ivan's "poem," the Inquisitor in sixteenth-century Spain confronts the returning founder of the now prevalent religion. Deeming Jesus an unwelcome intruder, an example of the kind of unstructured freedom that is anathema to his own ordered system, the Inquisitor uses his legal authority to convict and exile the very image of truth. But the confrontation, unlike the trial of Mitya, has no adversarial process, only a lengthy verbalization by the Inquisitor, an apology for the mode of externally imposed order at the expense of individual freedom.

Ironically, Ivan himself has become a formulator. In a sense, he reincarnates the Spanish priest, rejecting the medieval world view of the Inquisitor but preserving the Inquisitor's reactive formal approach to those who fall into his sphere of influence. Like the Inquisitor (and the novel's lawyers), Ivan demonstrates the urge to bring order to what is otherwise free and spontaneous. He transfers to the service of his theoretically nihilistic world view a paradoxical tendency to formulate, to create verbal structures. But, in the realm of human interaction, Ivan's mode, like the Inquisitor's, tends to stifle others (Lize, Katerina Ivanovna) or to lead them to violent thoughts (Smerdyakov, even Alyosha), not to inspire them with a sense of their own free potential. Ivan takes on his own sick and tortured soul the need to redirect and to reformulate the lives of those around him. But negativism can only breed negativism; like Jesus and his followers in the face of the Inquisitor, Alyosha, Katerina, Mitya, and Lize suffer the injury of externally imposed guilt from Ivan, the latter-day verbalizer.

For Ivan, life has become mere reaction. Just as the Grand Inquisitor's schemes are generated in reaction to the Nazarene example of freedom and spontaneity, and just as the law's forms contrive to undermine Mitya, so Ivan channels into everyone he meets the resentment within him against his father. He thus creates more than the story of the Inquisitor. While he cannot act himself, he can instill a violently reactive "idea" in the receptive mind of at least one member of his audience. Smerdyakov, like the Christian flock, absorbs the resentments of his leader and translates narrative structures into violent deeds. And, for this violence, an innocent person becomes condemned. Dmitri, an outsider by virtue of his relatively spontaneous, honorable, and nonverbal approach to reality, and despite the monk Alyosha's ineffective faith in his innocence, is convicted of the crime legally committed by his half brother, Smerdyakov, and actually "created" by none other than Ivan.

The structured word vanquishes the representation of life itself, both in the twin-leveled legal procedure depicted in this novel and in the intermediary between the two levels, the intellectual, Ivan. For if tacit love alone fails on this earth, so, too, does the bearer of the "narrative tendency," whether lawyer, intellectual, or literary artist. A just vision of the world requires a vigorous ethic of individual freedom, on a personal as well as on a comunal level. Love arises only as the end product of this ethic, a love based on a material awareness of the magnificence of the nonnarrative nature of human actualization. Dostoevsky's implicitly self-critical suggestion that the urge toward verbal formalism frequently conceals the obsessive negativism that the articulate individual hopes to extend outward to any willing audience ties him to other artists who have emphasized legal themes.

Thus does law relate to central meaning in a subtle structure of form and theme. We cannot discuss literarily *Crime and Punishment* or *Billy Budd, Sailor* outside the legal context any more than we can discuss Thomas Mann's *Doktor Faustus* outside the musical. Reliable interpretation often demands versatility.

II

Like the inquiry into "law in literature," that into "law as literature" may be divided into four sections. Seen as analogous academic pursuits, law and literature share a grounding in style and rhetoric (including the narrative expression of a vision of reality), hermeneutic function, value awareness, and imagination. Were it not for the uses to which we put the law, on the one hand, and literature, on the other, we would be struck immediately by their common epistemologies. Basically narrative in their formal aspects, law and literature rely on language to structure an otherwise amorphous and nonlinguistic reality. An event (or a series of events) occurs; the legal and literary individual strives to reconstruct the event, giving it by necessity a substantially personal imprint. As perhaps the most "poetic" of all lawyers, Benjamin N. Cardozo, once noted in a statement that recalls some of Gustave Flaubert's theories of narrative art:

> The important thing . . . is to rid our prepossessions, so far as may be, of what is merely individual or personal, to detach them in a measure from ourselves, to build them, not upon instinctive likes and dislikes,

but upon an informed and liberal culture, a knowledge (as Arnold would have said) of the best that has been thought and said in the world, so far as that best has relation to the social problem to be solved. Of course, when our utmost effort has been put forth, we shall be far from freeing ourselves from the empire of inarticulate emotion, of beliefs so ingrained and inveterate as to be a portion of our very nature. "I must paint what I see in front of me," said the elder Yeats to his son, the poet. "Of course, I shall really paint something different because my own nature will come in unconsciously." There is nothing new in all this.

The legal process, like the literary, moves from an experience in life toward a narrative re-creation of that experience. However tightly bound to evidence and the logic of events, the re-creation needs the bridging or collating powers of the imagination to put together the scene, or the picture, in all its details. Forming what we might call the legal "literature of narrative" — and excluding statutes and regulations for the moment — are, in descending order of definitive articulation, the judicial opinion, the legal brief, the parties' and witnesses' formal statement of fact (in affidavits, pleadings, or statements in court or at depositions), and the parties' informal accounts of the situation, usually to their attorneys. Ironically, the chain linking legal narrative to an event becomes authoritatively strong only as it achieves distance from the event. The ultimate statement, both of what originally occurred and of what the law of the case should be, comes from one or more judges whose rendition of the event is vicarious and sometimes fictional. Like the novelist, the appellate judge, furthering the fictive chain initiated by one or the other party's lawyers, employs the stuff of vicarious experience to forge an enduring reality in narrative prose. As Cardozo put it, again sounding like his fellow narrative craftsman Flaubert:

> [The ultimate] queries are slumbering within many a common law-suit, which can be lifted from meanness up to dignity if the great judge is by to see what is within. But as a system of case law develops, the sordid controversies of litigants are the stuff out of which great and shining truths will ultimately be shaped.
>
> It is a false and cramping notion that cases are made great solely or chiefly by reason of something intrinsic in themselves. They are great by what we make of them; McCulloch v. Maryland — to choose almost at random — is one of the famous cases of our history. I wonder, would it not be forgotten, and even perhaps its doctrine overruled, if [first Chief Justice John] Marshall had not put upon it the imprint of his genius.

In terms of pure exposition, we shall always be drawn to the magnetic prose of an Oliver Wendell Holmes (*Schenk* v. *U.S.*, dissent in *Abrams* v. *U.S.*) or a Learned Hand (*Schmidt* v. *U.S.*) or a William O. Douglas (dissent in *Den-*

nis v. *U.S.* and *Beauharnais* v. *Illinois*). Their grasp of, and respect for, language place them in the front rank of writers in the English language. As Cardozo said of another great stylist, Louis D. Brandeis, "his writing is communication rather than self-expression."

But appellate judges far less luminary than these, or less conscious of their re-creative powers, also use style, rhetoric, and form to narrate experience. So we contrast the effects of legal and literary prose only at our peril and only by narrowing our definition of "literature" to texts consciously created as such. Particularly when we consider that every legal document expresses the values of the surrounding culture itself, we may begin to ponder why we limit the uses of literature and law as we do.

Dramatic courtroom prose stands as the most obvious link between literature and the practice of law. Take, for instance, a comparison we might make between Plato's ubiquitously read *Apology* and the statement by Mahatma Gandhi (incidentally, a lawyer by training) to the tribunal of 1922. Socrates stands serenely before the court, facing the charge of having disbelieved in the gods and of having corrupted Athenian youth, thereby spreading the seed of resistance. But he knows, too, that it is his imperturbability that bothers the court, his belief that death is a summum bonum when one knows one has done one's duty. How can he not heed the voice of his conscience, especially when it comes to his fellow citizens' welfare? And while he feels that death would be unjust, Socrates suggests that the State must execute him, out of respect for its laws — until they are altered. In the crowded little courtroom in Ahmadabad similarly stands Gandhi, also old and tired, saying most of the things Socrates said, just as serene, just as imperturbable, and in an equally concise and artistically balanced form, inviting death for his posture of *satyagraha* 'holding on to truth,' which he actualized through his creed of nonviolent noncooperation. He ends with these words: "The only course open to you, the judge, is either to resign your post, and thus dissociate yourself from evil if you feel that the law you are called upon to administer is an evil and that in reality I am innocent, or to inflict on me the severest penalty if you believe that the system and the law you are assisting to administer are good for the people of this country and that my activity is therefore injurious to the public weal." Gandhi's statement is as much "literature" as Plato's dialogue.

Or let us look at Felix Frankfurter's account of the Nicola Sacco and Bartolomeo Vanzetti affair (*The Case of Sacco and Vanzetti*, 1927). The account is written with an immediacy and directness that would have drawn the praise of Stendhal, that admirer of the style of the Civil Code. Its pace-setting exposition, suspenseful development, powerful climax, and thoughtful denouement yield the cohesiveness, structural unity, and drama of the best novelistic fiction. *The Case of Sacco and Vanzetti*, vibrant as it is with emotional and ethical problems and moving characters like the protagonists (among other things, insecure in their command of English, facing a Brahmin judge like Webster Thayer) might be included profitably on our literary reading lists. It is not surprising that European intellectuals like Romain Roland, Anatole France, Tomáš Garrigue Masaryk, and Albert Einstein protested the verdict; it is equally not surprising that the cause célèbre gave rise to, or otherwise appeared in, works of literature by authors such as Edna St. Vincent Millay, John Dos Passos, James Thurber, and Upton Sinclair.

Similarly, the life and courtroom experience of Joan of Arc have provided steady inspiration over the centuries for writers like Friedrich Schiller, Mark Twain, Anatole France, George Bernard Shaw, and Jean Anouilh, and who is to say that the simple transcript of her trial (as found, condensed, in London, *The Law as Literature*) is not more powerful from the point of view of immediacy of style, drama, characterization, and meaning than the polished transpositions of the fiction writers? And, as a final example of the compelling similarities between courtroom utterance and fictive literature, we might consider E. L. Doctorow's *The Book of Daniel* as an evocative, wonderfully crafted scan on the actual Rosenberg case transcripts, appeals, and published letters.

Literary artist and courtroom lawyer must relate constantly to the constraints of their basic tool, language, and to the uses of rhetoric and style that suit, if not always a personal muse, at least an audience's perceived response. But a dynamic inner vision, an imaginative factor, ultimately obtains in much noncourtroom legal work, too. Lawyers are constantly interpreting, always bridging the hermeneutic gap and expressing values, consistently bringing an audience closer to their own perceptions of a text, an individual, or a reality. Most of the lawyer's work involves the imaginative (and goal-oriented) recasting of a prior reality into narrative form. A legal document such as a will expresses the entire humanity—the desires, quest for power, even the fantasies—of the testator. Aside from the jargon, as well as the stultifying repetition of synonyms that sometimes characterizes the legal idiom, even ordinary legal correspondence requires that legal writers interpret and understand the perspectives of a variety of possible readers of their texts. Admittedly, the interplay of the lawyer's subjective vision with the objective law (which may exist in a judicial opinion) should not dominate the final draft of a will, contract, or securities prospectus. These, to be sure, far less than the courtroom argument or judicial opinion, are palpably works of "literature" in the sense of being organized imaginative writings. Still, some of their genre achieve a higher "literary" status through the lucid transformation of the client's desires into prose, or through the convincing exposition of a human drama. This, too, as an act of interpretation, is narrative art.

As we elaborated the manner in which literature looks at the law in *The Brothers Karamazov*, so here we may elaborate strictly legal texts that suggest how the law "uses" literary devices. For, as the late Judge Harold Leventhal has put it, "I have been involved in enterprises such as 'Law and

Science' and 'Law and Economics.'. . . The case of Law and Literature is different, however. . . . There is a unique, complex, and profound inter-weaving of the various strands of both law and literature." Among the "strands" he might have recognized is interest in the intricacies of language. The legal or literary individual may embark upon any number of specialties or pursuits: the careful, imaginative, and effectively structured use of language will define all of them.

As the pinnacle of legal utterance, the judicial opinion achieves authority and endurance through linguistic craftsmanship. To some extent, the dynamism of the Anglo-American legal system derives from the necessity for style in the appellate opinion. Language may be used elegantly or carelessly, but it is the judge's medium. The opinion may be effectively organized or it may be haphazard in its explanation of the facts and issues, but it must have a form, which, as a part of style, contributes to the opinion's present and ultimate meaning. Cardozo put it this way:

> We find a kindred phenomenon in literature, alike in poetry and in prose. The search is for the just word, the happy phrase, that will give expression to the thought, but somehow the thought itself is transfigured by the phrase when found. There is emancipation in our very bonds. The restraints of rhyme or metre, the exigencies of period balance, liberate at times the thought which they confine, and in imprisoning release.

Cardozo's extrajudicial essays articulate a consistent theme: appellate judges work, consciously or not, within a linguistic medium that contributes a creative element to their everyday task of decision making. Judges are writers (or at least managers of writers); the way in which they use language will affect future law. A judge need not be a Cardozo, but the bare fact that the judicial medium is language moves that judge's efforts into the domain of narrative and its consequent ambiguities.

Our texts are two judicial opinions of unequal legal and literary merit. These texts are a form of "literature" whose meaning (for lawyer and lay person) is bound up in the operations of style, interpretation, imagination, and value-awareness. Each opinion written by a judge on an appellate bench forms a kind of narrative, a vision of reality framed in a structured discourse and almost always involving the imaginative recasting of that reality by the judge.

The first case is *Osterlind* v. *Hill*, written by a judge of little renown in a style that would be eminently forgettable were it not for the perennial fascination of its legal issue: is there in our law an affirmative duty to rescue? The court's answer is no, but its manner colors the meaning of the negative response and alters the effect that the opinion has had on its legal audience. A man named Hill rented a canoe to Osterlind and another man, both of whom may have been drunk at the time. The vessel overturned and Osterlind clung to it for a half hour screaming for help. Hill noted the incident from the shore, heard the screams, and although neither life nor limb would have been risked, failed to act. Osterlind finally lost his grip on the canoe and drowned.

Osterlind's relatives sued Hill on behalf of their "intestate," the drowned man. But the Massachusetts Supreme Court affirmed the lower court's dismissal of the tort action. The court used these words:

OSTERLIND v. HILL
160 N.E. 303 (1928)

Braley, J., delivered the opinion of the court:
. . .
The declaration must set forth facts which, if proved, establish the breach of a legal duty owed by the defendant to the intestate. Sweeney v. Old Colony & N. R. Co. 10 Allen, 368, 372, 87 Am. Dec. 644. The plaintiff relies on Black v. New York, N. H. & H. R. Co. 193 Mass. 448, 7 L.R.A. (N.S.) 148, 79 N.E. 797, 9 Ann. Cas. 485, as establishing such a duty on the part of the defendant. In that case the jury would have been justified in finding that the plaintiff was "so intoxicated as to be incapable of standing or walking or caring for himself in any way." There was testimony to the effect that, "when he fell, he did not seize hold anything, his arms were at his side." The defendant's employees placed a helpless man, a man impotent to protect himself, in a dangerous position.

In the case at bar, however, it is alleged in every count of the original and amended declaration that after the canoe was overturned the intestate hung to the canoe for approximately one-half hour and made loud calls for assistance. On the facts stated in the declaration the intestate was not in a helpless condition. He was able to take steps to protect himself. The defendant violated no legal duty in renting a canoe to a man in the condition of the intestate. The allegation appearing in each count of the amended declaration that the intestate was incapacitated to enter into any valid contract states merely a legal conclusion. The allegations, therefore, in the counts of the amended declaration to the effect that the intestate was incapable of exercising any care for his own safety is controlled by the allegations in the same counts that he hung to the side of the canoe for approximately one-half hour, calling for assistance.

In view of the absence of any duty to refrain from renting a canoe to a person in the condition of the intestate, the allegations of involuntary intoxication relating as they do to the issues of contributory negligence become immaterial. The allegations of willful, wanton or reckless conduct also add nothing to the plaintiff's case. The failure of the defendant to respond to the intestate's outcries is immaterial. No legal right of the intestate was infringed. . . . [Case dismissed]

In its style and approach, there is nothing to distinguish this opinion from many others. Its author, Henry K. Braley, was three years later to be eulogized for "his wide learning, his piercing discernment and . . . his elucidation, of the elemental and lasting, rather than the instant or ephemeral issues of any case at bar before him." Yet, for Braley, the human dimensions of Osterlind's case were undeserving of mention; clearly, he did not feel he could find, in Cardozo's phrase, "emancipation in the very bonds" of the legal precedents to which he owed allegiance.

The American legal system, unlike some others, imposes no affirmative duty to rescue upon an otherwise noninvolved bystander. Cardozo spoke of the rule this way:

> For years there has been a dogma of the books that in the absence of a special duty of protection, one may stand by with indifference and see another perish, by drowning, say, or fire, though there would be no peril in a rescue. A rule so divorced from morals was sure to breed misgivings. We need not be surprised to find that in cases of recent date, a tendency is manifest to narrow it or even whittle it away. We cannot say today that the old rule has been supplanted. The rulings are too meagre. Sown, however, are the seeds of scepticism, the precursor often of decay. Some day we may awake to find that the old tissues are dissolved. Then will come a new generalization, and with it a new law.

Judge Braley chose not to dissolve "the old tissues" of the rule. But since his rhetorical options were limitless, as immense as the language itself, nonetheless he moved toward Cardozo's "new generalization" subtly and perhaps unintentionally.

A piece of narrative discourse, this opinion evidences the infinite variety of approaches that all judges can take to any situation before them. Instead of a dry rearticulation of the plaintiff's claim, the adjudicator can set forth the facts with a narrative sense of their implicit moral and human dimensions. Instead Braley, having first found somewhat strangely that Osterlind's ability to hang on and scream disproved the plaintiff's claim that Osterlind was too drunk to have the canoe rented to him, reached the stylistic pinnacle of his opinion in the blandest of manners, articulated near the end of the opinion: "The failure of the defendant to respond to the intestate's outcries is immaterial."

Immaterial. The judge's language reflects not only his unwillingness to change the law, but, more significantly, his apparent approval of that law. His bland style seems least designed to plant Cardozo's "seeds of scepticism." But the starkness of his thirteen-word phrase has worked to give the opinion a different effect. Subsequent scholars and judges have been struck by the bloodless quality of Braley's response to the human dimension of the facts. Constrained to stylize, as judges in Anglo-American law are, Braley has influenced others to examine and criticize the rule that he himself supported. The case thus establishes an essential point about the appellate opinion: within it, willy-nilly, style serves the function of the law and is inseparable from it.

Therefore, as Harvey Couch declared, "It is no accident that Holmes, Brandeis, Cardozo and Hand are considered the greatest judges as well as the greatest writers of judicial opinions." The often dazzling style of these judges accounts in part for the continuing authority of so many of their opinions. Cardozo, in particular, took pains to articulate frequently the place of the "architectonics" of a successful judicial opinion. Since "right" or "wrong" answers so rarely inhered in the fact situations that arose in his court, Cardozo realized that the framing of his decision, structurally and linguistically, would often decide whether the intended audience would accept his legal reasoning. In his famous "Law and Literature" essay he put it this way: "The opinion will need persuasive force, or the impressive virtue of sincerity and fire, or the mnemonic power of alliteration and antithesis or the terseness and tang of the proverb, and the maxim; neglect the help of these allies, and it may never win its way."

When Cardozo speaks of an opinion's ability to "win its way," he is referring to its chances of convincing the other judges on the case and of gaining authority within the professional community. Much the same can be said about any piece of literature or criticism. In all narrative pursuits, the effective use of style can gain credibility for the idea proposed and lasting acceptance for its author. Let us not forget that Cicero won the acquittal of a mass murderer of kin with his eloquence.

To this extent, the judge is far more an artist than a logician or technician. Cardozo adds:

> The judge or advocate is expounding a science or a body of truth which he seeks to assimilate to a science, but in the process of exposition he is practicing an art. The Muses look at him a bit impatiently and wearily at times. He has done a good deal to alienate them, and sometimes they refuse to listen and are seen to stop their ears. They have a strange capacity, however, for the discernment of strains of harmony and beauty, no matter how diffused and scattered through the ether. So at times when work is finally done, one sees their faces change; and they take the worker by the hand. They know that by the lever of art the subject the most lowly can be lifted to the heights.

Cardozo's method articulates the reality for judges far less conscious of their craft than he; as we observed with Judge Braley, the way in which the adjudicator explains the case determines the ultimate meaning of the decision. As Karl Llewellyn has remarked, "adornment" is inseparable from legal function.

Let us take, as our second example, a Cardozo opinion. Like Braley's, it involves a tort claim by the surviving relatives of an individual killed while engaging in water sports.

HYNES v. NEW YORK CENT. R. CO.
Court of Appeals of New York, 1921
231 N.Y. 229, 131 N.E. 898, 17 A.L.R. 803

CARDOZO, J. On July 8, 1916, Harvey Hynes, a lad of 16, swam with two companions from the Manhattan to the Bronx side of the Harlem River, or United States Ship Canal, a navigable stream. Along the Bronx side of the river was the right of way of the defendant, the New York Central Railroad, which operated its trains at that point by high-tension wires, strung on poles and crossarms. Projecting from the defendant's bulkhead above the waters of the river was a plank or springboard, from which boys of the neighborhood used to dive. One end of the board had been placed under a rock on the defendant's land, and nails had been driven at its point of contact with the bulkhead. Measured from this point of contact the length behind was 5 feet; the length in front 11. The bulkhead itself was about 3½ feet back of the pier line as located by the government. From this it follows that for 7½ feet the springboard was beyond the line of the defendant's property and above the public waterway. Its height measured from the stream was 3 feet at the bulkhead, and 5 feet at its outermost extremity. For more than five years swimmers had used it as a diving board without protest or obstruction.

On this day Hynes and his companions climbed on top of the bulkhead, intending to leap into the water. One of them made the plunge in safety. Hynes followed to the front of the springboard, and stood poised for his dive. At that moment a crossarm with electric wires fell from the defendant's pole. The wires struck the diver, flung him from the shattered board, and plunged him to his death below. His mother, suing as administratrix, brings this action for her damages. Thus far the courts have held that Hynes at the end of the springboard above the public waters was a trespasser on the defendant's land. They have thought it immaterial that the board itself was a trespass, an encroachment on the public ways. They have thought it of no significance that Hynes would have met the same fate if he had been below the board and not above it. The board, they have said, was annexed to the defendant's bulkhead. By force of such annexation, it was to be reckoned as a fixture, and thus constructively, if not actually, an extension of the land. The defendant was under a duty to use reasonable care that bathers swimming or standing in the water should not be electrocuted by wires falling from its right of way. But to bathers diving from the springboard, there was no duty, we are told, unless the injury was the product of mere willfulness or wantonness—no duty of active vigilance to safeguard the impending structure. Without wrong to them, crossarms might be left to rot; wires highly charged with electricity might sweep them from their stand and bury them in the adjacent waters. In climbing on the board, they became trespassers and outlaws. The conclusion is defended with much subtlety of reasoning, with much insistence upon its inevitableness as a merely logical deduction. A majority of the court are unable to accept it as the conclusion of the law.

We assume, without deciding, that the springboard was a fixture, a permanent improvement of the defendant's right of way. Much might be said in favor of another view. We do not press the inquiry for we are persuaded that the rights of bathers do not depend upon these nice distinctions. Liability would not be doubtful, we are told, had the boy been diving from a pole, if the pole had been vertical. The diver in such a situation would have been separated from the defendant's freehold. Liability, it is said, has been escaped because the pole was horizontal. The plank when projected lengthwise was an extension of the soil. We are to concentrate our gaze on the private ownership of the board. We are to ignore the public ownership of the circumambient spaces of water and of air. Jumping from a boat or a barrel, the boy would have been a bather in the river. Jumping from the end of the springboard, he was no longer, it is said, a bather, but a trespasser on a right of way.

Rights and duties in systems of living law are not built upon such quicksands.

Bathers in the Harlem River on the day of this disaster were in the enjoyment of a public highway, entitled to reasonable protection against destruction by the defendant's wires. They did not cease to be bathers entitled to the same protection while they were diving from encroaching objects or engaging in the sports that are common among swimmers. Such acts were not equivalent to an abandonment of the highway, a departure from its proper uses, a withdrawal from the waters, and an entry upon land. A plane of private right had been interposed between the river and the air, but public ownership was unchanged in the space below it and above. The defendant does not deny that it would have owed a duty to this boy if he had been leaning against the springboard with his feet upon the ground. He is said to have forfeited protection as he put his feet upon the plank. Presumably the same result would follow if the plank had been a few inches above the surface of the water instead of a few feet. Duties are thus supposed to arise and to be extinguished in alternate zones or strata. Two boys walking in the country or swimming in a river stop to rest for a moment along the side of the road or the margin of the stream. One of them throws himself beneath the overhanging branches of a tree. The other perches himself on a bough a foot or so above the ground. Both are killed by falling wires. The defendant would have us say that there is a remedy for the representatives of one and none for the representatives of the other. We may be permitted to distrust the logic that leads to such conclusions.

The truth is that every act of Hynes from his first plunge into the river until the moment of his death was in the enjoyment of the public waters, and under cover of the protection which his presence in those waters gave him. The use of the springboard was not an abandonment of his rights as bather. It was a mere by-play, an incident, subordinate and ancillary to the execution of his primary purpose, the enjoyment of the highway. The by-play, the incident, was not the cause of the disaster. Hynes would have gone to his death if he had been below the springboard or beside it. The wires were not stayed by the presence of the plank. They followed the boy in his fall, and overwhelmed him in the waters.

. . . We think there was no moment when he was beyond the pale of the defendant's duty—the duty of care and vigilance in the storage of destructive forces.

This case is a striking instance of the dangers of "a jurisprudence of conceptions" (Pound, Mechanical Jurisprudence, 8 Columbia Law Review, 605, 608, 610), the extension of a maxim or a definition with relentless disregard of consequences to "a dryly logical extreme." The approximate and relative become the definite and absolute. Landowners are not bound to regulate their conduct in contemplation of the presence of trespassers intruding upon private structures. Landowners are bound to regulate their conduct in contemplation of the presence of travelers upon the adjacent public ways. There are times when there is little trouble in marking off the field of exemption and immunity from that of liability and duty. Here structures and ways are so united and commingled, superimposed upon each other, that the fields are brought together. In such circumstances, there is little help in pursuing general maxims to ultimate conclusions. They have been framed alio intuitu. They must be reformulated and readapted to meet exceptional conditions. Rules appropriate to spheres which are conceived of as separate and distinct cannot both be enforced when the spheres become concentric. There must then be readjustment or collision. In one sense, and that a highly technical and artificial one, the diver at the end of the springboard is an intruder on the adjoining lands. In another sense, and one that realists will accept more readily, he is still on public waters in the exercise of public rights. The law must say whether it will subject him to the rule of the one field or of the other, of this sphere or of that. We think that considerations of analogy, of convenience, of policy, and of justice, exclude him from the field of the defendant's immunity and exemption, and place him in the field of liability and duty. . . . [Action allowed]

Harvey Hynes is instantly personalized: a "lad of 16," he and his "companions" as well as other "boys of the neighborhood used to dive" from defendant's board into the "navigable stream" below. The *Hynes* narrative projects Cardozo's reader into the familiar world of innocent boyish fun; the imperfect tense with reference to the neighborhood boys reminds us that we all "used to" act this way, and the pluperfect—for "more than five years swimmers had used it as a diving board without protest or obstruction"—continues the stylistic implication that only the defendant railroad's behavior has interfered with a more idyllic past to which, if we do not find the railroad culpable, we may never again return.

"On this day," continues Cardozo, drawing our imaginations not only to a specific human being, but now also to a specific moment in history. The judge reminds us that one of Harvey Hynes' companions has just plunged safely from the diving board. The scene is readied for the fatal moment: "Hynes followed to the front of the springboard, and stood poised for his dive." We have before us not only a lawsuit, a dry series of issues, but a living lad, about to be killed by electrical wires falling from the defendant's pole.

Twenty-five lines of vivid factual narrative now give way to Cardozo's equally creative description of the second implied enemy of Harvey Hynes: "the courts" below. As much as Harvey gains tangibility in the opinion, "the courts" and the law that they have used to deny liability here become depersonalized. The pronoun "they" is superimposed on these opponents of Harvey Hynes: "They have thought it immaterial"; indeed, "they have said" that legal technicalities override human realities. Furthermore, "they" have said this to "us"—the opinion's author and its reader have become allies. "But to bathers diving from the springboard, there was no duty, we are told"; "we are to ignore the public ownership of the water and of air," They use "much subtlety of reasoning" and logic and find against Hynes; we see the larger picture, and the railroad must pay.

Cardozo's opening gambits in *Hynes* are not aberrational. They are but exceptional examples of what all appellate judges do: frame the facts and legal arguments in a manner supportive of the court's view. Rhetoric and style march along with legalisms. Precedents contra are denigrated, through style: form and language will assist the correct result not only to emerge but also to gain authority.

Hynes concludes with a series of visual images in harmony with the legal point being made. This was ever Cardozo's technique. Thus, starting in the middle of the opinion, the stylist matches metaphor to law in explaining why "the truth is" that this difficult case must go for the plaintiff:

"Rights and duties in systems of living law are not built upon such quicksands."

These lines, a paragraph unto themselves, cast our imaginations into a spatial sphere evocative of the boy's last moments on earth. The railroad's arguments, based on the "quicksands" of ancient property law concepts, are equated with the sad end of Hynes's life on the sands adjacent to the Harlem River. There begins a congruous stream of imagery, continuous until the end of the opinion, where, in its moving climax, the poet-judge seals his argument:

> Rules appropriate to spheres which are conceived of as separate and distinct cannot both be enforced when the spheres become concentric. There must then be readjustment or collision. . . . We think that considerations of analogy, of convenience, of policy, and of justice, exclude him from the field of the defendant's immunity and exemption, and place him in the field of liability and duty.

Just as the electric wires collided with Harvey Hynes, sending him into the spiral of his death, so the "spheres" of law supporting the railroad are sent to their demise by that simple, realistic justice with which they collide in this particular case. Harvey Hynes, excluded forever from "the field" of mature human development, at least can be posthumously situated by the poet-judge "in the field of [the defendant's] liability and duty." Justice and "the lad of 16" prevail, equally through style as through legal, indeed jurisprudential, logic.

Along with these examples of law as literature may be mentioned a work like Manzoni's *Storia della colonna infame*, which may claim as well the corollary distinction of being literature as law. The author of *I promessi sposi* accumulated reams of historical material about seventeenth-century Milan under Spanish rule that centered on criminal law and jurisprudence in the cases involving the *untori* ("smearers" falsely accused of spreading the 1630 plague). In a famous case, two commoners, a health commissioner (Guglielmo Piazza) and a barber (Giacomo Mora), were arrested, tortured, and executed brutally in the panicked city. Through much documentary evidence, Manzoni reconstructed the events and reversed the belief that the fault lay with the jurisprudence of the day; he laid it on the capricious and arrogant judges who throughout the inquiry felt the need to calm the volatile public and pin the blame for the urban ills on someone. The expendable commoners, themselves panicked and ready to confess and to accuse anybody rather than undergo further physical agony, played into their hands. Biased thinking, logical improprieties, legal negligence — nothing escapes Manzoni's careful eye. In presenting the case, the novelist uses dialogue (extracts from the original transcript); furthermore, since he does not proceed chronologically, he uses the flashback technique as a conveniently dramatic device. Characterization — not unlike Frankfurter's of Sacco and Vanzetti —

emerges as one of the main assets of the exposition, and psychological analysis (the psychopathology of torture) as one of the salient, propelling forces of the "quasi novel." The combination of extraordinary judicial, human, and artistic qualities makes this legal literature or literary jurisprudence a fascinating example of how law and literature may finally merge, each employing the virtues of the other to make a compelling statement of reality for the benefit of society.

The area of Law and Literature (not only in modern generic modes), then, can evoke a panoply of interpretive investigations, shape a vast panorama of study, all the more fertile because it remains relatively unexplored. Among literary critics, law in literature has enjoyed a little more recognition than its counterpart, perhaps because of the immediate necessity, when heeded, to deal with law within a given work. Yet the field remains esoteric to many, not because it is inaccessible but because it seems—however erroneously—dispensable. Law as literature, however, has been grossly neglected in literary consciousness. And it is in this area, we feel, that the study of literature may gain both insight and vitality.

Bibliography

Abraham, Kenneth S. "Statutory Interpretation and Literary Theory: Some Common Concerns of an Unlikely Pair." *Rutgers Law Review*, 32 (1979), 676–94.

Barricelli, Jean-Pierre. "Jurisprudence in the XVIIth Century from Manzoni's Viewpoint." *University of Hartford Studies in Literature*, 9 (1977), 141–63.

Bloch, R. Howard. *Medieval French Literature and Law.* Berkeley: Univ. of California Press, 1977.

Carbonneau, Thomas. "Balzacian Legality." *Rutgers Law Review*, 32 (1979), 719–26.

Cardozo, Benjamin N. "Law and Literature." In *Selected Writings of Benjamin Nathan Cardozo.* Ed. Margaret E. Hall. New York: Bender, 1947.

Christie, George C. "Vagueness and Legal Language." *Minnesota Law Review*, 48 (1964), 885–911.

Couch, Harvey. "Law and Literature: A Comment." *Vanderbilt Law Review*, 17 (1964), 911–16.

Cowan, Thomas. "The Law at Finnegan's Wake." *Rutgers Law Review*, 29 (1976), 259–77.

Danzig, Richard, and Richard Weisberg. "Reading List on Law and Literature." *Humanities*, 7, No. 3 (1977), 6–7.

Davenport, William H. "Law and Literature Once Again." *Law and Library Journal*, 50 (1957), 396–403.

Davis, David B. *Homicide in American Fiction, 1798–1860.* Ithaca, N.Y.: Cornell Univ. Press, 1957.

Frese, Jerry. "Swift's Houyhnhnms and Utopian Law." *University of Hartford Studies in Literature*, 9 (1977), 187–95.

Holdsworth, William S. *Charles Dickens as a Legal Historian.* New Haven: Yale Univ. Press, 1928.

Ives, C. B. "Billy Budd and the Articles of War." *American Literature*, 24 (1962), 31–39.

Jacobson, Richard. "Law, Ritual, Absence: Towards a Semiology of Law." *University of Hartford Studies in Literature*, 9 (1977), 164–74.

Koffler, Judith S. "The Platonic Assimilation of Law to Literature." *American Legal Studies Association Forum*, 3 (1978), 5–11.

Llewellyn, Karl. "On the Good, the True, the Beautiful in Law." *University of Chicago Law Review*, 9 (1942), 224–56.

London, Ephraim, ed. *The World of Law*. 2 vols. New York: Simon, 1960. Vol. I: *The Law in Literature*; Vol. II: *The Law as Literature*.

Mellinkoff, David. *The Language of the Law*. Boston: Little, 1963.

Michaels, Walter. "Against Formalism: The Autonomous Text in Legal and Literary Interpretation." *Poetics Today*, 1 (1979), 23–24.

Phillips, Owen Hood. *Shakespeare and the Lawyers*. London: Methuen, 1972.

Reinhard, J. R. "Setting Adrift in Medieval Law and Literature." *PMLA*, 56 (1941), 22–68.

Smith, J. Allen. "The Coming Renaissance in Law and Literature." *Maryland Law Forum*, 7 (1977), 84–92.

Suretsky, Harold. "Search for a Theory: An Annotated Bibliography of Writings on the Relation of Law to Literature and the Humanities." *Rutgers Law Review*, 32 (1979), 727–40.

Sussman, Henry. "The Court as Text: Inversion, Supplanting, and Derangement in Kafka's *Der Prozess*." *PMLA*, 92 (1977), 41–55.

Weisberg, Richard. "Comparative Law in Comparative Literature: The Figure of the 'Examining Magistrate' in Dostoevski and Camus." *Rutgers Law Review,* 29 (1976), 237–58. Rpt. Cornell Soviet Studies Reprints, No. 33. Ithaca, N.Y.: Cornell Univ. Press, 1976.

———. "How Judges Speak: Some Lessons on Adjudication in *Billy Budd, Sailor*, with an Application to Justice Rehnquist." *New York University Law Review*, 57 (1982), 1–69.

———. "Law, Literature, and Cardozo's Judicial Poetics." *Cardozo Law Review*, 1 (1979), 283–342.

———, and Karen Kretschman. "Wigmore's 'Legal Novels' Expanded: A Collaborative Effort." *Maryland Law Forum*, 7 (1977), 94–103.

White, James B. *The Legal Imagination: Studies in the Nature of Legal Thought and Expression*. Boston: Little, 1973.

Younger, Irving. "On Judicial Opinions Considered as One of the Fine Arts." *University of Colorado Law Review*, 51 (1980), 341–52.

9

Literature and Science

GEORGE SLUSSER AND GEORGE GUFFEY

The word "science" derives from the Latin *scientia* 'knowledge.' Today, when using the word, we normally have one of two etymologically relevant references in mind: first, to an activity that has as its goal the acquisition of knowledge; second, to the large body of knowledge generated by that activity. On the one hand we have, then, a process for acquiring—through rigorous observation and the formulation and testing of hypotheses—knowledge about human beings and nature, knowledge that is most efficiently expressed in the form of scientific "laws" (concepts). On the other hand, we have the great body of knowledge amassed through the application of scientific method and preserved in the literature of science. Much of this body of written materials is familiar to us all. In fact, most of what we today consider real knowledge is this kind of specially derived knowledge.

Though highly respected, science is, of course, not the only human activity widely admired and supported. Art is another such activity. Like "science," the term "art" is difficult to define adequately. For the purposes of this essay, D. W. Gotshalk's definition seems most productive: "art is the skillful use of instruments and materials to produce objects of value" (*Art and the Social Order*, p. 29). Using brush, pigment, and canvas, an artist can produce a painting of a wild, unpopulated landscape; using hammer, saw, wood, nail, and glass, an artisan can fashion a shelter for human beings. In both examples, instruments and materials have been skillfully used to produce objects of value, but the resulting objects are different in kind. The painting, if well executed, is valuable mainly for its intrinsic perceptual appeal. Such objects are said to have "fineness of art": "fine art is the production by man of objects intrinsically interesting to perceive" (Gotshalk, p. 29).

It is readily apparent, then, that objects of fine art differ radically from the products of science. The business of science is the construction of conceptual systems (knowledge structures). The business of fine art is the construction of perceptual systems (objects interesting to perceive). Quantum mechanics and symphonic music are, therefore, essentially poles apart;

for the value of the former arises chiefly from its central concern with concepts, the value of the latter principally from its emphasis on percepts. This distinction can perhaps be best imagined as a continuum with the purely conceptual at one terminus, the purely perceptual at the other. Obviously few literary constructs are as purely conceptual as quantum mechanics or as purely perceptual as symphonic music. Most of the works to be examined in this essay will fall nearer the middle of our imaginary continuum.

But what of the second example given above—that of shelters produced by artisans? In such cases, the central concern is with their effectiveness as shelters, not with their potential for perceptual interest. This is not to suggest that constructs like these must always be without perceptual appeal, but only to underline their essentially practical, instrumental nature. Objects like shelters, constructed not primarily for intrinsic perception but for instrumental functions, are best thought of as examples of "instrumental art."

Before turning to the main subject of this essay, literature and science, we must address one additional terminological problem—the ambiguous nature of the word "literature." In almost all dictionaries, something like the following definition of the word will surely be found: "Writings considered as having permanent value, excellence of form, . . ." With this meaning in mind, people frequently dismiss whole genres or subgenres of writing with statements like "That's not *literature*!" Curiously enough, such conflations of evaluative and classificatory content are infrequently met with outside the realm of the arts and art criticism. One would be greatly surprised to hear a zoologist say of a particularly awkward subspecies of *Felis catus*, "That's not a *cat*!" A second, less loaded definition of "literature" is also found in most dictionaries: "The total of preserved writings belonging to a given language or people." Thus, using terminology more consonant with that we employed earlier to define "art," "fine art," and "instrumental art," we might more economically and productively define "literature" as "verbal art."

This approach to the subject allows us a clearer vision of the great range of written materials available to us than would an approach heavily dependent upon evaluative as well as definitional parameters. More specifically, it allows us, after only a few moments of consideration, to see that some literary specimens are relatively pure examples of either instrumental art or fine art and that other specimens are of a more mixed nature.

Examples of each of these kinds of writing are easily adduced, and a specimen of instrumental literary art devoted to the elaboration of a scientific concept would appear an appropriate choice for beginning a series of illustrative examples. The following passage is taken from W. C. Krumbein and L. L. Sloss's textbook *Stratigraphy and Sedimentation* (San Francisco: Freeman, 1953, pp. 90–91):

One of the most important mass properties of a sediment is its permeability, which controls the relative ease of flow of fluids through the rock pores. Unlike porosity, permeability is strongly influenced by particle size. Coarse gravel has large openings among the pebbles, affording easy passage for fluids. As the particles become smaller, the pores also become smaller, and a greater force or a greater length of time is required to drive through a unit volume of fluid.

At the heart of this passage is the concept of permeability. Ignoring the explanatory phrases, one might reduce it to the following statement: "In sediments, permeability is proportional to the size of the pebbles constituting the sediments." Almost entirely without materials conducive to perceptual interest (and entirely devoted to the statement of a scientific concept), this is perhaps as pure an example of instrumental literary art as can be found.

Also focusing on a scientific subject, our next example is less purely instrumental. From George Gamow's well-known popularization *The Creation of the Universe* (New York: New American Library, 1957, p. 23), it is enlivened (given perceptual interest) by an extended birth metaphor:

At that early epoch, the moon must have hung motionless above the same point of the earth's surface, the point at which it was *born* by being *drawn out from the mother body* by the tidal forces of the sun. We may appropriately call this early state of our satellite a Hawaiian Moon, since in all likelihood its *birthplace* was the middle of the Pacific Ocean. In fact, there is evidence to support the assumption that the Pacific Basin is nothing but *a giant scar in the* granite *skin of Mother Earth*, a constant reminder of the *birth of her first and only daughter*.

(italics ours)

Powerfully descriptive and engagingly personal, our third passage, from a sonnet by Shakespeare, depends on numerous poetic devices for its perceptual appeal. Essentially without conceptual or scientific content, these lines have for hundreds of years moved millions of readers with their rhythms, sound effects, and figurative language:

That time of year thou mayst in me behold
When yellow leaves, or none, or few, do hang
Upon those boughs which shake against the cold,
Bare ruined choirs, where late the sweet birds sang.

The distinction we have been making thus far in this essay between literature that focuses primarily on concepts and literature that focuses primarily on percepts was first given definitive shape by Thomas De Quincey. In his essay "The Literature of Knowledge and the Literature of Power" (1848), he wrote:

In the great social organ which, collectively, we call literature, there may be distinguished two separate offices that may blend and often *do* so, but capable, severally, of a severe insulation, and naturally fitted for reciprocal repulsion. There is, first, the literature of *knowledge*; and, secondly, the literature of *power*. The function of the first is—to *teach*; the function of the second is—to *move*: the first is a rudder; the second, an oar or a sail. The first speaks to the *mere* discursive understanding; the second speaks ultimately, it may happen, to the higher understanding or reason, but always *through* affections of pleasure and sympathy.

De Quincey is here essentially circumscribing what are two distinct modes of discourse—the conceptual, whose primary goal is the conveyance of truth, and the perceptual, which aims principally at moving the feelings through powerful sensual appeal. What is more, he poses a crucial problem. For though these modes "may blend," they are nevertheless capable of "a severe insulation," are even perhaps at times natural contraries that tend to repel each other.

Beyond facile distinctions (such as that of fiction from fact) and beyond the Horatian dictum that poetry both teach and delight, there is, then, the deeper question of the compatibility of these modes. This is a basic problem which, in the case of prose, is perhaps best examined on the microtextual level—that of paragraph, speech, or scene. Our essay proper begins by examining various microtexts, within texts often carelessly designated as "literary" or "scientific," in hopes of characterizing the possible mixtures and repulsions of these modes as well as of defining the limits of their mutual permeability. This section, "Science and Literature," is followed by one that focuses on a related topic, "Science in Literature." Here we examine the impact of scientific method and world view on literary systems, stressing the increasing power of scientific speculation from the Renaissance onward to alter and reorganize the world of imaginative literature. On the one hand, in that world, we are confronted with the erosion of the privileged human center by the expansion of scientific knowledge; on the other, we witness the gradual development of fictional strategies to restore human values to what has increasingly become an indifferent material universe. This section seeks to measure the impact of scientific thought on three distinct aspects of imaginative literature: (1) the idea of a protagonist (the scientist as hero); (2) the world views of fiction (the thematics of science); (3) literary form itself.

I. Science and Literature

The potential for the "reciprocal repulsion" of the literature of knowledge and the literature of power is apparently not a modern one. In this regard, Plato's attitude toward his pre-Socratic predecessors—however tacit—is instructive. Not only does he (following Socrates) openly redirect his focus from the study of the nature of things to dialectic—the relation of human beings to things—but he appears in his own writing to discriminate between the two modes of discourse associated with these impulses. In Plato's work, the pre-Socratic disquisition, "thoughts" on the nature of the physical world, gives way to modes more fundamentally perceptual in nature: allegory and the mimetic form of dialogue. Interestingly, where the two modes of discourse coexist, as in the *Timaeus*, they tend to be incompatible. Despite Plato's attempt to frame it in dialogue, despite the fact that it is preceded by the overarching legend of Atlantis and richly overlaid with metaphor and allegory, Timaeus' long exposition of cosmic order—he is dubbed by his companions "the best astronomer among us"—usurps the perceptual apparatus and with its huge unàssimilable mass of concepts reduces all else to silence. The promised interrelation of modes is simply aborted.

To Cecil Schneer (*The Search for Order* [New York: Harper, 1960], p. 374), science differs from the arts mainly because it is "self-corrective." In order to be so within the framework of language, science has sought to eschew perceptual qualities in favor of a transparent, informational medium that offers as little resistence as possible to this endlessly developing cognitive content. Transposed to the context of human interaction and intercourse, however, this language of fact immediately appears digressive, intractable. In this web of textual relations it forms unwieldy masses of discourse that in turn isolate their utterers, render them socially uncouth, and, by extension, morally suspect. If the stigma against this kind of specialized opacity in imaginative literature has classical roots (see, for example, Horace's *Ars Poetica*), it continues to haunt this scientific voice down to modern times.

Perhaps our distinction finds its basic expression in Socrates' comparison of "dead" and "living" discourse in Plato's *Phaedrus*. Defined here are two distinct verbal cognitive modes, each related to the different media of writing and dialogue: the disquisitive and the dialectical. The first is "parentless," isolated both from maker and audience. The second is necessarily sensitive to the souls of others and the means of moving them. The communication of knowledge depends then not on sterile abstraction but on words that blend and integrate concepts into the living flow of human exchange. To be truly self-corrective, Plato is saying, scientific discourse must accept the mediation of qualities we call perceptual. In the *Phaedrus*, Socrates, discussing Pericles' use of the scientific speculations of Anaxagoras, makes it clear that conceptual discourse should function in both a complementary and clearly subordinate relation to the "art of rhetoric." If such discourse is not so placed, the result, in whatever verbal form imitating human thought in action, will be monstrosity.

Plato is also the source of a corollary to this vision of unmediated discourse: the portrait of the scientist as dreamer, the man with his head in the clouds. In his *Theaetetus*, he tells of Thales of Miletus, who "fell into a well as he was looking up at the stars." In mutating fashion a second corollary—that of the scientist as charlatan—has its locus classicus in Aristophanes' *The Clouds*, in which Socrates, suspended in a basket between heaven and earth, becomes the icon for all such scientific isolation. But if this Socrates is a sophist who eventually falls to earth, his medieval analogue, Nicholas in Chaucer's Miller's Tale (c. 1386), though warned of Thales' fate, turns the tables, puts the gullible carpenter in the basket, and in the end ultimately brings about his ignoble fall. In Ben Jonson's *Alchemist* (1610), a play that has as one of its themes the sterile clash of dead modes of discourse, Subtle employs unmediated jargon in his attempts to confuse and cozen the puritans: "*Subtle*: Can you sublime, and dulcify? Calcine? / Know you the *sapor pontic*? *Sapor styptic*? / Or, what is homogene, or heterogene? / *Ananias*: I understand no heathen language, truly." But in the wake of Face's much subtler rhetoric of social compromise, even this crafty use of technical discourse proves ultimately unviable. Increasingly, in the expanding social context of the novel, it is silenced altogether. Thus, in Honoré de Balzac's *La Recherche de l'Absolu* (1834), Balthasar Claës's long disquisitions on chemical theory serve only to open a chasm between the scientist and society. Here, Balthasar's impenetrable discourse (and the wasting force of the pure research it stands for) is methodically suppressed by the family whose material contours it threatens to engulf. In this utilitarian epilogue to Plato's protest against "dead discourse," we witness the ritual excision of the language of unmediated concept from both the fabric of society and prose fiction itself.

Yet not all examples of the interaction of this mode of discourse with the perceptual qualities of imaginative literature have necessarily terminated in such a grim rebuff. An important turn in literary attitudes toward conceptual discourse occurs in Sir Philip Sidney's *Defense of Poesie* (1595). Crucial here is Sidney's distinction between nature, the domain of the Fall, and man, who, formed in the likeness of his maker, is set "beyond and over all the works of that second nature." If most poesy, as Plato held, is mimetic, Sidney goes on to distinguish "several sorts," chief among which he emphasizes "natural" or "astronomical" kinds of imitation (such as those of Lucretius and Pontanus), in which language is "wrapped within the fold of the proposed subject," and a higher, poetical kind that transcends these natural, hence fallen, limits and imitates "what may be and should be." On the eve, then, of the awakening of the Baconian revolution, with its demand for tentative, correctible models and a descriptive language to match, Sidney's second category holds out a hope that later writers on scientific matters, like Sir Thomas Browne and Blaise Pascal, will in different ways realize. For by confronting physical fact (the recorded flux of natural phenomena) with poetic qualities and values, scientists might in their writing now hope to rescue their words from obsolescence and lift scientific observation to a state of literary permanence. A phrase of Sidney's fits this new, cognitively centered poesy exactly: "the sweet food of sweetly uttered knowledge."

Yet Sidney's phrase, if it characterizes the result, makes the task, for a writer like Browne, seem much too easy. If Lucretius may be said to have set "scientific" ideas to meter, Browne's task is of a different order and is executed on a higher level of tension between conceptual and perceptual elements. Browne's problem is less one of rhetorical embellishment than of existential dilemma. For why should this doctor, in his writings, want to look beyond antiquity to an eternity his scientific observations rendered doubtful at every turn? And why did he strive so hard to convert the factual mode into an oratorical vehicle that would help him transcend this same doomed world of fact? Not only did Browne follow what, for his age, were already becoming two necessary but irreconcilable vocations — man of science and man of God, he also spoke two languages, languages distinct yet so intertwined in his mind that he could hardly talk of spirit without mixing clinical detail: "There shall be no gray hairs in Heaven." For Browne, style is not just a secular strategy for rescuing a clutter of relics and theories from oblivion. Nor does it have a purely religious function, drawing spirit out of clay. Style is rather the instrument that enables him to exploit the tension between these two modes of discourse. Indeed, Browne's eloquence is a striving to "suck Divinity from the flowers of Nature," organizing this seemingly boundless discourse of the inquiring scientific mind and ultimately extracting from catalogs of fact periods of elevated prose.

This pursuit of "Reason to an O Altitudo!" is clearly visible in the structure of Browne's *Urn-Burial* (1658). The first four chapters uncover a welter of archaeological and scientific evidence against our hopes for immortality. With the fifth, however, the flickerings of poetry that had earlier dimly lit this maze are suddenly fanned to sustained eloquence. With the objective mode now clearly equated with transience and death and triumphant poetic rhythms with life, a pattern of "resurrection" is reiterated in cadence after cadence: "*Pyramids, Arches, Obelisks*, were but the irregularities of vainglory. . . . But the most magnanimous resolution rests in the Christian Religion." Transient things are caught up in strong, regular rhythms, carried and perhaps preserved by the music of poetry. Another example of this poetical transmutation of the language of science occurs in the "loadstone" chapter of his *Pseudodoxia Epidemica* (1646). Browne begins by grouping received opinions about this stone under the headings "natural," "historical," "medical," "magical." Such categories do little more than loosely collect a jumble of facts, experiments, opinions. We are exhausted by the endless possibilities of classification ("Other discourses there might be made of the Loadstone: as Moral, Mystical, Theological... but these fall under no Rule, and are as boundless as men's inventions") and yearn for sudden release. As if in response to our yearnings, in the final lines comes a leap — the creation of poetic order, miraculously wrested, from an impure mixture of pun and pomposity, scientific jargon and visions of God:

> And though honest minds do glorifie God hereby; yet do they most
> powerfully magnifie him, and are to be looked on with another eye,
> who demonstratively set forth its Magnalities; who not from postu-

lated or precarious inferences, entreat a courteous assent; but from experiments and undeniable effects, enforce the wonder of its Maker.

In regard to interpenetrating modes of discourse, it is interesting to compare Browne with his near-contemporary Pascal. Indeed, if one can dismiss Browne as an eccentric amateur scientist, not so Pascal, a brilliant mathematician and experimental physicist still cited in textbooks today. In Pascal's best writing, however, not only is there a similar refusal to choose between distinct forms of expression, there is also a cultivation and exploitation of the dynamic tension between them. But here tension between the language of physics and what Pascal calls "the language of the heart" is much more taut and agonizing. This tension, in a sense the subject of *Les Pensées* (assembled 1657-58) — where the title's promise of the aphorism, a form supremely suited to conceptual statement, is countered by flashes of some of the most poetical prose in French — eloquently redefines the individual's place in the universe. Pascal is capable of measuring the human condition in the most succinct physical terms: "Our soul is cast into the body, where it finds number, time, dimensions. It reasons on these and calls them nature, necessity, and can believe nothing else." This is essentially the Cartesian condition, but it is apprehended here less as an abstract duality of matter and spirit than as a dreadful *contrariété*. Typically, Pascal does not so much abandon the cogito as seek to redefine it within a paradoxical perspective of continual *renversement* of opposites. If "thought" is man's misery, it is also his grandeur: "All our dignity consists then in thought. By it we must elevate ourselves, and not by space and time which we cannot fill." This quandary leads him to posit two antithetical yet interacting forms of thought — what Pascal calls "esprit de géometrie" and "esprit de finesse." Throughout the *Pensées* this latter form functions most effectively by confronting the language of rational science with that of feeling, concept with percept. Thus Cartesian method encounters the image of man as a "thinking reed." The "thought" that guarantees human existence is a very different process from Cartesian reason, one of engagement rather than detachment. In the face of physical immensity and indifference, the individual's comprehension of existence becomes inseparable from the perception (however terrifying) of physical participation in this realm of matter: "A vapor . . . suffices to kill him. But, if the universe were to crush him, man would still be more noble . . . because he knows that he dies and the advantage the universe has over him; the universe knows nothing of this." Man's advantage then remains cognitional — he is because he thinks and matter does not — but cognition is all the richer because it is tragically qualified by a sense of its own fragility. In such passages, Pascal's rhetorical finesse subjects the language of logical demonstration to an ultimate *renversement*: the physical universe it would describe is not objectivized as a thing known, distanced from the individual, so much as given its raison d'être only by being drawn into the human verbal framework, where cognition is one with aspiration and fear: "The eternal silence of these infinite spaces frightens me."

Pascal and Browne lived in an age when both modes of discourse were open to a single individual. But barely. In the 1660s Bishop Thomas Sprat laid down rules of style for the Royal Society, admonishing scientists to renounce "all luxury and redundance of speech," to write with "mathematical plainness." What follows is an age of sectarian professionalism, of growing specialization in the sciences, specialization that will lead to the creation of variant "jargons." Years later, certain of the Romantics began openly to resist the incursions of the abstract sciences. In an oft-quoted passage in "Lamia" (1819), John Keats saw "cold philosophy"—here Newtonian physics—as not only conquering "all mysteries by rule and line" but also setting in place of the images of poetry a string of facts, measurements, and concepts: "the dull catalogue of common things." This lamentation against the depoetizing power of scientific language, spurred on perhaps by an accelerating abstraction of speculation coupled with an increasing impact of technology on the natural environment, became ubiquitous during the Victorian and post-Victorian eras, and among aesthetes and primitivists alike: John Ruskin, Matthew Arnold, D. H. Lawrence. A late and extreme expression of this Romantic reaction to the "cold equations" of science is to be found in Ray Bradbury's novel *Fahrenheit 451* (1953). This work obsessively juxtaposes the quantified sterilities of science with celebrations of nearly naked perceptual experience: "A glass of milk, an apple, a pear."

William Wordsworth, however, offers in his Preface to the second edition of *Lyrical Ballads* (1802), an alternative possibility for the poet faced with the inexorable advance of modern science:

> Poetry is the first and last of all knowledge—it is as immortal as the heart of man. If the labors of Men of science should ever create any material revolution, direct or indirect, in our condition, and in the impressions which we habitually receive, the Poet will sleep then no more than at present; he will be ready to follow the steps of the Man of science, not only in those general indirect effects, but he will be at his side, carrying sensation into the midst of the objects of science itself. The remotest discoveries of the Chemist, the Botanist, or Mineralogist, will be as proper objects of the Poet's art as any upon which it can be employed. . . . If the time should ever come when what is now called science . . . shall be ready to put on, as it were, a form of flesh and blood, the Poet will lend his divine spirit to aid the transfiguration, and will welcome the Being thus produced, as a dear and genuine inmate of the household of man.

Unwilling to concede the poets' supremacy, Wordsworth sees them carrying sensation to the objects of science, thus restoring the perceptual qualities of fine art—immortal beauty over material utility—to the discourse of science.

This process had, however, begun long before Wordsworth's day. An example is Johann Winckelmann's palimpsestic vision in his famous description of the Apollo Belvedere statue. The initial draft — a collection of precisely archaeological observations reported in a dry, factual style — was overlaid in successive revisions with passages of classical poetry, infused with archaisms, echoes of Greek hymns, of Luther's Bible. The result was the sonorous prose poem published in the *Geschichte der Kunst des Alterthums* (1764). To William Blake, this kind of transformation of scientific language into poetry seemed a far easier undertaking: "The Atoms of Democritus / And Newton's Particles of light / Are sands upon the Red sea shore, / Where Israel's tents do shine so bright." Indeed, Wordsworth's program was pronounced simultaneously in Germany, where Novalis, in a letter of 24 February 1798, issued the following challenge: "The sciences must all be poetized." And in their "Fragmente" — aphoristic "thoughts" now tossed off as playfully imperfect — Novalis and Friedrich Schlegel delighted in mixing what they called "chemically" explosive compounds, blending Old German vocables and the Latinate terminology of the new sciences, setting French phrases (at that time the sign of culture and art) jarringly against technical jargon from the "remotest" scientific disciplines.

In spite of their fascination with the concepts and language of the sciences, these men remain poets, exploiting scientific terms for their poetic charge. Ultimately, for writers during this period of unprecedented speculative expansion, scientific discoveries fail to become the proper objects of poetry. In successive drafts of Winckelmann's *Beschreibung*, for example, all trace of the earlier archaeological rigor is finally filtered out, not so much displaced as replaced by a consecrated Homeric form. Finally, to peruse Johann Wolfgang von Goethe's scientific writings — fourteen volumes in the Weimar Edition and the fruit of a lifelong endeavor — is to measure the gulf that remains between one mode of discourse and the other, and by implication between the scientific and poetic methods and world views that produce them. Goethe's scientific *Beschreibungen* are the driest prose, often no more than barren classifications and nomenclatures. Yet in their midst we suddenly come across a poem like "Metamorphose der Tiere" and are transported from morphology to classical gods and alexandrines. Such seemingly irreconcilable oppositions haunt the deepest levels of this text, where Bacon's desire to place nature on the empirical rack coexists with the assertion of the a priori unity of all natural phenomena — the *Urform*, or "original form."

Needless to say, during the nineteenth century, purely scientific writing was going its own way and flourishing. We may learn more, then, about Wordsworth's "breath and finer spirit of all knowledge" by ascertaining, from the other side, the degree to which the strategies of imaginative literature have penetrated scientific writing in this century. Two examples from the work of Charles Darwin will show the professional scientist drawing heavily on devices from the perceptual systems of imaginative literature to bolster his exposition of fact and concept. In *The Descent of Man* (1871), Darwin addressed the problem that many of his critics felt invalidated the central hypothesis of his *Origin of Species* (1859) — the enormous gap between the mental powers of human beings and those of the lower animals. In the later of these works, he is at pains to reinforce logical argument with anecdotes and examples — all observed and factual but, in their alternating humor and pathos, eminently "human." From passage to passage, there are often clever shifts of tone. We may have, for example, bemused personal observation: "In the Zoological Gardens I saw a baboon who always got into a furious rage when his keeper took out a letter or book and read it aloud to him; and his rage was so violent that, as I witnessed on one occasion, he bit his own leg till the blood flowed." But Darwin is also able, when necessary, to modulate to moving generalization: "Every one has heard of the dog suffering under vivisection, who licked the hand of the operator; this man, unless the operation was fully justified by an increase of our knowledge, or unless he had a heart of stone, must have felt remorse to the last hour of his life." The search for knowledge, then, like the expression of knowledge, is more complex than one might think, and one of Pascal's insights comes to mind: "The heart has its reasons, that reason does not know." Darwin's *Descent of Man* not only contributes greatly to the "literature of knowledge" but also contains numerous passages that are quintessentially "literature of power" as well.

II. Science in Literature

If the problems of science and literature — the repulsions and mixtures of two modes of discourse — have a long and complex history, those of science *in* literature are perhaps easier to circumscribe. As a hero in literature, the scientist or pseudoscientist is essentially a creation of the Renaissance. In Christopher Marlowe's seminal work *Doctor Faustus* (1604), we watch sin give way to the secular hubris of scientific curiosity. To the extent that diabolical mechanisms and pacts against God's order are replaced by human inquisitiveness and the lure of a purely material nature, the old didactic stage yields to one of new tragic possibility, and the medieval "trickster" to the flawed seeker after truth on a human scale. Marlowe's play, it might be argued, frees the protoscientist Faustus from the older medieval hegemony only to place him in a new one — that "brave new world" where the struggle is now between the individual and nature on one hand, the individual and society on the other, and where the "scientist" in the new role of literary hero must suddenly choose between these two. In *Faustus*, Mephistophilis stands on a stage that suggests the rigidly ordained geography of the morality play and yet is strangely vague about location. Not only is hell somewhere "under the heavens," but it now also appears coextensive with human existence in nature: "Hell hath no limits, nor is circumscribed / In one self place; but where we are is hell, / And where hell is, there must we ever be." In associating himself with the human condition ("we"), this devil in a sense becomes Faustus' double, and in doing so dissolves the metaphysical boundaries that formerly contained the hero's quest for knowledge. It is this secular option — the substitution of moral quandary for sin — that marks the turning point between the magician answerable to heaven and hell and the scientist terrifyingly alone, responsible only to the world and the self. Thus Faustus' fictional rival Cipriano in Calderón de la Barca's *El mágico prodigioso* (1637), though a much later figure, remains condemned to anachronism by the very title of his play, damned to challenge nature, only to discover the old and frustratingly absolute order of God.

The rise of the protoscientist to heroic stature, as experimenter and seeker after truth in nature, reveals the impact of the new humanist endeavors on Marlowe's generation. This ascension is striking if we measure it against the same figure's position in the medieval world view. If, for example, an actual early practitioner of experimental science, Albertus Magnus, finds his way into Dante's Circle of Lights (*Paradiso*, X), it is because he ultimately subordinated speculation to devotion and could turn his science to the exaltation of God's fixed order. Later in the same work, Thomas Aquinas sees Solomon's wisdom as the rejection of what we might call scientific curiosity for the exercise of right judgment. Thus Aquinas effectively confines knowledge to the legalistic interpretation of divinely ordained natural law and at the same time renders any human search for new laws or postulations purest folly. Indeed, if most of Dante's "scientists" are to be found in hell, they are invariably placed there for reasons other than those that lead to the fall of Faustus. Merely because they were pagans, Dante consigned some great Greek precursors — men like Heraclitus and Galen, whom his age could not read in the original — to limbo. Though Dante knew that Democritus "said the world was chance," his placing him indifferently in neutral space suggests the degree to which Dante's age not only overlooked but underestimated the potentially destructive force of protoscientific hypotheses on its world system. In fact it is the contemporary alchemists — in the eyes of modern science, much less subversive thinkers — who on the contrary are thrust deepest into hell. Significantly, these men are punished not for speculative boldness but for prideful imitation — they are poor "apes" of a nature that cannot be altered through human interaction but can merely be debased. In this sense Capocchio is branded a "betrayer of metals." What is more, in the last *bolge* of Circle VIII, the taxonomic link between the alchemists and the counterfeiters and imposters emphasizes the potentially antisocial force of their "scientific" doings. From Dante's Griffolino — a petty prankster and confidence man who comes into conflict with vested authority — a tradition of sorts begins. Running from the Renaissance to modern science fiction, from Robert Greene's Friar Bacon to filmdom's Dr. Frankenstein (who, insofar as he is linked in sequel after sequel to his own mis-

begotten monster, seems condemned to a special hell of his own), it stigma-
tizes scientists, strive though they may for heroic stature.

Marlowe inherits this same unsavory medieval figure but transforms
him. Indeed, his boldest leap—and this is not merely the product of different hands in a corrupt text—is to make Faustus at one and the same time a
trickster and an "overreacher" on the plane of speculative imagination. Because he is no longer simply an imitator, this thinker has become both master
and prisoner of nature, the scientist transcending the magician to postulate
a string of worlds better or worse than the one he inhabits, the magician in
turn reconjuring material limits that drag the scientist back to the tawdry
reality of earth. For if on one hand Faustus' triumphs are those of mental
agility over the spatially rigid order of the Middle Ages, his field of action
has at the same time shrunk to the totally secular one of physical quantity—
matter, energy, speed. Although Dante's alchemists never existed beyond
their fixed positions in hell, Faustus soars through the air, seeing old places
from new perspectives, and creates from resulting insights a radically new
vision that wrenches salvation and damnation from their polar frame by
converting them into spirits of the air. Yet what both energizes this new mobility of mind and sets terrible limits on its power is Faustus' confrontation
with time. It is significant that, in his race against the eleventh hour, this dis-
coverer of the fourth dimension ultimately turns not to science but to poetry.
Arrogating the powers of Sidney's poet to create ideal worlds beyond time,
Faustus in his evocation of Helen of Troy suspends the clock and transforms
himself into a conquerer of time: "I will be Paris, and for love of thee / Instead of Troy shall Wittenberg be sacked." But Wittenberg is small prey for
a thousand ships; and if, in this shrinking space, time returns to dispel Helen
and trap Faustus all the more cruelly, the beauty of poetic phrase has at least
momentarily suspended its course. Choosing a poet's solution to a physicist's dilemma, Faustus begins a line of development that eventually joins
artist and scientist in a common quest that links Icarian flight with the arti-
fices of Daedalus. For it is not only James Joyce's Stephen who seeks release
from space and time through heightened poetic vision but also Shevek, the
physicist hero of Ursula Le Guin's novel *The Dispossessed* (1974). Trapped
in the spatial and temporal antinomies of his world—on one hand the twin
planets with their seemingly irreconcilable social systems, on the other the
sequency-simultaneity paradox—Shevek achieves a theoretical breakthrough
in a moment of epiphany:

> He wandered around the room a little, touching things . . . for at this
> instance the difference between this planet and that one . . . was no
> more significant to him than the difference between two grains of sand
> on the shore of the sea. There were no more abysses, no more walls.
> There was no more exile. He had seen the foundations of the universe,
> and they were solid.

If Shevek acts here as distant legate of Faustus' revolt against natural time, he has completely reversed Faustus' approach; he has, in fact, exchanged defiance of the physical world for acceptance.

This heroic, speculative rebel is, however, not the only kind of scientist to descend from Marlowe. *Doctor Faustus*, in fact, raises the alchemist-prankster to such a degree of insistent activity—overachiever rather than overreacher—that it launches a second sort of scientist-hero into the literary mainstream—the technologist. If in his visionary boldness the speculative Faustus, though he defies the old divine order, still moves in a realm of metaphysical aspirations, his other side, the figure who engineers tricks, is operating in a natural and social context that during the Renaissance and after tends more and more toward the wholly secular. Indeed, as belief in diabolical possession gradually wanes in the Renaissance, this protoscientist emerges as the amoral servant of equally amoral physical processes, the dangerous disrupter who threatens a balance between society and the natural world, which during the neoclassical period grows increasingly fragile. As a challenge to moral and social structures, the antics of Faustus are similar to those of the greatest Renaissance "trickster," Don Juan Tenorio of Tirso de Molina's (1584–1648) *El burlador de Sevilla*. Though not specifically a scientist, Don Juan may in a sense be the purest embodiment of this line of technological heroes, for he ultimately defines himself not by pure mind but by pure energy, as a radical and eminently physical force of change. It is instructive to compare Don Juan's final moment with that of Faustus. For where the latter, in his great soliloquy, uses language to build a desperate monument against the dissipating power of time, Don Juan rushes headlong into a stone statue and sinks beneath the dead weight of social institutions. Although this sympathetic figure becomes, in theory at least, a hero to the practical Age of Enlightenment, he must in the nineteenth century face the ambiguities of a new scientific era in which the two realms of nature and human institutions, through a set of discoveries and conflicts that results in new limitations along with new powers, have become equally problematic. These problems emerge full-blown with Goethe's "technocratic" resurrection of the Renaissance disrupter in the second part of *Faust* (1808, 1832).

Although both are early nineteenth-century fictions about scientists and scientific research, E. T. A. Hoffmann's "Der Sandmann" (1816) and Balzac's *La Recherche de l'Absolu* (1834) are in a sense a world apart. Despite the development of radically new parameters, Hoffmann's story still focuses, in a traditional way, on a tragedy of the speculative mind. As defined by the maze of disjunctive observations that form this narrative—indeed, by the figurative play on seeing (speculation) and mirroring (speculum) that lies at its center—the limits encountered here by the scientist are no longer simply those of the physical world but rather those dependent on his own cognitive situation in that world, the fatal relativity of human knowledge itself. In Balzac's story, however, all generalized struggle – the scientist acting as a representative of mankind in a new scientific age – gives way to the parochial battles of the specialist operating in an increasingly restricted social and institutional context. Despite the capital *A* of the title's *Absolute*, chemist Claës is actually seeking knowledge with quite specific industrial applications: the discovery of a basic substance that would permit him to "repeat" nature, hence to fabricate the diamonds and precious metals he needs to replenish the family fortune that his research is consuming. It is precisely this newly developed dependence of science on material wealth – and Claës is not a resurrected quack seeking the "philosopher's stone" but a genuine experimental chemist whose research requires up-to-date laboratory equipment and research materials – that leads to a very different kind of downfall. For as Claës's science begins to threaten the economic stability of his family, his kin unite to curb it. The result is a ruthless power struggle that ends in what could be called institutionalized tragedy. In doing so, it provides a model for later fiction, such as Sinclair Lewis' *Arrowsmith* (1925), that chronicles the day-to-day compromises and defeats of the independent or "pure" researcher in a world where science itself has become but another institutional "complex."

Works like Mary Shelley's *Frankenstein* (1818) and Goethe's *Faust II* are, then, new because they explore what might be called the Promethean aspect of the scientist as literary hero – less the relatively easy theft of "fire" than the more difficult moral task of mediating scientific knowledge and developments in society. The attendant problems of the scientist operating on this level – those of responsibility to one's self and to one's fellow human beings – are elaborately examined in *Faust II*. Goethe here gives us repeated examples of experimenting scientists irresponsibly unleashing forces that they subsequently cannot control. Sometimes, as with Wagner's test-tube creation of Homunculus, the results are only potentially upsetting to the social order. As a creature both more than human and less than human, intellect both disembodied and disenfranchised, Homunculus is not so much a higher distillation of Faustian speculative power as its misbegotten offspring: the archetype of all such children of technology thrust back into the world to seek impossible, lost union with the elemental. Indeed, when such a creature is further forced, as is Frankenstein's "monster," to recapitulate the social evolution of mankind, forced to resume an innocence forever out of phase with our present institutions, the result leads beyond pathos to destructive violence. Furthermore, in *Faust II* the effects of such tampering with nature are thrust back on the scientist in the form of moral perplexity. Thus, Faust must stand by helplessly and witness the Icarian death of Euphorion, who has become, as the offspring of his time-traveling union with Helen, in a sense the ill-fated incarnation of his own scientific aspirations. This scene is highly portentous, for the scientist now seems doomed, in the impotence of the laboratory situation, to stand by helplessly and watch the rise and fall of the old Marlovian poetic response to the scientist's dilemma, reduced here to little more than another carefully controlled experiment. In the final pages of *Faust II*, however, the scientist's condition is again redefined. Faust's land-reclamation scheme is a classic example of technology, applied "for the good of humanity," in conflict with the entrenched social order, here represented by the old couple Philemon and Baucis, who claim "original" ownership of the land Faust covets. Having made life itself his laboratory, the scientist is at last free to experiment with the dynamic forces at his command to dissolve the static boundaries of codes, laws, and traditions. In a world of institutions with rival and absolute claims to existence, science moves, then, beyond good and evil by declaring itself also an institution — the one that represents power and change as values in themselves.

Significantly Mephistopheles' function as the scientist's diabolical helper has from Marlowe to Goethe irrevocably changed as well, the tempter has become a simple instrument, the agent who applies and misapplies the power delegated him by the abstracted scientist. This change is perhaps already present in embryo in *Doctor Faustus*, where Mephistophilis' real role in the action seems to be that of bridge between the contemplative and active worlds. With his oddly restless mind and fascination for human energy, he serves not only as Faustus' alter ego but also as Faustus' catalyst, converting the hero's speculative energy into corresponding displays of technical virtuosity. By the final scenes of *Faust II*, however, Mephisto has become an entirely new presence — an underling in the service of amoral science. When Faust orders Mephisto to "relocate" the old couple and then shuts his eyes to the consequences, he gives tacit sanction to an unscrupulous helper who, in burning them out, trades his old fire and brimstone for the new secular flames of technology. Science no longer honors the laws of God or man, but only those of efficiency; and, in Faust's own, oddly insensitive self-rebuke, haste seems now a purely physical rather than a moral category: "Quick ordered, and too quickly done." The old couple he and his emissary destroy are cast entirely in quantitative terms as well. As narrow and slow as Faust is fast and expansive, their self-righteousness is emptied of any broader significance; it becomes merely an impediment to "progress" and is swept away. With *Faust II* we have already entered our own mechanized and quantified age. In this world of instrumentality and efficacity, mankind no longer challenges time and space, but, like Philemon and Baucis, it is running out of both.

In our own century, the complex question of the scientist's responsibility to humanity and society is raised, in exemplary fashion, in Roger Martin du Gard's *Jean Barois* (1913) and Bertolt Brecht's *Leben des Galilei* (1947). In these works the lives and careers of scientists illustrate the complex, often unpredictable impact of theoretical speculation and technology on specific established institutions. Unlike *Doktor Faustus* and *Faust II*, these works restrict the scientist's actions to the social plane and present his relationship to society in terms of what may be called liberal and conservative impulses: the desire to alter old forms and the need to preserve them as fixed and "natural" in the wake of advancing science. In this context, the scientist can play various roles: he can conform to or rebel against the scientific "establishment" itself.

The confrontation between society and the scientific "establishment" is addressed in numerous works at the turn of the century. Henry Adams dealt with it in his opposition between the dynamo and the virgin. And Emile Zola illustrated it in the final scene of his novel *L'Œuvre* (1886), where Lantier's last rites in the new Parisian cemetery are interrupted by the incessant activity of machines ripping up old graves to make way for new and where the roar of a train ironically stifles the final *requiescat in pace*. Zola's stance in narrating this clash of worlds is ambiguous. Alternately we sense sympathy for stable values and exhilaration in response to change. What tips the scales is, perhaps, the stance of the hero Lantier, a man "enragé de modernité." And yet it is precisely this stance that destroys him.

"Enragé de modernité" describes the hero of *Jean Barois*. In dealing with the social struggles of the modern progressive scientist, this novel achieves a complexity lacking in more single-tracked works of science fiction where the scientist in revolt is merely branded "mad" and ritualistically excised from the body politic. Martin du Gard's novel recounts the life of the son of a provincial French physician who, rebelling against family and religion, takes up the study of the history of science and gradually seeks to apply the values of the new positivism to society. His career leads from ideas to actions — first polemics and then personal involvement in the Dreyfus case. The author is less interested, however, in examining ideas (or even institutions) in the light of this conflict than in chronicling the inevitable biological failure of such enlightened revolt. Through loneliness bred of shifting causes and alliances and through the onset of a hereditary disease, Barois is forced back into the flock. But if the scientist must compromise, it is not because entrenched institutions retain any ideal value; it is because they provide a palliative for physical suffering. Religion has lost both its metaphysical and moral foundations. Associated throughout with disease, it functions here as a negative force for social stability, the least socially disruptive balm for incurable mortality. In this context the scientist's quest is curiously debased. We need only measure Faustus' intellectual battles with time and matter in his last great soliloquy against Barois's pathetic renunciation of science and intellect in the face of wasting pain to ascertain the degree of that debasement. His ultimate return to faith satisfies no one, least of all his confessor. Though the novel is ambiguous — the author seems at times to admire the hero's militancy — it resolves finally with a conservative recognition of deep bonds between social institutions and nature, some absolute correspondence of religious ritual to the rhythms of season and blood. Indeed, Barois's little statue — a copy of Michelangelo's *Slave* — is emblematic, for the scientist is himself a slave here, not so much to unrelenting matter as to the human condition, mind within body. But in the end, some irony remains as well. For it is hardly consoling that, where the new science proves powerless, the conventional solution of art can elevate striving humanity to beauty and perpetuity only by turning life to stone, struggle to ever-frozen despair.

Brecht's play appears to deal with the problem of the scientist and society from a liberal viewpoint, but again there are ambiguities, pointing as in *Barois* to a conservative pessimism that transcends doctrine and inheres instead in the problem of scientific knowledge itself. The play, to be sure, has a clear social focus. In order to preserve truth, Galileo is forced to betray it, to renounce his discoveries publicly and submit to the cynical demands of society. His weakness is again that of the flesh—a love of good food and creature comforts—and, ironically, it proves science's strength, for after his humiliating defeat, Galileo embraces the rules of his society, completes his great opus in his comfortable prison, and has it smuggled over the border. All this is faithful to materialist dialectics perhaps. But a question remains: if scientific genius yields neither moral nor social benefit, what end does it serve? The brilliant final scene, in responding to this question, transcends doctrine. As Galileo's famulus Andrea steps across the border with the *Discorsi*, he comes of age. Turning back to address his audience—both the children in the play and us—he becomes the alchemist of old, revealing his magic to be natural occurrence, exhorting us to scientific activity, to open our eyes and observe. But in this moment the trickster is reborn as well. With one eye on the children and the other on us, Andrea develops a double perspective that transcends all borders of time and space. Suggesting that human beings may one day fly, he ironically summons our response from a vantage point of wisdom that has proved less than wise: we have learned to fly only to become more self-destructive in the process. Beyond the miniature spectacle of social injustice facing Andrea, we suddenly sense (through this expansion of perspective) deeper, ineradicable forces standing in the way of knowledge—superstition, human baseness. In this context all utopian hopes—that mankind can control nature and society through scientific method of any sort, dialectical or otherwise—are dashed. Indeed, the voice that finally pronounces the moral of the play does not lift our spirits with lofty poetry but taunts us with doggerel: "May you now guard science's light / Use it well and use it right / Lest it become a firefall / That one day consumes us all / Yes, us all." To seek traditional consolations here—either folk resiliency or some such sentimental cliché—is as futile as embracing the solution of art in *Jean Barois*. For if in the latter humanity was simply powerless to advance through science, here it is capable of terrible regression as old unregenerate mankind now threatens to turn science's light into the fires of a new holocaust.

Our second topic—the responsiveness of the thematic patterns of literature to scientific innovation—is also a product of the Renaissance. Indeed, such a topic would have been inconceivable in the Middle Ages. To the medieval writer, the forms of nature seemed to underlie and support, but never contend with, other planes of existence, including that of mankind. Renaissance science began to challenge and alter ideas about such fixed orders as the "great chain of being," and that process of reevaluation has become increasingly radical, and disquieting, as successive theories of the workings of the physical universe, backed by experimental evidence, have displaced humanity more and more from the center of things. The effect of these evolving theories on the themes and structures of imaginative literature has become increasingly noticeable. In the nineteenth and twentieth centuries, one such effect has been the rise of a new literary genre—science fiction. Isaac Asimov's definition of this form accurately reflects this interaction: "Science fiction is that branch of literature which is concerned with the impact of scientific advance upon human beings." It is primarily with this literary form that we shall be concerned in the remainder of our essay.

In terms of the impact of scientific advance on the human spiritual condition, we can distinguish two distinct problems. First, there is the physical impasse, the result of successive displacements of human life in the physical scheme of things through the development of successive revolutionary theories, such as heliocentricity, thermodynamics, entropy, evolution, and indeterminacy. Bertrand Russell has characterized the individual's existence as "brief and powerless"; "on him and all his race the slow, sure doom falls pitiless and dark."

Another line of development, however, leads to a different kind of impasse. Here, by a line of speculation that runs from the eighteenth century to Albert Einstein, the human empirical domain has itself been gradually narrowed, radically impoverished. Pascal, we recall, argued that the cognitive being achieves dignity in the face of blind and crushing physical forces. The modern observer, however, stands at what Samuel R. Delany calls the "Einstein intersection": "Einstein . . . defined the limits of man's perception by expressing mathematically just how far the condition of the observer influences the thing he perceives." Intersecting with Einstein's hypothesis, however, is Kurt Gödel's more recent theorem: "*In any closed mathematical system*—you may read 'the real world with its immutable laws of logic'—*there are an infinite number of true theorems*—you may read 'perceivable, measurable phenomena'—*which, though contained in the original system, cannot be deduced from it*—read 'proven with ordinary or extraordinary logic.'" At this intersection, the prospects for fictional worlds are frightening and exhilarating. Already in the works of writers like Philip K. Dick and Stanislaw Lem humanity has been depicted as having passed from a relativistic to a stochastic existence. Moving against a backdrop of phenomena no longer merely impersonal but random and indeterminate, the protagonists of these novels loop endlessly through a welter of probable theorems, all the while hoping against hope to recover the impossible stasis of an absolute system by finding a magical tear in this conceptual fabric, thereby regaining the certainty and repose of a world once more "immutable." Science fiction has long been fascinated with such concepts as time travel, alternate universes, and multidimensionality. And the fact that these loose categories have become increasingly focused on empirical dilemmas marks the importance of this "intersection" for the understanding of the genre. For if H. G. Wells's time machine carries its rider along a clearly physical continuum of devolution and entropy to a final observation of the death of the earth, the time traveler's experience, in more recent tales like Robert A. Heinlein's "By His Bootstraps," has itself become an observational quandary. The hero of Heinlein's story peoples his own universe with separate temporal manifestations of himself, entities created by the disjunctions of the observational process.

This cognitive dilemma has long been preparing in Western thought. Indeed, the rise of scientific method—the initiation and refinement of the inductive process of observation, hypothesis, and experimentation—must be seen in the larger context of a shift in emphasis in philosophical investigation from metaphysics to epistemology, from speculations on the ultimate nature of being to examinations into the nature and limits of knowledge. Since the birth of modern science, two distinct and somewhat contradictory epistemological lines have been evolving—Baconian technological optimism and cognitive skepticism. Indeed, if in his *Advancement of Learning* (1605) Francis Bacon hoped partially to reverse the effect of the Fall that haunted the pursuit of knowledge, a countercurrent running from Agrippa's *De Vanitate et Incertitudine Scientiarium* (1530) through Pascal and *Frankenstein* (1817) and into modern science fiction has warned against the limitations of the human mind and senses as valid investigative instruments. In encyclopedic compilations from Robert Burton's *Anatomy of Melancholy* (1621) to Gustave Flaubert's *Bouvard et Pécuchet* (1881), writers have mocked the folly of theorizing and ridiculed what they considered the hopeless Babel of contradictory scientific opinion. At the highest level of philosophic speculation, these differing attitudes have led, on the one hand, to Cartesian rationalism, the triumph of "method" and mathematical analysis, and on the other, to the eighteenth-century school of British skeptical empiricism.

While Isaac Newton found it necessary to posit absolutes—time and space—to guarantee the order of the eternal universe, Einstein later concluded that such attempts by scientific observers to construct an "objective" world view result in what are essentially only mental systems, systems that, although possibly closely related to reality, are not necessarily so. Ironically, in this system-making power of the mind, he found a way to relative freedom—from observational isolation to the theories of relativity. By means of "thought experiments," Einstein constructed a number of promising con-

ceptual systems; by exploring their possible relations to each other, he extrapolated a general vision of the relations amongst natural phenomena. Thus,
he posited, if on the level of special relativity the measure of time is dependent on the observer's system of reference, in the realm of general relativity
(in analogous fashion) the structure of the universe is equally dependent on
the sum of its contents, each planet and galaxy creating its own space-time
field. Einstein's speculations here rest on an edge of belief, for in his relativistic universe he has ultimately opted for mathematical unity: the connec-
tives guaranteeing the uniformity of natural law to these relative systems are
those transformational equations that regard time and space as variable
quantities. At another level, however, his thought merges with the mathematics of probability. For on the subatomic level the same empirical challenge operates. Observational inconsistencies here — the fact, for example,
that light, subjected to different modes of observation, behaves first like
waves, then like particles — have led scientists to reconsider the adequacy of
their earlier basic assumptions. On the plane of belief such dilemmas suggest
potentially opposite responses: we can retreat or advance, reaffirm some
traditional system of order or embrace discontinuity itself as a general principle, declaring "outright" with Niels Bohr "that there is an incomprehensible, irrational factor in physical events." To take this latter stand is to see
through what Frank Herbert calls "the eyes of Heisenberg," to embrace a vision that eschews all anthropocentric and anthropomorphic models. Much
of the best recent science fiction rests at this same point of intersection.

    We can distinguish, then, in terms of the impact of such scientific and
epistemological speculation, two distinct kinds of science fiction, clustering
around different nodes of scientific thought. The first kind, which we call
Pascalian, assumes a duality of mind and matter; and, on that assumption,
it generates fictional worlds in which the human mind is again and again
called on to assert its cognitive absoluteness amid physical flux, at the heart
of indifferent material process. The heroic prototype of this encounter between mind and universe is Faustus' final soliloquy. In his last moments,
this man who has declared himself free of the trammels of heaven and hell
runs head-on into the barrier of time. Faced with the horrors of a new damnation, this time in a seemingly endless sequence of leaden minutes, Faustus
seeks release through a series of wildly speculative leaps: "You stars that
reigned at my nativity / . . . Now draw up Faustus like a foggy mist / Into
the entrails of yon laboring cloud, / That when you vomit forth into the air,
/ My limbs may issue from your smoky mouths." Yet as we here see, mind
working to free itself from matter only succeeds in further twisting that matter into shapes that grotesquely imprison it. Fully secularized, this struggle
of mind against material limits is perhaps given its definitive modern expression in Baudelaire's cry in *Les Fleurs du mal*: "Ah, ne jamais sortir des
Nombres et des Etres!"

    In science fiction, this conflict of mind and matter has gradually degenerated into the "mad scientist" tale. Wells's Dr. Moreau (*The Island of Dr. Moreau* [1896]) claims to have struggled, in the name of higher human consciousness, against some brutish constant in organic nature: "I wanted . . . to find out the extreme limit of plasticity in a living shape." Yet here the context of these Faustian strivings—the island with its House of Pain—is at worst grotesque, at best ambiguous. The speculative mind's battle with matter further degenerates in Wells's *Invisible Man* (1897). In this novel, Griffin's discovery—a process that makes solid bodies invisible, hence, in a metaphorical sense, ethereal—is corrupted into an instrument of common violence. Where to Faustus invisibility was an end in itself, and the volatilization of spirit an act of heroism, to Griffin it has simply become the means by which basely material acts are performed—bank robberies and murders. The ultimate debasement of this pattern occurs, of course, in the science fiction film. In *The Fly* (1958), for instance, the central invention, a matter-transmitting machine, clearly suggests that scientific speculation no longer even hopes to challenge or elevate matter but is at best content to move it from one place to another. The grotesque transposition (Professor Delambre's head for that of a fly) is, in this regard, highly significant; the speculative consciousness of the scientist has, in other words, been irrevocably imprisoned in monstrous matter.

On the other side of this node, then, pivoting on Pascal's vision of man as a thinking reed, the heroic Faustian response to the thrust of blind physical forces yields to a response we can call elegiac. Increasingly in modern times, in the face of the bleak predictions of evolutionary and thermodynamic theory, defiance gives way to acceptance, as a progressively disenfranchised mankind seeks paradoxically to preserve its central role in the order of things by the very act of mourning its own passing. This line of response runs through a number of later nineteenth-century laments—for example, Thomas Hardy's "Darkling Thrush" and Matthew Arnold's "Dover Beach." It continues through Wells's *Time Machine* (1895), with the hero of that work elegiacally surveying the earth at the end of time, through Olaf Stapledon's account of the "last men," finally to the twilight figures of Arthur C. Clarke. The last scene of Clarke's *Childhood's End* (1953) sets the creation of a transcendent Overmind against the destruction of the solar system and humanity. As with Wells's Time Traveller, a lone survivor, Jan Rodericks, is here called on to observe the ultimate scientific spectacle of "heat death." Positioned at an optimal observation point—so to speak, at the eye of the storm that will annihilate him along with everything else—Jan learns that he can preserve the human presence only by the act of chronicling mankind's demise, by retracing the now obsolete history and aspirations of his race in the face of this spectacle of total destruction. In a sense, the recurring presence of this elegiac voice, in Clarke as in Wells, underscores the dilemma of the modern-day scientifically grounded writer. For if in Clarke the head has accepted the eventual obsolescence of humanity and the human form—he can coolly envision "cyborgs" replacing men on space missions—the heart apparently has not, and it must evolve tortuous strategies to reposition at least a ghost of mankind, in disembodied elegy, at the center of things. Thus, at the conclusion of *Childhood's End*, as mankind becomes Overmind, the Overlords, creatures openly equated with the fallen angels of Christian doctrine, carry away in their hearts all that remains of humankind—Jan's lament.

The second kind of science fiction—perhaps most appropriately called "Einsteinian"— focuses on observational quandaries, rather than on the basically existential ones of the Faustian and Pascalian traditions. Works of this kind transpose the old, dramatic defiance of the scientist-hero to a realm of observational uncertainty, placing the human observer at the interface between logically or observationally incompatible "worlds." They may explore either Einsteinian or Gödelian situations. An example of the first is Heinlein's "Universe" (1951, 1953), where a starship bound for Alpha Centauri becomes, after hundreds of years of travel, the entire known universe for the survivors, who, enclosed within its confines, have hypothesized a "geocentric" system very much like that formulated during the Middle Ages. An example of the Gödelian situation is Delany's *Nova* (1968). In this work Lorq von Ray's quest for the "heterotropic, psychomorphic" element Illyrion leads to an adventure that defies the logic in the table of elements or in any known physical system. All ground rules for heroism are altered in this landscape where prescriptive laws and codes are now no more than potential scenarios for action. In like manner, all theories have become conceptual grids thrown randomly (if desperately) over a phenomenal universe whose only consistency seems to be in its very indeterminacy: "Illyrion is many things to many men. . . . I wonder what it is to our captain?"

Equally significant is the emergence, within this general Einsteinian category, of two distinct modes of response to the problem of observational discontinuity. We call these modes "speculative fiction" and "science fantasy." The former accepts the uncertainty of speculation as axiomatic and portrays human beings acting within a context of discontinuity and acausality, human beings who are nonetheless able to work through to a redefinition of self and station. Classic examples of this "speculative" mode are Philip K. Dick's *The Man in the High Castle* (1962) and Brian Aldiss' *Cryptozoic* (1967). In Dick's novel, among possible available alternate versions of the outcome of World War II, none coincides with our own "real" version; and the closest to our version is that of a fictional account, a book whose every detail was determined by chance as its author threw *I Ching* straws. Aldiss' novel is more unsettling yet. All confidence in temporal continuity is here obliterated by the experiences of "mind travellers" who conceive and promulgate alternate theories of time that are not only contradictory but—like the assertion that, time really flowing backward not forward, our future is in fact our past—comically absurd. The final scene of this tour de force of simultaneously possible and preposterous visions involves a splendid Caligari situation, in which we cannot establish the primacy of any single version among overlapping and contradictory versions of reality (is there a government plot? is the hero insane?); in which, in fact, all possible connections between these versions are transposed to a level of linguistic "coincidence," a system of puns and assonantal ties that casts doubt on the relevancy of the very idea of purposeful human action.

Science fantasy, by contrast, posits uncertainty only to suspend it and seeks to recover or reassert, through eventual emotional release from situations of randomness, some idea of absolute order—be it solid foundations in time and space, a vision of "universal" human worth, or a metaphysical or religious destiny. This mode of fantasy is sophisticated, for it does not so much deny the radical conceptual frontiers of science as extend them to reaches of almost nightmarish contradiction, in order to force the reader, at a point of maximum psychological stress, to fall back critically on a solution that satisfies our emotional longings for a simpler order of things. A classic example of this type of subterfuge is found in John W. Campbell's "Twilight" (1934), a post-Einsteinian revision of Wells's *Time Machine*. In Campbell's story the time traveler, again arriving at an Eloi-Morlock nexus of will-less humans and dominant machines, this time acts to restore humanity to the center of the evolutionary process. The subtlety of this reinvestment becomes clear when we see that what is reinserted into the stream of time is not the human form but rather the human quality most necessary to man's role as speculator: "So I brought another machine to life. . . . I ordered it to make . . . a curious machine." Here is a thoroughly technological redemption that rejects the Adamic form for a machine-perpetuated curiosity, that once-fatal faculty which now, under this new dispensation, becomes a means of preserving a portion of the human spirit beyond the systems, be they those of flesh or of machine, that threatened to supersede it.

Such uncritical reassertions of an order scaled to human desires can result in egregious power fantasies of the sort one finds in Heinlein's "Waldo" (1942). In the world of this story, odd violations of known physical law indicate a condition of "leakage" in which energy generated in our space appears to be seeping away into what the hero, Waldo, calls "Other Space." Waldo not only fixes a precise and tangible place for this leakage in the synapses of the human brain but through magical feats of engineering and neurosurgery constructs an energy "pump" that can exchange our radiational garbage for an inexhaustible supply of clean energy. Not all science fantasy, however, involves literary colonization of this sort. In Arkady and Boris Strugatsky's *Definitely Maybe* (1977), for example, a series of savants pursuing unrelated research projects encounter a rash of illogical and irrational occurrences that thwart their efforts. Seeking an explanation, they come to an impasse, where they must either admit the possibility of irrational physical processes (for example, the possibility that "the Homeostasis of the Universe consists in maintaining the balance between the increase in entropy and the development of reason") or, beyond the urging of scientific data, "rehumanize" the problem by illogically positing some sentient, "alien" enemy. The final opting of these men for an "enemy" — and the heroic decision of one of them to engage in an absurd and lonely struggle against "it" — constitutes an existentialist revival in a post-Gödelian world.

Finally, we must consider the impact of scientific speculation on literary forms, a more recent problem in that it presumes the idea — not envisioned by classical poetics — of the relativity of such forms, of their susceptibility to the changing conditions of time and place, to successive "world views." In general, eighteenth-century doctrine still considered literary form as the "imitation" of a knowable nature. For unlike Sidney's earlier and more speculative approach (where the imitation of things not as they are but as they should be implies doubts as to nature's rightness, if not to its fixity), even those eighteenth-century theories of artistic imitation Meyer Abrams calls "empirical" remain fundamentally Aristotelian, hence involve a selective abstraction from nature, which only serves to confirm the absolute validity of the forms imitated. Alexander Pope can still echo this faith in "Unerring Nature" in his *Essay on Criticism* (1711). By the end of the eighteenth century, however, the problem of what constitutes this nature — and the corollary question of what method best imitates it, the poetic or the scientific — becomes more urgent as the results of scientific thought, most notably the genuinely empirical physics of Newton, begin to erode the facade of classical serenity. Keats, for instance, at the beginning of the nineteenth century, is painfully aware of two distinct and incompatible rainbows — the poet's "awful" form and Newton's "unwoven" spectrum of light. And side by side with this recognition of a variety of methods for approaching natural forms, we have in Stendhal's *Racine et Shakespeare* (1823) a statement of both the relativity of terms and the evolutionary nature of the literary forms themselves. Indeed, to Stendhal "romanticism" simply supplies the literary forms most suited to its day. Ironically, Stendhal's evolutionary vision has recently become the dogma of France's "new novelists." Such writers as Alain Robbe-Grillet and Nathalie Sarraute proclaim that, in an age that has produced the revolutionary visions of a Freud or a Ferdinand de Saussure, fiction can no longer rely on the forms of its Balzacian past. It must instead invent new forms to embody new visions of the workings of mind and language, new ways of expressing in fictional terms the theories, conditioned by the findings of modern science, that have radically altered the relationship between human activity and the phenomenal world.

At the basis, perhaps, of such alteration of forms is the idea, first adumbrated by the eighteenth-century empiricists, of observational uncertainty itself. Reflecting the investigations of Locke and Hume, the fiction of that century gave rise to first-person narration and to the self-conscious narrator, to the interplay of limited voices in epistolary novels such as Samuel

Richardson's *Clarissa* (1747–48) and Choderlos de Laclos's *Les Liaisons dangereuses* (1782). A direct line runs from these innovations to most modern experiments in literary form: preoccupation with point of view and reliability of narrator and, more recently, exploration of discontinuity in narrative focus, through such techniques as "interior monologue" and "subconversation," designed to register discrete and often contradictory levels of mental and observational activity. It is such preoccupation with formal innovation that characterizes the modern Western literary "mainstream." And if this revolution in literary form had a Copernicus, it was E. T. A. Hoffmann, whose "Der Sandmann" was perhaps the first narrative in which conscious dislocation of form functioned fully in response to observational uncertainty. In this tale, the closed narrative system of the Gothic, gruesomely homocentric in its fatal coincidences and incestuous family ties, is at every turn subverted in favor of an order that appears to have no connections whatsoever with human actions. Eyeglasses and other optical instruments, symbols of a scientific and epistemological revolution, now literally become agents of observational discontinuity as the protagonist, Nathanael, looks through them again and again only to find his "world" endlessly altered. Everywhere disorder is reflexively turned back on the perceiving self. Speaking and acting in utterly discontinuous manner throughout the story, the characters isolate themselves from any meaningful contact with what can to them be an objective "reality." The narrator himself cannot decide how to begin his tale even though it is already begun and moving toward a fatal conclusion. So unsettling is the narrative dislocation in "Der Sandmann" that Freud, in his essay "The Uncanny" (1919), sought to reposition the tale's relativistic vision in an absolute framework by attributing it to a single Oedipal cause.

But why has science fiction not shown more interest in such formal experimentation? If at the level of theme most sensitive to the impact of scientific advance, this genre seems curiously insensitive to it at the level of form, and perhaps nowhere more so than in its inability to incorporate into its narrative structures the observational relativity central to modern science. "Mainstream" critics, in the manner of a Robbe-Grillet, tend to dismiss science fiction as a secondary literature because of its seemingly constant recourse to old forms. But if we accept the consequences of relativity, we cannot consider the relativistic approach to narration any more of an absolute than the models it displaced. Despite its seeming fondness for time-worn devices, in particular the omniscient narrator, science fiction is widely read. Rather than impugn the taste of its readers, we will hazard a more generous speculation: perhaps the much-vaunted "mythic" force of science fiction — theoretically impossible in the new universe of contingent actions, where all remaining sympathetic ties between humanity and nature have finally been severed — comes precisely from this resurrection of an omniscient consciousness at the heart of the universe. Insofar as this is the result of deliberate

choice, we are entitled to see here something as progressive as it is regressive
— a further illogicality at the Einstein intersection in opting for these all-
knowing narrators to chronicle the very relativistic and probabilistic landscapes that obviate their existence. While the experimental "mainstream" increasingly depicts humanity as an isolated speaking or writing subject whose
linguistic acts turn endlessly back on themselves, signs signifying other signs
in a closed syntactical system, many of the best science fiction writers have
apparently chosen to ignore this problem, reinstating a firmly referential relation between subject and object, between the narrator and his or her world.

III. Conclusion: Science against Humanistic Literature

During this century the interrelations between science and imaginative
literature have been increasingly governed by a deepening antagonism between two world views, by what C. P. Snow has called the gap between the
"two cultures," scientific and humanistic. On the level of style and theme
this clash of cultures is itself perhaps most elaborately detailed in Thomas
Mann's novel *Der Zauberberg* (1924). In, for example, the chapter entitled
"Research," Hans Castorp's scientific investigations into the nature of life
lead (as technical detail and theory build to a critical linguistic mass) to literal dissolution of the human form: "This body . . . this individual and living I,
was a monstrous multiplicity of breathing and self-nourishing individuals."
In Mann's novel the symbol and instrument of the disintegrating power of
science is the X-ray machine. Looking through the new eyes now available
to him, Hans is led farther and farther from the humanistic vision his society
strives vainly to preserve, until its central myth of human progress becomes
for him no more than a blind devolutionary process in which the birth of life
now appears a "sickening of matter," and emerging spirit a mere "density."
All Mann's skills are therefore needed to anchor the traditions, ideals, and
future of humanity against the abysmal pull of the scientific vision.

On the level of literary form, recent attempts to close the two-cultures
gap may also bode ill for the humanist enterprise. Writers in France are, for
example, striving to produce, in concert with "structuralist" critics, fictions
that embody the vision of scientists and philosophers like Claude Lévi-
Strauss and Michel Foucault. For these thinkers, however, the individual —
surrounded by a field of intermeshing systems (cultural, linguistic, or otherwise) — has become less an entity or an agent than a "structure" determined
by various sets of relations. Norbert Wiener has expressed the same idea
succinctly: "We are not stuff that abides, but patterns that perpetuate themselves." Developing this view in increasingly antihumanistic directions,
writers like Philippe Sollers and Jean Ricardou create fictions that are no
longer dominated by human morals or manners but by systems — reflexive
word structures constructed from sets of interrelating elements that generate

fields of data (metaphoric comparisons and metonymic shifts) in a manner analogous to the closed, open, or looped structures of modern cybernetics. It is interesting that science fiction, as a formulaic literature with apparently apt terrain for metafictional games, has recently shown signs of taking up this structuralist challenge in order to subvert it. This is especially so in the work of Samuel R. Delany. If *Nova* is, for example, ostensibly metafictional space opera, it nevertheless ultimately (and incongruously) features an old-fashioned hero, a man seeking existence through purposive action, who moves through landscapes of reflexive systems in search of a new grail—the perhaps impossible restoration of human meaning at the core of this non-human welter of scientific and cultural models. Likewise in his *Einstein Intersection*, Delany sets alien (or alienated) creatures on a quest to become human—this time across a broken land of mythical roles and options, again the Babel modern science has created. If these novels offer few answers, at least they ask with persistence: "Is the human recuperable?"

On another plane, however, science fiction may be in the vanguard of what appears a more general (and serious) assault by scientific advance on the humanist vision. Increasingly the so-called media explosion heralded by Marshall McLuhan appears to be challenging that vision's technological base, the process of writing itself, a process that, according to McLuhan, has sanctioned, because it literally fixes it in the medium of the printed page, the linear logic of individuation that informs all major Western literary genres. However circular McLuhan's argument may seem, there is nevertheless real evidence that the electronic media, with their demands for "global" observation, are altering reader expectations along with reader ability. Moreover, recent science fiction, as an eminently paperback literature, shows signs of undergoing a formal transformation designed to accommodate itself to these new modes of observation and communication. The paperback novels of Frank Herbert, for instance, could qualify as "vast mosaic worlds in depth." Not only are they permeated with the thematics of communication but their narrative structures seem to be increasingly "mosaic" in nature. The *Dune* novels are prime examples. The text of these works continuously draws the reader into radial involvement with the ramifications of each narrative moment, in a manner that tends to obscure or suspend all linear sense of plot or character development. Often praised for its "ecological" dimensions, Herbert's writing demands a global participation by the reader, an ability to pursue multiple connections across and through the text at any given point of observational contact. Again, this radical reorganization may not be so much a conscious development as an instinctive survival response by imaginative literature in the face of threatening technological changes. To study these formal changes, if McLuhan is correct, is to measure the sensitivity of print to other media that are perhaps on their way to usurping the storytelling process itself.

Bibliography

Barnett, Lincoln. *The Universe of Dr. Einstein.* New York: Harper, 1948.

Chihara, Charles S. *Ontology and the Vicious-Circle Principle.* Ithaca, N.Y.: Cornell Univ. Press, 1973.

Drachman, Julian M. *Studies in the Literature of Natural Science.* New York: Macmillan, 1930.

Gamow, George. *One, Two, Three . . . Infinity: Facts and Speculations of Science.* 1947; rpt. New York: New American Library, 1953.

Gotshalk, D. W. *Art and the Social Order.* 2nd ed. 1947; rpt. New York: Dover, 1962.

Hofstadter, Douglas R. *Gödel, Escher, Bach: An Eternal Golden Braid.* New York: Basic, 1979.

Huxley, Aldous. *Literature and Science.* New York: Harper, 1963.

Jeffares, A. Norman. *Language, Literature, and Science.* Cambridge: Leeds Univ. Press, 1959.

Kuhn, Thomas. *The Structure of Scientific Revolutions.* Chicago: Univ. of Chicago Press, 1962.

Levy, Hyman, and Helen Spalding. *Literature for an Age of Science.* London: Methuen, 1952.

Popper, Karl. *Conjectures and Refutations.* London: Routledge and Kegan Paul, 1963.

———. *The Logic of Scientific Discovery.* New York: Basic, 1959.

Scholes, Robert, and Eric S. Rabkin. *Science Fiction: History, Science, Vision.* New York: Oxford Univ. Press, 1977.

Snow, C. P. *The Two Cultures and the Scientific Revolution.* New York: Cambridge Univ. Press, 1959.

Suvin, Darko. *Metamorphoses of Science Fiction.* New Haven: Yale Univ. Press, 1979.

Whitehead, Alfred North. *Science and the Modern World.* New York: Macmillan, 1925.

Wiener, Norbert. *The Human Use of Human Beings: Cybernetics and Society.* 2nd ed. Garden City, N.Y.: Doubleday, 1954.

10

Literature and Psychology

MURRAY M. SCHWARTZ AND DAVID WILLBERN

I. Introduction

The interrelations of literature and psychology derive from the inherently psychological dimensions of literature as well as from the uses of psychology in the interpretation of literary texts. For literature is an institutionalized idiom of interpersonal communication, which contributes to our imaginings of personal experience as fully as any theory of motivation that enables us to map literary effects and meanings. Literary works carry their psychology within themselves, in the very structure of relations they embody and invite us to form with them as readers. In some way, however obscure, the literary work contains its origins and significance as a psychologically coherent act. This much we assume, and seek to experience and understand as readers and critics.

But if literature in some sense always includes a psychology, it is also true that psychological assumptions always govern the interpretation of literary texts. The psychology we bring to the literary experience affects that experience; the language and concepts we use to engage and comprehend a text will transform the text we discover and the meaning we formulate. There is always literature *and* psychology, just as there is always literature and history or literature and the sounds of words.

The interplay of literary and psychological modes of representing and understanding experience is as old as each discipline. Their relations can be studied in the psychological poetics of Plato and Aristotle, especially their notions of aesthetic experience as inspired "phrensy" or emotional "catharsis." Later psychological speculation revived Aristotelian and Platonic ideas in the Renaissance but combined them with an awareness of human individuality as a dilemma and a possibility rather than a given "natural" state of affairs. Where there is a literary, as opposed to a sacred or mythical, language of representation, we also find a historical concern with the nature and problem of individual existence in society, and hence some psychology of the individual, however schematic or rudimentary. Renaissance faculty psychology, for example, with its categorizations of individual functions such as "will," "spirit," "appetite," or "reason," coincides and intersects with interpretations of the consequences of desire that pervade the literature of the period. We can move readily from the language of Marsilio Ficino to the language of *Love's Labour's Lost*.

One relation of literature and psychology is thus historical: the study of the prevailing interactions, continuities, and conflicts between literary representations and psychological theories in specific times and places. In this kind of study one would ask, for example, how the psychology of Thomas Hobbes's *Leviathan* is reflected in the drama of the Restoration, or how Samuel Taylor Coleridge projects psychological assumptions in his commentary on Shakespeare. Both literature and psychology would be treated as subcategories of intellectual history, and the critic would seek to understand each within a larger cultural context. In its most sophisticated forms, this type of research transcends naive adherence to ideas of "influence" that claim to understand authors when some contemporary psychological theory is found to underlie their literary creations and instead seeks to formulate the mutual effects of psychology and literary expression, thus avoiding a unilateral subordination of one to the other. The result is neither literature reduced to an illustration of psychology nor psychology made a mere scaffolding for literary structure but a conception of the conditions that ground their coexistence.

At its best a historical perspective explores the intrinsic interdependence of literature and psychology. As Geoffrey Hartman has remarked, "the necessity for theory arises when a skill disintegrates or must be reintegrated on a wider, more conscious basis. The wound nurtures the bow" (*The Fate of Reading*, p. 27). Theory arises (when it does) in response to a personal or cultural lack, just as literature answers a social desire. Adaptation to historical actuality is one goal of both theoretical and literary works. With this in mind, we can turn from a general conception of their interrelation to some specific forms of psychological thought that have proved especially integrative for twentieth-century writers and critics.

II. Psychological Theories

The revolution in depth psychology that began in the late nineteenth century has affected both the interpretation and creation of literary works. It continues to yield rereadings of every dimension of the literary experience: authorship, textual meaning, and the act of reading. We would be mistaken, however, to isolate this psychology — especially the works of Sigmund Freud and Carl Jung — from other major fields of psychological inquiry with which it has come to share significant concepts and methods. Contemporary psychology is various and heterogeneous in its own development and in its effects on literary study. Gestalt ideas, cognitive psychology, learning theories, and conceptions of the life cycle have become interrelated dimensions of many psychological studies of literature. Often even Freudian and Jungian ideas and speculations about personality and creative activity are reread by subsequent generations with all the freshness and ambiguity we would expect of encounters with complex and exploratory texts; their work is as overdetermined as the experience it addresses. Simultaneously, there has been a continuous revision and expansion of psychoanalytic theory. As a result, older concepts have been transformed, and contemporary depth psychology aims at the inclusiveness of a general psychology that makes many earlier oppositions obsolete (the controversy over Freud *or* Jung) or irrelevant (was there a "primal horde"?). Taken together, these changes make for a paradoxical progress not unlike the narrative structure of some contemporary novels. The result of this syncretic history is a difficult discipline, and the student of its present uses should avoid the impulse toward the reductive or exclusive choices of which psychoanalysis has been so frequently accused.

For all their difficulty, however, varieties of psychoanalysis deserve to be privileged in our discussion for several reasons. First, psychoanalytic insight has generated a greater body of significant work in relation to literature than any other psychology. This is not always obvious, because some of the best critics have succeeded in addressing a general audience by eschewing jargon: Leon Edel, for example, in his exemplary biography of Henry James. Second, the theory connects deep human motives to specific human actions and thereby uniquely attends to emotional and linguistic aspects of literature, through careful analysis of the language, image, and metaphor of a text. Third, psychoanalytic approaches have become interwoven with other psychologies and general theories, such as semiotics and information theory (see Peterfreund). As a result, our focus on the evolution of psychoanalytic theory and practice will lead us to consider a spectrum of contributions, including many rejected in some earlier definitions of the term "psychoanalysis." For example, Charles Rycroft's recent book, *The Innocence of Dreams*, cannot be easily labeled "Freudian," "Jungian," or "cognitive," although its author is a "Freudian" psychoanalyst. Nor can Northrop Frye's *A Natural Perspective* be dubbed "Jungian" without ignoring its frequent use of "Freudian" metaphors. Even in apparently orthodox journals, such as *American Imago* or *The Psychoanalytic Review*, which have given play to essays in literature and psychology for over thirty years, one finds imaginative expansions of and radical questions about the field.

We begin our conceptual summary with the most fundamental idea psychoanalysis has brought to literary study: that of dynamically repressed unconscious mental actions. To be fully appreciated, all other psychological concepts that address subsequent questions about personal intentions must be related to this idea. It asserts that the mind is not a simple unity but a divided unity, and that motives and the meanings of actions are actively kept from consciousness in the interest of self-protection and self-delusion. With this idea we must also accept the concept of resistance to knowing painful aspects of ourselves and our relations to others. The "unconscious" is an assumption about the way we structure reality in relation to our wishes and fears; it makes it impossible for naive trust or the idea of unmediated expression to govern our understanding of discourse.

Freud's theory of representation is consistent with his dualistic conception of mind. In *The Interpretation of Dreams* (1900), he maintained that the goal of dreaming is both biological and psychological: to preserve sleep while attempting to find expression for the dreamer's psychic preoccupations. The dream is "a (disguised) fulfillment of a (repressed) wish." It is chronologically layered, with an immediate motive (the "day residue") joining forces with an unconscious, infantile one. The manifest dream becomes a coproduction of past and present that fantasizes a future (fulfillment). It is a regression in the service of a progression, a compromise formation mediating the urges of the wish and the inhibitions of the repressive force (the "censor"). This model characterizes early theories of dream, joke, art, and literature as conservative governments of subversive energies.

In a successful dream, the wish evades the censor and finds fulfillment through various defensive transformations: the dreamwork's processes of condensation, displacement, representability, and secondary revision. These intrapsychic modes, as Lionel Trilling noted, are essentially artistic. The dream is thus a kind of poem—a reciprocal analogy to Freud's notion of poetry as a kind of dreaming. Both represent styles of thought and expression closer to "primary process" than to "secondary process" mentation, yet moving along a continuum between these two modes. The dreamwork's eventual production reveals and conceals its origins, through a manifest content that hides yet deviously derives from a latent content. The goal of classic psychoanalytic interpretation is to discover the latent, through the dreamer's free associations, symbolism, and the interpreter's special attentiveness. Interpretation reorders dream elements, translating arbitrary contiguity to meaningful continuity, parataxis to syntax. Since the dream itself is an instance of condensation, the concept of overdetermination allows for various and even contradictory meanings. Because the expressed dream, like the literary work, exists in a continuing and changing relation between creator and interpreter, its meaning may change as interpretations develop. Meanings are thus multiple, mutable, and historical. These complexities qualify the popular notion of "Freudian symbolism," since the relation of sign to signified in psychoanalysis is a function of individual and cultural contexts, historical as well as linguistic. A snake, for example, may provisionally function as a phallic substitute for some observers in some contexts, but it is not always or essentially such a substitute.

Both Freud and Jung expressed belief in an archaic symbolic vocabulary, or "collective unconscious," an idea tangential to Freud's theory but central to Jung's. Both relied on dream interpretation and free association in therapy, but Jung's goal was to place the patient's personal history within a mythological scheme to which a language of immutable symbols holds the key. Jung's analytical psychology populates the unconscious with superpersonal agencies, such as "shadow," "anima," "animus," and a pantheon of "archetypes." His theory favors this "collective unconscious" over the "personal unconscious," and subordinates the familial and sexual to the mythical and systematic, locating personality types on a grid of "thinking versus feeling," "sensation versus intuition."

Jungian literary studies typically expand from the characterological to the mythical. For instance, Herman Melville's narrative of Ahab and the whale may be reimagined as the adventures of the Hero and the Terrible Mother. Freudian literary studies tend to focus on details of personal history or language in order to describe a convergence of themes within a work or to connect an individual author or reader to a text. A similar difference in focus may be found in theory. Freud's idea of the Oedipus complex is universal yet specific: it refers to an individual child's actual incestuous wishes and fears. For Jung, such wishes are the symbolic expression of an "incest archetype" to be interpreted in terms of infantile nostalgia for (or terror of) the Great Mother. Hence for Jung infantile sexuality is less a set of psychological and physiological events to be observed in human development than a set of superpersonal symbols to be amplified and deciphered. His theory describes a broad taxonomy of cultural myths, useful for general analogies (our modern Superman is a type of Herakles) but less so for specific human relations. Jung's is an allegorical system; causality is replaced by synchronicity, individual development by collective repetition. This emphasis on recurrent mythic patterns gives Jungian criticism a special value in genre studies (such as Northrop Frye's *Anatomy of Criticism* or Maud Bodkin's *Archetypal Patterns in Poetry*) and places it in close relation to studies in anthropology and religion.

Classic psychoanalytic interpretive strategies have two major intents. First, to uncover the basic wish that motivates the fantasy; second, to note the specific defenses that transform the wish into licit expression. Yet literary creativity is not only the defensive transformation of infantile wishes. What we might call the "literature work" (by analogy to the dreamwork) intends to communicate to others in order to make a difference in the writer's relation to the outside world. Such a perspective emphasizes the positive, synthetic functions of the ego in reimagining past and present for the future. Art is not merely a regression, nor is the ego merely defending against primitive demands. Art also attempts to restore a lost relation between present and past or between self and others, and to establish a new synthesis of conscious and unconscious. It is analogous to the play of children, which stakes out a magical area of protected yet fluid boundaries in which experimentation is personally and culturally permissible.

Freud elaborates this analogy in *Beyond the Pleasure Principle* (1920), when he describes his 1½-year-old grandson inventing a new game with a small wooden reel. The boy throws the reel from his crib and then retrieves it by the attached string. In this game of *Fort* 'gone' and *Da* 'here,' Freud sees the child's symbolic representation of his mother's absences and reappearances. In his recreation, these anxiety-provoking events are imaginatively in the child's own hands: he is actively mastering what he once passively suffered. This behavior is not simply a symptomatic act of sublimated substitution. It is an adaptive and synthetic achievement that indicates the tractable exigencies of his environment. It is an original act of psychic and physical coordination that offers a new perspective on the classic notion of "defense" and provides an exemplary illustration of the Freudian theory of representation.

Shifting from a notion of defense to adaptation or mediation signals the development of ego psychology: the theory of autonomous functions with energies and intents neither simply dependent on nor defending against primitive demands from id or superego. The shift represents an advance from instinct theory to "object relations": a movement away from the body and psyche of the infant toward the infant's relation to an external (maternal) environment, from a somatic to a social world. Whereas classic Freudian theory frequently images the self as a body, nurtured by mother and threatened by father, object-relations theory centers on the relation between self and (m)other and the gradual emergence of ways of being in that environment for that infant, primarily the development away from early symbiosis toward adaptation to separation and individuation. Older models of biological determinism give way to interrelational models of feedback between self and other. For instance, the idea of an oral stage is not simply a matter of libidinal pleasure or aggression located at the mouth (sucking, biting, teething) but a complex process of learning to summon gratification and to tolerate its delay or absence, thereby making a gradual distinction between self and other and symbolizing relations between them. Thus understood, the psychoanalytic conception becomes compatible with other theories of development, such as Jean Piaget's distinction between assimilation and accommodation.

Psychoanalytic theories and interpretive strategies have been most elaborated by such post-Freudian writers as Erik Erikson and Jacques Lacan and modified by recent revisions of Freud's patriarchal and phallocentric biases (e.g., Juliet Mitchell's *Psychoanalysis and Feminism* and Nancy Chodorow's *The Reproduction of Mothering*). Erikson's extensive reinterpretation of Freud's central "dream of Irma's injection" exemplifies the wider contexts of applied psychoanalysis (see "The Dream Specimen of Psychoanalysis"). By "giving new depth to the surface" (Erikson's phrase), this essay offers an example of how to bring personal, social, and cultural contexts to bear on a single analysis. Erikson has also developed a theory of play that stresses social as well as intrapsychic purposes. Art becomes a reconstitution of relations, and the wish exists in the reconstitution, not merely in the unconscious "core fantasy." Further, in describing life as a sequence of stages, Erikson locates the meanings of symbolic actions in the person's present relations, avoiding excessive emphasis on origins.

British theorists have developed similar ideas, starting with Melanie Klein's reunderstandings of Freud's notion of art as reparation for loss and continuing in the work of Marion Milner and D. W. Winnicott, who characterizes the wish to restore by re-creation in terms of shifting boundaries between self and other within an interrelational arena that he terms "potential space." Here occur the earliest events between child and mother, and the lattices of this early space form the framework for later events between child and environment. Indeed, this intermediate region prefigures the locus for all cultural relations. An initial way of grasping the reality of this magical space is through what Winnicott calls the "transitional object": an object simultaneously presented by the mother and wishfully created by the infant (security blankets and teddy bears are examples). The transitional object is neither within nor without, neither here nor there: it embodies experiences between attachment and separation. The concept has added to psychoanalytic literary theory, since the creation and reception of texts can be seen as transitional phenomena (see Schwartz, "Where Is Literature?").

By focusing on this interrelation, contemporary theories observe the emerging development of a particular self for and with an other in a particular space and time. This focus enables new perspectives on individual identity, seen not simply in intrapsychic or psychobiological terms but in terms of how one self learns to *be* for and within the specific environment that sustains it (see, for example, Lichtenstein's and Holland's uses of "identity themes"). Analogously, theories of interpretation focus on the relations between author and text, text and audience, interpreter and text (see Iser's interactive model of reading). Recent studies have shifted from the process of artistic creativity toward the reciprocal creativity of response. Contemporary psychological criticism has absorbed earlier ideas and acknowledges an interpretation work analogous to the classic dreamwork. Critical analysis is an agent of transformation and reconstitution, with its own wishes, fears, shadowy motives, and projected audiences. The interpretive process is bound up with the individual and social identity of the interpreter. No longer is the bipolar notion of nineteenth-century science, with its neutral observer of external "objective" phenomena, deemed adequate to the study of human behavior or of literature. Even perceptual cognition is an act of individual re-creation, as experimental psychologists have demonstrated (see Ulric Neisser). Increasingly, psychological literary critics, like many contemporary poets and fiction writers, have become intimately and self-consciously implicated in their interpretations.

III. Psychological Criticisms

Most early psychoanalytic interpretation of literature assumes a coherent interrelation between an author's life, fantasies, and fictions. It seeks to discover hidden motives in the author and in characters considered as persons. Its subjects are typically drama and story; its discoveries are typically Oedipal (incest and parricide). Freud's initial remarks on the Oedipus complex were literary, involving *Hamlet* and *Oedipus Tyrannus*. Hamlet was "the hysteric" who delays because he is paralyzed by guilt over Claudius' enactment of his own unconscious wishes. From these brief remarks sprang Ernest Jones's elaborations in *Hamlet and Oedipus* (1910, rev. 1923 and 1949), and an analytic stance premised on the presumption that imaginary characters are real people with infantile histories and unconscious minds. (For a contemporary critical attitude that sustains this tradition, see Kaplan and Kloss, *The Unspoken Motive*.) Freud also wrote several interpretations of literary works, such as his analysis of Wilhelm Jensen's *Gradiva* and E. T. A. Hoffmann's tale, "Der Sandmann" (in "The Uncanny" [1919]). His psychobiographical essay "Dostoevsky and Parricide" (1928) explains the novelist's criminal fantasies, epilepsy, sadomasochism, gambling mania, even banishment by the czar, in terms of Dostoevsky's guilt over his unconscious patricidal wish.

Other examples of classic psychobiographical analyses, which lean heavily on the neurotic model of creativity, are Phyllis Greenacre's study of Jonathan Swift and Lewis Carroll and Marie Bonaparte's study of Edgar Allan Poe. More recent work integrates ego psychology and an appreciation for the ways in which genius transforms private issues into public utterances, and the books of (for example) Leon Edel on James, Bernard Meyer on Joseph Conrad, Frederick Crews on Nathaniel Hawthorne, John Irwin on William Faulkner, and David Lynch on William Butler Yeats demonstrate a variety of finely tuned analyses of the interrelations among biography, psychological theory, and literary criticism.[1]

Such critical studies rely on post-Freudian theories of creativity and response, such as those of Ernst Kris, who advanced the idea of "regression in service of the ego" to explain the creative process, especially as it relates to the visual and plastic arts of caricature and the comic. Kris's emphasis is on the ego's attempts to achieve mastery over anxiety through play. The artist reenacts earlier modes of representation in the interest of creating a new order that transforms present reality. Simon Lesser's *Fiction and the Unconscious* (1957) and Norman Holland's *Dynamics of Literary Response* (1968) present more systematic theories of literary form and reader response, moving away from the classical emphases on Oedipal triangles and essential symbolism. Lesser and Holland emphasize two major aspects of psychoanalytic literary theory: pre-Oedipal developmental stages (oral, anal, phallic) and specific defense mechanisms (like denial or undoing). In their view, the text transforms a basic infantile fantasy into an acceptable and pleasurable experience for a reader. Holland develops Lesser's notion of form as defense into more precise correlations, so that (for instance) irony is a kind of denial. Other critics have analyzed literary genres, arguing, for example, that allegory is a species of obsession-compulsion (see Angus Fletcher's *Allegory: Theory of a Symbolic Mode*) or that detective stories are based on primal-scene fantasies (see Charles Rycroft, *Imagination and Reality*).

These various efforts to correlate literature and psychology can be viewed against a background of literary theory illustrated by the work of I. A. Richards. Richards' assertions that poetic experience organizes mental responsiveness in salutary ways, leading to both synaptic and social improvements, are based on a sui generis quantum theory of nervous excitations through "uniform impulses." His theories have influenced two apparently disparate fields of twentieth-century criticism: New Criticism, with its iconography of the text as autonomous artifact, and "reader-response criticism," with the reader as re-creator of the literary experience. The issue of bridging the distance between the poem-as-object and the reader-as-subject is one that Richards made clear, even if his theoretical assertions about it hardly cleared it up. It remains at the core of today's psychologies and phenomenologies of reading—"affective stylistics," "subjective criticism," "transactive criticism," "hermeneutics," and *"Rezeptionsesthetik."*

In reaction to the array of idiosyncratic responses demonstrated by student subjects such as Richards' (see *Practical Criticism*), New Criticism tried to exclude individual readers' vagaries from the experience of the "poem itself," through such notions as the "affective fallacy"—"a confusion between the poem and its results (what it *is* and what it *does*)." The poem was to be "an object of specifically critical judgment," not to be confused with its "psychological effects" (see Wimsatt and Beardsley, *The Verbal Icon*). Much recent critical theory has openly embraced this "fallacy" and argued that what a poem "does" is essentially what it "is." Not only should the poem not be separated from its reader, it cannot meaningfully be so separated.

The importance and value of readers' reconstructions of texts are implicit in *Practical Criticism* and explicit in Richards' later writings (see *Speculative Instruments*). Although Richards did not develop his ideas into a coherent theory that would locate the form of a text in the structuring of a reader's satisfactions and frustrations, Kenneth Burke developed just such an idea (see "Psychology and Form"). Its themes and variations are being played out in many contemporary theories of reading.

Most such theories acknowledge that reading, like any act of perception and comprehension, is an activity. We are not passive audiences to the sights and sounds of a text, though our common metaphors reify and animate its words. We do not in fact look at a sign to "see what it says." Experiments in cognitive psychology since the 1950s have demonstrated that sensory perceptions are personal constructions (see Piaget and Neisser), and various psychologies of reading explore the (re-)creation of a literary work by an individual relating to a text. As Louise Rosenblatt wrote forty years ago, "The experience of literature, far from being for the reader a passive process of absorption, is a form of intense personal activity. The reader counts for at least as much as the book or poem itself" (*Literature as Exploration*). Wolfgang Iser makes a now-standard distinction between the idea of the text (what is written) and the work (what is read). He carefully examines the "dynamic interaction between text and reader," an interaction that is the focus of several other theorists of readers' responses, such as Norman Holland, David Bleich, Walter Slatoff, and Stanley Fish.

Describing the "virtual dimension" created by this interaction of reader and text, Iser notes: "This 'gestalt' must inevitably be colored by our own characteristic selection process. For it is not given by the text itself; it arises from the meeting between the written text and the individual mind of the reader with its own particular history of experience, its own consciousness, its own outlook" ("The Reading Process," p. 284). A resulting emphasis on individual readings has led to psychological analyses known as reader-response criticism. This perspective has evoked concerns that criticism will end in impressionism and sheer subjectivity, uncontrolled by any stringencies of the words on the page. Most theorists try to balance on the thin line between an "objective" text and a "subjective" reader or wish to erase that line without allowing one territory fully to overlap the other. However, David Bleich asserts the primacy of subjectivity and considers objects such as texts to be the results of provisional agreements among a group of perceivers who determine to "objectify" some thing and then behave accordingly. Critical discussion then becomes a set of negotiations among private interpretations, some of which may win out over others but none of which is essentially privileged owing to fidelity to some objective text.

Another position, less extreme than Bleich's, is taken by Norman Holland (modifying his earlier views in *The Dynamics of Literary Response*). Holland argues that individual responses disclose essential psychological characteristics of the individuals responding. He believes that readers use literature to rediscover themselves through "transactions" with texts (see *Poems in Persons* and *5 Readers Reading*). Bleich and Holland, in thus modifying psychoanalytic models of literary response to allow for individual differences, have moved the "fantasy" out of the text and into the reader, or into the relation between reader and text. Each reader makes sense out of the text, thus making that text in important ways his or her own. Early interpretive models of fantasy-and-defense become more sophisticated designs of transaction between an author's characteristic psychic style and a reader's, with Holland's interpretive goal the demonstration and distillation of an "identity theme" for both author and reader. There remain many similarities with the earlier scheme of *Dynamics*, however, as the centrality of the identity theme as an all-explanatory unifying principle of the reader dislodges the centrality of the core fantasy as the all-explanatory unifying principle of the text.[2]

Other critics speculate psychoanalytically on the nature of poetry and language, or the intertextual relations of poems and poets. Harold Bloom's *Anxiety of Influence*, for example, argues that prior (paternal) poets haunt every writer, so that John Keats feels the constant presence and pressure of William Wordsworth, just as Wordsworth finds John Milton inhabiting his Pierian spring. Bloom's model is Oedipal, a variation of Freud's "family romance," and leads to a constant, anxious rhythm of rivalry and imitation from poet to poet. As Geoffrey Hartman has noted, Bloom's Freudian thesis stresses intrafamilial conflict (son against father, brother against brother) in literary history, as opposed to Northrop Frye's ahistorical mythic criticism, wherein the son replicates the father, not in anxious rivalry, but in ritual reenactment (see "War in Heaven," in *The Fate of Reading*).

Among other important contributors to contemporary psychological understandings of literature would be Lionel Trilling, who opened up the analogy of poetry and dreaming and did much to make Freud respectable in academia; William Empson, whose elaborations of ambiguities in language demonstrated the benefits of combining close New Critical readings with psychoanalytic assumptions; and Geoffrey Hartman, who has developed a "psychoesthetics" of creative criticism. Hartman sees interpretation as a species of literature, and the goal of the critic to develop an "answerable style" to that of the text, through the interplay of linguistic and semantic potentialities, literary allusions, and unconscious associations.

Hartman's critical style is related in spirit to French structuralism and deconstruction, especially as represented by Roland Barthes and Jacques Derrida.[3] Barthes's psychoanalytic and linguistic (Freudian and Saussurean) readings of Jean Baptiste Racine and Honoré de Balzac, for example, construct images of the authors through a systematic yet playful dismantling and restructuring of the texts, in an effort to unveil not latent contents but latent structures (see *On Racine* and *S/Z*). Both Barthes and Derrida express in their unique ways a radical philosophical questioning of culture and language that discloses the complex linguistic bases of social and psychological assumptions. In Derrida's more recent work, Barthes's energetic *plaisir du texte* becomes ascetic verbal play as he juxtaposes Hegel and Genet in a French philosophical version of *Finnegans Wake* (see his split-text *Glas*).

The most increasingly insistent figure among French claimants to contemporary psychoanalytic style is Jacques Lacan. Through a combination of conservative theoretical loyalties (e.g., the Oedipal paradigm, the castration complex) and original, provocative, and sometimes obscure reinterpretations of basic concepts (e.g., the "unconscious" as a second order of representations structured like a language), Lacan has revived among some critics the sense of a special relevance of psychoanalysis to literature and literature to psychoanalysis. He rejects the biological orientation of much American theory, substituting his own conception of the ego as the locus of an illusory unification of desires that can never be captured through signifying systems.

His style thus subverts the idea that we can master literature through the application of theory and enacts instead an ironic attitude toward the possession of textual meaning.

IV. Conclusion

Contemporary psychological critical practice embodies responses to several commonly perceived issues and problems. Its various forms exemplify the explosion of terminologies in intellectual discourse at large. The field is undergoing a transformation that is both a source and an effect of new assumptions about reality. This process has made the field newly sophisticated and complexly questionable. New combinations of ideas are emerging from developments in perceptual and cognitive theory and from the expansion and reinterpretation of psychoanalysis. The questionability of this sophistication derives from the closeness of recent theoretical debate to contemporary critical concerns with the self, with the nature and function of language in interpretive discourse, and with the possibility of unification both in personality and in fiction making. Ironically, psychological approaches to literature have begun to reveal the very possibilities and problematics associated with literary uses of language.

The most outstanding development concerns the relation between theory and the process of interpretation. Whereas more traditional uses of psychoanalysis frequently assigned unconscious meanings to literary works unhistorically and impersonally, contemporary writing reflects awareness of the role of transference and countertransference in creative and critical practice. In clinical psychoanalysis, the analyst can discover the meanings of the patient's discourse only by understanding the interpersonal relations through which it is engendered. The analyst must become aware of how the patient repeats past relationships in the present, assigning roles to each of the participants in ever-changing ways. Likewise, the analyst must become aware of how his or her own thoughts and feelings are specifically related to the patient's conscious and unconscious formation of the relation between them. The meaning of the patient's language thus becomes woven into the therapeutic process.

Although the analogy does not pertain in every detail, the literary uses of psychology also involve an open-ended process of discovering meanings through the interpreter's emotional as well as intellectual relations to texts. Both readers and critics restructure texts to fit their own desires as they accommodate themselves to the internal requirements of those texts. Consequently, contemporary practice requires more than theoretical understanding on the critic's part; this understanding must be integrated into the critic's personal experience of the work he or she would interpret, and conversely, his or her interpretation will become part of a dialectical interaction of self and literature. In taking this dialectic more seriously than before, psychological criticism has invited a wider range of critical styles and drawn on a wider range of theories even as it has become more difficult to encompass as a totality.

Closely related to this awareness of meaning making as a dialectical process is the question of the "subject" or "person." There are postmodern psychologies as well as postmodern fictions. In each we see a radical questioning of the assumption of a unified self or identity or subjectivity. French psychoanalysis has been especially effective in challenging the positivist reductions of some American criticism, while contemporary American and British writing derives from newer concepts of narcissism and identity that account for the relational, rather than objectivist, meanings of experience. As a novel by John Barth plays out questions of self-identity in the author's relation to his material, treating a fixed perspective as an ironic illusion, so an essay by Norman Holland brings Holland's own subjectivity explicitly into the interpretive process, making his personal choices more consciously available even as he implicitly raises the question of whether the critic can practice such honesty without also donning a defensive mask.

Active critical play with language has made the boundaries between criticism, theory, and fiction more difficult to define and justify. The "fictional" status of theory has become an issue for psychologists as well as critics, and controversy continues as to the appropriate language for theoretical formulations. Full-scale attempts to rewrite the theory, such as Roy Schafer's *A New Language for Psychoanalysis* (1976), are symptomatic of the problems and possibilities facing the field. Awareness of theory as a "languaging" of experience leads to a fresh sense of choice at the same time that it reveals several philosophical foundations and political ramifications of differing schools. This self-consciousness exposes the inevitable interest of the theorist in his or her formulations. In relation to critical practice, the same kind of self-consciousness about language can lead to explorations of the uses of critical voice in psychological interpretation. Such considerations are more than merely rhetorical. They are central, for example, to feminist criticisms of the inherent patriarchal bias, not only of literature and literary tradition, but of language itself (see Gilbert and Gubar, *The Madwoman in the Attic*). Any interpretation puts into language a relation to a text that can never be emotionally or ideologically neutral. From this basic premise, both a sense of crisis and a sense of new beginnings have grown. Perhaps the best result is to make the relations of literature and psychology explicitly more mutual than before.

Notes

[1] We note that Crews has altered his view of psychoanalysis. He now disclaims many of the strategies of his earlier book (see his more recent *Out of My System*).

[2] Two contemporary psycholinguistic models of the reading process provide a schematic representation of the fundamental "text versus reader" problem. Termed

(a) "bottom-up" and (b) "top-down" models, they respectively assert that (a) reading is a process of systematically decoding discrete units of meaning in a text, and (b) reading is a process of the mental set of a reader as that reader generates hypotheses, in his or her own style, about what he or she is reading. On the issue of misreading: for the first model, correction is mandatory (it's an erroneous decoding); for the second, the "error" is a clue to the reader's style or mode of hypothesizing. See Michael Kamil and P. David Pearson, "Theory and Practice in Teaching Reading." *New York University Education Quarterly*, 10 (Winter 1979).

[3] For a brief history of the development of psychoanalytic critical styles in France, see Leo Bersani, "From Bachelard to Barthes," *Partisan Review*, 2 (1967), 214–32. The most influential contemporary figures are Lacan, Foucault, and Derrida. A more recent account is Sherry Turkle's *Psychoanalytic Politics: Freud's French Revolution* (New York: Basic, 1978).

Bibliography

This bibliography represents three areas: (1) actual historical and contemporary relations between literature and psychology; (2) psychological theories that a student should attempt to master; (3) sources for further reading.

I. Dictionaries and Bibliographies

These basic source books are supplemented by reading lists and bibliographies included in items listed in other sections.

Grinstein, Alexander. *Index of Psychoanalytic Writings*. 12 vols. New York: International Universities Press, 1956–76. A basic bibliography.

Kiell, Norman. *Psychoanalysis, Psychology, and Literature*. 2nd ed. 2 vols. Metuchen, N.J.: Scarecrow, 1982. A basic bibliography.

Laplanche, Jean, and J.-B. Pontalis. *The Language of Psycho-Analysis*. Trans. Donald Nicholson-Smith. New York: Norton, 1973. The fullest dictionary of psychoanalytic terms and concepts, and an indispensable book in the field.

Rycroft, Charles. *A Critical Dictionary of Psychoanalysis*. New York: Basic, 1968. Less historical than Laplanche and Pontalis, but accurate and imaginative.

II. Readings in Theory

These books and articles represent major schools of theory that have had an important impact on literary study and continue to inform contemporary criticism.

Bleich, David. *Subjective Criticism*. Baltimore: Johns Hopkins Univ. Press, 1978.

Bollas, Christopher. "The Transformational Object." *International Journal of Psycho-Analysis*, 60 (1979), 97–107.

Chodorow, Nancy. *The Reproduction of Mothering: Psychoanalysis and the Sociology of Gender*. Berkeley: Univ. of California Press, 1978.

Dewey, John. *Art as Experience*. New York: Putnam, 1934.

Ehrenzweig, Anton. *The Hidden Order of Art: A Study in the Psychology of Artistic Imagination*. Berkeley: Univ. of California Press, 1967.

Erikson, Erik H. *Childhood and Society*. 2nd ed. New York: Norton, 1963. Especially useful for developmental theory and a psychosocial view of adaptation.

———. "The Dream Specimen of Psychoanalysis," *Journal of the American Psychoanalytic Association*, 2 (1954), 5–56. Rpt. in *Psychoanalytic Psychiatry and Psychology: Clinical and Theoretical Papers*. Ed. Robert P. Knight and Cyrus

R. Friedman. New York: International Universities Press, 1954, III, 131–70. A major restatement of the interpretive process using Freud's original "specimen dream."

Foucault, Michel. *Madness and Civilization: A History of Insanity in the Age of Reason.* Trans. Richard Howard. New York: New American Library, 1965.

Freud, Sigmund. *Beyond the Pleasure Principle* (1920). Trans. James Strachey. 2nd ed. New York: Liveright, 1961.

———. "Dostoevsky and Parricide" (1928). In *Character and Culture.* Ed. Philip Rieff. New York: Macmillan, 1963, pp. 274–93.

———. *The Interpretation of Dreams* (1900). Trans. James Strachey. 1955; rpt. New York: Avon, 1965.

———. *Jokes and Their Relation to the Unconscious* (1905). Trans. James Strachey. New York: Norton, 1960.

———. *On Creativity and the Unconscious: Papers on the Psychology of Art, Literature, Love, Religion.* Ed. Benjamin Nelson. Trans. Joan Riviere et al. New York: Harper, 1958. See, among other papers, "The Relation of the Poet to Daydreaming" (1908), pp. 44–54; and "The Uncanny" (1919), pp. 122–61.

Frye, Northrop. *Anatomy of Criticism: Four Essays.* Princeton: Princeton Univ. Press, 1957.

Greenacre, Phyllis. *Emotional Growth: Psychoanalytic Studies of the Gifted and a Great Variety of Other Individuals.* 2 vols. New York: International Universities Press, 1971.

Hillman, James. *Re-Visioning Psychology.* New York: Harper, 1975.

Iser, Wolfgang. *The Act of Reading: A Theory of Aesthetic Response.* Baltimore: Johns Hopkins Univ. Press, 1978.

———. "The Reading Process." In *The Implied Reader: Patterns of Communication in Prose Fiction from Bunyan to Beckett.* Baltimore: Johns Hopkins Univ. Press, 1974, pp. 274–94.

Jones, Ernest. "The Theory of Symbolism" (1916). *Papers on Psycho-Analysis.* 5th ed. Boston: Beacon, 1961, pp. 87–144.

Jung, C. G. *Analytical Psychology: Its Theory and Practice.* New York: Random, 1968.

———. *Psyche and Symbol: A Selection from the Writings of C. G. Jung.* Ed. Violet S. de Laszlo. Garden City, N.Y.: Doubleday, 1958.

———. *Symbols of Transformation: An Analysis of the Prelude to a Case of Schizophrenia* (1912). Trans. R. F. C. Hull. Bollingen Series, 20. New York: Pantheon, 1956.

Klein, George S. *Psychoanalytic Theory: An Exploration of Essentials.* New York: International Universities Press, 1976. A major statement of contemporary American psychoanalysis.

Kohut, Heinz. *The Analysis of the Self: A Systematic Approach to Psychoanalytic Treatment of Narcissistic Personality Disorders.* New York: International Universities Press, 1971. Theory of narcissism.

Kristeva, Julia. *La Révolution du langue poétique.* Paris: Seuil, 1974.

Lacan, Jacques. *Ecrits: A Selection.* Trans. Alan Sheridan. New York: Norton, 1977. A French alternative to American ego psychology.

———. *The Language of the Self: The Function of Language in Psychoanalysis.* Trans. Anthony Wilden. Baltimore: Johns Hopkins Univ. Press, 1968.

Lemaire, Anika. *Jacques Lacan.* Trans. David Macey. London: Routledge and Kegan Paul, 1977.

Lichtenstein, Heinz. "Identity and Sexuality." *Journal of the American Psychoanalytic Association,* 9 (1961), 179–260. Source of the identity concept in the work of Norman N. Holland and others.

Loewald, Hans W. "Ego and Reality." *International Journal of Psycho-Analysis*, 32 (1951), 10–18. A summary of ego development.

Mahler, Margaret S. *On Human Symbiosis and the Vicissitudes of Individuation.* New York: International Universities Press, 1968. Contemporary developmental theory.

Milner, Marion. *On Not Being Able to Paint.* 2nd ed. New York: International Universities Press, 1957.

Mitchell, Juliet. *Psychoanalysis and Feminism.* New York: Pantheon, 1974.

Modell, Arnold H. *Object Love and Reality: An Introduction to a Psychoanalytic Theory of Object Relations.* New York: International Universities Press, 1968.

Neisser, Ulric. *Cognitive Psychology.* New York: Appleton, 1967.

Peterfreund, Emanuel, with J. T. Schwartz. *Information, Systems, and Psychoanalysis.* Psychological Issues, Nos. 25 and 26. New York: International Universities Press, 1971.

Phillips, John L., Jr. *The Origins of Intellect: Piaget's Theory.* 2nd ed. San Francisco: Freeman, 1975.

Piaget, Jean. *Six Psychological Studies.* Ed. David Elkind. Trans. Anita Tenzer and David Elkind. New York: Random, 1967.

——. *Structuralism.* Trans. Chaninah Maschler. New York: Basic, 1970.

Pontalis, J.-B. "Dream as an Object." *International Review of Psycho-Analysis*, 1 (1974), 125–33.

Poulet, Georges. "Phenomenology of Reading." *New Literary History*, 1 (1969), 53–68.

Richards, I. A. *Principles of Literary Criticism.* New York: Harcourt, 1925.

Rogers, Robert R. *Metaphor: A Psychoanalytic View.* Berkeley: Univ. of California Press, 1978.

Rosenblatt, Louise. *The Reader, the Text, the Poem: The Transactional Theory of the Literary Work.* Carbondale: Southern Illinois Univ. Press, 1978.

Rycroft, Charles. *Imagination and Reality.* New York: International Universities Press, 1968.

——. *The Innocence of Dreams.* New York: Pantheon, 1979.

Schafer, Roy. *A New Language for Psychoanalysis.* New Haven: Yale Univ. Press, 1976.

Spivak, Gayatri C. "The Letter as Cutting Edge." *Yale French Studies*, 55–56 (1977), 208–26.

Strouse, Jean, ed. *Women and Analysis: Dialogues on Psychoanalytic Views of Femininity.* New York: Viking, 1974.

Swan, Jim. "Giving New Depth to the Surface: Psychoanalysis, Literature, and Society." *Psychoanalytic Review*, 62 (1975), 5–28.

——. "*Mater* and Nannie: Freud's Two Mothers and the Discovery of the Oedipus Complex." *American Imago*, 31 (1974), 1–64.

Waelder, Robert. "The Principle of Multiple Function: Observations on Over-Determination." *Psychoanalytic Quarterly*, 5 (1936), 45–62.

Winnicott, D. W. *Playing and Reality.* New York: Basic, 1971. The central representative of British object-relations theory.

III. Criticism: Anthologies

These collections of essays and special journal issues span the range of modern psychological literary criticism from its earliest to its latest forms. They include examples of the uses of American, British, and French theoretical ideas.

Crews, Frederick, ed. *Psychoanalysis and Literary Process.* Cambridge, Mass.: Winthrop, 1970. Contains a guide to reading in psychoanalytic theory.

Faber, M. D. *The Design Within: Psychoanalytic Approaches to Shakespeare.* New York: Science House, 1970.

Felman, Shoshana, ed. *Literature and Psychoanalysis: The Question of Reading: Otherwise.* Special issue of *Yale French Studies*, 55–56 (1977).

French Freud: Structural Studies in Psychoanalysis. Special issue of *Yale French Studies*, 48 (1972). Rpt. New York: Kraus, 1976.

Hartman, Geoffrey H., ed. *Psychoanalysis and the Question of the Text.* Selected Papers from the English Institute, 1976–77. Baltimore: Johns Hopkins Univ. Press, 1978.

Klein, Richard, ed. *The Tropology of Freud.* Special issue of *Diacritics*, 9 (Spring 1979).

Manheim, Leonard, and Eleanor Manheim, eds. *Hidden Patterns: Studies in Psychoanalytic Literary Criticism.* New York: Macmillan, 1966.

Phillips, William, ed. *Art and Psychoanalysis.* New York: World, 1963.

Psychology and Literature: Some Contemporary Directions. Special issue of *New Literary History*, 12 (Autumn 1980).

Roland, Alan, ed. *Psychoanalysis, Creativity and Literature: A French-American Inquiry.* New York: Columbia Univ. Press, 1978.

Ruitenbeek, Hendrik, ed. *Psychoanalysis and Literature.* New York: Dutton, 1964.

Schwartz, Murray M., and Coppélia Kahn, eds. *Representing Shakespeare: New Psychoanalytic Essays.* Baltimore: Johns Hopkins Univ. Press, 1980. Contains a complete bibliography of psychological studies of Shakespeare since 1964.

Smith, Joseph H., ed. *Psychiatry and the Humanities.* 5 vols. New Haven: Yale Univ. Press, 1976–81. Vol. IV: *The Literary Freud: Mechanisms of Defense and the Poetic Will.*

Tennenhouse, Leonard, ed. *The Practice of Psychoanalytic Criticism.* Detroit: Wayne State Univ. Press, 1976.

Third Force Psychology and the Study of Literature. Special issue of *Literary Review,* 24 (Winter 1981).

IV. Criticism: Books and Articles

These items represent styles of psychological criticism as practiced in America and Europe. Each work is an example in its theoretical perspective and its way of relating theory and practice. (Some important authors are not included because their work is represented in the anthologies.)

Aronson, Alex. *Psyche and Symbol in Shakespeare.* Bloomington: Indiana Univ. Press, 1972.

Barthes, Roland. *On Racine.* Trans. Richard Howard. New York: Hill and Wang, 1964.

———. *The Pleasure of the Text.* Trans. Richard Miller. New York: Hill and Wang, 1975.

Bernheimer, Charles. *Flaubert and Kafka: Studies in Psychopoetic Structure.* New Haven: Yale Univ. Press, 1982.

Bersani, Leo. *Baudelaire and Freud.* Berkeley: Univ. of California Press, 1977.

———. "From Bachelard to Barthes." *Partisan Review,* 2 (1967), 215–32.

Bickman, Martin. *The Unsounded Centre: Jungian Studies in American Romanticism.* Chapel Hill: Univ. of North Carolina Press, 1980.

Bleich, David. *Readings and Feelings: An Introduction to Subjective Criticism.* Urbana, Ill.: National Council of Teachers of English, 1975.

Bloom, Harold. *The Anxiety of Influence: A Theory of Poetry.* New York: Oxford Univ. Press, 1974.

Bodkin, Maud. *Archetypal Patterns in Poetry: Psychological Studies of Imagination*. 1934; rpt. New York: Oxford Univ. Press, 1971.

Bonaparte, Marie. *The Life and Works of Edgar Allan Poe: A Psychoanalytic Interpretation*. 1949; rpt. New York: Humanities Press, 1971. Selections included in Phillips, *Art and Psychoanalysis*.

Burke, Kenneth. *Language as Symbolic Action: Essays on Life, Literature, and Method*. Berkeley: Univ. of California Press, 1966.

———. "Freud—and the Analysis of Poetry." Included in Phillips, *Art and Psychoanalysis*.

———. "Psychology and Form" (1924). *Counter-Statement*. 2nd ed. Chicago: Phoenix, 1952, pp. 29–44.

Crews, Frederick. *Out of My System: Psychoanalysis, Ideology, and Critical Method*. New York: Oxford Univ. Press, 1974.

———. *The Sins of the Fathers: Hawthorne's Psychological Themes*. London: Oxford Univ. Press, 1966.

Davis, Robert Con. *The Fictional Father: Lacanian Readings of the Text*. Amherst: Univ. of Massachusetts Press, 1981.

Derrida, Jacques. *Glas*. Paris: Editions Galilée, 1974.

———. *Of Grammatology*. Trans. Gayatri C. Spivak. Baltimore: Johns Hopkins Univ. Press, 1976.

———. "White Mythology: Metaphor in the Text of Philosophy." Trans. F. C. T. Moore. *New Literary History*, 6 (1974), 5–74.

Edel, Leon. *Literary Biography*. Garden City, N.Y.: Doubleday, 1959.

———. *Henry James*. 5 vols. Philadelphia: Lippincott, 1953–72.

Eissler, K. R. *Discourse on Hamlet and Hamlet: A Psychoanalytic Inquiry*. New York: International Universities Press, 1970.

Empson, William. *Some Versions of Pastoral*. 1935; rpt. New York: New Directions, 1960.

Fiedler, Leslie. *Love and Death in the American Novel*. 2nd ed. New York: Stein and Day, 1966.

———. "Archetype and Signature." Included in Phillips, *Art and Psychoanalysis*.

Fish, Stanley. "Literature in the Reader." *New Literary History*, 2 (1970), 123–62.

Fletcher, Angus. *Allegory: Theory of a Symbolic Mode*. Ithaca, N.Y.: Cornell Univ. Press, 1964.

Fruman, Norman. *Coleridge, the Damaged Archangel*. New York: Braziller, 1971.

Frye, Northrop. *A Natural Perspective: The Development of Shakespearean Comedy and Romance*. New York: Columbia Univ. Press, 1965.

Gilbert, Sandra, and Susan Gubar. *The Madwoman in the Attic: The Woman Writer and the Nineteenth-Century Imagination*. New Haven: Yale Univ. Press, 1979.

Greenacre, Phyllis. *Swift and Carroll: A Psychoanalytic Study of Two Lives*. New York: International Universities Press, 1955.

Harding, D. W. *Experience into Words*. New York: Horizon, 1964.

Hartman, Geoffrey H. "A Touching Compulsion: Wordsworth and the Problem of Literary Representation." *Georgia Review*, 31 (1977) 345–61. An example of psychoaesthetics.

———. *The Fate of Reading*. Chicago: Univ. of Chicago Press, 1975.

Hoffman, Frederick. *Freudianism and the Literary Mind*. 2nd ed. Baton Rouge: Louisiana State Univ. Press, 1957.

Holland, Norman N. *The Dynamics of Literary Response*. New York: Oxford Univ. Press, 1968. Develops an objective model of literary creation and meaning. Contains a glossary of psychoanalytic terms.

———. *5 Readers Reading*. New Haven: Yale Univ. Press, 1975. Psychoanalytic model of reader response based on the concept of identity themes.

――――. *Poems in Persons: An Introduction to the Psychoanalysis of Literature.* New York: Norton, 1973. Contains a guide to reading in literature and psychology.

Irwin, John T. *Doubling and Incest, Repetition and Revenge: A Speculative Reading of Faulkner.* Baltimore: Johns Hopkins Univ. Press, 1975.

Jones, Ernest. *Hamlet and Oedipus.* New York: Norton, 1949.

Kahane, Claire. "Flannery O'Connor's Range of Vision." *American Literature*, 46 (1974), 54–67.'

Kahn, Coppélia. *Man's Estate: Masculine Identity in Shakespeare.* Berkeley: Univ. of California Press, 1981.

Kaplan, Morton, and Robert Kloss. *The Unspoken Motive: A Guide to Psychoanalytic Literary Criticism.* New York: Free Press, 1973.

Kris, Ernst. *Psychoanalytic Explorations in Art.* New York: International Universities Press, 1952.

Lesser, Simon O. *Fiction and the Unconscious.* Boston: Beacon, 1957.

Lynch, David. *Yeats, the Poetics of the Self.* Chicago: Univ. of Chicago Press, 1979.

Macksey, Richard, and Eugenio Donato, eds. *The Structuralist Controversy: The Languages of Criticism and the Sciences of Man.* Baltimore: Johns Hopkins Univ. Press, 1972.

Marcus, Steven. "Freud and Dora: Story, History, Case History." *Psychoanalysis and Contemporary Science*, 5 (1976), 389–442.

Mauron, Charles. *Introduction to the Psychoanalysis of Mallarmé.* Trans. Archibold Henderson, Jr. and Will L. McLendon. Berkeley: Univ. of California Press, 1963.

Meyer, Bernard C. *Joseph Conrad: A Psychoanalytic Biography.* Princeton: Princeton Univ. Press, 1967.

Onorato, Richard J. *The Character of the Poet: Wordsworth in* The Prelude. Princeton: Princeton Univ. Press, 1971.

Orlando, Francesco. *Toward a Freudian Theory of Literature, with an Analysis of Racine's* Phèdre. Trans. Charmaine Lee. Baltimore: Johns Hopkins Univ. Press, 1978.

Paris, Bernard J. *A Psychological Approach to Fiction: Studies in Thackeray, Stendhal, George Eliot, Dostoevsky, and Conrad.* Bloomington: Indiana Univ. Press, 1974.

Peckham, Morse. *Man's Rage for Chaos: Biology, Behavior, and the Arts.* New York: Schocken, 1967.

Pops, Martin. *The Melville Archetype.* Kent, Ohio: Kent State Univ. Press, 1970.

Richards, I. A. *Practical Criticism: A Study of Literary Judgment.* New York: Harcourt, 1929.

Rogers, Robert. *A Psychoanalytic Study of the Double in Literature.* Detroit: Wayne State Univ. Press, 1970.

Said, Edward. *Beginnings: Intention and Method.* New York: Basic, 1975.

Schwartz, Murray M. "Where Is Literature?" *College English*, 36 (1975), 756–65.

Shechner, Mark. *Joyce in Nighttown: A Psychoanalytic Inquiry into* Ulysses. Berkeley: Univ. of California Press, 1974.

Skura, Meredith Anne. *The Literary Use of the Psychoanalytic Process.* New Haven: Yale Univ. Press, 1981. Good overview of the field.

Slatoff, Walter. *With Respect to Readers: Dimensions of Literary Response.* Ithaca, N.Y.: Cornell Univ. Press, 1970.

Trilling, Lionel. "Freud and Literature." Included in Phillips, *Art and Psychoanalysis.*

Wheeler, Richard P. *Shakespeare's Development and the Problem Comedies: Turn and Counter-Turn*. Berkeley: Univ. of California Press, 1981.

Willbern, David. "Freud and the Inter-penetration of Dreams." *Diacritics*, 9 (1979), 98–110.

Wolff, Cynthia Griffin. *A Feast of Words: The Triumph of Edith Wharton*. New York: Oxford Univ. Press, 1977.

V. *Periodicals*

The following representative quarterlies and annuals are of two sorts: (1) psychological journals receptive to essays on literature and (2) literary journals amenable to psychological approaches:

(1) *American Imago, The International Review of Psycho-Analysis, Psychiatry and the Humanities* (annual), *The Psychoanalytic Quarterly, The Psychoanalytic Review.*

(2) *College English, Comparative Drama, Contemporary Literature, Critical Inquiry, Criticism, Diacritics, English Literary Renaissance, Hartford Studies in Literature, Literature and Psychology, New Literary History, PMLA, Texas Studies in Literature and Language.*

11

Literature and Music

STEVEN PAUL SCHER

Poets and musicians are members of one church, related in the most intimate way: for the secret of word and tone is one and the same.

E. T. A. HOFFMANN

What demon pushes the composer so inexorably to literature? What is the power that compels him in emergency to become a poet himself? Is it merely the longing for the lost Paradise, for that original unity which can never be regained?

PIERRE BOULEZ

To find a true word in music is as lucky as to find true music in words.

WILLIAM W. AUSTIN

That music and literature share their origin is a notion as old as the first stirrings of aesthetic consciousness. Even a cursory glance at the evolution of the arts confirms that "histories of both have remained in many ways mutually contingent."[1] As the two arts developed, diverse theories were advanced about their comparability as basic media of artistic expression. From early on, juxtapositions now all too familiar, like "music and poetry," "word and tone," and "sound and poetry," recur with formulaic frequency in critical discourse. Though rarely substantiated by a precise definition, such commonplace juxtapositions lend a deceptively axiomatic aura of legitimacy to comparisons of the two arts. Indeed, by their cumulative presence alone, these clichés seem to authenticate what has been traditionally viewed in aesthetic speculation as a relation of mutual dependency. But as scrutiny of critical theory and practice reveals, the relation is precarious and beset with interpretive pitfalls: while in many instances the two arts are virtually inseparable, there are also apparent correlations that ultimately prove to be illusory or at best metaphorical.

225

It may seem odd to begin a discussion of the manifold alliance of literature and music on a skeptical note. Yet it is necessary here as a preventive measure, for the study of this correspondence — perhaps more than any other study of interart parallels — holds "a fatal attraction for the dilettante, the faddist and the crackpot."[2] One reason for this attraction may be the tacit endorsement in aesthetics and art criticism of the cliché that music is the art most closely allied with literature. A generalization of this sort, however true, often fosters the illusion that scholars in the field require little if any specialized background. To be sure, the spectrum of possible parallels between the two arts is vast. But that most of these parallels are also enormously complex is not readily evident even to musically sophisticated students of literature or, for that matter, to musicologists with considerable literary erudition. Precisely here lies the difficulty for prospective practitioners of musico-literary study: namely, that more often than not they make the decisive initial contact with this "interarts borderland"[3] of literary and musical aesthetics on too high a level of generalization. Uninitiated parallel seekers thus enter the happy hunting ground of musico-literary relations with insufficient ammunition, yet expect to emerge with a handsome booty. What awaits them behind the unassuming conjunction "and" is an infinite variety of affinities, interplays, and analogies as well as divergencies; to master the complexities, they need a knowledge of the fundamental principles, creative potentialities, and interpretive possibilities of both arts.

No matter how similar literature and music may appear on occasion, they are only analogous, never identical. In addressing some of the basic issues and preoccupations of musico-literary criticism, an attempt will be made to maintain a reasonable balance between the literary and the musical perspectives. A systematic and a historical overview of the interrelation will be included as well as consideration of more general questions concerning the boundaries between the two arts: where and how do they overlap or transgress their individual confines; what are the typical, concrete manifestations of the interaction, based on specific affinities; which are the major areas and commonly practiced types of comparative investigation; and to what extent can legitimate comparisons succeed and be fruitful for the literary scholar? To facilitate orientation, the parallels between the two arts will be divided into three categories: music and literature, literature in music, and music in literature.[4]

Manifestations of what we generally call "vocal music" fall under the heading "music and literature." In vocal music, literary text and musical composition are inextricably bound. Together they constitute a symbiotic construct that qualifies as a full-fledged work of art only if components of both are simultaneously present. Most common among such combinations of text and music in a single work are operas and lieder (art songs), along with a host of other forms familiar from past centuries of European musical and theatrical history, such as oratorios, cantatas, masses, motets, madrigals, a cappella choruses, ballads, the English masque, and the German singspiel. From its early seventeenth-century beginnings, opera has been a unique and indestructible form of artistic expression fusing poetry and music into a theatrical spectacle, and it has generated memorable partnerships between poets and composers of stature; in the twentieth century, for example, Richard Strauss collaborated with Hugo von Hofmannsthal, and Igor Stravinsky with Jean Cocteau and W. H. Auden. Perhaps even better known are those cases in which composers drew inspiration from existing literary works to create operatic masterpieces or outstanding examples of the lied: Giuseppe Verdi's *Macbeth*, *Otello*, and *Falstaff*; Modest Mussorgsky's *Boris Godunov*; Alban Berg's *Wozzeck*; Benjamin Britten's *Billy Budd*; Franz Peter Schubert's settings of Goethe poems; and Robert Schumann's Eichendorff songs readily come to mind. In the interaction between text and music, poets and musicians no doubt recognized an opportunity to transcend the communicative limitations of the individual art forms. The manifold aspects of where and how word interacts and intersects with tone have proved most rewarding for musico-literary study.

Traditionally, in spite of the obvious points of reciprocal contact between the two arts, vocal music has been regarded as a primarily musical genre. No one would seriously think of, say, Verdi's operas based on Shakespeare plays or Schubert's Goethe lieder as first and foremost literary creations. Yet interpreters of such works cannot dispense with the literary aspect of the relation. After all, it is almost always a given text that inspires the composer's musical realization, even if it undergoes alteration in the creative process. For a long time, opera criticism and lied scholarship have been practiced almost exclusively by musicologists. As a result, the poetic elements in the word-tone synthesis have rarely received due attention.[5] In recent years, however, remarkable progress has been made by musically informed literary critics toward a correction of this imbalance, notably by Ulrich Weisstein, Gary Schmidgall, Peter Conrad, and Jack M. Stein. Analysis of the complex artistic conditions conducive to a realization of optimal musical settings of poetic texts; discussion of matters of priority, such as the recurring dilemma of collaborating composers, poets, and librettists about the relative merit of the text or the music — "prima le parole e dopo la musica" or "prima la musica e poi le parole"; speculation about the particular choice, nature, and aesthetic value of the text to be set to music; and inquiry into specific theoretical and interpretive problems generated by the diverse attempts to achieve an ideal word-tone synthesis: these are only a sampling of the most frequently treated topics concerning composite instances of music and literature.

"Literature in music" conveniently designates works customarily referred to as "program music." Though, like vocal music, a primarily musical genre, program music invites the scrutiny of the literary scholar inasmuch as it often exhibits an impact of literature on music. Particularly in nineteenth-

and early twentieth-century music, this impact has been so considerable that we may say that most examples of program music represent attempts on the part of their composers at "literarization" of music. In contradistinction to "absolute" or "abstract" music that possesses no extramusical connotations, program music is defined as instrumental music inspired by or based on "a nonmusical idea, which is usually indicated in the title and sometimes described in explanatory remarks or a preface."[6] In 1854 Franz Liszt coined the term "symphonic poem" (later also known as "tone poem") for what has since become the most common type of such expressive instrumental music. Liszt's own pioneering symphonic poems like *Tasso* or *Hamlet* and his Dante and Faust symphonies were followed by a host of others similarly inspired by specific literary works, as for example Hector Berlioz' *Harold en Italie* (based on Lord Byron's *Childe Harold*), Hugo Wolf's *Penthesilea* (after Heinrich von Kleist's tragedy), Richard Strauss's *Don Juan* (after Nikolaus Lenau), Paul Dukas's *L'Apprenti sorcier* (after Johann Wolfgang von Goethe's ballad "Der Zauberlehrling") and Claude Debussy's *Prélude à l'après-midi d'un faune* (after Stéphane Mallarmé's eclogue). Some of the best-known pieces of program music, however, were inspired by nonliterary sources such as impressions of landscape and events in nature (Ludwig van Beethoven's *Pastoral Symphony*), nationalistic themes (Bedřich Smetana's *Má Vlast*), specific paintings (Mussorgsky's *Pictures at an Exhibition*) and quasi-philosophical writings (Strauss's *Also sprach Zarathustra*, after Friedrich Nietzsche).

Critical consideration of the theoretical and interpretive ramifications of program music is contingent on a grasp of the history and aesthetics of music. Particularly relevant in this context is the controversy that arose in response to Eduard Hanslick's 1854 treatise *Vom Musikalisch-Schönen* (*The Beautiful in Music*) between "formalist" and "expressionist" aestheticians about the meaning of music.[7] This ongoing controversy harbors implications for the correlation of music and literature: the issue intimated here is the incomparability of the two arts. Clearly, "since any literary work is composed of words conveying some sort of definite conceptual meaning, through proper combination of words literature can communicate, express, or evoke a wide range of possibilities beyond itself. Music, on the other hand, is not composed of words and therefore lacks conceptual meaning" (Scher, *Verbal Music*, p. 163). Directed at the time against the overtly dramatic, illustrative tendency in Richard Wagner's and Liszt's compositional approach, Hanslick's definition "Moving patterns of sound are the sole content and object of music" (p. 32) confirms the essential difference in expressivity between the two arts. This difference continues to separate the formalists or absolutists (champions of absolute music) from the expressionists or programmatists (champions of program music). Two contrasting statements illustrate the irreconcilability in basic outlook. Almost a century later the convinced formalist Igor Stravinsky still echoes Hanslick: "I consider that music is, by its very nature, powerless to *express* anything at all, . . . if, as is nearly always the case, music appears to express something, this is only an illusion, and not reality."[8] The British musicologist Deryck Cooke, in his polemical *The Language of Music*, espouses the opposite extreme: "The 'literary' aspect of music is to be found, to a greater or lesser extent, in most Western music written between 1400 and the present day, since music is, properly speaking, a language of the emotions, akin to speech. . . . Music is, in fact, 'extra-musical' in the sense that poetry is 'extra-verbal,' since notes, like words, have emotional connotations . . . " (p. 33).

So far, few literary critics have ventured beyond source study into the aesthetics of program music and grappled with the implications of the problematic presence, nature, and effectiveness of the literary model as reflected in the musical realization.[9] The best treatment of these and related aspects can be found in Calvin S. Brown's *Music and Literature: A Comparison of the Arts* (1948). In several chapters devoted to what he terms "literary types in music," Brown offers comprehensive analytical surveys of the kinds of program music, evaluates their literariness, and makes distinctions between descriptive and narrative types of program music.

"Music in literature" is the only one of the three areas of the interrelation that encompasses exclusively literary works of art. While unalterably bound to the literary medium of expression, in one way or another all these works represent attempts at "musicalization" of literature or verbalization of music. No matter how similar to music purely verbal constructs may be, in the nature of their material they remain fundamentally different from works whose medium is primarily musical, such as absolute, vocal, or program music. Literary texts cannot transcend the confines of literary texture and become musical texture. Literature lacks the unique acoustic quality of music; only through ingenious linguistic means or special literary techniques can it imply, evoke, imitate, or otherwise indirectly approximate actual music and thus create what amounts at best to a verbal semblance of music. Firmly anchored in the literary realm, manifestations of music in literature promise to be most rewarding for literary study. But the possibilities of literary treatment of music are so numerous and diverse that only the three basic kinds can be discussed and illustrated here in some detail: "word music," musical structures and techniques in literary works, and "verbal music." They will be reviewed as part of a larger framework of the major methodological strategies practiced by critics who deal with musico-literary parallels: the synchronic approach concerning the systematic relations and the diachronic approach concerning the historical relations between the two arts.

The essential distinction between affinity in material and affinity in structure determines the nature and extent of systematic analogies between literature and music. Organized sound serves as basic material for both arts, a shared feature that immediately suggests the idea of comparability. But caution is in order, for the literary sound unit differs substantially from the

musical sound unit: the individual word can (and usually does) carry semantic connotations, whereas the individual tone cannot. Word music, for example, is a rather common type of poetic practice that aims primarily at
imitation in words of the acoustic quality of music (frequently also of nonmusical sound) and that is realizable because of affinities in basic material
(Yoshida, "Word-Music"). "Experimenters with such 'pure' poetry or prose
of intense sound attempt to evoke the auditory sensation of music by com-
posing verbal structures consisting predominantly of onomatopoeic words
or word clusters" (Scher, *Verbal Music*, p. 3). Onomatopoeia is, of course,
the technique most often used to approximate in words the effect of sound.
Particular constituents superimposed on organized sound structures and
patterns in both music and language likewise substantiate affinity in material:
rhythm, stress, pitch (intonation), and timbre (tone color) are all applicable
in literature, more or less effectively, to create musiclike textures. Selected
strategies of versification such as alliteration, assonance, consonance, and
rhyme schemes are purely literary and have also been successfully utilized
for this purpose. A sampling of characteristic examples from the last two
centuries shows that poetic preoccupation with the phenomenon of word
music is by no means confined to any one national literature: we often encounter it in allusive poems by Clemens Brentano, Joseph von Eichendorff,
Edgar Allan Poe, Charles Baudelaire, Paul Verlaine, Mallarmé (and other
French symbolists); in Edith Sitwell's "poésie pure"; in the nonsense lyrics
of the Dadaists Hugo Ball, Hans Arp, and Kurt Schwitters; in the imaginative sound poems (*Lautgedichte*) of the Austrian Ernst Jandl; and in virtuo-
so prose passages of James Joyce's *Ulysses* and *Finnegans Wake*. The first
stanza of Verlaine's poem "Chanson d'automne" illustrates word music at
its suggestive best:

> Les sanglots longs
> Des violons
>   De l'automne
> Blessent mon cœur
> D'une langueur
>   Monotone.[10]

But even here the successful imitation of musical timbre—through transparent interplay of appropriate diction, assonances, and rhymes—depends on
the poet's naming of the violin, whose timbre is being imitated. Without this
suggestive aid (comparable to the function of suggestive literary titles in
program music) even a reader endowed with the most fertile imagination
would find it difficult to identify the instrument in question, supposing that
he or she could associate the imitative verbal timbre with a musical instrument at all.

In the traditional classification of the fine arts, music and literature are
viewed as closely akin, because they both are auditory, temporal, and dy-

namic art forms. (Painting, sculpture, and architecture, on the other hand, resemble one another on account of their visual, spatial, and static nature.) Without the auditory quality inherent in both music and literature, for example, imitative experiments with word music would be inconceivable. That by nature both arts are also temporal and dynamic becomes particularly relevant when we consider their affinities in structure. Since in an abstract sense receptive comprehension of both arts requires attentive tracing of a certain movement to be completed in time, both "music and literature are *activities* to be realized; they ... create ... 'things to be done' (a score to be performed or a book to be read), i.e. processes which still need to be decoded" (Scher, "Literature and Music," p. 38). In terms of musico-literary critical practice, decoding here means recognition and interpretation of certain corresponding formal designs and organizing strategies in literature that create the impression of comparable progressive movement. Clearly, imitation of standard musical forms and features based on concrete structural affinities deserves special critical attention when the "musiclike" organization is integrated as unobtrusively and fully as possible into the literary work. In such rare instances analysis can advance beyond mere recognition to a critical evaluation of the contours similar to music. The demonstrable correspondences occasioned by the interart transfer constitute an additional interpretive dimension within the musically inspired literary work.

In spite of the difficulties involved, many authors susceptible to music's formative impact have found the borrowing of musical strategies for literary purposes an irresistible challenge. Two major types of such borrowing are the adaptation of larger musical structures and patterns and the application of certain musical techniques and devices common to both arts. Aldous Huxley, an avid and not inept practitioner of music in literature, provides an illuminating theoretical digression in his novel *Point Counter Point* on how some musical techniques might be translated into novelistic practice:

> The musicalization of fiction. Not in the symbolist way, by subordinating sense to sound. ... But on a large scale, in the construction. Meditate on Beethoven. The changes of moods, the abrupt transitions. ... More interesting still, the modulations, not merely from one key to another, but from mood to mood. A theme is stated, then developed, pushed out of shape, imperceptibly deformed, until, though still recognizably the same, it has become quite different. In sets of variations the process is carried a step further. Those incredible Diabelli variations, for example. The whole range of thought and feeling, yet all in organic relation to a ridiculous waltz tune. Get this into a novel. How? The abrupt transitions are easy enough. All you need is a sufficiency of characters and parallel, contrapuntal plots. ... More interesting, the modulations and variations are also more difficult. A novelist modulates by repudiating situation and characters. He shows several people falling in love, or dying, or praying in different ways—

dissimilars solving the same problem. . . . In this way you can modulate through all the aspects of your theme, you can write variations in any number of different moods.[11]

From a musical point of view, Huxley's methodological musings verge on dilettantism. But as a writer of fiction Huxley is entitled to a laxer usage of terms like theme, modulation, or variation; as a precondition for creative reflection, he must be allowed to contemplate the other medium from a distance and interpret its ground rules with flexibility.

Among the larger structures, the theme and variations, the sonata, the fugue, and the rondo form have been attempted most frequently—and at times quite successfully—in literature. Based on the principles of repetition and variation indispensable to both music and literature, the literary set of variations comes perhaps closest to approximating its musical counterpart. In a recent article, "Theme and Variations as a Literary Form," Calvin S. Brown has examined some effective uses, found as early as in Eve's morning song to Adam in John Milton's *Paradise Lost* (IV.641–56). Later examples include Ludwig Tieck's romantic comedy *Die verkehrte Welt*, Robert Browning's *The Ring and the Book*, and Raymond Queneau's *Exercise de style*. Interpretive insights have been derived from the sonata form as an inconspicuous but demonstrable overall design in prose works such as Thomas Mann's *Tonio Kröger* and Hermann Hesse's *Der Steppenwolf*.[12] Thomas De Quincey's "Dream Fugue" and Paul Celan's "Todesfuge" are considered the most convincing literary realizations of the fugue. As for the literary rondo, here is a compact passage from the "sirens" section of Joyce's *Ulysses*:

> From the saloon a call came, long in dying. That was a tuning fork the tuner had that he forgot that he now struck. A call again. That he now poised that it now throbbed. You hear? It throbbed, pure, purer, softly and softlier, its buzzing prongs. Longer in dying call.[13]

In music the rondo is essentially an extended A-B-A form that resembles the tripartite (exposition-development-recapitulation) sonata form. The usual scheme for the musical rondo is A-B-A-C-A-D-A. . . . In this passage Joyce succeeds in approximating the musical scheme in miniature. A "call" constitutes the regularly recurring basic theme or refrain (A). In between its recurrences, distinctly different contrasting themes or episodes (B and C) appear and linger on a while before they are finally abandoned so that the refrain (A) can once again return.[14]

Organizing principles such as repetition, variation, balance, and contrast pervade both musical and literary textures; and the straightforward way they usually function in the respective arts yields many points of contact for legitimate comparison. Only the leitmotiv—a unique, more sophisticated repetition technique of truly mixed origin—needs special comment. The term itself was coined by the Wagnerite critic Hans von Wolzogen to denote the recurring musical themes (*Grundthema* was Wagner's own designation) attached to characters, objects, situations, and ideas that together form the associative network underlying the Wagnerian *Gesamtkunstwerk*. But the technique in literature can be traced back to the principle of formulaic repetition evident in the Homeric *epitheton ornans* and has been refined and employed in epic tradition ever since: "a verbal formula which is deliberately repeated, which is easily recognized at each recurrence, and which serves, by means of this recognition, to link the context in which the repetition occurs with earlier contexts in which the motive has appeared" (Brown, *Music and Literature*, p. 211). Indiscriminate use of the leitmotiv as a catchword for any kind of literary repetition has resulted in horrendous misinterpretations familiar to readers of modern and contemporary criticism. However disconcerting these critical blunders may be, they should not deter us from realizing that the literary leitmotiv — responsibly defined — provides a rare instance of genuinely reciprocal impact of music and literature: an associative technique that, as an overall structural principle, can be analogously employed in dramatic vocal music, in instrumental music, and in epic (less frequently also in dramatic) literature. As Marcel Proust's *A la recherche du temps perdu* and Thomas Mann's oeuvre clearly demonstrate, the impact of the Wagnerian leitmotiv on modern literature can hardly be overestimated. More specifically, documentary evidence confirms that there is a direct line from the musical leitmotiv — from Wagner through Eduard Dujardin and Italo Svevo to Joyce — to the stream-of-consciousness technique.

Transplantation of other standard musical devices and features into literature has also been tried, though with disappointing results. Not even the favorably disposed reader's total suspension of disbelief can help the author to suggest the actual impression of a musical phrase that is attempted in a text only through punctuation or syntax; resemblance to tonality in music cannot be conveyed specifically enough by a main theme, idea, or topic that permeates a literary work; and modulation from one key to another in a composition is something very different from what Huxley calls modulation "from mood to mood" in a novel. The outcome of such interart transfers is usually so vague that even the endeavor itself seems hardly worthwhile. Yet we cannot dismiss these attempts as fascinating aberrations, for no matter how hopeless, they represent an aesthetic impulse on the part of their authors to transcend the limitations of their own medium of expression (in this case literature) and cross over into another medium (in this case music), while still remaining necessarily confined to the original medium. Given the impossibility of the task and the fascination that it has elicited, the improbable notion of a literary equivalent to counterpoint warrants a closer look.

Counterpoint denotes "music consisting of two or more lines that sound simultaneously."[15] In order to achieve a semblance of polyphonic construction, literature would have to be able to present and sustain two or more ideas or narrative strains simultaneously — which, by the nature of its medium, it cannot do. That the notion of literary counterpoint continues nevertheless to be entertained by authors and critics is a telling example of the aesthetic intent to overcome a fundamental difference between the two arts, namely, that the idea of fusing sequentiality and simultaneity is achievable in music but only conceivable in literature. Interestingly enough, even in a mixed medium like vocal music, which is not primarily literary, quasi-contrapuntal simultaneity has a restricting effect: the simultaneous presentation of words and music may retard or impede full comprehension of the text. In the lied, for example, the musical dimension represents a continuous distraction for the listener who wants to understand the words. Or in operatic ensemble singing, say, in a quartet where the four characters sing different lines simultaneously, total comprehension of the individual lines is severely limited, if not impossible. According to Calvin S. Brown, in literature proper the genuine pun comes closest to contrapuntal simultaneity, though still not close enough (*Music and Literature*, p. 42). For in a pun, only one idea can actually be told, which, during its telling, simultaneously implies another idea; that idea, if the pun is understood, can be simultaneously perceived but has not actually been told. Theodore Ziolkowski takes Brown's cue one step further when he claims that in Hermann Hesse's *Der Steppenwolf* "double perception achieves the effect of a sustained pun, and the interplay of the two levels of reality produces a genuine contrapuntal effect."[16] Prominent modern experimenters with counterpoint in literature include Aldous Huxley (*Point Counter Point*), André Gide (*Les Faux-Monnayeurs*), and, of course, James Joyce, who invented words like *bespectable* and even "had a special theory about what he called the 'polyphonic' word which would emit two meanings just as a chord emits several notes in one sound."[17] In a recent book on *Laurence Sterne and the Origins of the Musical Novel*, William Freedman has tried to make a case for polyphonic construction as the predominant narrative technique in *Tristram Shandy*, but Erwin Rotermund's discussion of the sustained effort of quasi-contrapuntal simultaneity created by the two alternating, continually converging narrative strains in E. T. A. Hoffmann's remarkably modern romantic novel *Kater Murr* seems more convincing.[18] It should be clear, however, that any parallel between musical and literary counterpoint can only be metaphorical; and the term itself, as used widely in literary criticism, translates in plain language to mean various forms of contrast.

"Verbal music" as a general designation has been gaining wide currency in recent musico-literary criticism; it refers to the third basic kind of imitative approach to music in literature, which may draw on any, all, or none of the affinities discussed above. In critical usage verbal music must not be confused with seemingly similar terms such as word music, vocal music, or literary music (sometimes used for program music) that, as we have seen, mean something different. I have defined verbal music as "any literary presentation (whether in poetry or prose) of existing or fictitious musical compositions: any poetic texture which has a piece of music as its 'theme.' In addition to approximating in words an actual or fictitious score, such poems or passages often suggest characterization of a musical performance or of subjective response to music" (Scher, *Verbal Music*, p. 8). In many ways verbal music is the most genuinely literary among musico-literary phenomena, perhaps because successful attempts to render poetically the intellectual and emotional import and intimated symbolic content of music tend to be less specific and restricting in mimetic aim and thus less obtrusive than direct imitations of particular sound effects or elements of musical form. Prominent poets like Brentano, Franz Grillparzer, Verlaine, and Algernon Charles Swinburne (as well as all too many less prominent ones) have experimented with verbal music in lyric poetry, on the whole with unconvincing results. Calvin S. Brown, who has studied these attempts exhaustively in his *Tones into Words*, assesses them as "distinctly minor verse" (p. 2), containing little more than vague, dilettantish effusions about the intoxicating beauty and power of music. Verbal music in prose, however, possesses greater aesthetic potential. As a versatile combination of rhetorical, syntactical, and stylistic strategies, it can create plausible literary semblances of actual or fictitious music as well as integrate musiclike verbal textures unobtrusively into a larger epic context, which is normally sustained by a network of anticipatory and retrospective allusions. Diverse examples of verbal music in prose abound in German literature since 1800 (notably, E. T. A. Hoffmann, Kleist, Grillparzer, Heinrich Heine, Eduard Mörike, Thomas Mann, Hesse, and more recently Wolfgang Hildesheimer) but can also be found frequently in French, Russian, and English works.[19] The following excerpt from Chapter xv of Thomas Mann's *Doktor Faustus*, a veritable "verbal score" of the Prelude to Act III of Wagner's opera *Die Meistersinger von Nürnberg*, demonstrates the connotative quality and far-reaching interpretive possibilities inherent in the phenomenon of verbal music. In a candid letter to his musical mentor, the hero, Adrian Leverkühn, an avant-garde composer, offers an ironically tinged illustration to justify his rejection of the traditional concept of the beautiful as it culminates in cadence-conscious Wagnerian music:

> It goes like this when it is beautiful: the cellos by themselves intone a melancholy, pensive theme, which, in a manner both highly expressive and decorously philosophical, questions the world's folly, the wherefore of all the struggle and striving, pursuing and plaguing. The cellos, head-shaking and deploring, enlarge upon this riddle for a while, and at a certain point in their remarks, a well-chosen point, the choir of wind instruments enters with a deep, full breath that makes your shoulders rise and fall, in a choral hymn, movingly solemn, richly harmonized, and produced with all the muted dignity and mildly restrained power of the brass. Thus the sonorous melody presses on up to nearly the height of a climax, which, in accordance with the laws of economy, it at first avoids, yielding, leaving open, holding in reserve,

remaining very beautiful even so, then withdrawing and giving way to another subject, a songlike, simple one, now jesting, now grave, now popular, apparently robust by nature, but sly as can be, and, for someone seasoned in the arts of analysis and transformation, astoundingly full of possibilities of significance and refinement. This little song is managed and deployed for a while, cleverly and charmingly. It is taken apart, looked at in detail and varied. Out of it, a delightful figure in the middle register is led up into the most enchanting heights of fiddles and flutes, lulls itself there a little, and then, when it is at its most artful, the mild brass again takes up the word with the earlier choral hymn and moves into the foreground—not, however, starting with a deep breath from the beginning as it did the first time, but as though its melody had already been going all along—and it continues, solemnly, to that climax from which it had so wisely refrained the first time, in order that the surging feeling, the Ah-h effect, might be the greater, now, that, mounting unchecked and with weighty support from the passing notes of the bass tuba, it can gloriously bestride the theme, looking back, as it were, with dignified satisfaction on the finished achievement, singing its way modestly to the end.[20]

An ingenious blend of imitation, description, analysis, and interpretation, this single, self-contained paragraph reflects the musical essence and suggests the metaphorical dimensions of Wagner's Prelude. But beneath the descriptive surface texture that allows initiated readers to re-create in their reading experience the effect of listening to this orchestral composition, other contextual and structural levels of meaning crucial to the interpretation of the entire novel may be discerned. For instance, the exegesis of the Prelude can be read as a camouflaged confession in which the evoked musical outlines and events symbolically correspond to certain formative influences and major events in Leverkühn's life: allusions to his early years as well as anticipations of his extraordinary musical career made possible by his encounter with the mysterious Hetaera Esmeralda, who embodies the diabolical.[21]

Verbal music is a literary phenomenon and as such must be distinguished from the nonliterary verbalization of music that is practiced by music critics and musicologists, usually in the form of program notes accompanying a musical performance, reviews of performed music, or technical descriptions of music. G. B. Shaw's parody of the nonliterary style and diction of contemporary music reviewing accentuates the difference:

Here the composer, by one of those licences which are, perhaps, permissible under exceptional circumstances to men of genius, but which cannot be too carefully avoided by students desirous of forming a legitimate style, has abruptly introduced the dominant seventh of the key of C major into the key of A flat, in order to recover, by a forced modulation, the key relationship proper to the second subject of a movement in F—an awkward device which he might have spared himself by simply introducing his second subject in its true key of C.[22]

The following diagram presents the relations of literature and music in a systematic typology and shows how the major areas of musico-literary study and the basic kinds of musico-literary phenomena are interconnected:

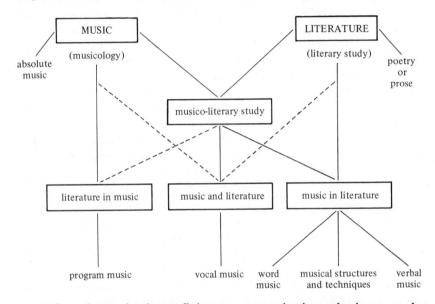

A few other topics do not fit into our categorization as basic approaches to music in literature but have generated significant critical response. Ever since the advent of European Romanticism, for example, experimentation with music's role in literary synesthesia—"poetic interpretation of musical experiences in terms of specific colors or visual images" (Scher, *Verbal Music*, p. 166)—has been a trend, from the German and English Romantics to the French symbolists and beyond (more recently in the poetry of Hart Crane and Wallace Stevens). *Doppelbegabung* is a phenomenon that has been studied for its effect on the artistic physiognomy of extraordinary multiple talents like E. T. A. Hoffmann, Wagner, and Nietzsche.[23] Both musicologists and literary critics have found it rewarding to investigate the music criticism of such authors as Hoffmann, Stendhal, G. B. Shaw, and Ezra Pound from the point of view that they also excelled as competent music critics (see Braun and Graf). But most common are studies that treat musician figures in fiction (Schoolfield) like Hoffmann's Johannes Kreisler (*Kater Murr*), Romain Rolland's Jean Christophe (Sices), and Thomas Mann's Leverkühn and analyze the creative influence of music on literary periods and individual writers.

The latter topic—music's influence on periods and authors—suggests that the synchronic, systematic relations between music and literature must be viewed together with diachronic, historical correlations such as periodization, reception, dissemination, and influence. Take for instance the highly problematic area of periodization.[24] To what extent are we justified in assuming a parallel development in music and literature during a given cultural period, for example, that of the so-called Romantic era? Is the period term "impressionism" more or less equally applicable to a certain identifiable style in both arts? Is there an expressionistic style in twentieth-century music comparable to the stylistic traits we commonly associate with literary expressionism? Since scholarly opinion on these questions differs widely (and wildly), do we side with Kurt Wais, who believes in what he called the "parallel development of the arts"? Or do we espouse René Wellek and Austin Warren's conviction that "'classicism' in music must mean something very different from its use in literature for the simple reason that no real classical music (with the exception of a few fragments) was known and could thus shape the evolution of music as literature was actually shaped by the precepts and practice of antiquity" (*Theory of Literature*, pp. 127–28)? Until we develop a solid theoretical and methodological foundation for period comparisons, no definitive answers can be provided; and diachronic interart analogies will remain limited, both in scope and in interpretive validity.

A historical overview of the development of aesthetics, however, is necessary at this point, for "the system of aesthetics is its history: a history which is permeated with ideas and experiences of heterogeneous origin."[25] As reflected in the theories and methodologies that have shaped musicoliterary scholarship, such an overview will complement the foregoing systematic consideration of the parallels and differences between the two arts. Although philosophers of classical antiquity like Plato and Aristotle engaged in speculation concerning the nature, relative merits, and comparability of literature and the other arts, including literature and music, scholarly activity in the modern sense, focusing specifically on interart relations, is of more recent origin: it evolved during the eighteenth century as part of general aesthetics, which by then had established itself as a more or less independent discipline. The first comparative treatments regard music and literature as separate but parallel "sister arts." Appropriately, Hildebrande Jacob's early attempt to determine the fundamental affinities and correspondences between the two arts and their relative ranking within the contemporary hierarchy of the arts bears the title *Of the Sister Arts* (London, 1734). In this hierarchy, still based on the Aristotelian mimetic principle, poetry occupied first place, with painting second and music only an inferior third. But around mid-century, expressive theories of music—derived from the influential *Affektenlehre* 'doctrine of affections' of the baroque period—began to undermine the reigning concept of imitation in the arts.[26] Charles Avison was the first critic to stress, in his *An Essay on Musical Expression* (London,

1752), the emotive aspect of music and convincingly challenge the primacy of the traditional mimetic principle, still firmly upheld by French aestheticians like Charles Batteux and Jean-Baptiste Du Bos.[27] Avison's treatise inspired the first specific scholarly comparisons of poetry and music as "sister" arts by fellow British aestheticians John Brown, Daniel Webb, James Beattie, and Thomas Twining.[28] Clearly, for these critics poetry and music, rather than poetry and painting, were the true "sister" arts.

This British trend of specific comparisons was sympathetically received and further refined in German by aestheticians like Johann Georg Sulzer, Johann Nikolaus Forkel, and Johann Gottfried von Herder.[29] And it is this very trend that culminated a few decades later in the emotion-oriented aesthetics of "melomaniac" Romanticists like Wilhelm Wackenroder, Ludwig Tieck, Novalis, and E. T. A. Hoffmann, who proclaimed the supremacy of music among the arts: in the new hierarchy, music, and not poetry, was "the art most immediately expressive of spirit and emotion."[30] Ever since 1800, Romantic aesthetics, openly advocating the elimination of boundaries between literature and music in theory and poetic practice, has had a major impact on the development of the interrelation. Musicalization of literature is a quintessentially Romantic notion, after all: it was first attempted in earnest by Romantic authors whose works inspired all later musico-literary experimenters, including the French symbolists, Joyce, and Thomas Mann. Also part of the Romantic legacy, throughout the nineteenth century and beyond, is the radical impulse toward literarization of music in the form of program music (Beethoven, Berlioz, Liszt), the lied (Schubert, Schumann, Johannes Brahms, and Hugo Wolf), and the literary opera (Wagner's music dramas). And without the lingering climate of Romantic aesthetics, even Eduard Hanslick's formalist manifesto *Vom Musikalisch-Schönen* of 1854 —categorically rejecting the expressive principle in music—could not have been written.

Jules Combarieu's *Les Rapports de la musique et de la poésie, considérées au point de vue de l'expression* of 1894 marks a new departure for musico-literary scholarship. Of clearly antiformalist persuasion, Combarieu presents for the first time a philologically as well as musicologically reliable comparative study of the correspondences. The next landmark is Oskar Walzel's pioneering treatise of 1917, *Wechselseitige Erhellung der Künste*, along with his comprehensive *Gehalt und Gestalt im Kunstwerk des Dichters* of 1923, which contains several analytical chapters on the interrelations of "Dichtkunst und Musik" in the light of his concept of "reciprocal illumination of the arts." Also in 1923, though independent of Walzel, André Coeuroy published his traditional, more musicologically oriented *Musique et littérature: Etudes de musique et de littérature comparées*. Until today, René Wellek's historical survey of 1942, "The Parallelism between Literature and the Arts," constitutes the most informative critical assessment of twentieth-century international research concerning interart analogies; and in retrospect his timely skepticism toward vague analogizing in the arts remains justified.

The period since World War II shows definite signs of a renewed scholarly interest in the exploration of the parallels between literature and the other arts. The rekindling of this interest in musico-literary studies is due chiefly to the efforts of Calvin S. Brown, whose contributions to the field over the last thirty years have made him its central, most influential figure. In his *Music and Literature: A Comparison of the Arts* of 1948, the only comprehensive modern scholarly treatment of the interrelation to date, Brown systematically surveys, analyzes, and evaluates virtually all musico-literary phenomena with sound judgment, common sense, and admirable terminological rigor. Similarly exemplary is the article "Musico-Literary Research in the Last Two Decades," the only recent review of scholarship in the field that is of truly international scope, in which Brown surveys significant or representative studies published between 1950 and 1970 and assesses the emerging theoretical, methodological, and interpretive trends and perspectives. His description of this undisciplined discipline is still apt today:

> There is no organization of the work or the workers in the field of musico-literary relationships. Many a scholar publishes a single article in the field, usually involving a writer or aspect of literature in which he regularly works, and never returns to the relationship of the arts. A small number of scholars have a primary interest in the field and work in it intensively, but they do not form anything that could be called a group or coterie. Similarly, there are no organized or conflicting schools of thought, as there is no official point of view and no standard methodology. The entire field of study remains essentially individual and unorganized (pp. 5–6).

Brown also served as guest editor of the special issue of *Comparative Literature* (Spring 1970) devoted to music and literature. The definition of comparative literature he offers in his introductory essay to this issue—"any study of literature involving at least two different media of expression" (p. 102)—strikes me as the most persuasive plea so far for the legitimacy of literature-based interart comparisons, including that of literature with music, as an integral branch of comparative literature.

During the last decades, then, active interest in the serious study of musico-literary relations has increased considerably, not only among literary scholars. Many of the ablest minds in music have been attracted by the field: along with Thrasybulos Georgiades, Joseph Müller-Blattau, Walter Wiora, and Frederick Sternfeld of the older generation, the musicologists Joseph Kerman, Leonard B. Meyer, Edward Cone, Carl Dahlhaus and the composers Karlheinz Stockhausen, John Cage, Pierre Boulez, Luciano Berio, and Luigi Dallapiccola. As more musicologists contribute to musico-literary research, certain methodological questions will continue to be raised. To what extent, for example, should we insist on thorough academic training and equal competence in both arts when contemplating the interrelation? Aware of the unavoidable overlaps, where, if at all, are we to draw the line separating the hunting ground of musico-literary comparatists from the domain of musicologists? Is there a definable minimum of musical knowledge necessary for fruitful musico-literary study? Above all, we must beware of the potential danger of dilettantism and set our standards accordingly: the individual scholar's ability, critical rigor, and background in both arts must be commensurate with the degree of competence required for a particular comparison. But beyond this general standard, there is no need for specific prescriptions. After all, in interart comparisons it often proves to be a definite advantage if the critic remains unencumbered by overly technical vocabulary and analytical practices borrowed from one or the other art. As a recent contribution by a historian of music demonstrates, however, a reliable working knowledge of music can provide profitable new insights into literary works that exhibit "a substantial analogy to, and in many cases an actual influence from, the art of music" (Frye, *Sound and Poetry*, pp. x–xi): Hermann Danuser's 1975 study of the phenomenon of *musikalische Prosa* succeeds because it rests on a solid musicological foundation that complements but never overshadows the informed analyses of the topic's literary aspects.

All too many potentially promising interart comparisons by literary scholars, however, have been severely flawed by a lack of sophistication in musical matters. A case in point is the frequently inexact and inconsistent usage in literary criticism of specific terms undiscriminatingly borrowed from the vocabulary of musical analysis, such as melody, harmony, counterpoint, cadence, tonality, modulation, and orchestration. Perhaps even more crucial and frustrating is the terminological confusion that results from the notorious abuse and misuse of designations like "musical," "musicality," and "the music of poetry." The following sample of the vacuous and most deplorable kind of pseudocritical discourse is cited here as a warning example:

> Everybody who can sense the difference between "Ruh ist über allen Gipfeln" and "Über allen Gipfeln is Ruh" is aware of what is involved. The 'meaning' is the same, but the meaning is different, because in the true form there is contrapuntal correspondence between 'meaning' and melody and sound quality and rhythm, since here the words are used musically, not analogous to music.[31]

In my "How Meaningful Is 'Musical' in Literary Criticism?" I discerned three types of critical usage of the term: the acoustic, the evocative, and the structural. Only the third type of usage, "alluding to...artistic arrangement in musiclike sequence" in literary works, seems potentially meaningful. Ideally, the adjective "musical" should be left to poets. If used at all in criticism, it should denote only literary phenomena that relate specifically to some aspect of actual music. Whenever this is not the case, instead of "musical" or "musicality" in the impressionistic sense, reference to the acoustic or phonetic quality of poetry or prose is most appropriate: and within this broader acoustic context it might be practicable to distinguish between the euphonious and the cacophonous.

In view of the continuing terminological dilemma, one of the tasks for serious musico-literary scholars ought to be to evolve a set of clearly defined critical terms that would put an end to the persisting "trend towards the loose metaphorical use of technical terms" (Brown, "Musico-Literary Research," p. 6), clearly a remnant of Romantic aesthetics bent on amalgamation and confusion of the arts. There is also an immediate need to assess the numerous contributions since 1970, following the model of Calvin Brown's review of scholarship and based on the musico-literary sections of the annual *Bibliography on the Relations of Literature and the Other Arts*, covering the international scene since 1953. Rather than contemplaté the many still unsolved theoretical issues of the interrelation, during the last decade scholars have concentrated on musical connections demonstrable in individual authors or specific literary works, with authors like Jean-Jacques Rousseau, Diderot, Wackenroder, Kleist, Hoffmann, Heine, Honoré de Balzac, Giuseppe Mazzini, Nietzsche, Hofmannsthal, Thomas Mann, Brecht, and T. S. Eliot receiving a great deal more critical attention than others. Important new work has also been done on the literary connections of composers such as Franz Joseph Haydn, Berlioz, Liszt, Debussy, Paul Hindemith, Kurt Weill, and Hanns Eisler. Appreciable theoretical advances were made only in lied and opera research (Kerman).

Literature and music today is a vigorous and steadily growing field of comparative inquiry. But for some time to come it will remain a pioneering field that could accommodate more terminologically and methodologically solid interpretive studies of the diverse systematic relations—especially of structural parallels based on demonstrable points of tangency—and innovative, informed analyses of the historical correlations between the two arts. The time is also ripe for a critical and comprehensive historical survey of the theory and practice of musico-literary scholarship. Such a survey would also have to account for the feasibility and potential usefulness of the semiotic approach in comparing literature and music. To date only the semiotic features of music and language—not of literature—have been explored in depth by scholars like Roman Jakobson, Roland Barthes, Nicolas Ruwet, Roland Harweg, and Jean-Jacques Nattiez.[32] Perhaps it is too early to tell, but it seems probable that future work in musical, linguistic, and literary semiology will help to illuminate certain aspects of the interrelation between music and literature.[33]

Notes

1. John Hollander, "Music and Poetry," in Alex Preminger, ed., *Encyclopedia of Poetry and Poetics* (Princeton: Princeton Univ. Press, 1965), p. 533.

[2] Calvin S. Brown, "Comparative Literature," *Georgia Review*, 13 (1959), 175.

[3] Breon Mitchell's felicitous designation in *Yearbook of Comparative and General Literature*, 27 (1978), 5.

[4] The following presentation draws extensively on my publications treating musico-literary topics (see bibliography). Whenever possible, an attempt has been made to improve upon earlier definitions and formulations. Direct quotations from previous material are acknowledged in the text.

[5] Prominent exceptions are studies by such musicologists as Joseph Kerman, Thrasybulos Georgiades, and Walter Wiora.

[6] *Harvard Concise Dictionary of Music*, comp. Don M. Randel (Cambridge: Harvard Univ. Press, 1978), p. 402.

[7] John Hospers' *Meaning and Truth in the Arts* (Chapel Hill: Univ. of North Carolina Press, 1946) is still the most informative account of this controversy. See esp. pp. 78–98. See also Scher, *Verbal Music*, p. 163.

[8] Igor Stravinsky, *Stravinsky: An Autobiography* (New York: Norton, 1936), pp. 83–84.

[9] See, for example, W. H. Hadow, *The Place of Music among the Arts* (Oxford: Clarendon, 1933); John Hospers, *Meaning and Truth in the Arts*; M. P. T. Leahy, "The Vacuity of Musical Expressionism," *British Journal of Aesthetics*, 16 (1976), 144–56; and Luigi Ronga, *The Meeting of Poetry and Music*, trans. Elio Gianturco and Cara Rusanti (New York: Merlin, 1956).

[10] Paul Verlaine, *Œuvres poétiques*, ed. Jacques Robichez (Paris: Garnier, 1969), p. 39.

[11] Aldous Huxley, *Point Counter Point* (Garden City, N.Y.: Doubleday, 1928), pp. 349–50.

[12] Harold A. Basilius, "Thomas Mann's Use of Musical Structure and Techniques in *Tonio Kröger*," *Germanic Review*, 19 (1944), 284–308, and Theodore Ziolkowski, "Hermann Hesse's *Steppenwolf*: A Sonata in Prose," *Modern Language Quarterly*, 19 (1958), 115–40.

[13] James Joyce, *Ulysses* (1922; rpt. New York: Random, 1961), p. 264.

[14] Wolfgang Hildesheimer's novel *Tynset* has been convincingly analyzed as the latest example of the literary rondo. See Patricia H. Stanley, "The Structure of Wolfgang Hildesheimer's *Tynset*," *Monatshefte*, 71 (1979), 29–40.

[15] *Harvard Concise Dictionary of Music*, p. 121.

[16] Ziolkowski, "Herman Hesse's *Steppenwolf*," p. 124.

[17] Stephen Ullmann, *Style in the French Novel* (Cambridge: Cambridge Univ. Press, 1957), p. 12.

[18] See William Freedman, *Laurence Sterne and the Origins of the Musical Novel* (Athens: Univ. of Georgia Press, 1978), and Erwin Rotermund, "Musikalische und erzählerische 'Arabeske' bei E. T. A. Hoffmann," *Poetica*, 2 (1968), 48–69.

[19] To mention only a few prominent authors: Balzac, Proust, Gide, and Romain Rolland; Turgenev and Tolstoy; and E. M. Forster, Virginia Woolf, Joyce, and Huxley.

[20] Michael Steinberg's unpublished translation of Thomas Mann, *Doktor Faustus* (Stockholm: Fischer, 1947), pp. 207–08:
So geht es zu, wenn es schön ist: Die Celli intonieren allein, ein schwermütig sinnendes Thema, das nach dem Unsinn der Welt, dem Wozu all des Hetzens und Treibens und Jagens und einander Plagens bieder-philosophisch und höchst ausdrucksvoll fragt. Die Celli verbreiten sich eine Weile kopfschüttelnd und bedauernd über dieses Rätsel, und an einem bestimmten Punkt ihrer Rede, einem wohl erwogenen, setzt ausholend, mit einem tiefen Eratmen, das die Schultern emporzieht und sinken läßt, der Bläserchor ein zu einer Choral-Hymne, ergreifend feierlich, prächtig harmonisiert und vorgetragen mit aller gestopften Würde und mild gebändigten Kraft des Blechs. So dringt die sonore

Melodie bis in die Nähe eines Höhepunktes vor, den sie aber, dem Gesetz der Ökonomie gemäß, fürs erste noch vermeidet; sie weicht aus vor ihm, spart ihn auf, sinkt ab, bleibt sehr schön auch so, tritt aber zurück und macht einem anderen Gegenstande Platz, einem liedhaft-simplen, scherzhaft-gravitätisch-volkstümlichen, scheinbar derb von Natur, der's aber hinter der Ohren hat und sich, bei einiger Ausgepichtheit in den Künsten der orchestralen Analyse und Umfärbung, als erstaunlich deutungs- und sublimierungsfähig erweist. Mit dem Liedchen wird nun eine Weile klug und lieblich gewirtschaftet, es wird zerlegt, im Einzelnen betrachtet und abgewandelt, eine reizende Figur daraus wird aus mittleren Klanglagen in die zauberischsten Höhen der Geigen- und Flötensphäre hinaufgeführt, wiegt sich dort oben ein wenig noch, und wie es am schmeichelhaftesten darum steht, nun, da nimmt wieder das milde Blech, die Choralhymne von vorhin das Wort an sich, tritt in den Vordergrund, fängt nicht gerade, ausholend wie das erste Mal, von vorne an, sondern tut, als sei ihre Melodie schon eine Weile wieder dabei gewesen und setzt sich weihesam fort gegen jenen Höhepunkt hin, dessen sie sich das erste Mal weislich enthielt, damit die 'Ah!'-Wirkung, die Gefühlsschwellung desto größer sei, jetzt, wo sie in rückhaltlosem, von harmonischen Durchgangstönen der Baßtuba wuchtig gestütztem Aufsteigen ihn glorreich beschreitet, um sich dann, gleichsam mit würdiger Genugtuung auf das Vollbrachte zurückblickend, ehrsam zu Ende zu singen.

[21] For a detailed interpretation of this passage, see Scher, *Verbal Music*, pp. 106–42.

[22] G. B. Shaw, "Sir George Grove," in Shaw, *Pen Portraits and Reviews* (London: Constable, 1931), p. 106.

[23] See esp. Herbert Günther, *Künstlerische Doppelbegabungen*, 2nd ed. (Munich: Heimeran, 1960).

[24] See Hubert P. H. Teesing, *Das Problem der Perioden in der Literaturgeschichte* (Groningen: Wolters, 1949); Lawrence Lipking, "Periods in the Arts: Sketches and Speculations," *New Literary History*, 1 (1970), 181–200; and Jost Hermand, "Musikalischer Expressionismus," in Hermand, *Stile, Ismen, Etiketten: Zur Periodisierung der modernen Kunst* (Wiesbaden: Athenaion, 1978), pp. 65–79.

[25] Carl Dahlhaus, *Musikästhetik*, p. 10.

[26] René Wellek, *A History of Modern Criticism, 1750–1950*, I (New Haven: Yale Univ. Press, 1955), p. 115.

[27] Charles Batteux, *Les Beaux Arts reduits à une même principe* (Paris, 1747) and Jean-Baptiste Du Bos, *Réflexions critiques sur la poésie et sur la peinture* (Paris, 1719).

[28] The titles of these contributions are revealing: John Brown, *A Dissertation on the Rise, Union, and Power, the Progressions, Separations, and Corruptions of Poetry and Music* (London, 1763); Daniel Webb, *Observations on the Correspondence between Poetry and Music* (London, 1769); James Beattie, *Essays on Poetry and Music, as They Affect the Mind* (London, 1770); and Thomas Twining, *Aristotle's Treatise on Poetry Translated: . . . and Two Dissertations on Poetical, and Musical Imitation* (London, 1789). For a summary of aesthetic developments in this period, see James S. Malek, *The Arts Compared: An Aspect of Eighteenth-Century British Aesthetics* (Detroit, Mich.: Wayne State Univ. Press, 1974).

[29] J. G. Sulzer, *Allgemeine Theorie der schönen Künste* (Leipzig, 1771–74); J. N. Forkel, *Allgemeine Geschichte der Musik*, 2 vols. (Leipzig, 1788, 1801); and J. G. von Herder, *Kritische Wälder* (Riga, 1769).

[30] M. H. Abrams, *The Mirror and the Lamp: Romantic Theory and the Critical Tradition* (New York: Oxford Univ. Press, 1953), p. 50.

[31] Heinrich Meyer in *Books Abroad*, 43 (1969), 602.
[32] Roman Jakobson, "Musikwissenschaft .und Linguistik," *Prager Presse*, 7 Dec. 1932; Roland Barthes, *Mythologies* (Paris: Seuil, 1957); Nicolas Ruwet, *Langage, musique, poésie* (Paris: Seuil, 1972); Roland Harweg, "Sprache und Musik." *Poetica*, 1 (1967), 390–414 and 556–66; and Jean-Jacques Nattiez, *Fondements d'une sémiologie de la musique*.
[33] For preliminary considerations, see esp. Rose Subotnik, "The Cultural Message of Musical Semiology: Some Thoughts on Music, Language, and Criticism since the Enlightenment," *Critical Inquiry*, 4 (1978), 741–68.

Bibliography

A. Bibliographies

A Bibliography on the Relations of Literature and the Other Arts 1952–1967. New York: AMS, 1968. Continued in annual installments under the editorship of Calvin S. Brown (until 1972) and Steven P. Scher (1973–). Coverage includes contributions on literature and music.

Scher, Steven Paul. "Literatur und Musik. Eine Bibliographie." In *Literatur und Musik: Ein Handbuch zur Theorie und Praxis eines komparatistischen Grenzgebietes*. Ed. Steven P. Scher. Berlin: Schmidt, 1982. Over three hundred selected items provide up-to-date, comprehensive coverage of international musico-literary scholarship.

B. Reviews of Research

Brown, Calvin S. "Musico-Literary Research in the Last Two Decades." *Yearbook of Comparative and General Literature*, 19 (1970), 5–27.

Just, Klaus Günther. "Musik und Dichtung." In *Deutsche Philologie im Aufriss*. Ed. Wolfgang Stammler. 2nd ed. Berlin: Schmidt, 1962, III, 699–738. Excellent survey of scholarship on vocal music, with exhaustive bibliography.

Reichert, Georg. "Literatur und Musik." In *Reallexikon der deutschen Literaturgeschichte*. Ed. Paul Merker and Wolfgang Stammler. 2nd ed. Berlin: de Gruyter, 1965, II, 143–63. Concentrates on vocal and program music, with extensive bibliography.

Werner, Theodor W. "Musik und Literatur in ihren Wechselbeziehungen." in *Reallexikon der deutschen Literaturgeschichte*. Ed. Paul Merker and Wolfgang Stammler. 1st ed. Berlin: de Gruyter, 1925–31, II, 431–40. Limited coverage of vocal music only.

C. General: Aesthetics, Theory, Methodology

Boulez, Pierre. "Poésie—centre et absence—musique." *Melos*, 30 (1963), 33–46.

Bronson, Bertrand H. "Literature and Music." In *Relations of Literary Study. Essays on Interdisciplinary Contributions*. Ed. James Thorpe. New York: MLA, 1967, pp. 127–50. This unsystematic treatment of the various aspects of the interrelation has limited introductory value: Bronson concentrates on the problems of text and music in song and draws his examples exclusively from English literature.

Brown, Calvin S. *Music and Literature: A Comparison of the Arts*. Athens: Univ. of Georgia Press, 1948. The most comprehensive, systematic modern critical survey of the interrelation.

————. "The Relations between Music and Literature as a Field of Study." *Comparative Literature*, 22 (1970), 97–107. A concise and informative introductory essay.

————, ed. *Comparative Literature*, 22 (1970), 97–190. Special number on music and literature, includes important contributions to musico-literary theory by Brown, Ulrich Weisstein, and Steven P. Scher and analysis by Jack M. Stein, Nan C. Carpenter, Frederick W. Sternfeld, and Mary J. Chan.

Coeuroy, André. *Musique et littérature: Etudes de musique et de littérature comparées.* Paris: Bloud and Gay, 1923.

Combarieu, Jules. *Les Rapports de la musique et de la poésie, considerées au point de vue de l'expression.* Paris, 1894.

Cooke, Deryck. *The Language of Music.* London: Oxford Univ. Press, 1962.

Cupers, Jean-Louis. "Etudes comparatives: Les approches musico-littéraires." In *Publications de l'Institut de Formation et de Recherches en Littérature. Fascicule 4⁰. La littérature et les autres arts.* Ed. A. Vermeylen et al. Paris: Les Belles Lettres, 1979, pp. 63–103. The first ambitious, up-to-date introduction to modern musico-literary research in French.

Dahlhaus, Carl. *Musikästhetik.* Cologne: Gerig, 1967.

Danuser, Hermann. *Musikalische Prosa.* Regensburg: Bosse, 1975.

Eliot, T. S. *The Music of Poetry.* Glasgow: Glasgow Univ. Publications, 1942.

Friederich, Martin. *Text und Ton: Wechselbeziehungen zwischen Dichtung und Musik.* Hohengehren: Schneider, 1973. A concise historical treatment of the interrelation, confined to German literature and music.

Frye, Northrop. "Music in Poetry." *University of Toronto Quarterly*, 11 (1941), 167–79.

————, ed. *Sound and Poetry.* New York: Columbia Univ. Press, 1957. Valuable contributions by Frye, Edward T. Cone, Frederick W. Sternfeld, John Hollander, Craig La Drière, Ants Oras, and Harold Whitehall.

Georgiades, Thrasybulos G. *Musik und Sprache: Das Werden der abendländischen Musik dargestellt an der Vertonung der Messe.* Berlin: Springer, 1954. A primarily musicological study, important for its theoretical insights.

Gruhn, Wilfried. *Musiksprache, Sprachmusik, Textvertonung: Aspekte des Verhältnisses von Musik, Sprache und Text.* Frankfurt am Main: Diesterweg, 1978. Historical and systematic treatment of the problem of word and tone, with a pronounced linguistic orientation.

Hanslick, Eduard. *Vom Musikalisch-Schönen: Ein Beitrag zur Revision der Ästhetik der Tonkunst.* Leipzig, 1854.

Hollander, John. "The Music of Poetry." *Journal of Aesthetics and Art Criticism*, 15 (1956), 233–44.

Huxley, Aldous. "Music and Poetry." In *Texts and Pretexts.* London: Norton, 1932, pp. 237–54.

Lipking, Lawrence. *The Ordering of the Arts in Eighteenth-Century England.* Princeton: Princeton Univ. Press, 1970. A general survey of eighteenth-century British aesthetics, with three comprehensive chapters on "The Ordering of Music" (Avison, Hawkins, and Burney).

Nattiez, Jean-Jacques. *Fondements d'une sémiologie de la musique.* Paris: Danel, 1975.

Scher, Steven Paul. "How Meaningful Is 'Musical' in Literary Criticism?" *Yearbook of Comparative and General Literature*, 21 (1972), 52–56.

————, ed. *Literatur und Musik: Ein Handbuch zur Theorie und Praxis eines komparatistischen Grenzgebietes.* Berlin: Schmidt, 1982. A collection of twenty-four essays, reflecting the state of modern musico-literary scholarship on an international scale. Includes extensive bibliography.

———. "Literature and Music: Comparative or Interdisciplinary Study?" *Yearbook of Comparative and General Literature*, 24 (1975), 37–40.

———. "Notes toward a Theory of Verbal Music." *Comparative Literature*, 22 (1970), 147–56.

———. "Temporality and Mediation: W. H. Wackenroder and E. T. A. Hoffmann as Literary Historicists of Music." *Journal of English and Germanic Philology*, 75 (1976), 492–502.

Schnitzler, Günter, ed. *Dichtung und Musik: Kaleidoskop ihrer Beziehungen*. Stuttgart: Klett-Cotta, 1979. A collection of fourteen essays dealing exclusively with the problem of setting literary texts to music. No comprehensive bibliography.

Schueller, Herbert M. "Literature and Music as Sister Arts: An Aspect of Aesthetic Theory in Eighteenth-Century Britain." *Philological Quarterly*, 26 (1947), 193–205.

Springer, George P. "Language and Music: Parallels and Divergencies." In *For Roman Jakobson*. Ed. Morris Halle et al. The Hague: Mouton, 1956, pp. 504–13. Helpful introduction to the linguistic implications of the interrelation.

Wais, Kurt. *Symbiose der Künste: Forschungsgrundlagen zur Wechselbeziehung zwischen Dichtung, Bild- und Tonkunst*. Stuttgart: Kohlhammer, 1936. A critical survey of modern research devoted to literature-based interart parallels.

———. "Vom Gleichlauf der Künste." *Bulletin of the International Committee of the Historical Sciences*, 9 (1937), 295–304.

Walzel, Oskar. "Dichtkunst und Musik." In *Gehalt und Gestalt im Kunstwerk des Dichters*. Berlin-Neubabelsberg: Athenaion, 1923, pp. 347–67.

———. *Wechselseitige Erhellung der Künste: Ein Beitrag zur Würdigung kunstgeschichtlicher Grundbegriffe*. Berlin: Reuther and Reichard, 1917.

Weisstein, Ulrich. "Die wechselseitige Erhellung von Literatur und Musik: Ein Arbeitsgebiet der Komparatistik?" *Neohelicon*, 5 No. 1 (1977), 92–123.

Wellek, Albert. *Musikpsychologie und Musikästhetik*. Frankfurt am Main: Akademische Verlagsgesellschaft, 1963. Two seminal chapters on vocal and program music.

———. "The Relationship between Music and Poetry." *Journal of Aesthetics and Art Criticism*, 21 (1962), 149–56. Important discussion of terminological distinctions.

Wellek, René. "The Parallelism between Literature and the Arts." In *English Institute Annual 1941*. New York: Columbia Univ. Press, 1942, pp. 29–63.

———, and Austin Warren. "Literature and the Other Arts." In *Theory of Literature*. 3rd ed. New York: Harcourt, 1962, pp. 125–35.

Winn, James Anderson. *Unsuspected Eloquence: A History of the Relations between Poetry and Music*. New Haven: Yale Univ. Press, 1981.

Yoshida, Minoru. "Word-Music in English Poetry," *Journal of Aesthetics and Art Criticism*, 11 (1952), 151–59.

D. *Program Music*

Niecks, Frederick. *Programme Music in the Last Four Centuries: A Contribution to the History of Musical Expression*. London: Novello, 1906. A comprehensive critical survey of encyclopedic tone and dimensions, still indispensable for its thoroughness and sound judgments.

Orrey, Leslie. *Programme Music: A Brief Survey from the Sixteenth Century to the Present*. London: Davis-Poynter, 1975. A brief, up-to-date introductory survey.

Stockmeier, Wolfgang. *Die Programmusik*. Cologne: Gerig, 1970.

E. Vocal Music: Lied, Opera, etc.

Cone, Edward T. "Words into Music: The Composer's Approach to the Text." In *Sound and Poetry*. Ed. Northrop Frye. New York: Columbia Univ. Press, 1957, pp. 3–15.

Conrad, Peter. *Romantic Opera and Literary Form*. Berkeley: Univ. of California Press, 1977. Conrad's thesis that "opera is more musical novel than musical drama" is persuasively argued but debatable.

Flaherty, Gloria. *Opera in the Development of German Critical Thought*. Princeton: Princeton Univ. Press, 1979. Informative survey of eighteenth-century German writings on opera, with an extensive bibliography of primary sources.

Georgiades, Thrasybulos G. *Schubert: Musik und Lyrik*. Göttingen: Vandenhoeck and Ruprecht, 1967. A definitive analytical treatment of Schubert's lied composition in a theoretical framework.

Kerman, Joseph. *Opera as Drama*. New York: Random, 1956. A classic work of modern opera criticism, viewing opera as "dramma per musica."

———. "Opera, Novel, Drama: The Case of *La Traviata*." *Yearbook of Comparative and General Literature*, 27 (1978), 44–53.

Müller-Blattau, Joseph. *Das Verhältnis von Wort und Ton in der Geschichte der Musik*. Stuttgart: Metzler, 1952. A short, historical account of the relations of text and music.

Schmidgall, Gary. *Literature as Opera*. New York: Oxford Univ. Press, 1977. Covering operatic history from Handel to Britten, Schmidgall offers readable analyses of text and music in twelve operas based on well-known literary works.

Smith, Patrick J. *The Tenth Muse: A Historical Study of the Opera Libretto*. New York: Knopf, 1970. The first critical history of the libretto; informative and introductory rather than comprehensive and definitive.

Stein, Jack M. *Poem and Music in the German Lied from Gluck to Hugo Wolf*. Cambridge: Harvard Univ. Press, 1971. Stein's approach to word-tone synthesis is primarily literary; he critically surveys the faults and merits of musical settings of lyric poetry by the great German masters of the art song.

———. *Richard Wagner and the Synthesis of the Arts*. Detroit: Wayne State Univ. Press, 1960.

Weisstein, Ulrich, ed. *The Essence of Opera*. New York: Free Press, 1964. An indispensable collection of representative texts by composers, poets, librettists, and critics, reflecting the history and aesthetics of opera from the Florentine Camerata to W. H. Auden.

———. "The Libretto as Literature." *Books Abroad*, 35 (1961), 14–22.

———. "Reflections on a Golden Style: W. H. Auden's Theory of Opera." *Comparative Literature*, 22 (1970), 108–24.

Wiora, Walter. *Das deutsche Lied: Zur Geschichte und Ästhetik einer musikalischen Gattung*. Wolfenbüttel and Zürich: Möseler, 1971. The musicologist Wiora covers essentially the same ground as Stein, but with an emphasis on theory rather than on interpretation of individual lieder. Includes excellent bibliography.

F. Musical Structures and Techniques in Literature

Brown, Calvin S. "The Musical Structure of De Quincey's 'Dream-Fugue.'" *Musical Quarterly*, 24 (1938), 341–50.

———. "The Poetic Use of Musical Forms." *Musical Quarterly*, 30 (1944), 87–101.

———. "Theme and Variations as a Literary Form." *Yearbook of Comparative and General Literature*, 27 (1978), 35–43.

Cluck, Nancy Anne, ed. *Literature and Music: Essays on Form.* Provo, Utah: Brigham Young Univ. Press, 1982.

Peacock, Ronald. *Das Leitmotiv bei Thomas Mann.* Bern: Haupt, 1934.

Petri, Horst. *Literatur und Musik: Form- und Strukturparallelen.* Göttingen: Sachse and Pohl, 1964. This short and polemical book is the only comprehensive survey so far on structural parallels between the two arts.

Smith, Don N. "Musical Form and Principles in the Scheme of *Ulysses.*" *Twentieth-Century Literature*, 18 (1972), 79–92.

G. Verbal Music

Brown, Calvin S. *Tones into Words. Musical Compositions as Subjects of Poetry.* Athens: Univ. of Georgia Press, 1953.

Scher, Steven Paul. *Verbal Music in German Literature.* New Haven: Yale Univ. Press, 1968.

Stanley, Patricia H. "Verbal Music in Theory and Practice." *Germanic Review*, 52 (1977), 217–25.

H. Synesthesia

Erhardt-Siebold, Erika von. "Harmony of the Senses in English, German, and French Romanticism." *PMLA*, 47 (1932), 577–92.

O'Malley, Glenn. "Literary Synaesthesia." *Journal of Aesthetics and Art Criticism*, 15 (1957), 391–411.

I. Music Criticism

Braun, Werner. *Musikkritik: Versuch einer historisch-kritischen Standortbestimmung.* Cologne: Gerig, 1972.

Graf, Max. *Composer and Critic: Two Hundred Years of Musical Criticism.* New York: Norton, 1946. A highly readable and comprehensive general history of music criticism on an international scale.

J. Interpretive Studies: Authors, Composers, Works, Periods

Barricelli, Jean-Pierre. "Romantic Writers and Music: The Case of Mazzini." *Studies in Romanticism*, 14 (1975), 95–117.

Bowen, Zack. *Musical Allusions in the Works of James Joyce: Early Poetry through Ulysses.* Albany: State Univ. of New York Press, 1974. The first systematic and comprehensive study of music in Joyce.

DiGaetani, John L. *Richard Wagner and the Modern British Novel.* Rutherford, N.J.: Fairleigh Dickinson Univ. Press, 1977. Traces Wagner's influence and the presence of Wagnerian patterns in Joseph Conrad, D. H. Lawrence, E. M. Forster, Virginia Woolf, and Joyce.

Hollander, John. *The Untuning of the Sky: Ideas of Music in English Poetry, 1500–1700.* Princeton: Princeton Univ. Press, 1961. An erudite and informative critical survey of music-related English poetry from Chaucer to Dryden, with cogent interpretations of selected individual poems.

Jensen, H. James. *The Muses' Concord: Literature, Music, and the Visual Arts in the Baroque Age.* Bloomington: Indiana Univ. Press, 1976. A genuinely comparative study, especially valuable for methodological and interpretive insights concerning rhetorical theory and practice in the arts.

Jones, John A. "The Analogy of Eighteenth Century Music and Poetry: Bach and Pope." *Centennial Review*, 21 (1977), 211–35.

Kanzog, Klaus, and Hans Joachim Kreutzer, eds. *Werke Kleists auf dem modernen Musiktheater*. Berlin: Schmidt, 1977. A collection of essays on contemporary operas based on Kleist's texts. Includes an up-to-date bibliography on Kleist and music.

Koller, Hermann. *Musik und Dichtung im alten Griechenland*. Bern: Francke, 1963. The most convincing analysis to date of the varieties of meaning behind the elusive word *musikē* in ancient Greece.

Mellers, Wilfrid. *Harmonious Meeting: A Study of the Relationship between English Music, Poetry, and Theatre, c. 1600–1900*. London: Dobson, 1965. Mellers' numerous individual interpretations focus on the word-tone synthesis in song and drama.

Mittenzwei, Johannes. *Das Musikalische in der Literatur: Ein Überblick von Gottfried von Strassburg bis Brecht*. Halle: VEB Verlag Sprache und Literatur, 1962. Covering music-related works of only German authors, Mittenzwei quotes generously but offers little critical commentary.

Phillips, James E., and Bertrand H. Bronson. *Music and Literature in England in the Seventeenth and Eighteenth Centuries*. Los Angeles: Clark Library, 1953.

Schafer, R. Murray. *E. T. A. Hoffmann and Music*. Toronto: Univ. of Toronto Press, 1975. A musicologist's informative introductory survey of Hoffmann the writer, composer, and music critic. Includes English translations of selected music-related works.

Scher, Steven Paul. "Carl Maria von Weber's *Tonkünstlers Leben*: The Composer as Novelist?" *Comparative Literature Studies*, 15 (1978), 30–42.

———. "Kreativität als Selbstüberwindung: Thomas Manns permanente 'Wagner-Krise.'" In *Rezeption der deutschen Gegenwartsliteratur im Ausland*. Ed. Dietrich Papenfuss and Jürgen Söring. Stuttgart: Kohlhammer, 1976, pp. 263–74.

Schering, Arnold. *Beethoven und die Dichtung*. Berlin: Junker and Dünnhaupt, 1936. An influential though dubious attempt by the well-known musicologist to prove definitively that Beethoven modeled certain symphonies, quartets, and sonatas on specific literary works.

Schmid, Martin E. *Symbol und Funktion der Musik im Werk Hugo von Hofmannsthals*. Heidelberg: Winter, 1968.

Schoolfield, George C. *The Figure of the Musician in German Literature*. Chapel Hill: Univ. of North Carolina Press, 1956.

Sices, David. *Music and the Musician in "Jean-Christophe": The Harmony of Contrasts*. New Haven: Yale Univ. Press, 1968.

Stein, Jack M. "From *Woyzeck* to *Wozzeck*: Alban Berg's Adaptation of Büchner." *Germanic Review*, 47 (1972), 168–80.

Sternfeld, Frederick W. *Music in Shakespearean Tragedy*. London: Routledge and Kegan Paul, 1963. This definitive scholarly treatment of the topic includes an informative "Retrospect of Scholarship on Shakespeare and Music."

———. "The Musical Springs of Goethe's Poetry." *Musical Quarterly*, 35 (1949), 511–27.

Thomas, R. Hinton. *Poetry and Song in the German Baroque: A Study of the Continuo Lied*. Oxford: Oxford Univ. Press, 1963. Includes an appendix of musical examples and a selected bibliography.

Wenk, Arthur B. *Claude Debussy and the Poets*. Berkeley: Univ. of California Press, 1976. A musicologist's critical commentary of Debussy's settings of poets like Banville, Verlaine, Baudelaire, and Mallarmé.

Zuckerman, Elliott. "Nietzsche and Music: *The Birth of Tragedy* and *Nietzsche contra Wagner*." *Symposium*, 28 (1974), 17–32.

12

Literature and the Visual Arts

ULRICH WEISSTEIN

Keine einzige Muse mahlt und so viele musiziren.

A. W. SCHLEGEL

I

In the second volume (1799) of the periodical *Athenäum*, which he coedited with his brother Friedrich, August Wilhelm Schlegel published an "imaginary" conversation about painting, "Die Gemählde," which offers descriptions of pictures in the famous Dresden museum and concludes with a set of *Bildgedichte* 'iconic poems' in sonnet form. Toward the end of the lengthy and somewhat rambling exchange of views between a painter named Reinhold, a writer named Waller, and a female connoisseur named Louise, the relation of literature (*Poesie*) and painting is touched on and Waller observes correctly that Greek mythology knows no protector of the plastic arts, a fact that Louise underscores by noting, half jestingly: "Not a single Muse paints, and so many make music." Picking up the thread, Waller retorts: "That's their duty since music gets its name from them. Apollo has charge of the poets, Vulcan of the artisans, Minerva of the feminine crafts; but the visual arts are invariably left out in the cold." And Reinhold, introducing a historical perspective, adds: "This probably results from the fact that they flourished later than music and poetry, when all the gods had already been assigned." Waller then extends the argument to the ancient heroes and demigods by remarking: "Nor can they boast of an Orpheus, Linos, Amphion or the like. The only figure they can claim for themselves is Daedalus, who is relevant to sculptors but not painters," who, as he subsequently notes, found their patron, belatedly, in the evangelist St. Luke.[1]

Although the tone of this portion of Schlegel's dialogue is slightly ironic and bantering, the gap in the aesthetic pantheon of the Greeks to which it calls attention is genuine, as is shown by a glance at the ancient modes of classification, that is, what might be called antiquity's rudimentary "system of the arts." As O. B. Hardison, Jr., points out in this analysis of Chapter i of Aristotle's *Poetics*, the Greeks seem to have distinguished between the often symbiotic arts of rhythm (= dance), harmony/melody (= music), and speech (= literature) presided over by the Muses, on the one hand, and activities subsumed under the label *techne* (= Latin *ars*), on the other, it being understood that painting and sculpture, whose means of imitation are color and form respectively, ranked only slightly above the crafts or arts of making. This was to be the lot of the visual arts through much of antiquity and the Middle Ages. Thus Paul Oskar Kristeller ("Modern System," p. 170) reports that Seneca specifically denied painting a place among the liberal arts; and this iniquity was perpetuated by the Scholastics, from whose academic curricula it was banished, while music, subordinate to mathematics, and literature, attached to rhetoric, were included.

Nevertheless, the gradual emancipation of literature (Aristotle's "nameless" art) from music, exemplified by the evolution of verbal genres of no longer truly lyric poetry, resulted in a realignment of forces and in the rehabilitation of painting and sculpture in Hellenistic times. The bond that united literature and the visual arts, it was now increasingly felt, was their vital concern with imitation (mimesis), which, naturally, was not shared by music, an art that tended to become more and more strictly instrumental and hence "absolute." As early as the late sixth or early fifth century B.C., Simonides of Ceos is supposed to have stated—as Plutarch reports in the section "On the Fame of the Athenians" of his *Moralia*—that painting is mute poetry and poetry a speaking picture. That dictum was to be as crucial and omnipresent in the debate that raged from the Renaissance down to the eighteenth century as any except Horace's widely misunderstood and misinterpreted *ut pictura poesis*. Parallels of this kind, on different grounds and from different perspectives, are commonplace in subsequent centuries; we encounter them in Cicero (from an evolutionary angle in the Brutus portion of his *Orator*), Dionysius of Halicarnassus (regarding kinds of excellence in sculptors and rhetoricians, in the essay on Isocrates), Lucian of Samosata (on the artistic and historiographical use of raw materials in "How to Write History"), and Quintilian (on different styles in painting, sculpture, and rhetoric in Book XII of the *Institutiones Oratoriae*).

In late antiquity, several literary genres linked to the plastic arts made their appearance. The iconic poem—an artistic variant of the rhetorical *ekphrasis* 'description'—reached the height of its popularity with the *eikones* 'images' of Philostratus the Elder (fl. c. 150 A.D.), his grandson Philostratus the Younger, and Callistratus. It was given a new lease on life in Justinian, sixth-century Byzantium, where Paulus Silentiarius wrote a long poem describing the Hagia Sophia and its treasures. (Its true and uniquely medieval equivalent is the *titulus*, another form of the epigram or inscription.) One of the most intriguing discussions of the genre occurs in a dialogue written by Lucian (fl. mid-second century A.D.), "Eikones," where one of the speakers, Polystratus, calls for the creation of a verbovisual mini-*Gesamtkunstwerk* aimed at depicting concurrently the physical and the moral and spiritual beauty of the "sitter," a young woman from Smyrna:

Lycinus, I have a proposal to make. Let us combine our portraits, yours of the body and mine of the soul, and throw them into a literary form, for the enjoyment of our generation and of all posterity. Such a work will be more enduring than those of the painters [Apelles, Parrhasius, and Polygnotus]; it will be far removed from creations of wood and wax and color, being inspired by the Muses, in whom alone is that true portraiture that shows forth in one likeness a lovely body and a virtuous soul.[2]

Unlike the iconic poem, which is a product of conscious and highly reflective artistry, the *carmen figuratum* (*technopaignia* 'pattern poem') seems originally to have served a ritual purpose, being a dedicatory inscription on a religious or cult object whose external shape it verbovisually reproduced. The Greek Anthology (Book XV) contains several such pieces: the Pipe of Theocritus, the Wings of Love, the Axe and the Egg of Simias, and the Altars of Besantinus and Dosiades — anticipations of poems by George Herbert, Dylan Thomas, and Christian Morgenstern, not to mention Guillaume Apollinaire's playful or playfully sentimental *calligrammes* and certain concrete poems of more recent vintage.

In the Middle Ages, the theological attitude toward painting was divided. On the one hand, the eye, being the window of the soul, was regarded as the most spiritual organ of sense perception; on the other, it was also seen as the mirror in which the sensuous and sensual nature of the world was most palpably reflected. Aesthetically, the latter view seems to have prevailed. For Isidore of Seville, the great seventh-century encyclopedist, *pictura* was essentially *fictura*, that is, a feigned representation, rather than a truthful rendering, of reality; and Christian thinkers like Saint Augustine preferred music and architecture, the least representational of the arts, to painting and sculpture.

The aesthetic emancipation of the visual arts, coupled with the social emancipation of the painters and sculptors (whose exodus from the artisan guilds culminated in the foundation of academies of what then became known as the fine arts), occurs in the Italian Renaissance, where *ut pictura poesis* is literally taken to imply the equality of the two arts, if not, as subsequently, the superiority of painting over poetry. The reversal is effected in Leonardo da Vinci's comparison of the arts. According to the scale of values presented in Leonardo's so-called *Paragone*, painting excels over both music (because it "does not fade away as soon as it is born") and literature:

Painting is poetry which is seen and not heard, and poetry is painting which is heard but not seen. These two arts, you may call them both either poetry or painting, have here interchanged the senses by which they penetrate to the intellect. Whatever is painted must pass by the eye, which is the nobler sense, and whatever is poetry must pass through a less noble sense, namely the ear, to the understanding.[3]

The hierarchy of the arts is here, at the height of the early Renaissance, finally in keeping with the hierarchy of the senses established in the Middle Ages (Dante Alighieri and Thomas Aquinas, whom in *Portrait of the Artist as a Young Man* James Joyce quotes as the author of the aesthetic tenet *pulcra sunt quae visa placent*).

In the baroque, the balance destroyed by Leonardo was partly, though precariously, restored as a call was sounded for the fusion of the arts in the architectural and theatrical (operatic) *Gesamtkunstwerk*. In spite of the "neoclassical," and slightly atavistic, linkage of music and poetry in the *dramma per musica* spawned in Florence, the bonds between literature and the visual arts were firmer and more pervasive. In the tradition of the *biblia pauperum*, the ancient epigram or inscription was revived and elaborated in the quickly standardized triadic form of the emblem, or *Sinnbild*, with its moralistic and frequently allegorical overtones. Here lies one of the most cogent and historically viable reasons for the enormous proliferation of descriptive poetry and literary pictorialism of the seventeenth and early eighteenth centuries that Gotthold Ephraim Lessing, anticipated by Jean-Baptiste Du Bos in his *Réflexions critiques sur la poésie et la peinture* (1719), fulminated against in his *Laocoön* (1766).

With regard to the baroque and the rococo, it can be said that, as John Dryden puts it in his rendition of C. A. Du Fresnoy's posthumously published *De Arte Graphica* (1668), which he graced with a preface entitled "A Parallel of Poetry and Painting" (1695): "Painting and poetry are two sisters, which are so like in all things that they mutually lend to each other both their Name and Office." The intimacy of that relation, hinted at by ancient writers like Cicero and patristic authors like Tertullian, was most strongly expressed by Giovanni Paolo Lomazzo, whose *Trattato dell'arte della pittura, scultura e architettura* (1585, Dryden trans., 1716), refers to painting and poetry not only as siblings but as twins, "quasi nate ad un parto."

In contrast to what Ernst Robert Curtius, and he alone, would have us call manneristic ages (including the baroque and the rococo), classicist and neoclassical eras tend to look askance at mixed and symbiotic forms and invariably proclaim the dogma of the purity of kinds. Thus it comes as no surprise that Lessing, inveighing against word painting and pictorial narrative alike, demands a separation "of bed and board" and sets strict limits for the visual and verbal arts:

> If it be true that painting, in its imitation, makes use of entirely different means and signs from those which poetry employs: the former employing figures and colors in space, the latter articulating sounds in time . . . it follows that bodies, with their visible properties, are the proper objects of painting. Objects which succeed, or the parts of which succeed, to each other are called generally actions. It follows that actions are the proper objects of poetry.[4]

It is the differences, then, rather than the similarities between the two arts and the media to which they are tied that Lessing emphasizes, without ignoring that "bodies do not exist only in space, but also in time," and that "actions cannot subsist by themselves but must attach to specific objects." Hence his choice of the "pregnant moment" (a commonplace in eighteenth-century criticism, as evidenced by Shaftesbury among others) as the one to be focused on by sculptors and painters in their visual and plastic representations. Here is one kind of mutual illumination that aestheticians like Theodore Meyer Greene and Etienne Souriau have favored. Our postnaturalistic age has lent itself especially well to this approach on account of the many spatializing trends in poetry (imagism, concrete poetry, and the kind of reflexive reference discussed by Joseph Frank) and temporalizing trends in painting (futurism and, in an ambiguous but symptomatic sense, impressionism).

Regarding the accepted hierarchy of the arts—which is surely in part responsible for the way, and the spirit, in which comparisons between them are conducted in a given age—it must be stated that in Lessing's time it was not literature, his preferred medium, but sculpture that reigned supreme. In other words, the hero of the day, aesthetically speaking, was Johann Jakob Winckelmann, originator of the *Gedancken über die Nachahmung der griechischen Werke in der Malerei und Bildhauerkunst* (1755), and he, rather than the author of the *Hamburgische Dramaturgie*, set the tone. The fact that sculptural ideals engendered by the contemplation of Roman copies of Greek statuary dominated the artistic scene invalidates the argument, set forth by René Wellek and Austin Warren in Chapter xv of their *Theory of Literature* (p. 117), that "'Classicism' in music [and painting] must mean something very different from its use in literature [as well as sculpture and architecture]," since practically no ancient music and, until the excavations at Pompeii and Herculaneum, no ancient paintings were known and could therefore shape the evolution of these arts "as literature was actually shaped by the precepts and practice of antiquity." For, as H. P. H. Teesing persuasively argues, "Gluck and other composers as well as the Classicist painters abstracted the sculptural principles of their art from literature, sculpture, and architecture, thereby showing that the organizing principle can be transplanted from one art to another" (p. 33).

Toward the end of Lessing's enlightened century, the wall that that critic had erected between the arts began to crumble as the French pre-Romantics and German Romanticists preached and practiced the twin gospel of synesthesia and symbiosis (the fusion—subsequently, with Charles Baudelaire and his decadent heirs down to Joris-Karl Huysmans, the confusion—of the arts and senses). In doing so, they subverted the classicist hierarchy of the arts; Marcel Proust, for example, could insist that taste and smell, the most "primitive" senses, are precisely those that allow us to recapture the past and thus to restructure our lives. The synesthetic ravings of E. T. A. Hoffmann's mad musician Kreisler, Baudelaire's exhortations in the sonnet "Correspondances" ("Comme de longs échos qui de loin se confondent / Dans une ténébreuse et profonde unité, / Vaste comme la nuit et comme la clarté, / Les parfums, les couleurs et les sons se répondent"), and A. W. Schlegel's express desire, voiced in the previously mentioned "Die Gemähl-de," to "bring the arts closer to each other, and to look for transitions from one to the other" reflect a mentality that seeks reciprocal enlightenment not in rational comparisons but in the creative intuition.

If sculpture was the paradigm of the arts in the eighteenth century, as architecture had been in the Middle Ages and painting in the Renaissance and post-Renaissance, so music, in the view of many scholars, came to dominate the Romantic phase of the nineteenth century. Arthur Schopenhauer took music to be an abstract but sensuous (hence, direct and immediate) reflection of the universal will; Richard Wagner, his disciple, found that it added psychological depth and temporal breadth to the total work of art; and Søren Kierkegaard praised its sensual immediacy in his essay on the musical and erotic. Literature took its turn by shaping the art of realism (inspired, to be sure, by pictorial models offered by Dutch seventeenth-century and English early nineteenth-century paintings like those of John Constable).

The visual arts came again to the fore after the turn of the century. In the decades of the avant-garde, which determined the course of twentieth-century art in all its branches, literature turned to the plastic arts for help, borrowing many of their techniques—especially after the ascent of cinematography. It was not coincidentally at this juncture that the "mutual illumination of the arts," now widely though not universally regarded as a branch of comparative literature, made its debut as a scholarly discipline. Logically, under the circumstances, it looked for, and found, its models in art history rather than in the younger science of musicology. In his 1917 lecture, which is the magna charta of the comparative arts, Oskar Walzel, the founding father, leans rather too heavily on Heinrich Wölfflin, the Swiss art historian, whose five "kunstgeschichtliche Grundbegriffe" (basic concepts of art history) he sought to apply to literature, focusing initially on Shakespeare's dramas as paragons of the baroque style. (The subtitle of the lecture, "Ein Beitrag zur Würdigung kunstgeschichtlicher Begriffe," frankly acknowledges this debt.)

Appropriately, the comparative arts, in their infancy and childhood, have shown a decided preference for visual phenomena as opposed to auditory phenomena, among which the operatic genre alone has found widespread favor. And as of today we have relatively few equivalents—such as Wilfrid Mellers' *Harmonious Meeting: A Study of the Relationship between English Music, Poetry, and Theatre, c. 1600–1900* (London: Dobson, 1965)—of the sweeping surveys authored by Hatzfeld, Praz, and Sypher. *Geistes-* and *Stilgeschichte*, usually in conjunction with each other, have done their job, and throughout the scholarly community the feeling persists that the visual arts and literature have much more in common than do music and literature, because both are basically mimetic, and that, accordingly, their parallel course can be more fruitfully studied in the context of the history of ideas. Hence the enormous significance that attaches to the example set by the Warburg School (as discussed by Herbert Weisinger) and, in particular, by Erwin Panofsky, the greatest art historian of our age, whose lucid and methodologically persuasive essay on iconography and iconology should be required reading for the historian and critic of literature as well. The skepticism evinced by Paul and Svetlana Alpers in this regard may be justified ("It seems to us that art criticism and literary criticism are the same activity only in the most general—though therefore in the most important—ways. The specific nature of the criticism depends on the specific nature of the art work" [p. 457]); but it loses much of its bite when viewed in the light of the benefits that *Literaturwissenschaft* 'literary science' has derived, and is likely to derive, from its companion science.

The history of comparative literature as an academic discipline also shows a clear-cut bias in favor of the visual arts. Thus as early as 1887 Max Koch, founder and editor of the *Zeitschrift für vegleichende Litteraturgeschichte*, singled out the mutual illumination of painting and literature (he points to Italian Renaissance frescoes as a source for certain portions of Johann Wolfgang von Goethe's *Faust*, Part II); and only a decade ago, Simon Jeune, working in a long tradition that includes Jean-François Sobry's *Poétique des arts, ou Cours de peinture et de littérature comparées* (Paris: Delaunay, 1810) as well as Paul Maury's pamphlet *Arts et littérature comparées: Etat présent de la question* (Paris: Les Belles Lettres, 1934) and Louis Hourticq's *L'Art et la littérature* (Paris: Flammarion, 1946), stressed the need for studying "les liaisons existantes entre la littérature d'une part et les beaux-arts de l'autre." Although he also includes architecture, sculpture, and even music among the latter, his preference is marked: "Mais c'est surtout avec le dessin et la peinture que les rapports de la littérature semblent plus étroites."[5]

The mutual illumination of the arts in general, and the study of literature in its relation to the plastic arts in particular, is a discipline in its fledgling years that has not found its proper bearings and lacks a sound methodological foundation and a solid terminological framework. Its long but not always distinguished prehistory includes more or less systematic attempts to show either similarities or differences, to demonstrate the superiority of one art over the other, to polemicize against the fusion or separation of the arts, or to reduce all arts to one and the same—usually the mimetic—principle (as Charles Batteux did in his famous treatise *Les Beaux-Art reduits à un même principe* of 1746). The need for comparing and contrasting the arts objectively and without *parti pris* was first stressed by Denis Diderot, whose "Lettre sur les sourds et les muets" (1751) directly attacks Batteux.[6]

A century and a half had to pass before a serious effort was made to raise the mutual illumination of the arts to the level of unimpassioned scholarship. Walzel's Berlin lecture marks the beginning of a scholarly debate that, initially at least, was more or less limited to the German-speaking countries and to individuals steeped in the German tradition. (The fact that Jost Hermand, working in and writing about that tradition, produced a book on *Literaturwissenschaft und Kunstwissenschaft* serves as proof.) The results have been uneven and, on the whole, disappointing for a number of reasons: the attempt either stuck too closely to the art-historical model (Walzel) or dealt with the problem too stringently in the context of *Geistesgeschichte* (from Oswald Spengler to Wylie Sypher and Arnold Hauser); or the discussion was too theoretical (Fritz Medicus, Karl Vossler, and, more recently, Pierre Dufour and Dionyź Ďurišin)[7]; or the issue was treated with too much skepticism (Wellek) or tackled with undisguised and sometimes unqualified enthusiasm (Wais). Yet, while we remain in need of a coherent theoretical exposition of the entire gamut of intermedial relations, we can take pride in possessing several exemplary historical surveys of specific genres and problems (or notions) involving literature and the visual arts: Jean Hagstrum's treatment of literary pictorialism, Henkel and Schöne's handbook of emblematics, Gisbert Kranz's survey of iconic poetry, and Ulrich Ernst's work on the *carmen figuratum*, as well as, from the art-historical point of view, Rensselaer W. Lee's monograph on *ut pictura poesis*.

II

Having explored the historical dimension of the interrelation between literature and the visual arts in theory and practice, I shall now address myself to its nature and aesthetic or scholarly value.

Unlike aesthetics, which is a branch of philosophy and operates with the help of a priori categories, the mutual illumination of the arts is, or might be, preoccupied with all manner of specific, tangible relations involving works of art executed in two or more artistic media. (Books like Thomas Munro's *The Arts and Their Interrelations*, "a general survey of the arts and of ideas about them" that largely focuses on problems of classification, and Theodore M. Greene's *The Arts and the Art of Criticism*, which discusses the categories and forms intrinsic to the major arts but "is also concerned with those aspects of art criticism [and theory] which lend themselves to philosophical analysis," occupy a middle ground between the purely aesthetic and the strictly critical approaches.) Because of its scholarly origins it has been the nearly undisputed domain of literary science, deriving sustenance from, and making inroads into, the companion disciplines without turning into an *Allgemeine Kunstwissenschaft* 'general science of art.' Insofar as the present volume addresses itself primarily to students of literature, this line of demarcation will be honored. The visual arts (*beaux-arts* 'fine arts'), on which the present chapter centers, can be subdivided in several ways. For the present purpose, it may suffice to indicate that the most important among them are painting, sculpture, the graphic arts, photography, and architecture. In the field of comparative arts, architecture and sculpture are clearly less significant than painting and the graphic arts[8]; and it is on these latter that I lavish most attention in the following pages. Specifically, I intend to offer a catalogue raisonné of the various types of interrelations that are of interest to the literary scholar, followed by annotated references to selected works exemplifying these modes.

The list of actual or possible types of intermedial linkage that follows presupposes an orientation that is mainly, though not solely, that of the literary critic/historian; and exceptions to that rule will be duly noted. Following the advice implied in René Wellek's assertion (*Theory of Literature*, p. 119) that "the most central approach to a comparison of the arts is based on an analysis of the actual objects, and thus of their structural relationships," I start by naming kinds of cohabitation and interpenetration that are manifest "to the naked eye."

1. *Literary works that describe or interpret works of art*. These include the so-called iconic poems that Gisbert Kranz seeks to classify in his *Das Bildgedicht in Europa* (pp. 66–79, esp. p. 77). The iconic poem, derived from the ancient epigram or inscription, must be regarded as the poetic strain of *ekphrasis*. Rainer Maria Rilke's *Dinggedichte*, by contrast, are poetic adumbrations of nonartistic objects.

2. *Literary works that re-create or literally constitute the things that they delineate*. These are the so-called pattern poems. In modern times, they include Apollinaire's *Calligrammes* and that brand of concrete poetry which regards the poem as a visual object.

3. *Literary works whose outward appearance partly or wholly depends on design or graphic elements*, such as the use of hieroglyphs or Chinese characters (Ezra Pound's ideographic poetry) or the spatial distribution of letters or words on the page (Stéphane Mallarmé's "Un Coup de Dés").

4. *Literary works so designed as to stimulate the reader's visual sense*, be it through the use of images, metaphors, or similes, as in imagist poetry (Pound's "In a Station of the Metro") or through "sculpturesque" treatment (the Parnassians).

5. *Literary works seeking to reproduce movement styles in the visual arts*, such as the impressionistic pictorialism of Katherine Mansfield (see example 1 below), the "impressionist" syntax of certain French and Spanish authors at the turn of the century, Oskar Kokoschka's expressionist use of color and movement in his early play *Mörder, Hoffnung der Frauen*, Gertrude Stein's cubism in her "Portrait of Picasso."

6. *Literary and art works that are linked with each other through manifestos and programmatic statements reflecting a common viewpoint and purpose*. Wellek, like the New Critics, is particularly wary of the inten-

tional fallacy to which they might be subject. For example, whereas Emile Zola's naturalist manifestos are limited to literature, the programs issued by the editors of the periodical *Réalisme* (1856) combine literary with pictorial elements. In the case of futurism, a general manifesto was followed by various technical manifestos focusing on literature, painting, music, and so on.

7. *Literary works in whose creation certain techniques or modes borrowed from the visual arts have been employed*, such as the "grotesque" style of E. T. A. Hoffmann, the application of collage to poems and novels, the camera-eye technique in Alain Robbe-Grillet's *La Jalousie*.

8. *Literary works concerned with art and artists, whether real or imagined*. Examples are Honoré de Balzac's *Le Chef-d'œuvre inconnu*, Somerset Maugham's *The Moon and Sixpence*, Joyce Cary's *The Horse's Mouth*, Virginia Woolf's *To the Lighthouse* (see example 2 below); the works discussed in Jeffrey Meyers' *Painting and the Novel*; the function of Michelangelo in T. S. Eliot's "Love Song of J. Alfred Prufrock" and of Lucas Cranach's eccentric version of "Adam and Eve" in Georg Kaiser's play *Von morgens bis mitternachts*.

9. *Literary works that, without directly referring to specific art works or particular artists, require art-historical expertise for a fully adequate interpretation*, such as W. B. Yeats's "Sailing to Byzantium" (see example 3 below) and Heinrich Mann's narrative transposition of paintings in his novel *Die Göttinnen*.

10. *Literary works that share themes or motifs with works of art* but show no sign of an actual, tangible influence. This analogical relation is one of the most popular targets in the comparative arts. Interdisciplinary exercises of this kind tend to be facile or inconclusive since what emerge are mostly parallelisms.

11. *Literary works that, jointly with other literary works produced in a given era and civilization, as well as together with contemporary music, painting, philosophy, science, and so forth, display features of a common style*. This is the basic assumption underlying the method known as *Geistesgeschichte*, which, in its worst practitioners, seems to presuppose a belief in the actual existence of "time spirits," but which, in its best representatives, makes *Geistesgeschichte* the handmaiden of *Stilgeschichte*. Indiscriminately practiced, as throughout Mario Praz's *Mnemosyne* and, intermittently, in Sypher's *Rococo to Cubism in Art and Literature* and Helmut Hatzfeld's *Literature through Art*, it fully deserves the charge leveled against it by René Wellek (*Theory of Literature*, p. 111): "We are only convinced that the solutions offered by the usual *Geistesgeschichte* with its excessive reliance on contraries and analogies, its uncritical presupposition of the seesaw alterations of styles and *Denkformen*, and its belief in a complete integration of all activities of man, have been premature and, frequently, immature." Wellek attacks the excrescences of the method; he does not reject the need for, or deny the validity of, interarts periodization, a problem to which Alastair

Fowler addresses himself. A healthy antidote to generalizations of the kind perpetrated by *Geistesgeschichte* is to be found in the notion of the noncontemporaneity of the contemporary ("Ungleichzeitigkeit des Gleichzeitigen"), which Wilhelm Pinder adumbrates in the first chapter of his *Das Problem der Generation in der Kunstgeschichte Europas* (Leipzig: Seemann, 1928).

12. *Synoptic or symbiotic genres*, such as the masque, the emblem, the *livre d'artiste*, the picture story à la Wilhelm Busch, and, in the realm of *Trivialliteratur*, the cartoon and its equivalents.

13. *Synesthesia*, which is the psychological correlate of artistic symbiosis, and which, in its literary manifestations, may well concern the student of the comparative arts.

14. *Book illustration proper*, as surveyed by Alain-Marie Bassy. This is the first of two types of intermedial linkage involving literature and the visual arts where, traditionally, the scholarly perspective is an art-historical one. But there is no reason why astute critics and historians of literature should not study the phenomenon from their standpoint.

15. *Paintings, drawings, and so on, that hark back to literary antecedents or exist in a literary context without being outright illustrations.* Here the literary critic or historian, using the iconological method outlined by Panofsky, may benefit from the pictorial evidence of one of several literary texts (see the discussion of Pieter Bruegel's *The Fall of Icarus* in example 4 below as well as the examples from Hoffmann, Baudelaire, and Proust cited above). Rensselaer W. Lee's *Names on Trees: Ariosto into Art* (Princeton: Princeton Univ. Press, 1977) exemplifies this mode of investigation.

16. A rather special case is that constituted by the multiple talent (*Doppelbegabung*). Wellek is skeptical with regard to the appropriateness and significance of studies analyzing such phenomena, whose *tertium comparationis* lies in the artist's elusive psyche. He maintains that "the 'medium' of a work of art . . . is not merely a technical obstacle to be overcome by the artist in order to express his personality, but a factor preformed by tradition and having a powerful determining character which shapes and modifies the approach and expression of the individual artist" and bolsters his argument by pointing to the allegedly "grotesque little animal . . . supposed to illustrate 'Tiger! Tiger! burning bright,'" and William Makepeace Thackeray's "smirky caricature of Becky Sharp" (*Theory of Literature*, p. 117). But this is hardly cogent proof; for while Thackeray may well have dashed off the portrait of his fictional heroine, William Blake's artistry at its best is hardly embodied in the qualitatively inferior copies of the etching in question. Wellek's view is just as one-sided as that which, at the other end of the spectrum, claims that all creative activities of an artist working in several media are perfectly aligned and hence aesthetically compatible. For there are instances (Michelangelo, Dante Gabriel Rossetti, Ernst Barlach, and so on) where enduring works were created in two media, as well as those where this was decidedly not the case.

In raising the issue of multiple talent—a heading under which one might also treat the work of writers (Diderot, Zola, John Ruskin, Apollinaire) who served as art critics and whose art criticism, an applied form of *ekphrasis*, had a bearing on their literary activities—we have left the safe realm of tangible objects and structural relations and entered the precarious domain of psychology. Methodologically, psychological approaches, focusing on the artistic mentality and predisposition rather than on tangible works, are less rewarding in the comparative study of the arts and are best left to those better equipped to deal with the mind and its myriad manifestations, unless, that is, there is concrete evidence of mental processes (their residue, as it were) to be found in the completed work or the preparatory stages (sketches, drafts, etc.). Here are a few examples illustrating the difficulties one encounters in the course of such investigations:

(a) The moment of inspiration, which marks the beginning of the creative process and is, therefore, of the utmost importance in the evolution of the work of art, must by definition be opaque to the scholarly mind; it defies scientific explanation. Nevertheless, this moment may be precious to the student of the comparative arts when the spark is lit by a work executed in another medium. Inspiration, however, acquires scholarly value only when traces of the source can be found in the finished product.

(b) The mood present in, or engendered by, a work of art cannot properly be the subject of scholarly investigation because, whether conceived of as present in the artist, in the work of art, or in the beholder, "mood" is intangible and, hence, nonproductive as a research goal, as Wellek, polemicizing against Emil Staiger and Käte Hamburger, has argued in "Genre Theory, The Lyric and *Erlebnis*."[9] The comparative study of moods prevalent in works executed in different media with a view toward their mutual illumination would be equally preposterous.

(c) The way in which we perceive, through the different senses, works of art belonging to different artistic realms is a matter of considerable importance and well worth studying, as Rudolf Arnheim does in "The Unity of the Arts: Time, Space, and Distance" (pp. 7–12). Whether, and how much, it can contribute to the mutual illumination of the arts, I am not prepared to say. Yet insofar as the psychology of art is a field tangential to the study of art per se, we should relegate it to a second plane in our still precarious and methodologically fickle comparative endeavors.

III

In choosing examples that illustrate modes of significant interrelation between literature and the visual arts, I draw heavily on two previous publications of mine: the paper entitled "Verbal Paintings, Fugal Poems, Literary Collages and the Metamorphic Comparatist" ("Lilly Conference," pp. 7–18) and my contribution to a volume edited by Horst Rüdiger.

Example 1 (literary work seeking to reproduce a movement style in the visual arts): Katherine Mansfield's story "Her First Ball" is a text produced in consequence of what, in the absence of documentation amounting to proof, must be regarded as an attempt to use in one art form techniques germane to another. As her model, the author chose impressionism (better called sensationism), a style based on the assumption that things exist only insofar as they are seen or, by extension, apperceived by the other senses. The universe of impressionism is, consequently, one of eternal flux in which the self drifts like a sponge absorbing sense data. Owing to the limitation placed on their medium, painfully felt but never overcome, the impressionist painters could accommodate only one of the senses. Literature, by contrast, manages to produce something of a total work of the senses because words, though abstract signs, are capable of providing sensory stimuli of many kinds. Thus in "Her First Ball" sight and sound are joined by taste and touch. In this way, literature recoups some of the losses incurred by not being a visual art and by being compelled to substitute description for depiction. By existing in a spatiotemporal medium, the written text has the advantage of being inherently dynamic and conveying the sense of incessant, undirected motion in which, according to the philosophy of impressionism, things are caught up as if in a gentle vortex.

Oblivious of the law of gravity, Mansfield's characters are literally swept off their feet; and if they are not pushed or tossed, they float, flutter, glide, rush, or drift. On this characteristically impressionist occasion, a ball (and the breathless anticipation thereof), the inanimate objects that surround them in this Heraclitean world follow their lead: a jet of gas light dances in the ladies' dressing room, and the lampposts, houses, fences, and trees lining the road waltz, as if to confirm the validity of Einstein's theory of relativity. Throughout, objects perceived by people moving past them lose their accustomed shape and have their outlines blurred. There is, in addition, a carefully controlled progression from the observation, occurring halfway through the piece, that "the azaleas were separate flowers no longer: they were pink and white flags streaming by" to the culmination at the end where "the lights, the azaleas, the dresses, the pink faces, the velvet chairs, all [become] one beautiful flying wheel."

"Her First Ball" is an extraordinarily successful attempt to draw the reader into a fleeting and essentially fragile world of sensations in which perception is shallow, reflection painful, and memory so brittle that individuals, shorn of their personality, tend to forget who and where they are.

Example 2 (literary work concerned with art and artists): Virginia Woolf's *To the Lighthouse* is a novel in which art and artists play an important role. The tension between Mrs. Ramsay, who represents the deepest life force, and Lily Briscoe, who finds consolation in art, forms the axis around which the internalized action revolves. Both women have embarked on a quest. Consciously as well as unconsciously, Mrs. Ramsay aims for a stable, impersonal center from which will radiate that profound humanity that, while she lives, causes the world to be a patterned order in which all things and all people have their place — but always in relation to her. It is attained in the eleventh section (p. 96, Harcourt ed.): "There was freedom, there was peace, there was, most welcome of all, a summoning together, a resting on a platform of stability. Not as oneself did one find rest ever, in her experience . . . but as a wedge of darkness. Losing personality, one lost the fret, the hurry, the stir. . . . "

By contrast, the stable center toward which her "opponent," Lily Briscoe, strives pertains to art, not life. From the standpoint of art history, Lily's quest recapitulates the postimpressionist dilemma, more specifically, Paul Cézanne's stubborn search for permanence on his way to cubism, which is characterized by progressive abstraction and the substitution of shape (Roger Fry's "significant form") for color. Thus impressionism (of the Edgar Degas variety) appears in the person of Mr. Paunceforte, after whose visit to the seaside resort where the Ramsays spend their summers the pictures painted by Sunday artists tend to be "green and grey, with lemon-colored sailing boats and pink women on the beach" (p. 23), since it has become customary to see "everything pale, elegant, semitransparent" (p. 32). But Lily, like the recluse from Aix-en-Provence who initiated twentieth-century art, moves resolutely away from that style. Frustrated in her desire to be like Mrs. Ramsay, who radiates life but tries to find peace for herself outside of it, she scores her admittedly modest victory by painting her rival as a "triangular purple shape" (p. 81). Having seen "the color burning on a framework of steel; the light of the [impressionistic] butterfly wing lying upon the arches of a cathedral" (p. 75), Lily finally has her vision. But lacking the genius of Cézanne, she completes the painting she was preoccupied with throughout the novel realizing that the canvas, "with all its greens and blues, its lines running up and across, its attempt at something," might well be "hung in the attics" or even destroyed (p. 310).

Example 3 (literary work requiring art-historical expertise for full understanding): Yeats's "Sailing to Byzantium" has been the object of close readings in the neocritical vein, and its highly personal, as well as symbolic, message has not escaped the attention of its readers. Its important art-historical implications are usually ignored, even though they have a bearing on the interpretation, as can be shown by reference to the numerous drafts that Curtis Bradford made available twenty years ago.[10] In a nutshell: the persona's journey originally led to the real Byzantium; but in time the poet realized that he was facing a problem, for the mosaics on the walls and the ceiling of the circular dome of Hagia Sophia had been defaced or covered up after the Turkish conquest of Constantinople in 1453. They were not fully restored to view until after Yeats, who never journeyed to the East, had completed "Sailing to Byzantium." The poet chose to substitute Ravenna as his locus, where the sixth-century mosaic friezes of Sant'Apollinare Nuovo, depicting both saints and holy virgins, offer a perfect view of figures standing "in God's holy fire / As in the gold mosaic of a wall." The title of the poem in its "authorized" version, then, is metaphorical, Byzantium representing not the capital of the Justinian empire but a world view and soul state. In the light of a more pedantic, literal reading, the piece probably should have been called "A Trip to Ravenna."

Example 4 (painting harking back to literary antecedent): the study of the two versions of Pieter Bruegel's painting *The Fall of Icarus*, placed in its literary context, serves a double purpose, for it raises both an iconographical problem of the kind hitherto erroneously thought to concern solely the art historian and a series of questions relevant for the literary scholar charged with the mutual illumination of the arts. The iconographical search is bound to focus initially on the works' literary source, Book VIII of Ovid's *Metamorphoses*, which tells the story of Daedalus and Icarus; and no account of the paintings will be satisfactory unless it explains the striking omissions (the absence of Daedalus, who appears in the alternate version), modifications (only one of the three witnesses glances upward), and additions. Nor can the scholar ignore the visible impact of certain medieval and Renaissance traditions, whether proverbial, emblematic, hermetic, or broadly humanistic.

Literaturwissenschaft is clearly charged with "reading" the dozen or so iconic poems—most of them written in the present century—that have focused on *The Fall of Icarus*. Among these, W. H. Auden's "Musée des Beaux-Arts" excels, not only because it is artistically superior but also because it seems to have created its own tradition. In studying this body of poetry and in determining the exact nature of the relation between each poem and its pictorial referent, the critic will have to explain, and justify, the choice of details, the order in which these are presented, and the nature of the poetic "message" extracted from Bruegel's picture. (The critic may, in passing, wish to inquire whether a poet has seen the painting in situ or has relied on reproductions.)

IV

Once an academic discipline has been surveyed and its history outlined, it is proper to inquire what methods can be legitimately used in studying the relevant phenomena. While I cannot hope to do justice to the methodological complexities that are innate in the study of the comparative arts, I can touch on some basic issues and indicate, with the aid of a few examples, the possible margin of error.

Addressing myself to the closely intertwined questions of methodology and terminology, I should like to emphasize that the practitioners of our "art" often reflect inadequately on the status of a given relation and particularly on the crucial distinction between contactual and noncontactual relations. The first type invites the scholar to look for verifiable links between two objects belonging to different spheres of art. Here, the flow is unidirectional, moving from the work (or person) exerting an influence to the work (or person) exposed to it. Studies of this kind, which are intrinsically historical, aim at proving or disproving influence; and where no documentary proof is available, evidence may be provided by "mutually exclusive parallels" (Sven Linnér's term) that make it unlikely that no contact has existed.[11]

The second class of phenomena, difficult enough to encompass in a purely literary context, comprises cases involving parallels ("sets of features inherent in two entities which are closely similar or corresponding, as in purpose, tendency . . . or essential parts") and analogies ("similarities in some respects between things otherwise unlike or unrelated"), affinities that have been studied by Moriarty and Weisstein with an eye toward the comparative arts. One could justifiably argue that whenever works belonging to different artistic realms are compared, we deal with analogies (on account of the qualitative leap) on which parallels may be superimposed. As previously indicated, the most brazen practitioners of *Geistesgeschichte* usually ignore this fact and, to the justifiable scorn of the critics of mutual illumination, treat analogies as parallels by maintaining that all works created in a given period, regardless of medium or provenance, share essential features. Thus Wylie Sypher, in *Rococo to Cubism in Art and Literature*, claims that, although the rococo is wedged in between the baroque and Romanticism, "Pope's verse, like Lepautre's architecture and Watteau's painting, belongs to a distinguishable style" (p. 34) and that "technically there is a deep similarity between Keats and Delacroix, both enriching conventional forms of composition by a fine poetry of excess" (p. 70). Mario Praz, whose *Mnemosyne* continues—and, one hopes, terminates—this "impressionistic" tradition, entertains the notion that in a portrait by Hans Eworth the sitter "is represented against a background full of accessories, which give the effect of a flat arabesque, the same effect we note in so many stanzas of Spenser's *The Faerie Queene*" (pp. 110, 112). In all three instances, the method, leading itself ad absurdum, shows its madness.

The study of analogies between two works not otherwise linked merely serves the function of throwing light on each of them by pointing out similarities and differences outside of any historical framework. It constitutes a procedure that French comparatists of the old school, such as Jean-Marie Carré, have denounced as futile, theoretical exercises. In the words of Fernand Baldensperger, founder of the *Revue de Littérature Comparée*, "no explicatory clarity results from comparisons restricting themselves to a glance cast simultaneously at two different objects, to that appeal, conditioned by the play of memories and impressions, to similarities which may well be *erratic* points furtively linked by the mind's caprice."[12] At best such exercises show that universal laws are operative in the arts and that there are anthropological (Emil Staiger) or aesthetic (René Etiemble) constants. In the comparative arts, even more than in the already overextended field of comparative literature, it is imperative, as Jean Seznec suggests, to eschew vast syntheses and brilliant generalizations and to concentrate, instead, on monographic studies "limited in their object and rigorous in their form" ("Art and Literature," p. 574).

In interdisciplinary endeavors one would, accordingly, do well to proceed discreetly and with measured pace from the small to the large and from the particular to the general. One's choice of topic in undertakings of this kind ought to be gauged, precisely and narrowly, to the subject matter at hand, and one's investigation should be conducted in a "controlled" environment. One should pay particular attention to the logical progression of the argument; for nothing is easier in the comparative arts than to shift, imperceptibly, the grounds of the intended comparison. In his two-part essay "The Parallel of the Arts: Some Misgivings and a Faint Affirmation," James D. Merriman proffers sensible advice:

> In the study of the interrelations of the arts, the problem of the selection of features for comparison is of the greatest importance, and . . . it may be worth reviewing the criteria which any feature must satisfy if it is to be workable. Clearly, the feature must be at least a possible feature of all the objects to be compared; a feature possible to one art but definitionally impossible to others can only show non-relationships. . . . At the same time, at least ideally, it should be a feature possible only to the arts, for otherwise we shall not so much be discovering the particular relations of the arts, as we shall be merely observing the common relationships of the arts with all other sorts of objects [the fallacy of *Geistesgeschichte*]. . . . Thirdly, the feature must be capable of literal presence in all the objects to be compared. One of the most frequent methodological errors in interarts comparisons has been the failure to recognize that a feature literally present in one art is only figuratively present in another. (p. 57)

Based on Kenneth Burke's notion of "innate forms," Merriman's catalog of features to be noted in interarts comparisons unfortunately lacks the specificity that he himself so wisely calls for; for categories like contrast, balance, repetition, expansion, reversal, are too broad, and they are even less indigenous to the arts than are Theodore M. Greene's "intermedial factors of artistic unity," that is, simplicity or complexity, integration and rhythm.

A particularly interesting part of Merriman's program—and a convenient point of departure for a brief discussion of the terminological aspect of the question—is his assertion that all features to be used in interarts comparisons "must be capable of literal presence in all the objects to be compared" and that "one of the most frequent methodological errors . . . has been the failure to recognize that a feature literally present in one art is only figuratively present in another." Indeed, how often does an identical feature inhere in two works belonging to two different spheres of art? Usually only the names of apparently common elements are identical while the elements themselves are either parallel or analogous, meaning that in one work—most frequently the one involving the art that has borrowed the term from its companion—the designation is clearly metaphorical. (In the range of phenomena under study, the transfer is usually made from the visual arts to literature.) Here are some examples that demonstrate the truth of this contention:

1. While it is customary to call poets painters (as Lucian does in the case of Homer in the aforementioned dialogue "A Portrait Study"),[13] there is an unbridgeable gap between visual depiction and verbal description. Words can be sufficiently evocative to excite the visual imagination; but a literal transfer from one medium to another is impossible.

2. Much the same is true of the verbal equivalent of the grotesque, which, as Wolfgang Kayser and others have shown, has its roots in the visual arts, where it took hold when the Pompeian-style wall decorations of Nero's Golden House were unearthed in the Renaissance and imitated by artists like Raphael and Luca Signorelli. In literature, the term—which Michel de Montaigne first used, metaphorically, to characterize the stylistic and structural idiosyncrasies of his *Essais*—gradually acquired a host of meanings, some of them almost completely devoid of pictorial implications, while writers such as E. T. A. Hoffmann, in his emulation of Jacques Callot, continued to appeal to the visual imagination. Methodologically, it would therefore be well to do what is historically impossible, that is, to reserve the literary use of the term for works with distinctly visual implications.

3. Certain literary uses of the technique of collage, as discussed in Klotz and Weisstein, on the other hand, are barely metaphorical, and the application of the identical term is justified in regard to novels like John Dos Passos' *Manhattan Transfer* and Alfred Döblin's *Berlin Alexanderplatz*, where newspaper headlines, billboard signs, and street vendors' cries are introduced as casually encountered random bits of undigested reality. Yet there remains a basic difference, in intention, between what Georges Braque and Pablo Picasso did in 1909 and what the two novelists did in the twenties; for whereas the fathers of cubism sought to reintroduce reality into canvases that had been on the point of becoming abstract, their fellow artists merely wished to enhance the concreteness of a fictional world already bursting with reality.

4. By way of contrast, and conclusion, we offer an example where the purely metaphorical nature of a term transplanted from one medium to another is so obvious that there are clearly no grounds for using it for the anal-

ogous literary phenomenon. In his essay "On the Concept and Metaphor of Perspective," Claudio Guillén has shown how the art-historical term "perspective," so admirably explicated by Erwin Panofsky,[14] gradually lost its mathematical and art-historical specificity and, although originally limited to the visible world and the visual arts, began to acquire a measure of universality that seemed to justify its use in literary discourse. But what is the literary equivalent of a technique that serves the double purpose of suggesting, through an optical illusion, depth to the beholder who actually faces a flat surface and of clarifying, through variance in size, the relative position of figures and objects in a unified three-dimensional space? It would be hard to find, since literature is mostly concerned with mental attitudes and thought processes, a fact that Proust comments on in the following passage from his magnum opus:

> A real person, profoundly as we may sympathise with him, is in great measure perceptible only through our senses, that is to say, he remains opaque, offers a dead weight which our sensibilities have not the strength to lift. . . . The novelist's happy discovery was to think of substituting for those opaque sections, impenetrable by the human spirit, their equivalent in immaterial sections, things, that is, which the spirit can assimilate to itself.[15]

Hence the preference justly given by literary critics to "point of view" (a term coined by Percy Lubbock in an early book on Henry James), as manipulated by writers like Virginia Woolf (in whose *To the Lighthouse* it is sometimes — in the section "Time Passes," for instance — conspicuous by its absence) and William Faulkner (in whose novels *As I Lay Dying* and *The Sound and the Fury* the various points of view are deliberately scrambled).

The four examples just adduced must suffice as evidence that caution is called for in interdisciplinary studies whenever choices of terminology, invariably involving decisions of a methodological kind, have to be made; for the human mind is, unfortunately, so constituted as to believe that things named alike must be alike and, conversely, that things bearing different labels must be different. (A case in point: the indiscriminate use of the terms "collage" and "montage" in literary criticism aimed at elucidating T. S. Eliot's *Waste Land*.) What is urgently needed is a companion piece to Robert Escarpit's *Dictionnaire international des termes littéraires* (now in process of publication), a *Dictionnaire international des termes interdisciplinaires* that will settle, if only by consensus, the problems of nomenclature besetting the student of the comparative arts. In the meantime, if we do not go out of our way to conduct our business wisely and with great discretion, our pedagogical, methodological, and terminological efforts will either go unheeded or result in the obfuscation (*Verdunklung*) of the arts rather than in their mutual illumination (*Erhellung*).

Notes

[1] Quoted from the fascimile edition of the *Athenäum* (Stuttgart: Cotta, 1960), pp. 39–151.

[2] Quoted from "A Portrait Study," in *The Works of Lucian of Samosata*, ed. and trans. H. W. Fowler and F. G. Fowler (Oxford: Clarendon, 1905), III, 23.

[3] Quoted from *A Documentary History of Art*, ed. Elizabeth G. Holt, I (New York: Doubleday-Anchor, 1957), 277–78.

[4] From Chapter xvi of Lessing's *Laocoön* in the translation of Sir Robert Phillimore (New York: Dutton, 1974).

[5] Simon Jeune, *Littérature générale et littérature comparée: Essai d'orientation* (Paris: Les Lettres Modernes, 1968), pp. 18–19.

[6] "Balancer les beautés d'un poète avec celles d'un autre poète, c'est ce qu'on a fait mille fois. Mais rassembler les beautés communes de la poésie, de la peinture et de la musique: en montrer les analogies; expliquer comment le poète, le peintre et le musicien rendent la même image; saisir les emblêmes fugitifs de leur expression; examiner s'il n'y aurait pas quelque similitude entre ces emblêmes, etc., c'est ce qui reste à faire, et ce que je vous conseille d'ajouter à vos *Beaux-Arts reduits à un même principe.*" Denis Diderot, *Œuvres complètes*, ed. J. Assézat (Paris: Garnier, 1875), I, 385.

[7] Fritz Medicus, "Das Problem der vergleichende Geschichte der Künste" in *Philosophie der Literaturwissenschaft*, ed. Emil Ermatinger (Berlin: Juncker and Dünnhaupt, 1930), pp. 188–239; Karl Vossler, "Über gegenseitige Erhellung der Künste" in *Heinrich Wölfflin-Festschrift* (Dresden: Jess, 1935), pp. 160–67; and Dionyź Ďurišin, "Comparative Investigation in Literature and Art." *Neohelicon* 5, No. 2 (1977), 125–40.

[8] Webster's *New World Dictionary of the American Language* offers two definitions of "graphic arts," one more and one less inclusive: "1. any form of visual artistic representation, esp. painting, drawing, photography, etc.; 2. now sometimes only those arts in which impressions are printed from various kinds of blocks or plates, as etching, lithography, drypoint, offset, etc."

[9] Originally published in the *Festschrift für Richard Alewyn*, ed. Herbert Singer and Benno von Wiese, (Cologne: Böhlau, 1967), the essay was subsequently included in Wellek's book *Discriminations: Further Concepts of Criticism* (New Haven: Yale Univ. Press, 1970), pp. 225–52.

[10] Curtis Bradford, "Yeats's Byzantium Poems: A Study of Their Development." *PMLA*, 75 (1960), 110–25.

[11] The nature of influence and its application to literature in general and comparative literature in particular has been the subject of numerous essays and symposia, many of them listed in the appropriate section (p. 289) of my *Comparative Literature and Literary Theory*. To these should now be added Sven Linnér's "The Structure and Functions of Literary Comparisons" in *Journal of Aesthetics and Art Criticism*, 26 (1967), 169–79, and a book by the Swedish art historian and aesthetician Göran Herméren, *Influence in Art and Literature* (Princeton: Princeton Univ. Press, 1971).

[12] Fernand Baldensperger, "Littérature comparée: Le mot et la chose," *Revue de Littérature Comparée*, 1 (1921), 7.

[13] The metaphorical equation poet = painter continues to operate well into the eighteenth century, when the Swiss critics Bodmer and Breitinger use it with regard to Martin Opitz in the ninth of their *Discourse der Mahlern* (1721).

[14] Erwin Panofsky, "Die Perspektive als symbolische Form," *Vorträge der Bibliothek Warburg*, ed. Fritz Saxl (Leipzig: Teubner, 1924–25), pp. 258–330.

[15] *Swann's Way*, trans. C. K. Scott Moncrieff (New York: Modern Library, 1928), pp. 118–19.

Bibliography

A. Bibliographies

A Bibliography on the Relations of Literature and the Other Arts 1952-1967. New York: AMS, 1968. Compiled for the General Topics 9 Discussion Group of the MLA. Continued in annual installments under the editorship of Calvin S. Brown (until 1972) and Steven P. Scher (1973-   ). The installment for 1974 appeared in *Hartford Studies in Literature*, 7 (1975), 77-96. Coverage includes music, the visual arts, and, since 1974, film.

"Selected Current Bibliography for Aesthetics and Related Fields." Annually in the *Journal of Aesthetics and Art Criticism*, from 4 (1945-46) to 31 (1972-73). Now discontinued.

B. Reviews of Research

Rousseau, André-M. "Arts et littérature: Un Etat présent et quelques réflexions." *Synthesis* (Bucharest), 4 (1977), 35-52. Lists and briefly evaluates over four hundred items published in the last twenty-five years.

Weisstein, Ulrich. Chapter ix ("Wechselseitige Erhellung der Künste") of *Vergleichende Literaturwissenschaft: Erster Bericht, 1968-1977.* Bern: Lang, 1982.

C. General and Methodological

Dufour, Pierre. "La Relation peinture/littérature: Notes pour un comparatisme interdisciplinaire." *Neohelicon*, 5, No. 1 (1977), 141-90. Proposes a semiotic model based on Hjelmslev's *Prolegomena to a Theory of Language*.

Giovanni, G. "Method in the Study of Literature in Its Relation to the Other Fine Arts." *Journal of Aesthetics and Art Criticism*, 8 (1950), 185-95. More general and, hence, less useful than the Merriman essay below.

Greene, Theodore Meyer. *The Arts and the Art of Criticism.* 1940; rpt. New York: Gordian, 1973. A systematic attempt to classify the six major arts (music, dance, architecture, sculpture, painting, literature) according to matter, form, and content. "Three Inter-Medial Factors"—simplicity or complexity, integration, and rhythm—are considered in Ch. xi.

Hardison, O. B., Jr. "*Poetics*, Chapter I: 'The Way of Nature.'" *Yearbook of Comparative and General Literature*, 16 (1967), 5-15. An analysis of the opening portion of Aristotle's treatise, with emphasis on the classification of the arts.

Merriman, James D. "The Parallel of the Arts: Some Misgivings and a Faint Affirmation." *Journal of Aesthetics and Art Criticism*, 31 (1972-73), 154-64, 309-21. A comprehensive and (overly?) cautious treatment of basic questions.

Munro, Thomas. *The Arts and Their Interrelations.* Rev. ed. Cleveland: Case Western Reserve Univ. Press, 1967. Primarily concerned with classification. Part II is devoted to the "Relations between the Arts" as seen from various angles.

Teesing, H. P. H. "Literature and the Other Arts: Some Remarks." *Yearbook of Comparative and General Literature*, 12 (1963), 27-35. A reply to and partial refutation of Wellek's "Parallelism between Literature and the Arts."

Wais, Kurt. *Symbiose der Künste: Forschungsgrundlagen zur Wechselberührung zwischen Dichtung, Bild- und Tonkunst.* Stuttgart: Metzler, 1937. Highly suggestive but poorly organized.

Walzel, Oskar. *Wechselseitige Erhellung der Künste: Ein Beitrag zur Würdigung kunstgeschichtlicher Grundbegriffe.* Berlin: Reuther and Reichard, 1917. Application of Wölfflin's "kunstgeschichtliche Grundbegriffe" to literature.

Weisstein, Ulrich. "Comparing Literature and Art: Current Trends in Critical Theory and Methodology." *Literature and the Other Arts*, ed. by Steven P. Scher and Ulrich Weisstein. Vol. III of the *Proceedings* of the IXth Congress of the

International Comparative Literature Association (Innsbruck, 1981), pp. 19–30.

———. "Die wechselseitige Erhellung von Literature and Musik: Ein Arbeitsgebiet der Komparatistik?" *Neohelicon*, 5, No. 1 (1977), 92–123. The comparative arts as a subfield of comparative literature.

———. Chapter x ("The Mutual Illumination of the Arts") of *Comparative Literature and Literary Theory: Survey and Introduction*. Trans. William Riggan. Bloomington: Indiana Univ. Press, 1973, pp. 150–66.

———. "Zur wechselseitigen Erhellung der Künste." In *Komparatistik Aufgaben und Methoden*. Ed. Horst Rüdiger. Stuttgart: Kohlhammer, 1973, 152–64. Analyzes works by Katherine Mansfield, Virginia Woolf, and W. B. Yeats.

Wellek, René. "The Parallelism between Literature and the Arts." In *English Institute Annual for 1941*. New York: Columbia Univ. Press, 1942, pp. 29–63. A shortened version of this incisive critique appears as Chapter xi of Wellek and Austin Warren's *Theory of Literature*. 3rd ed. New York: Harcourt, 1962.

D. Influences, Parallels, Analogies

"Analogy." Two entries in the *Dictionary of the History of Ideas*. New York: Scribner, 1973. Vol. II: "Analogy in Early Greek Thought" by G. E. R. Lloyd (60–63) and "Analogy in Patristic and Medieval Thought" by Armand Maurer (64–67).

Herméren, Göran. *Influence in Art and Literature*. Princeton: Princeton Univ. Press, 1975. Primarily addressed to art historians. The intermedial aspect is briefly touched on on p. 261.

Moriarty, Michael. "The Uses of Analogy: An Essay in the Methodology of Comparative Literature." Diss. Indiana Univ. 1971. The comparative arts seen as furnishing one of five purposes of analogy in the field.

Weisstein, Ulrich. "Influences and Parallels: The Place and Function of Analogy Studies in Comparative Literature." In *Teilnahme und Spiegelung: Festschrift für Horst Rüdiger*. Ed. B. Allemann and E. Koppen. Berlin: de Gruyter, 1975, pp. 593–609.

E. Time and Space

Frank, Joseph. "Spatial Form in Modern Literature." In *The Widening Gyre: Crisis and Mastery in Modern Literature*. New Brunswick, N.J.: Rutgers Univ. Press. 1963, pp. 3–62. Originally published in the *Sewanee Review*, 53 (1945) and often—sometimes incompletely—reprinted. Walter Sutton's essay "The Literary Image and the Reader: A Consideration of the Theory of Spatial Form" (*Journal of Aesthetics and Art Criticism*, 16 [1957-58], 112–23) is a rather unconvincing rejoinder.

Sauvage, Micheline. "Notes on the Superposition of Temporal Modes in Works of Art." In *Reflections on Art: A Source Book of Writings by Artists, Critics, and Philosophers*. Ed. Susanne Langer. 1958; rpt. New York: Oxford Univ. Press, 1961, pp. 161–73. Appeared originally in *Revue d'Esthétique*, 6 (1953),

Souriau, Etienne. "Time in the Plastic Arts." *Journal of Aesthetics and Art Criticism*, 7 (1949), 294–307. Rpt. in Langer, pp. 122–41.

F. Multiple Talent

Günther, Herbert. *Künstlerische Doppelbegabungen*. 2nd ed. Munich: Heimeran, 1960. A dictionary preceded by an introductory survey.

Scheidegger, Ernst, ed. *Malende Dichter/Dichtende Maler*. Zurich: Die Arche, 1957. An anthology of poems by painters, and paintings and drawings by writers.

G. Synesthesia

Schrader, Ludwig. *Sinne und Sinnesverknüpfungen: Studien und Materialien zur Vorgeschichte der Synästhesie und zur Bewertung der Sinne in der italienischen, spanischen und französischen Literatur.* Heidelberg: Winter, 1969. Comprehensive bibliography on pp. 272–87. Of particular significance are the various contributions by Albert Wellek listed on p. 286.

Vinge, Louise. *The Five Senses: Studies in a Literary Tradition.* Lund: Glerup, 1975.

H. Some Key Concepts Historically Surveyed

Babbitt, Irving. *The New Laocoön: An Essay on the Confusion of the Arts.* Boston: Houghton, 1910. The classical and "pseudoclassical" theories of imitation pitted against the Romantic theory of spontaneity. A biased and polemical account.

Hagstrum, Jean. *The Sister Arts: The Tradition of Literary Pictorialism and English Poetry from Dryden to Gray.* Chicago: Univ. of Chicago Press, 1958. Part I reviews the tradition of parallelizing literature and the visual arts from antiquity through the Middle Ages, the Renaissance, the baroque and English neoclassicism.

Kristeller, Paul Oskar. "The Modern System of the Arts." (1951–52). In *Renaissance Thought II: Papers on Humanism and the Arts.* New York: Harper, 1965, pp. 163–227. Traces the evolution of the system from antiquity to Batteux.

Lee, Rensselaer W. *"Ut pictura poesis": The Humanistic Theory of Painting.* New York: Norton. 1967. An art historian's account, covering the fifteenth, sixteenth, and seventeenth centuries.

Park, Roy. "*Ut pictura poesis*: The Nineteenth-Century Aftermath." *Journal of Aesthetics and Art Criticism,* 28 (1969), 155–64. A sequel to Lee's monograph.

Trimpi, Wesley. "The Meaning of Horace's *Ut pictura poesis.*" *Journal of the Courtauld and Warburg Institutes,* 36 (1973), 1–34. A scholarly and primarily philological study.

I. Periodization

Fowler, Alastair. "Periodization and Interart Analogies." *New Literary History,* 3 (1972), 487–509.

J. Some Historical Surveys by Period

(a) General

Hatzfeld, Helmut. *Literature through Art: A New Approach to French Literature.* 1952; rpt. Chapel Hill: Univ. of North Carolina Press, 1969. Approach by way of *Geistes-* and *Stilgeschichte,* as theoretically outlined in Hatzfeld's "Literary Criticism through Art Criticism and Art Criticism through Literary Criticism," *Journal of Aesthetics and Art Criticism,* 6 (1947-48), 1–21.

Praz, Mario. *Mnemosyne: The Parallel between Literature and the Visual Arts.* Bollingen Series, 35. A. W. Mellon Lectures, 16. Princeton: Princeton Univ. Press, 1970. A combination of *Geistesgeschichte* and stylistic analysis derived from Bernard Berenson.

(b) Antiquity

Webster, T. B. L. *Greek Art and Literature, 530–400 B.C.* Oxford: Clarendon, 1939. A parallel history, since "there is little evidence of cross influences between literature and art." Complemented by the same author's *From Mycenae to*

Homer (London: Methuen, 1958), *Greek Art and Literature, 700–530 B.C.* (London: Methuen, 1959) and *Art and Literature in Fourth Century Athens* (London: Athlone, 1956).

(c) Middle Ages

Frühmorgen-Voss, Hella. *Text und Illustration im Mittelalter: Aufsätze zu den Wechselbeziehungen zwischen Literatur und bildender Kunst.* Ed. N. H. Ott. Munich: Beck, 1975. On pp. ix–xxi, the editor surveys studies concerning "Text und Illustration im Mittelalter."

Pickering, F. P. *Literature and Art in the Middle Ages.* Coral Gables, Fla.: Univ. of Miami Press, 1970. German version: *Kunst und Literatur im Mittelalter.* Berlin: Schmidt, 1966. Methodological questions are raised on pp. 1–71 of the English and pp. 1–55 of the German version.

Stammler, Wolfgang. *Wort und Bild: Studien zu den Wechselbeziehungen zwischen Schrifttum und Bildkunst im Mittelalter.* Berlin, Schmidt, 1962.

(d) Renaissance and Baroque

Hocke, Gustav René. *Manierismus in der Literatur: Sprach-Alchimie und esoterische Kombinationskunst.* Hamburg: Rowohlt, 1959.

———. *Die Welt als Labyrinth: Manier und Manie in der europäischen Kunst.* Hamburg: Rowohlt, 1957. Mannerism understood in the way suggested by E. R. Curtius, i.e., all "mannerisms" from late antiquity to surrealism.

Jensen, H. James. *The Muses' Concord: Literature, Music, and the Visual Arts in the Baroque Age.* Bloomington: Indiana Univ. Press, 1976. Chapter ix ("Comparisons of the Arts") is methodologically oriented.

Sypher, Wylie. *Four Stages of Renaissance Style: Transformations in Art and Literature, 1400–1700.* New York: Doubleday-Anchor, 1955. Renaissance, mannerism, baroque, late baroque. Chapter i of this rather strained exercise in *Geistesgeschichte* treats "The Analogy of Forms in Art."

(e) Eighteenth to Twentieth Century

Sypher, Wylie. *Rococo to Cubism in Art and Literature.* New York: Random, 1960. A sequel to the above.

Kamber, Gerald. *Max Jacob and the Poetics of Cubism.* Baltimore: Johns Hopkins Univ. Press, 1971.

Moser, Ruth. *L'Impressionisme français: Peinture, littérature et musique.* Geneva: Droz, 1952.

Weisstein, Ulrich. "Expressionism: Style or *Weltanschauung?*" *Criticism*, 9 (1967), 42–62.

———. "Romanticism: Transcendentalist Games or 'Wechselseitige Erhellung der Künste'?" *Colloquia Germanica*, 1–2 (1968), 47–69.

K. Science of Literature and Science of Art

Alpers, Svetlana, and Paul Alpers. "*Ut pictura noesis?*: Criticism in Literary Studies and Art History." *New Literary History*, 3 (1972), 437–58.

Hermand, Jost. *Literaturwissenschaft und Kunstwissenschaft: Methodische Wechselbeziehungen seit 1900.* Stuttgart: Metzler, 1965. Limited to German-language area.

Panofsky, Erwin. "Iconography and Iconology: An Introduction to the Study of Renaissance Art" (1939). In *Meaning in the Visual Arts: Papers in and on Art*

History. New York: Doubleday-Anchor, 1955, pp. 26–54. Pp. 26–40 are of particular relevance to the study of the comparative arts.

Seznec, Jean. "Art and Literature: A Plea for Humility." *New Literary History*, 3 (1972), 569–74.

Weisinger, Herbert. "What the Literary Historians Can Learn from the Warburg School." *Bulletin of the New York Public Library*, 67 (1963), 455–64.

L. Literary Critics as Art Critics

Brookner, Anita. *The Genius of the Future: Studies in French Art Criticism.* London: Phaidon, 1971. French writers from Diderot to Zola.

Fosca, François. *De Diderot à Valéry: Les Ecrivains et les arts visuels.* Paris: Michel, 1960.

Seznec, Jean, and Jean Adhémar, eds. *The Salons of Denis Diderot.* 4 vols. Oxford: Clarendon, 1957–67.

M. Conferences

"Comparing the Arts: Methods, Terms, Teaching." Conference held at Indiana University, March 12–14, 1976. Partial Proceedings in *Yearbook of Comparative and General Literature*, 25 (1976), 5–30. Includes major addresses by Rudolf Arnheim ("The Unity of the Arts: Time, Space, and Distance") and Decio Pignatari ("The Metalanguage of Art").

"Lilly Conference on Literature and the Other Arts," Indiana University, March 2–4, 1978. Proceedings in *Yearbook of Comparative and General Literature*, 27 (1978). Major papers by Ulrich Weisstein ("Verbal Paintings, Fugal Poems, Literary Collages and the Metamorphic Comparatist") and Claus Cluever ("Painting into Poetry"), as well as workshop reports on concrete poetry (Mary Ellen Solt) and Renaissance art and literature (Giancarlo Maiorino).

"Second Lilly Conference on Literature and the Other Arts," Indiana University, March 1979. Privately printed on behalf of the Eli Lilly Company (Indianapolis, 1979). Unifying theme: "Metamorphosis and the Arts."

Ninth Congress of the International Comparative Literature Association, Innsbruck, Austria, August 20–24, 1979. About ninety papers, over half of which concern the relation between literature and the visual arts. Published as *Literature and the Other Arts*, ed. Steven P. Scher and Ulrich Weisstein. Vol. III of the *Proceedings* of the IXth Congress of the International Comparative Literature Association. Innsbruck, 1981.

N. Pedagogy

Cluever, Claus. "Teaching Comparative Arts." *Yearbook of Comparative and General Literature*, 23 (1974), 79–92. The comparative arts at Indiana University, 1954 to 1974.

Frenz, Horst, and Ulrich Weisstein. "Teaching the Comparative Arts: A Challenge." *College English*, 18 (1956), 67–71. Analytical description of the first comparative arts course offered at Indiana University.

O. Special Topics

(a) Techniques Transferred from Art to Literature

Guillén, Claudio. "On the Concept and Metaphor of Perspective." In *Literature as System: Essays toward a Theory of Literary History.* Princeton: Princeton

Univ. Press, 1971, pp. 283–371. Originally published in *Comparatists at Work.* Ed. S. G. Nichols, Jr., and R. B. Vowles. Waltham, Mass.: Blaisdell, 1968.

Kayser, Wolfgang. *The Grotesque in Art and Literature* (1957). Trans. Ulrich Weisstein. Bloomington: Indiana Univ. Press, 1964.

Klotz, Volker. "Zitat und Montage in neuerer Literatur und Kunst." *Sprache im technischen Zeitalter,* 60 (1976), 259–77.

Weisstein, Ulrich. "Collage, Montage and Related Terms: Their Literal and Figurative Use in and Application to Techniques and Forms in Various Arts." *Comparative Literary Studies,* 15 (1978), 124–39.

(b) Genres

Albrecht-Bott, Marianne. *Die bildende Kunst in der italienischen Lyrik der Renaissance und des Barock: Studien zur Beschreibung von Porträts und anderen Bildwerken unter besonderer Berücksichtigung von G. B. Marinos "Galleria."* Wiesbaden: Steiner, 1976. Contains a comprehensive list of sixteenth- and seventeenth-century Italian iconic poems.

Bassy, Alain-Marie. "Iconographie et littérature: Essai de réflexion critique et méthodologique." *Revue Française d'Histoire du Livre,* 3 (1973), 1–33. Book illustration.

Buch, Hans-Christoph. *"Ut pictura poesis": Die Beschreibungsliteratur und ihre Kritik von Lessing bis Lukács.* Munich: Hanser, 1972. Limited to German literature. The opening section, "Enzyklopädisches Stichwort: Was ist Beschreibung?" (pp. 10–25), is of more general interest.

Downey, Glenville. "Ekphrasis." In *Reallexikon für Antike und Christentum.* Ed. Theodor Klauser. Vol. IV. Stuttgart: Hiersemann, 1959, cols. 922–44.

Ernst, Ulrich. "Die Entwicklung der optischen Poesie in Antike, Mittelalter und Neuzeit." *Germanisch-romanische Monatsschrift,* 26 (1976), 379–85. Pattern poems.

Friedländer, Paul. "Über die Beschreibung von Kunstwerken in der antiken Literatur." In Johannes von Gaza und Paulus Silentiarius, *Kunstbeschreibungen justinianischer Zeit.* Ed. Friedländer. Leipzig: Teubner, 1912, pp. 1–103.

Garvey, Eleanor M. *The Artist and the Book, 1860–1960, in Western Europe and the United States.* Exhibition catalog. Boston: Museum of Fine Arts, 1961. See also *Beyond Illustration: The Livre d'Artiste in the Twentieth Century.* Exhibition catalog, Lilly Library, Bloomington, Ind., 1976, prepared by Breon Mitchell.

Henkel, Arthur, and Albrecht Schöne, eds. *Emblemata: Handbuch zur Sinnbildkunst des 16. und 17. Jahrhunderts.* 2nd ed. Stuttgart: Metzler, 1976. A compendium containing an exhaustive bibliography on the subject.

Kranz, Gisbert. *Das Bildgedicht in Europa: Zur Theorie und Geschichte einer literarischen Gattung.* Paderborn: Schöningh, 1973. Contains a *bibliographie raisonnée* of iconic poems (pp. 121–200) and a catalog of artists to whose works iconic poems have been devoted (pp. 201–217).

——, ed. *Gedichte auf Bilder: Anthologie und Galerie.* Munich: Deutscher Taschenbuch-Verlag, 1975. An anthology of iconic poems and reproductions.

Rosenfeld, Hellmut. *Das deutsche Bildgedicht: Seine antiken Vorbilder und seine Entwicklung bis zur Gegenwart: Aus dem Grenzgebiet zwischen bildender Kunst und Dichtung.* Leipzig: Mayer and Müller, 1935. Limited to German-language literature.

Solt, Mary Ellen, ed. *Concrete Poetry: A World View.* Bloomington: Indiana Univ. Press, 1970. An anthology of poems and theoretical statements.

Wojaczek, Günther. "Technopägnien des Simias und der koischen Dichter." In *Daphnis: Untersuchungen zur griechischen Bukolik.* Meisenheim am Glan: Hain, 1969, pp. 67–125. Greek pattern poems.

(c) Art and Artists in Literature

Bowie, Theodore. *The Painter in French Fiction: A Critical Essay.* Chapel Hill: Univ. of North Carolina Press, 1950.

Goebel, Gerhard. *Poeta faber: Erdichtete Architektur in der italienischen, spanischen und französischen Literatur der Renaissance und des Barock.* Heidelberg: Winter, 1971. Comprehensive bibliography on pp. 242–250.

Meyers, Jeffrey. *Painting and the Novel.* Manchester: Manchester Univ. Press, 1975. Thirteen studies on nineteenth- and twentieth-century novels from Dostoevsky to Camus.

13

Literature and Film

GERALD MAST

The first deliberate attempts to make films of well-known literary works can be traced to 1907, the year that the Kalem Company in America produced a fifteen-minute, unauthorized version of General Lew Wallace's *Ben-Hur* and the year the Film d'Art, a company dedicated to bringing serious plays and stories to the screen, was founded in France. But from their very beginning, once they had discovered the possibility of recording life in motion, motion pictures attempted to organize that recording and that life according to fictional narrative patterns. Although Edwin S. Porter's *The Great Train Robbery* (1903) is frequently cited as the first motion picture to tell a story, the rudiments of storytelling (character, incident, and plot) can be glimpsed in the Edison Company's *The Execution of Mary, Queen of Scots* (1895), the Vitagraph Company's *Burglar on the Roof* (1896), James A. Williamson's *A Big Swallow* (Great Britain, 1899), Ferdinand Zecca's chase films in France (1899–1905), and in thousands of other short films made in America, England, France, and Germany in the first decade of the motion picture.

Since moving pictures and, after 1927, moving pictures synchronized with recorded sounds could be used to tell stories, describe events, imitate human actions, expose problems, and urge reforms, it is not surprising that such uses of motion pictures would provoke speculative comparisons with that other major human system for telling, describing, imitating, exposing, and urging—verbal language. The history of these comparisons between film and literature has been a history of splitters and lumpers, of those who argue for the distinctness of the two media—the effects, purposes, pleasures, and possibilities of two separate arts that are, ought to be, or must be distinct—as opposed to those who argue that the aims, effects, and means of the two media are similar, parallel, or analogous. One of the earliest splitters to publish an extended theoretical defense of film's uniqueness was the American poet Vachel Lindsay, whose *The Art of the Moving Picture* (1915) loudly and lengthily proclaimed the legitimacy of the motion picture as a "great, high art" on the basis of its parallels with all the arts and its separateness from any one of them. One of the earliest lumpers to argue that making

278

meaning with visual images paralleled making meaning with words was Sergei M. Eisenstein, the Russian filmmaker and theorist, whose essays of the twenties and thirties defended the legitimacy of film as an art on the basis of its parallels with literary processes and literary works.[1]

Although Lindsay and Eisenstein may have disagreed about the relation of film to literature, both wrote to assert the legitimacy of film as an art. Theoretical comparisons of film and literature have frequently been colored by issues of value, assumptions about artistic superiority and "legitimacy" that have themselves rarely been argued or even articulated, an accumulation of covert values arising inevitably from the historical circumstances in which both films and we find ourselves. First, film is a "new art," the only new art to be invented in thousands of years of Western civilization (with the exception of its parent mechanical art, photography); indeed, like photography, film is the only art to be invented at all (at the end of a century devoted to the invention of all sorts of machines), and the only art whose year of birth can, with some justification, if not certainty, be fixed — 1895. Inevitably, the new art must be compared to and judged by the standards of the existing arts.

Second, those interested in making such theoretical comparisons have necessarily been trained, formally or informally, by the standards and values of older arts, particularly by the standards and principles of writing about those arts. Only a certain sort of person would find it interesting or valuable to compare the theoretical aims and purposes of the various arts. Virtually all these people have been educated in universities (guaranteeing the influence of certain principles and traditions of aesthetic argument), most of them have earned doctorates in philosophy (guaranteeing a commitment both to writing and to writing about other written works), and many of their degrees have been in literature.

Third, there has been, at least until recently, a cultural and economic difference (in effect, a class difference) between those who have taken their primary cultural pleasure from reading and those who have taken their primary cultural pleasure from films. The earliest audiences for films either did not or could not read (either less-educated Europeans or immigrant Americans who spoke little English). Throughout the decades of the motion picture's greatest popularity — the first five of this century — those who regularly went to films tended to be less educated and less affluent than those who spent their time with novels, or at plays, concerts, operas, and ballets, or in art galleries and museums. The artistic values of those more educated and more affluent people necessarily tended to be imposed on films in any comparisons between film and the other arts, for only the educated and affluent people wrote or read or cared about such issues. In the 1960s, the conversion of the educated and affluent to a recognition of the legitimacy and importance of motion pictures as an art (as evidenced by the growing cultural importance of films in weekly magazines and daily newspapers, the proliferation of film courses in university curricula, the founding of a Film Division by the Modern Language Association, and, indeed, by the appearance of this article in this collection) was accomplished, ironically, not by the conversion of the educated and affluent to the values of the old moviegoers but by the conversion of the movies to the values of the educated and the affluent.

What were these values, and what assumptions lay beneath them? There were three. First, a respect for the integrity, perhaps even the sanctity, of the original literary text. A film adaptation of an important literary work has an obligation to be faithful to the spirit (or, even, the letter) of the original text and, at the same time, to be a cogent and unified work in its own terms. But what if the urge faithfully to adapt a work conflicts with the urge to make a whole and cogent work in its own terms? Indeed, if form and content are inextricably wedded in the greatest and densest works of literary art, how can one preserve the identical content in a new form? Akira Kurosawa's *Throne of Blood* (1957), thought by many to be one of the finest film adaptations of a Shakespearean text (preserving the spirit of *Macbeth* yet a stirring work in its own terms), does not preserve a single line of Shakespeare's play; whereas Roman Polanski's film of *Macbeth* (1971), thought by many to be a terrible distortion of Shakespeare, probably contains a higher percentage of Shakespeare's verse than any other film adaptation (as opposed to recorded performance) of a Shakespearean play. How can a film be simultaneously most and least faithful? One of the first and fullest academic examinations of adapting literary works into film, George Bluestone's *Novels into Film* (1957), summarized a previous generation's attitude toward "film and literature" by demonstrating the ways most films distorted, shrunk, or enfeebled the power of the original literary material.

But does one apply such criteria when comparing Shakespeare's *Othello* with Guiseppe Verdi's *Otello*? Or, more to the point for literary scholars, does one condemn Shakespeare or Chaucer for their alterations of their source materials, for their hammering the original Boccaccio story or Holinshed chronicle into the form they needed for their own particular concerns in that particular narrative? Although the filming of a literary work has been called "adaptation" by some and "translation" by others, both terms imply (indeed demand) a respect for the original text as the fixed foot of a compass around which the film version must revolve. If one terms the film work an "interpretation" of the original text (as Verdi's *Otello* is an operatic interpretation of Shakespeare's play or as Shakespeare's *Henry V* is a dramatic interpretation of Holinshed's history), the burden for artists becomes the wholeness and integrity of their artistic interpretations, not their loyalty to the original. Further, critics who claim that a film violates the integrity of the original material can only mean that the film violates either their own interpretations of the original or the general consensus regarding the interpretation of the original work. Seen in this manner, the critical problem is not of two competing works of art (film versus literary text) but of two competing interpretations (the critic's and the filmmaker's) of the same work of art. While the critical interpretation owes its loyalty to the original work, the artistic interpretation becomes an original work in its own right.

The second assumed value was closely related to the first—the tendency to prefer the reflective, the contemplative, and the intellectual aesthetic pleasures to the more passionate, intensely sensual, and stimulating ones. When Verdi makes an opera of *Othello*, he takes something out—words—and puts something else in—music. The elimination of words reduces intellectual ironies and subtleties, psychological shading and detail—indeed the very stuff that makes Shakespeare's *Othello* Shakespeare's *Othello*. In place of these internalized subtleties, Verdi substitutes a passionate vocal and orchestral score that attempts to concretize and externalize intense human feeling, asking its listeners not to savor its subtleties and ambiguities but to feel its immensities and intensities. So too, any filmed version of a literary work must take something out—words—and put something else in—sights and sounds. These direct, physical appeals to two senses make the cinema an even more intensely physical experience than opera, pushing the work even farther from the intellectual richness of verbal subtlety, attempting to convey an intensely sensuous metaphor for the experience of an event rather than an ironic or reflective understanding of its significance (an especially pervasive aim of films in the last decade, with their use of the immensely wide screen and their overwhelming, multichannel stereophonic sound tracks). Because literary pleasure is a much quieter, more solitary, contemplative one, those who devote their lives to it and its study might find any diminution of that pleasure and the substitution of another an inherent debasement. It would also tend to produce a preference for contemplatively ironic films like *The Rules of the Game* (1939), *The Seventh Seal* (1957), and *Dr. Strangelove* (1963) as opposed to aggressively passionate ones like *Scarface* (1932), *Stagecoach* (1939), and *Star Wars* (1977).

This contempt for genre films leads to the third assumed value that influenced the comparison of literature and film: the modernist assumption that a work must be a unique, indeed radical, creation in both form and content, neither stemming from generic conventions nor appealing to the mass who feel comfortable with the generic and the conventional.[2] The experimental delving into both conscious and unconscious mental processes in the modern novel, the playing with authorial point of view, the subversion of the very conventions and assumptions on which the writing of novels, plays, and poetry depends in the works of James Joyce, Ezra Pound, Virginia Woolf, William Faulkner, Samuel Beckett, Eugène Ionesco, and many others has led many modernist and modernist-influenced literary scholars to expect that same sort of value and innovation in films (modernists are far more likely to take a professional interest in film than, say, medievalists). Indeed, there have been many films—particularly the best European films of the last twenty-five years—that satisfied precisely this kind of modernist taste (the films of Federico Fellini, Michelangelo Antonioni, Bernardo Bertolucci, Pier Paolo Pasolini, François Truffaut, Jean-Luc Godard, Alain Resnais, Ingmar Bergman, and many others). Indeed, the European film tradition has consistently paddled in the modernist stream, from the silent days of German expressionism, French surrealism, and Soviet montage through the prewar French sound films of Jean Renoir, Jean Vigo, and Marcel Carné. Unfortunately, the modernist value excludes the serious consideration of a huge body of cinema works—almost every American film made between D. W. Griffith's *The Birth of a Nation* in 1915 and the collapse of the American studio system some fifty years later, films that did not explicitly and aggressively subvert the conventions and procedures of film storytelling but simply wanted to tell good stories that would entertain as many people as possible.

It was easy to exclude such films from serious consideration by serious people on the grounds of their patent unseriousness (for the same reason that teachers of American literature ignore the popular novels of Herman Wouk, Irving Wallace, and Jacqueline Susann). One could dismiss all "Hollywood films" (a generic category that includes some 25,000 titles) for being commercial (made by big business for big profits), factory productions (cranked out by a studio system rather than shaped by a single imagination), genre pictures (westerns, gangsters, screwball comedies, and—worst of all—musicals) that made the dreadful error of pleasing (and continuing to please) a large number of people everywhere in the world. The one widely accepted exception to this studio rule, Orson Welles's *Citizen Kane* (1941), achieved its reputation because it was the one American studio film that was in style, subject, and spirit, a modernist film (although Pauline Kael's "Raising Kane" argues that it was truly an American genre film beneath its modernist surface).[3]

Although the modernist denigration of the American studio-film tradition is understandable, it has been subjected to scrutiny in the last decade (just as the modernist assumption in general has been subjected to the scrutiny implied by the critical term "postmodernism"). First, one cannot substitute the seriousness of an intention for the solidity of an accomplishment. Literary excellence is recognized by the excellence of the literary work. We respect the work of a Shakespeare and a Dickens, who simply tried their best to please their audiences, because the best they could do was very good indeed. Second, neither Shakespeare nor Dickens aggressively subverted the conventions and procedures of playwriting or novel writing. Although Shakespeare's plays are subtle explorations of such generic structures as revenge tragedies and pastoral romances (just as the best Hollywood westerns, mysteries, screwball comedies, and musicals are subtle explorations of their generic structures), a Shakespeare, Dickens, John Ford, or Howard Hawks explores a genre from within, ultimately creating another work in that tradition rather than a work that subverts and explodes the traditional genre altogether. Such artists inherit their forms and accept the task of telling as good a story within those forms as they can. What does a "good story" mean in such a context? Not just a well-structured, interesting tale but also a probing of the depth of the characters' souls, the author's offering perceptive social and psychological insight, manipulating a literary style both lucidly communicative and richly evocative, and, finally, creating a complex vision of human experience that we infer from the work as a whole. In such traditional works, the seriousness and depth of the author's moral-social-psychological vision is implicit rather than explicit, inferred from the action as a whole and the paradigmatic relations of characters rather than that vision's serving as the logical premise that generates the style and structure of the whole work, as it does in modernist works.

Hollywood films can be judged only as individual works, not as an immense generic category. Some westerns (say, John Ford's *Stagecoach* [1939], *My Darling Clementine* [1946], and *The Searchers* [1956] or Howard Hawks's *Red River* [1948]), contain penetrating analyses of the interrelation between human character and the destiny of the American nation; certain gangster films (Hawks's *Scarface*, Mervin LeRoy's *Little Caesar* [1931], and Fritz Lang's *The Big Heat* [1953]) develop an interesting relation between American crime and the American success ethic; some screwball comedies (Hawks's *Bringing Up Baby* [1938], Preston Sturges' *The Lady Eve* [1941], or Leo McCarey's *The Awful Truth* [1937]), explore the necessary ingredients for a fulfilling domestic and sexual existence; and even some musicals (the Astaire films, Vincente Minnelli's *The Pirate* [1948] and *An American in Paris* [1951], Gene Kelly and Stanley Donen's *Singin' in the Rain* [1952]) develop the simultaneous qualities of joyous exuberance, technical perfection, and absolute grace, a combination that may be one of the ultimate aspirations of American spiritual life.

Perhaps the best (or worst) example of where such assumptions could lead can be found in a single sentence of Robert Richardson's *Literature and Film* (1969), with which I want to quarrel because it is so indicative of the previous decade's thinking:

> And the screen version of Hemingway's *To Have and Have Not*, prepared by William Faulkner, shows how Hollywood could preside over a conjunction of geniuses only to produce, by a sort of cross-sterilization, a perfectly ordinary vehicle for Humphrey Bogart.[4]

First, how ordinary is "a perfectly ordinary vehicle for Humphrey Bogart," even if the film is indeed such an ordinary vehicle? Humphrey Bogart, a "mere" movie actor (worse, movie star) is, in fact, one of the great archetypes of twentieth-century culture, more familiar spiritually (and not just facially) to the citizens of our planet than all the Nick Adamses, Nick Caraways, Sutpens, Marlowes, Marcels, even Kurtzes and Gatsbys put together —

and probably, sad for literary scholars to contemplate, more influential on both writers and citizens of future generations than all these as well. As the semioticians would point out, Humphrey Bogart is as much a "text" as the novel of *To Have and Have Not*. His combination of the tough outside and sensitive inside, the gravelly voice and the soft eyes, the method of casually yet purposefully handling or dangling a cigarette (which has produced a new verb in English, *to bogart*) is a mask, an archetype, a persona, a symbol of human behavior that will last, like our notions of Oedipus, and Achilles, and Hector, as long as the physical material that is capable of transmitting that mask. It is difficult for literarily trained critics to understand the power of such archetypal presences, who, simply by their being, moving, and speaking, convey a whole attitude toward human existence and aspiration.

Although the literary critic may not be sensitive to a star presence, he or she should be sensitive to the narrative structure in which that star presence is embedded, and the film of *To Have and Have Not* is no "ordinary vehicle" at all. First, it is the film in which Bogart met Bacall — that is, one of those archetypal presences met another of those archetypal presences — a meeting that not only produced a highly publicized off-screen romance but generated the highly charged, subtextual, on-screen sparks as well (such electricity beneath the surface usually generates the best movie acting and interacting). Second, *To Have and Have Not* was "presided over" not by an anonymous "Hollywood" but by Howard Hawks, who was not employed by a Hollywood studio but remained a semi-independent producer, who was a writer of scripts (he coauthored every film he shot), who was the close friend of both Ernest Hemingway and Faulkner (he was the first man in Hollywood to recognize Faulkner's talent and to purchase the screen rights to one of his novels), and whose name is mentioned repeatedly in this essay and in any discussion of American genre films. *To Have and Have Not* is rich in the social themes, psychological preoccupations, moral vision, and stylistic traits that concern and distinguish Howard Hawks, a personal style and vision that can be inferred from the narrative of this single film and that informs every film Hawks made.

Then there is the alleged genius of the "conjunction of geniuses" that resides primarily, one presumes, in the original Hemingway novel. But this presumption is startlingly innocent of the jocular beginnings of this film project: Howard Hawks told Hemingway that he could make a good movie of Hemingway's worst novel. And Hemingway agreed to both the project and the assessment. Indeed, the Hemingway novel, written quickly for money, is one of those "interesting experiments" (like Faulkner's *The Wild Palms* and *The Old Man*) that try to make two stories into one novel: the first half, a story about Harry Morgan, a rum-running owner of a power boat in the Caribbean, and the second half about Richard Gordon, a burned-out hack author who makes his living by writing about the Harry Morgans of the world but cannot feel or understand anything about them. Hawks and Faulkner made a coherent narrative out of Hemingway's divided tale by staying with Harry Morgan, by building the plot around a crisis that forces him to balance his moral, personal, and romantic commitments and by making the archetype of Humphrey Bogart the center of that narrative conflict (in this sense, the film is a perfect vehicle for Bogart, but not a "perfectly ordinary" one).

I spend so much time with this one sentence from Richardson, not to beat a dead horse (indeed, many of the attitudes it implies are still very much alive),[5] but to reveal where certain literary assumptions and values have led when blindly applied to comparisons of "literature and film." In the end, we can invoke our personal values in comparing specific film and literary works, in preferring certain films to others, in regarding the form of film in general as more or less satisfactory at accomplishing certain ends. But we cannot begin with such normative assumptions if we wish to describe, either as splitters or as lumpers, the relation between literature and film. Where might we begin?

I

There is a Film Division within the Modern Language Association, and there are two reasons the study of film might be the proper province of an organization devoted to literary and language study. On the one hand, films are works—indeed works of art—sequential, patterned, temporal wholes that begin and end and, progressing from beginning to end, elaborate some kind of content in some kind of style that illuminates, reflects, or reveals that content. As works, films are analogous to plays, novels, poems, and essays, the specific kinds of works implied by the general study of literature. On the other hand, film is a modern "language"—a complex communicative system for making and conveying meaning. Of all the alternative modern "languages" that semioticians have investigated—the "languages" of clothing, of traffic signs, of human gesture, and the like—film is the only semiotic system that can rival verbal language's ability to construct lengthy and complex messages. Any comparison of film and literature must, therefore, begin with a distinction between the comparison of formal wholes and the comparison of systems (or media) of communicating messages.

Pedagogically and practically, the literary discipline classifies whole literary works into four broad categories: (1) prose fiction (novels, novellas, stories); (2) plays; (3) poems (narrative and lyric); and (4) nonfiction prose, a category for which there is no commonly accepted term. Three of these categories can be defined by their physical characteristics as printed type on a page—prose fiction in sentences and paragraphs, plays in speeches, and poems in lines—while the fourth is distinguishable from prose fiction only in its intention (or "final cause"), which is not to tell stories but to inform or persuade about facts. Such mixed categorization produces grave theoretical difficulties: more theoretically tidy would be either three categories based on the physical organization of lines of type—plays, poems, and prose narratives—which would include two (fiction, nonfiction) or more (fiction, history, biography, etc.) subclasses or the four classical categories—history, philosophy, poetry, and rhetoric—that are purely and consistently generated by their final causes. But the four mixed classes of prose fiction, drama, poetry, and nonfiction prose accurately reflect the way that members of the literary profession divide the works of their study.

Film scholars also divide film works into four broad classes for practical and pedagogical purposes: (1) narrative films—fictional stories ("narrative" in this sense has been equated with fictional storytelling) of either feature length (100 minutes, plus or minus 30) or shorter (a very few, of course, are much longer); (2) documentary films (also called nonfiction films)—films that claim not to be telling fictions but somehow informing or persuading about facts; (3) experimental films—a very broad category with no commonly accepted name (avant-garde, underground, abstract, and independent films are among them) and no clearly unified purpose other than a tendency to be about themselves, to be visually or psychologically strange and formally innovative, and to be short (less than 30 minutes, although there are many exceptions); (4) animation—films that use drawn pictures rather than photographs, although some methods of animation use photographs, but shot in some noncontinuous way. In contrast with the four classes of literary works, three of these four film categories are determined by intentional rather than formal criteria. Narrative films tell fictional stories; documentary films inform or persuade about the factual; and experimental films, many of which indeed tell stories or document facts, somehow wish to experiment with cinema processes, visual perception, or states of human consciousness. At the same time, only one of the classes owes its basis to a physical characteristic—the method of making an animated film. Indeed, animated films are themselves either fictional narratives, nonfictional explications, or abstract experiments. As with the categories of literary works, this division is a theoretical one, and others can be devised; classification might be based on some single and consistent principle as into two broad material classes (photographic and nonphotographic) with three subclasses (narrative, nonfiction, experimental) or into three intentional classes (to narrate, to document, to experiment) with two subclasses (animated, photographic). But the four-class system seems functional and, again, accurate in terms of the way film scholars view their field. Indeed, international film festivals use these four classes for inviting and awarding entries.

This system reveals some relevant and interesting comparisons with the categories of literary works. Two of the literary categories, prose fiction and plays, are analogous to a single kind of film work, narrative films. In fact, most comparisons of literature and film in the past have tacitly shrunk the term "literature" into novels and plays and the term "film" into narrative films, the kind of film that is most like a novel or play and the kind of film into which novels and plays are adapted. Shrinking the terms in this manner produces inaccuracies and shows an insensitivity to the broad range of both literary and filmic possibilities. Are novels and plays, for example, so ontologically similar that we could justify their being lumped together as "literature"? Properly speaking, is a play literature at all (if we define literature as that kind of art or enterprise which is composed of letters — writing, words)?[6]

On its first, physical level of apprehension, a novel is nothing but letters, words. One can easily define what a novel concretely, physically is: it is that piece of matter one holds in one's hand, its letters printed on paper and bounded by the covers in which those pieces of paper have been gathered.[7] But a play has no similar concrete, physical existence. The object that one can hold in one's hand is not a play but the script of a play. Nor is a performance of that text the play but a performance or production of the play. A play, then, is not a physical thing at all but an imaginary ideal: either the imaginary combination of all possible performances and productions of that script or the idealized "best" performance that can be imagined (by whom? at what time?) from that script. As teachers of literature we frequently pretend that the text of the play is the play, as if it were a novel written in speeches.

But, in point of fact, none of the meaning of Shakespeare's plays is transmitted to the audience by letters. When Aristotle claimed that plays contained everything in epics (i.e., narrated as opposed to dramatized stories) and more, the "more" he mentioned were melody and spectacle (what we hear and what we see). All the verbal information of a play comes to us as "melody," as sounds, and the quality of those sounds often conveys the play's meaning and values as much as the meanings of the words ("diction") do; imagine Gertrude's voice as opposed to Ophelia's (say, a bassoon as compared to a clarinet), or Hamlet's voice as opposed to Claudius' as opposed to Polonius' as opposed to Osric's (perhaps, trumpet, French horn, tuba, and oboe). Although such musicalization is certainly implied by the words of the printed text (such instrumentation is itself an interpretation of the literary text), the experience of hearing these voices must influence, deepen, and enliven our understanding and enjoyment of the work.

Although the printed texts of Shakespeare's plays seem complete and although little meaning may seem to come to us visually, as spectacle (other than the pleasing display of color and costume), a purely visual cue, such as the side of the stage where a character makes an entrance or exit, may inform us where the scene takes place (in the Greek or the Trojan camp, in Rome or Alexandria, in England or France). In modern plays like Chekhov's, Beckett's, and Pinter's the deliberate scoring of the text with dozens, perhaps hundreds, of pauses makes silence itself communicative, forcing the audience to infer why this character at this moment has fallen silent (thus the notion of the subtext, the not verbalized but merely implied, becomes so important in a discussion of modern drama). Such pauses do not merely influence the rhythms, the musicality, the "melody" of the play; they actually convey its meaning.

While the communicative system of a novel is composed solely of words (or letters and other typographic symbols), the communicative system of a play is composed of sounds and sights, adorning and suggested by a verbal text. This distinction bears an obvious relevance to film, which also communicates with sights and sounds and in which many of those sounds are human speeches. In certain ways films resemble plays more than novels, but in others resemble novels rather than plays.

As with a novel, it is possible to state what a film concretely, physically is, for a film is a physical object that can be held in the hand—the lengths of cellluloid wrapped around however many reels. Like a novel, a narrative film is a narrated fiction, controlled by a narrative voice, a teller (the camera lens) that lets us see only what it wishes. And like a novel, a film is capable of leaping nimbly in time and space, a common characteristic of narrated fictions. Although deliberately realist dramas have chosen to equate "realism" with the unities of time and place, ritualized, stylized, presentational, or epic theater can take us anywhere as quickly as a film does, essentially by using the same tools that the novel uses to transport us—words that ask our imaginations to see the characters in some new time or place. Films, however, make their leaps in time and space with the same physical concreteness and detail that the realistic theater reserves for its invisible-fourth-walled drawing rooms and bedrooms. Although the usual distinction between drama and film is between the stable space of the theater and the dynamized, shifting space of cinema, only "realist" theater space remains stable, while cinema retains its realist connection with the physical world by depicting the visual concreteness of each of its shifting spaces.

Like a play and unlike a novel, a film is a sort of performance art, presented for a group of persons gathered together at a specific place and time. Like other performance arts, a film is usually limited to the amount of time it is believed that people wish to spend. Unlike a novel, then, a feature film must be compact, its length even closer to that of a concert or dance program than to the 2½-hour play. And like a play, a film concretely presents scenes between physical beings rather than between abstract "characters," beings who seem to be enacting their thoughts and feelings directly for us. But because every shot in a film is controlled by the guiding narrative presence of the camera's lens, even those scenes that seem to be played for us as if the players stood before us directly on a stage are really interpreted for us as if they were narrated in a novel.

The film's midway position between a novel and a play explains why these two literary forms collapse into a single kind of film. A narrative film collapses Aristotle's distinction between the "dramatic mode," which presents characters and actions to us directly, and the "epic mode" (i.e., narrative or narrated mode), which tells us about the characters and their actions. While some sequences of a narrative film seem entirely dramatic (the dialogue scenes) and others seem entirely "epic" (e.g., the montage sequences that assemble many different shots to imply a progression or development over a period of time), every shot in a film is a simultaneous hybrid between dramatic showing and narrative telling.

From these considerations and distinctions it would follow that the three problems of filming a novel are those of enclosing it within an approximately two-hour form, converting its purely verbal text into a succession of sights and sounds (only some of which are verbal), and dramatizing its narrated scenes. It would also follow that the hardest novels to film would be those whose size is an inherent element of their conception and our experience of it, whose verbal style is unique and essential in their conception and our experience of it, and whose action cannot readily be broken into scenes of human interaction. Bluestone has argued that one essential and insurmountable difference between films and novels is that because films are photographs of physical objects, human or otherwise, they are incapable of revealing the inner and abstract states of human consciousness and unconsciousness. But Bluestone's book appeared before the New Wave films of the 1960s — Alain Resnais's *Hiroshima Mon Amour* (1959) and *Last Year at Marienbad* (1964), Michelangelo Antonioni's *L'Avventura* (1959) and *Red Desert* (1964), Federico Fellini's *8½* (1963), Ingmar Bergman's *Persona* (1967), and others; all these manipulate abstract mental states as fluidly as any modern novel does (significantly, none of these films was adapted from a novel).[8] If the films of *Ulysses*, *Lord Jim*, and *The Sound and the Fury* have disappointed many admirers of these literary works, it is probably because the novels' actions could not be trimmed to the two-hour limit without losing their texture, subtlety, and complexity; their structures could not be conveyed by a series of dialogue scenes; and their verbal styles defied translation into visual imagery.

Conversely, if Alfred Hitchcock's film of John Buchan's *The 39 Steps* or Howard Hawks's film of Raymond Chandler's *The Big Sleep* seem, for many, far richer and subtler than their originals, it is probably because the originals' actions could be unfolded in two hours without shrinking them; the original incidents could be easily broken down into a series of dramatized confrontations; and the verbal styles of the novels displayed less dexterity, virtuosity, and uniqueness than the visual styles of the two films. The thinner narrative skeletons of these smallish novels allowed both Hitchcock and Hawks to exercise their own narrative artistry. Hitchcock added an ironically humorous sexuality to the Buchan novel by building every encounter around an embarrassing or titillating confrontation between the fleeing protagonist and a provocative woman (not a single major female figure exists in the novel). Hawks injected a sensually hypnotic sexuality into the Chandler novel by building the narrative as a sexual journey through a maze of murders that allows Marlowe-Bogart and Vivian-Bacall to come to know, and trust in, each other's love (no such action and no such Vivian Rutledge exist in the novel). Ultimately, neither film merely decorates the thrilling incidents of the original narratives with human or sexual touches, and neither merely subscribes to the romantic and sexual obligations of genre films; both use the succession of external incidents as the means to explore internal human psychology, producing completely new, self-contained, richly internalized narratives. The smallish size of these two novels, their emphasis on external incident, their more functional, less idiosyncratic prose style, and their lack of cultural reverence gave Hawks and Hitchcock the freedom and the means to remake them.

From these considerations and distinctions it would follow that the three problems of filming a play are realizing the verbal text in a succession of sights and sounds (both words and other sounds), converting theatrical decor into cinematic decor, and converting a dramatic work into an "epic" (i.e., narrated) work. The length of the original play does not cause the same structural problems as the length of a novel, since a play and a film are already about the same length. It is possible to film a play by setting the camera up in the appropriate indoor and outdoor settings and staging the entire verbal text, from beginning to end, for the observing lens. However, the attempts to make precisely this kind of cinematic recording (pejoratively called "canned theater") have been unsuccessful, striking their viewers as dull, static, lifeless, and boring, conveying neither the vibrancy and intimacy of living theater nor the energy of true cinema.

The reasons for the feebleness of these dramatic transcriptions remain quite mysterious. The art historian Erwin Panofsky, who argued that one of the cinema's essential powers was the "dynamization of space," found that such "canned" plays were insufficiently dynamized; space itself was as immobile in the film as it would be in the theater.[9] The Soviet theorist Sergei Eisenstein argued similarly; such films were not constructed cinematically, by editing the different pieces of celluloid, the different shots (which, by implication, means the different pieces of space) to establish meaning. The French film critic and theorist André Bazin, however, argued differently.[10] He maintained that the core of a play, its verbal text, was written to be presented in a certain stylized setting, within a certain architecture, while films take place within the world, within nature itself. To stage a dramatic text within the real world will either diminish the words (for there is no reason for such stylized speech to exist in the real world) or diminish the world (for there is no reason that the world should agree to serve as the supporting player for a dramatic text).

Interestingly enough, one hears little theoretical or practical argument against television's "canning" of dramatic texts. This lack of critical antagonism suggests a genuine difference between film and television as artistic and cultural media. The physical characteristics of the television image (small screen, a picture reduced in brilliance, subtlety, and resolution, viewed in the light at home rather than in the dark in public) may lead us to expect less of it as a powerful artistic entity in its own right, and the cultural role that television has come to fulfill as our primary means of recording or transcribing preexisting events (sports events, news events, concerts) may also make it acceptable for recording productions of plays.

Most filmed versions of plays have recognized these theoretical difficulties in a very practical way by "opening up" the stage work, in effect, either dropping certain scenes into interestingly varied visual settings where the stage version could not go or interrupting the flow of dialogue scenes with essentially nonverbal ones in which the characters go for a walk in the park, a drive in the car, a dance in a disco, and so forth. Unfortunately, such films frequently give the impression of being artistic layer cakes — chunks of dramatic dialogue separated by segments of cinematic frosting. As opposed to alternating theatrical (indoor) and cinematic (outdoor) spaces, the cinema's task in adapting a play (or in constructing any film narrative) is to charge all its space and spaces with meaning. While space in the theater can indeed be meaningful, the meaning tends to be a single and stable metaphor that remains constant for the entirety of the stage performance. But in its shifting spaces, and its shifting camera positions within spaces, the cinema can endow every element in every space (walls, windows, furniture, objects, shapes, colors, patterns of light) with significant relations to the characters, action, and themes of the film. According to the orthodoxies of film history, the cinema did not successfully separate itself from theatrical assumptions until D. W. Griffith discovered and developed the procedures and principles of editing between 1908 and 1915. The years preceding 1908 are seen as a "dark age" when poor, benighted filmmakers went about the erroneous business of slavishly recording whole scenes in long, single shots. What these primitive directors were discovering, however, between 1898 and 1908 was precisely the way to make the individual spaces as communicative and as meaningful as possible, a technique that Griffith brought to perfection simultaneously with his innovations of editing.[11]

The ultimate solution to the problem of filming plays is the creation of a seamless weave of verbal and visual style that, through editing, narrative construction, and decor, renders the dramatic work into the "epic" (i.e., narrated) mode. Jean Renoir, for example, constructed his film version of Maxim Gorky's *The Lower Depths* (1936) as the narrative of two major figures (the Baron, who falls into the lower depths, and the thief, who climbs out of it — passing each other along the way) rather than as Gorky's whole dramatized society of fallen types. By alternating between Gorky's imprisoning indoor theatrical space and the open cinematic space of the outdoors, Renoir adds his own visual metaphor and thematic vision to Gorky's claustrophobic play — a contrast between the openness, freedom, and naturalness of the unfettered human spirit outside society and society's architecture as opposed to the restrictive tyrannies of civilized, bourgeois, materialistic society. But Akira Kurosawa filmed the same work (1957) by retaining the social microcosm, by retaining a large proportion of the dramatic text (which Renoir did not), and by keeping the action mercilessly enclosed in its indoor claustrophobic setting. Instead of "opening up" the play, Kurosawa deliberately closes it down, preserving claustrophobia as one of the film's metaphors. In confining his camera to the enclosed setting, shooting the various social groupings from different visual perspectives, Kurosawa converts his camera into an invisible narrator who is one more member of the microcosm, unseen and unnamed; this conversion of narrative focus converts the viewing audience itself into inside rather than outside observers of the social microcosm.

For his filmed version of Arthur Schnitzler's *La Ronde* (1950), Max Ophuls created a seen (but unnamed) narrative voice, a debonair master of ceremonies who wanders in and out of the action (just as Ophuls' camera wanders), controlling both our visual and moral view of the film's social and sexual commentary. Howard Hawks converted two Ben Hecht–Charles MacArthur plays (*Twentieth Century* and *The Front Page*) into dynamic narrative works identically — by adding a thirty-minute prologue to each, a major sequence that sketches and establishes the spiritual biographies of the two major figures before they confront each other in the central conflict that is the basis of the original play. Ironically, although plays are much closer to films than novels in their size and shape, more works of narrative fiction (which already exist in the narrated mode) have probably served as the basis for effective films.

Before moving from this comparison of novels, plays, and films to other comparisons between film and literature, some space must be devoted to the one Aristotelian element of poetic works that has not yet been developed: character. Aristotle's discussion of character applies equally well to the dramatic and epic modes because there is no ontological difference between character in a play and a novel. In plays as well as narrated fictions, characters are preexistent bundles of created traits — speeches, actions, thoughts, feelings — that take vague shape in our imaginations when we read a novel and more concrete shape on stage in a production of a play. With both, the characteristics that have been conceived for the human figure, the things he or she chooses to say or do or think or feel, preexist and therefore determine any specific embodiment of that figure. But character in a film is ontologically different from that in a play or novel. The existence of the physical being precedes and determines the traits that the human figure will demonstrate in the work. Harry Morgan in the film of *To Have and Have Not* is that specific being, embodied by Humphrey Bogart, and no other. It is impossible to determine whether Humphrey Bogart is Harry Morgan or Harry Morgan is Humphrey Bogart. The same character's name can be used in several different films, but the Philip Marlowes embodied by Bogart, James Garner, Elliot Gould, and Robert Mitchum are no more the same character than Jean Cocteau's Oedipus is the same as Sophocles'.

The discussion of character in film most frequently appears unknowingly disguised as a discussion of film acting (as in Richardson's reference to a "perfectly ordinary vehicle for Humphrey Bogart"). The assumed standards of great acting are really corollaries of the ontological status of character in plays and novels. The preexisting model is the gospel to whose authority the actor submits, his or her obligation being the exploration and fulfillment of that model.[12] The greatness of stage actors is therefore measured by their ability to fulfill as wide a range of these models as possible and to fulfill them as completely as possible. In comparison, film actors (especially film stars) are criticized for failing at precisely these tasks: for demonstrating as narrow a range of personalities as possible and for always being themselves. So too, many stage actors feel themselves both shrunken and restricted when they switch to making films.[13]

There are great stage actors—Marlon Brando and Laurence Olivier come immediately to mind—who have also demonstrated a great range of character playing in films. But the worst film performances of stage performers seem to be those in which we can see that they are performing, that they are pretending to be the characters they are embodying rather than embodying them. Given the ontological fact that a character in a film is that physical being and nobody else, and given the fact that a camera brings us close enough to human faces to reveal when they are pretending instead of being the figures they embody, there is a genuine aesthetic advantage for films in using actors who have little range and always play themselves.[14] Richardson, for example, does not question Humphrey Bogart's convincingness as Harry Morgan; he merely disparages the actor's being Humphrey Bogart and the Hemingway character's enslavement in the body of Bogart. No one has criticized Cary Grant's believability as David Huxley, Gary Cooper's as Longfellow Deeds, John Wayne's as Thomas Dunson, Greta Garbo's as Anna Karenina, Humphrey Bogart's as Philip Marlowe, and so forth. To some extent, the great "mistake" these movie stars make (and the greatest movie stars make it most often) is the apparent effortlessness of their convincing embodiment of these characters (and the greatest movie stars betray the least apparent effort).

As opposed to character in plays (and, by extension, in novels), character in narrative films moves not from a series of abstractly elaborated traits to a concrete physical embodiment but from a concrete physical embodiment to our inferences about traits, feelings, and commitments. The greatest movie stars (Humphrey Bogart, Clark Gable, Katharine Hepburn, Cary Grant, John Wayne, Gary Cooper, Jimmy Stewart, Bette Davis, Greta Garbo, and so forth) have been the richest "texts," suggesting most fully, clearly, powerfully, and immediately the traits that lie beneath the surface. The immediacy, instantaneousness, and effortlessness with which they establish their characters have a very great advantage for film, because it is more structurally compact than a novel or even a play. The audience's immediate recognition of a star's internal traits (aided by the familiarity of the star and the fact that the star has repeatedly demonstrated many of these traits in a number of films) allows a film to curtail the most necessary and least interesting narrative section of every play or novel, the exposition — who and where the characters are, why they are there, and what they want. The opening of Howard Hawks's *His Girl Friday* (1940) can plunge the two major figures into immediate verbal (and spiritual) battle because the shot's background lets us know where they are (a newspaper office) and the stars let us know who they are (Cary Grant and Rosalind Russell); those two central adversaries in *The Front Page*, named Walter Burns and Hildy Johnson, on whom the Hawks characters are based, do not face each other until the middle of the second act, after all the characters and the atmosphere and the issues of the play have been ploddingly defined. The intelligibility of star presences is a powerful narrative advantage in narrative films, and to expect character in films to conform to our models from literature is to inflict yet another normative literary prejudice on our judgment of films.[15]

Critical studies have paid far less attention to those other types of film works that parallel poetic or expository-rhetorical works of literature, just as this survey devotes far less space to them than to the relations of narrative films to plays and prose fiction. One of the few books to suggest a connection between expository prose and film is *Nonfiction Film* by Richard Meran Barsam, its very title implying a parallel that the more traditional term, "documentary film," does not; it is also one of the few books by a literary scholar about films other than fictional narratives.[16] One might think of nonfiction films, like nonfiction prose, as broadly divided between the expository and the rhetorical, and in both media, the line between the purely expository and the deliberately rhetorical is frequently blurry. Even the most purely informational films — newsreels and training films, for example — contain a particular attitude toward the news and the training, but the same must be said of a story in a news magazine or a sequence of instructions in a training manual. Travel films not only describe the place they visit but attempt to convince an audience that this place is a nice place to be. And the most complex tensions between the expository and the rhetorical are generated by those films, some of feature length, that begin with the far more general and less utilitarian purpose of producing a nonfiction work of art that simultaneously documents some real-life person, process, or event and affects us emotionally.

The first of these nonfiction classics, Robert Flaherty's *Nanook of the North* (1922), might be seen as an interesting and informative document about the way an Eskimo survives in the frozen wilderness and/or the ways that the physical conditions of human existence determine the way life can be lived. But the film makes other choices that clearly are artistic, personal choices of the filmmaker, which reflect his own concerns rather than those of the reality he was filming. Why, for example, does Flaherty choose Nanook and not some other Eskimo? (Nanook is indeed a supreme example of a life-style; might an Eskimo less successful than Nanook in this frozen world have produced a very different document of that world?) Why does Flaherty begin his film in the spring—warm, fertile, vibrant—and end it during the depths of a winter storm? (If the structure had been reversed, wouldn't it have implied a more hopeful view of life's continuity rather than the inevitable victory of the icy landscape?) Is it legitimate for Flaherty to have reconstructed in a studio scenes that could not be shot any other way (for example, Nanook's life inside an igloo)? (And how different does that make Flaherty's film from any other studio-created film?)

Almost every major nonfiction film raises similar questions about its nonfictionality. Is Sergei Eisenstein's *Potemkin* (1925) a nonfictional description of events in 1905 (like, say, Edward Gibbon's history of Rome), or a fictional historical romance (like *Gone with the Wind*), or a rhetorical history inculcating certain moral and social values (like Parson Weems's *Life of Washington*)? Is Dziga-Vertov's *The Man with the Movie Camera* (1929) a nonfictional document of life in the Soviet Union or a hymn of praise to that life? Is Basil Wright's *Night Mail* (1936) a nonfictional study of transporting the mail from England to Scotland or a hymn to the modern methods of cooperation between people and machines? Is Frank Capra's *Prelude to War* (1942), one of the Why We Fight series, merely an explanation of the historical conditions that produced the war or an assurance that because the causes of the war are understandable they are controllable and surmountable? Is Frederick Wiseman's *Meat* (1976) a detailed analysis of the meat industry's process of turning living animals into food for the American dinner table or a powerful indictment of the waste, brutality, yet necessity of that process? Most controversial of all, is Leni Riefenstahl's *Triumph of the Will* (1935) a mere document of a major Nazi political conference and its attendant visual ceremony, or is it mythic propaganda to advance the Nazi aims and ethic?

These questions are familiar enough in relation to literary texts. How much is Gibbon's history of Rome a study of that ancient culture and how much is it a modern interpretation of events by a scholarly gentleman of the late eighteenth century? How factual is *The Education of Henry Adams* or *Mein Kampf*? The difficulty, perhaps, is that the four classical categories of poetry, philosophy, history, and rhetoric are neater in definition than in fact—no less in film than in literature. Do the problems with film works of this kind differ from those with prose works? That question is dependent on a comparison between words and pictures as conveyers of fact and carriers of argument. Ironically enough, the presumption about the film image is that it is simultaneously more true and more false in its relation to reality than the written word.

On the one hand, the veracity of the film image is indisputable—for on film, reality concretely, photographically seems to exist instead of being reduced to verbal signifiers, no matter how full or apt. On the other hand, film seems capable of tricking up that reality so that the indisputable truth of what we see has been assembled by such falsehoods as editing, camera angle, staging events in a studio, and so forth. Further, because a film flies by so inexorably without stopping to let us consider its arguments (certain recent Third World films break the flow of film images for periods of discussion and analysis, but the pause is merely another sort of rhetorical ploy), because a film image is so dense compared with the single word or sentence, and because those images are usually underscored by music that is effective and affective precisely because it is undetectable, viewers who trust words develop a Platonic suspicion of film rhetoric, which makes lies go down like stirring truths. The experience of reading seems more contemplative and analytical than that of watching a film: perhaps because we have been educated to analyze and evaluate the deductive structures and inductive data of verbal arguments but have not been trained to recognize the methods and devices of film rhetoric; perhaps because we can control our pace of reading but not the pace of a film. A systematic comparison of film's expository and persuasive powers with those of verbal language will probably come from philosophers or social scientists rather than from literary scholars.

Literary scholars have paid even less attention to the relations between poetry (particularly lyric poetry) and the type of film that has been vaguely called "experimental," despite the striking parallels between the two. Like lyric poems, experimental films tend to be short rather than full-length works. Like lyric poems, experimental films tend to explore more abstract, internalized states of human thought and feeling than do narrative works, which are obligated, by definition, to develop a coherent narrative of external human action. Like lyric poems, experimental films play most richly, complexly, densely, and, indeed, elliptically with the stylistic devices—in effect, the grammatical, syntactical, and semantic conventions—of the medium itself. They both do so to explore the processes of language and meaning in themselves and/or to make these abstract states, experiences, and sensations of human consciousness concrete.

Historically, the origins of this type of film can be traced to Paris in the 1920s, to the film experiments of the surrealists and dadaists, two terms that proclaim their literary analogues: the films of Luis Buñuel, Jean Epstein, Man Ray, Alberto Cavalcanti, Fernand Léger, Marcel L'Herbier, and others. To some extent, the differences between these two types of experimentation have defined the two traditions of experimental films that descended from them. The surrealist films (*Un Chien andalou* [1929] and

L'Age d'or [1931] of Luis Buñuel and Salvador Dali are the best examples) manipulated concrete images of the real world so that they spoke directly to the immaterial, impossible dreams, imaginings, and sensations of the human unconscious. Cinema was an ideal medium for this immaterial conversation since its individual images could be so concrete, and yet the methods of joining those images (by editing) could be so elliptical. The essential cinematic method of the surrealists was the creation of an irrational continuity (as if the flow of images corresponded to the impossible mental meanderings of a dream) from individual images that in themselves were recognizable and, therefore, comprehensible. The dadaists, however, concentrated on the purely formal characteristics of the individual film image, stripping it of the recognizable and, consequently, making it incomprehensible.[17] Since the 1920s these two experimental approaches have continued to coexist, primarily as an important American tradition. In Europe, the surrealists, including Luis Buñuel, have joined the narrative, feature-film tradition (Buñuel's films continue to juxtapose individually comprehensible images with an irrational, discontinuous continuity), while the aims of the dadaists seem trivially fanciful and formalist in the socially conscious, Marxist-oriented intellectual climate that has dominated European thought since World War II.

Maya Deren's *Meshes of the Afternoon* (1943) and Kenneth Anger's *Fireworks* (1947) are two classics of the American surrealist tradition, dreamlike examinations of the sexual and spiritual health of the two filmmakers, who also appear as the major human figures in the two films (like the "I" who is so frequently both the speaker and the subject of a lyric poem). The films of Stan Brakhage also attempt to construct a spiritual autobiography in lyric terms, combining the modern poet's taste for revolutionary grammar and syntax with the Wordsworthian adoration of nature and childhood. The first section of Brakhage's most mythic autobiographical work, *Dog Star Man* (1967), is entitled "Prelude"—as Wordsworthian a title as one might find. Films in the dadaist experimental tradition do not so much examine the poet-filmmaker's soul as explore the processes of cinematic illusion, meaning, and signification themselves, just as the poetry of Gertrude Stein or Tristan Tzara explores the interrelation between phonemes, morphemes, grammar, and syntax. Robert Breer's abstract animated films examine the way that the inevitable movement of celluloid through the projector at twenty-four frames per second produces the impression of movement and connection between still images. Michael Snow's *Wavelength* (1967) examines the cinema's use of both deep and flat spaces by almost imperceptibly pushing a zoom lens for forty-five minutes through a room whose primary inhabitant is space itself, while Hollis Frampton's *Zorn's Lemma* (1970) compares printed letters with filmed images as systems of signification and methods of expanding human vision. Given the clear relation of these types of films to the concerns of lyric poetry, particularly modern poetry, it seems strange that literary critics have abandoned this class of film works to their colleagues in departments of art or art history.

II

From this comparison of film and literary works our attention shifts to a comparison of film and literary "languages." Like literary works, works of cinema are constructed according to a system of signification that makes them intelligible and therefore capable of informing, persuading, or moving. Like literary makers, filmmakers manipulate the signifying system according to its conventions, enabling the receiver of the work to re-create those identical manipulations and thereby receive its information. Like the literary system of signification, the cinema system is additive (individual signs are added to one another), cumulative (each addition progressively increases and specifies meaning and understanding), progressive (the direction of its progressive meaning cannot be reversed; previously established significances cannot be erased), and, therefore, temporal (the signification process unfolds over a period of time and requires time for its operation). Like the literary process of signification, the cinema process can be extended infinitely, guaranteeing the infinitely complex cumulativeness and progressiveness of its messages. Given these striking parallels, it is no wonder that scholars and theorists have been attracted to compare verbal language and film "language," both informally (Eisenstein) and formally (the French semiotician Christian Metz and others he has influenced).

To put the word "language" in quotation marks in reference to film implies that however much the cinematic processes of making and receiving messages parallel the linguistic process, these two "languages" are not languages in the same sense at all. Indeed, one of the primary accomplishments of semioticians thus far has been the elaboration of clear distinctions between the linguistic and cinematic systems of signification.[18] First, as opposed to the double articulation system of language—phonemic and morphemic—films usually manipulate only a single articulation system, the filmed image itself. One consequence of lacking such a double system is that the maker of cinema signification does not exercise a choice analogous to that of the verbal maker—either to speak or to write. The only way to make film signification is to make a film. Another consequence is that film signification is not a general cultural activity practiced informally by all members of the culture who speak and write daily. Film is "spoken" only formally and by a few to the many, whose activity consists not in making new utterances but in making sense of the utterances that have been previously constructed. Although the increasing popularity of home-movie cameras and projectors makes it possible for everyone to "speak" cinema, even these amateur utterances, once "spoken," acquire the status of formal, finished works rather than informal quotidian cultural communication.

Second, whereas verbal language operates according to clearly established paradigmatic and syntagmatic codes, film "language" seems to lack any paradigmatic codes, and those syntagmatic codes that have been identified in film fail to explain much and have failed to convince many. In ordinary terminology, verbal language operates by the combination of previously defined words (the paradigmatic activity, since a definition is determined by the definition of something else — snow rather than ice, cow rather than dog, walk rather than run, etc.) according to grammatical rules for their combination (the syntagmatic activity, distinguishing between subjects and objects, nouns and verbs, so that one can construct "the dog runs" but not "runs dog the"). One can construct new words (say, *polyester*) by paradigmatic analogy, and one can shift words from one syntagmatic category to another ("Shall we McDonald's or Burger King it tonight?") without being misunderstood because the comprehensibility of such innovation is guaranteed by the analogous operations and structures of a system that is highly encoded.

But film "language" is not highly encoded in this way, and some argue that it is not encoded at all.[19] Paradigmatically, the shot, recognized as the smallest indivisible unit of cinematic meaning, is not equivalent or even analogous to the word (despite Eisenstein's argument to the contrary). A shot can vary from a single frame (less than 1/15 second in a silent film) to thousands of frames (lasting many minutes, as some single shots do in the films of Jean Renoir and Orson Welles). Indeed, Eisenstein's analogy between words and shots was based on his assumption that a shot should be very brief so that it could function like a word. But even the briefest shots convey an immense amount of information simultaneously: foreground and background action; physical setting; patterns of light, composition, and shadow; camera distance and angle; variations in either the color or monochromatic spectrum; sounds; music; even, perhaps, spoken words themselves. As Metz has shown, the shot is at least equivalent to a sentence — an assertion such as "There is a cat" — if not to a whole paragraph.

Given the immense number of variables in every shot, it is not surprising that shots cannot be compared paradigmatically. It is probably impossible to construct a shot that is absolutely identical to another (hence, a director prefers one take of a shot to another on the basis of some very subtle difference) while, in a functional paradigmatic system, it is necessary that a rose first be a rose be a rose if it is to be meaningfully compared with a carnation. The black and white hats of western films have been suggested as one paradigmatic code, but the code holds truer of cheap westerns (of the Ken Maynard and Hoot Gibson variety) than of major ones (John Wayne and Montgomery Clift wear various hats of varying shades in *Red River*), suggesting that the hats are less a code than an easy and stale metaphor. Others suggest that individual filmmakers establish their own paradigmatic codes (e.g., the communal dance in John Ford films and the communal sing in Howard Hawks films are codes of social coherence).[20] Such a claim, however, differs only verbally from calling such dances and songs recurring motifs, metaphors, or devices of these filmmakers; one could also call fishing and hunting "codes" in the novels of Hemingway.[21]

The semioticians have been more successful at identifying syntagmatic codes. Christian Metz, for example, has identified the "alternating syntagma" (the alternation between various locations, either temporally linked, as in D. W. Griffith's last-minute rescues, or temporally unrelated, as in the intellectual crosscuts that conclude Eisenstein's *Strike*).[22] Metz has also attempted to identify the "grand syntagma" of narrative film construction—the various temporal and causal connections between two shots. In response to Metz's arguments, some claim that Metz's syntagmas are not codes at all but mere analyses of structural patterns that underlie only certain kinds of films —narrative feature films of the "classic Hollywood" style (one could just as well call the rising and falling action of tragedies a code).[23] Others might claim that our ability to understand an alternating syntagma proceeds not from the encoded operation of the syntagma but from our understanding of the whole narrative; since no relevant temporal connection could possibly exist between the slain workers and the slaughtered ox at the end of Eisenstein's *Strike*, the connection between the two shots must necessarily be nontemporal, that is, metaphorical or symbolic rather than causal. The single syntagmatic law of cinema is that two successive shots are *somehow* related; it is this syntagmatic law that the surrealists exploit, for in their films our minds search for a connection between shots without success. (This exploitation does not violate the syntagmatic necessity of connection: it is simply an alternative principle of connection—a deliberately nonconnected connection.) Such a discussion suggests that the syntagmatic principles of connecting shots are not encoded at all, as the connection of subjects, predicates, and objects is in sentences. Understanding a connection between shots is more properly analogous to understanding a poetic trope than to understanding a sentence—relating the specific device to the contextual grid of the specific work rather than to a preexisting code.

The only way to apply the notion of a code (on which semiotic precision depends) to the cinematic "language" is to put "code" in quotation marks as well. The reason, perhaps, is that the cinematic "language" might more properly be termed the cinematic "languages." Comprehending verbal language requires the use of a single sense (either seeing or hearing) and a single (yet extremely complex) encoded system of translating the physical stimuli into meaning. Comprehending a film requires the use of two senses (both seeing and hearing at the same time) and of several different systems (or "codes") for translating physical stimuli into meaning. Even within each of these systems, we must exercise different kinds of mental operations to understand the information. For example, although a camera angle, a dominant color, a human face, and the connection between two shots are all received as visual information, different systems of perception are required to "read" each of these stimuli: the "code" of camera angles, the color "code," the "code" of human physiognomy and gesture, and an editing "code." The problem with such individual "codes"—the color "code," for example—is that, like the color spectrum itself, the "code" is a line without any points. Language is so highly encoded because it can so easily be broken into its points, its units. Although points in the color spectrum have been translated into words—in effect, into points—so that we can recognize the differences between cardinal, carmine, and crimson, the colors themselves can only be experienced (and, in this sense, "understood") in terms of their subtle differences. So too, although the terms "close-up," "medium shot," and "far shot" suggest a paradigmatic series of camera distances, only the terms (rather than the shots they approximately describe) are paradigmatic. The descriptions are merely approximate because there is no precise definition of how close a close-up or how far away a far shot is from its subject—merely the continuum that a close-up is closer than medium, which is closer than far.

While the verbal code, because of its units, permits both denotation and connotation, a "code," such as the color or shot "code," tends to permit only connotation. The complexity of language as a system arises from the ability to add its units infinitely and complexly, but the complexity of color as a system of meaning comes from subtle shades of difference within a continuum that exists as a whole. All sources of meaning in a film—with the exception of words (either uttered or written) and, possibly, of certain syntagmas of editing—are "codes" of the color and shot sort rather than of the linguistic sort. Even music, an important source of meaning in cinema, operates according to a system that resembles that of colors as much as that of words. Although music has definable paradigmatic units (the notes) and encoded syntagmatic relations between those units (major and minor, 3/4, 4/4, etc.), its messages are primarily connotative, not denotative.[24]

It is not difficult to understand the explicit or tacit preference of certain film theorists for the silent film. It manipulated only a single sense (let us forget about the piano, organ, or orchestra in the pit) and a single system of information (let us forget about all those printed titles between the moving pictures). Sound, according to a theorist like Rudolf Arnheim, not only destroyed the purity of film art by making it a "mixed art" (appealing to more than a single sense) but also debased the cinematic language by redundantly adding the verbal language to it.[25] Even today, there is a decided prejudice in favor of defining film as something seen rather than as something seen and heard. For example, synonyms for cinema like "moving picture" or "moving image" refer only to the visual, like "cinema" itself, which is descended from cinematograph, the recording of motion. Whatever happened to all those words that referred to the recording of life, like "biograph"? Sounds are very much a part of life. But even if one grants the visual prejudice its legitimacy, the visual "language" of cinema is itself composed of many "languages"—a "language" of faces, gestures, shapes, light, color, composition, editing, and so forth—if by language we mean a single system in which we not only receive the signifiers identically but understand what they signify according to a single code of signification.

This fact makes it difficult to identify, classify, and codify the individual systems of cinema communication and impossible to systematize the interaction of all these systems. While linguistics has revealed the organization and principles of verbal communication, the application of semiotics to the cinema has revealed how little we know about the rules of cinematic communication, how unlike verbal language the cinematic "language" is. Indeed, the application of the term "language" to cinema is purely a metaphor for the many simultaneous human mental activities that allow cinema works to be comprehensible. Although the systematic operations of cinema remain mysteries, even the average moviegoer does a good job at understanding films, even their most audacious and innovative devices, without understanding how it is we understand them. The great landmarks of film history —D. W. Griffith's films; those of Eisenstein, Chaplin, and Renoir; *Citizen Kane, Open City, Breathless, L'Avventura, 2001: A Space Odyssey*, and many others—are said to owe their reputations to their expansion of the cinematic language. What such films accomplished was the discovery of new cinematic tropes, ways of telling a story, revealing a character, or making a point that was simultaneously new, clear, creative, and compelling. They were also demanding, requiring their "readers" to make nimble mental leaps, to connect complex pieces of information in totally new ways. Although such a trope could then be frozen into an established cinematic "code" for the use of future films, a new syntagma or variation on an extant syntagma, the evidence of film history is that the most creative "speakers" of cinema refuse to rest on their syntagmas and insist on perpetually casting for fresh ones—of which the audience must perpetually make fresh sense. This vital process—of perpetually making and "reading" new formal devices, of perpetually making and "reading" new uses and variations of familiar generic structures—may well explain the cinema's cultural and aesthetic vitality throughout the century.

I think that future comparative studies of film and literature will pay increasing attention to the ways that audiences of films and readers of literature make sense of these kinds of works. The application of semiotics to film in the last decade is evidence of the increasing interest in how we make sense of films, just as the most recent trend in literary criticism, the deconstructing of a text, shifts the critical emphasis from the maker of the work to the reader of the work. The Marxist cinema critics and theorists, most of them European semioticians or structuralists, also want to know how films manipulate audiences and underscore a culture's political, economic, and moral values without an audience's awareness of this manipulation or underscoring. The fact that film is now so widely taught in American universities (and what is taught, whatever the course title, is essentially film rhetoric —how specific devices in specific films produce specific meanings)[26] suggests that cinema has been recognized as a powerful cultural and artistic force. It is time to try to understand how it does what it does and how we do whatever we do that allows it to do what it does.

Notes

[1] See such essays as "The Cinematographic Principle of the Ideogram," "Film Language," and "Dickens, Griffith, and the Film Today," in *Film Form*, ed. and trans. Jay Leyda (New York: Harcourt, 1949).

[2] Leo Braudy traces this modernist prejudice to the eighteenth century and the Romanticist rebellion against genre and convention. See *The World in a Frame* (Garden City, N.Y.: Doubleday-Anchor, 1977), pp. 104–14. Braudy is one of the literary scholars whose film writings of the past decade have challenged the literary prejudices of previous ones.

[3] See *The Citizen Kane Book* (Boston: Little, 1971).

[4] Robert Richardson, *Literature and Film* (Bloomington: Indiana Univ. Press, 1969), p. 48

[5] For example, Keith Cohen's *Film and Fiction: The Dynamics of Exchange* (New Haven: Yale Univ. Press, 1979), one decade more recent than Richardson's book, contents itself with the identical assumption that only "art films" bear any relation to serious fiction.

[6] Aristotle did not have this problem, since his subject was poetry, not literature. Although my notion of literature may seem terribly book- and print-bound, the term "literature" itself seems to have little meaning except in reference to writing words, and the means for recording the written word and transmitting it is the printed text. It may be obvious to the reader that I cannot embark on a comparison of "film and literature" without understanding what the monolithic term "literature," which we all take for granted, means. Apart from the four operational classes of works that I list in the essay (prose fiction, plays, poems, and nonfiction prose), the term "literature" may have no meaning at all.

[7] One may object that the entire experience of a novel does not exist within the covers of the printed book—that readers subvocalize the words as they read, or that they imaginatively "perform" the novel's events and characters in their minds. Such a performance, called "narrativity" in Robert Scholes's "Narration and Narrativity in Film" (in Gerald Mast and Marshall Cohen, eds., *Film Theory and Criticism: Introductory Readings*, 2nd ed. [New York: Oxford Univ. Press, 1979], pp. 417–33), certainly accompanies the reading of words and, in effect, makes sense of them. But, as the Scholes article indicates, this kind of performance must also take place in experiencing any kind of narrative work, even those performed (like plays) or screened (like movies).

[8] Keith Cohen's *Film and Fiction* answers Bluestone's charge by demonstrating that some of the most radical techniques of modernist novels have precise analogues in modernist films.

[9] Erwin Panofsky, "Style and Medium in the Motion Pictures," in Mast and Cohen, pp. 243–63.

[10] André Bazin, "Theater and Cinema," in Mast and Cohen, pp. 378–93.

[11] My own *A Short History of the Movies* has been guilty of disseminating this orthodoxy, an error I have tried to remedy in the third edition of the book (Indianapolis: Bobbs-Merrill, 1981). Perhaps the best demonstration of the way

that cinematic narrative imbues space with meaning and then uses that meaning to convey the narrative is V. F. Perkins' *Film as Film: Understanding and Judging Movies* (Baltimore: Penguin, 1972). Perkins makes this meaningful use of space, rather than editing, the essence of cinema narrative art.

[12] Stanley Cavell describes stage acting as parallel to playing third base; the expectations of the position already exist, and the player sets about fulfilling them as richly, deeply, and brilliantly as possible. In *The World Viewed: Reflections on the Ontology of Film* (New York: Viking, 1971), pp. 25–29.

[13] See, for example, Lillian Ross and Helen Ross, "The Player: Actors Talk about Film Acting," in James Hurt, ed., *Focus on Film and Theatre* (Englewood Cliffs, N.J.: Prentice-Hall, 1974), pp. 99–115.

[14] According to Charles Eidsvick: "The crux of good acting is that actors not only make us believe in their persons; they also convince us of the 'validity' of the stories they are in," *Cineliteracy: Film among the Arts* (New York: Random, 1978), p. 91. This little-known film book by a literary scholar has probably suffered from looking like a textbook but reading like a sophisticated theory. Leo Braudy makes a similar link between acting, character, and narrative probability in film:

The basic nature of character in film is omission—the omission of connective between appearances, of reference to the actor's existence in other films, of inner meditation, in short of all possible other worlds and selves except the one we see before us. . . . Film character achieves complexity by its emphasis on incomplete knowledge, by its conscious play with the limits a physical, external medium imposes upon it. The visible body is our only evidence for the invisible mind. (*The World in a Frame*, p. 184)

[15] This is why Stanley Cavell calls movie stars one of the "media" of movies—one of the ways that movies "make sense" (*The World Viewed*, pp. 27–37).

[16] Richard Meran Barsam, *Nonfiction Film: A Critical History* (New York: Dutton, 1972).

[17] See William Earle, "Revolt against Realism in the Films," in Mast and Cohen, pp. 33–44, for a fuller discussion of these two experimental types.

[18] For example, see Christian Metz's "Some Points in the Semiotics of the Cinema," in Mast and Cohen, pp. 169–83.

[19] See Gilbert Harman, "Semiotics and the Cinema: Metz and Wollen," in Mast and Cohen, pp. 204–16.

[20] See, for example, Peter Wollen, *Signs and Meaning in the Cinema*, 3rd ed. (Bloomington: Indiana Univ. Press, 1972), pp. 116–54.

[21] There is, of course, a code of honor attached to hunting and fishing in the Hemingway novels, but that use of the term "code" has an altogether different sense. These multiple meanings of "code" lead Gilbert Harman to charge that the only way semioticians have developed the appearance of a single science is by an equivocal use of the central term "code" (Mast and Cohen, pp. 212–16).

[22] "Some Points in the Semiotics of the Cinema," Mast and Cohen, pp. 178–80.

[23] See Alfred Guzzetti, "Christian Metz and the Semiology of the Cinema," in Mast and Cohen, pp. 184–203.

[24] In *Film/Cinema/Movie: A Theory of Experience* (New York: Harper, 1977), pp. 216–20, I describe several denotative functions performed by the musical score of George Cukor's *Camille* (1936). A brief example of music's performing a denotative function in a film is in the prologue of Howard Hawks's *Red River* (1948) when the approach of a distant rider is accompanied by a shift to Mexican-style music on the sound track, conveying the denotative information that the rider is Mexican. Although music serves primarily connotative pur-

poses in film (to control or intensify a scene's emotional tone), it can serve denotative purposes when very specific musical shifts (into a new theme, into a new orchestration, from major to minor or vice versa) accompany specific visual imagery and narrative cues.

[25] Although Arnheim's attitude can be found throughout *Film as Art* (1957; rpt. (Berkeley: Univ. of California Press, 1966), his most rigorous (and most desperate) theoretical assault on synchronized sound is in "A New Laocoön: Artistic Composites and the Talking Film," pp. 199–230 of *Film as Art*.

[26] There are many such film-rhetoric books on the market, textbooks designed to acquaint the student with the terminology and techniques of film meaning and expression. Among the most popular and respected are Louis D. Giannetti, *Understanding Movies*, 3d ed. (Englewood Cliffs, N.J.: Prentice-Hall, 1982); James Monaco, *How to Read a Film* (New York: Oxford Univ. Press, 1977); John L. Fell, *Film: An Introduction* (New York: Praegers, 1975); and Bernard F. Dick, *Anatomy of Film* (New York: St. Martin's, 1978). The greatest theoretical problem that these rhetorics must encounter is whether a particular cinematic device inevitably generates a particular meaning or whether the meaning and effect of the device is itself the product of the narrative and stylistic context in which the device is employed. Those rhetoric textbooks that are least sensitive to this kind of question are most dogmatic and most schematic in their description of a film "language."

Bibliography

In addition to the works cited in the notes, the following books and articles consider the issues of this essay.

Affron, Charles. *Star Acting: Gish, Garbo, Davis*. New York: Dutton, 1977.

Balázs, Béla. *Theory of the Film: Character and Growth of a New Art*. Trans. Edith Bone. New York: Dover, 1970.

Barthes, Roland. *Elements of Semiology*. Trans. Annette Lavers and Colin Smith. New York: Hill and Wang, 1967.

———. *S/Z*. Trans. Richard Miller. New York: Hill and Wang, 1974.

———. *Writing Degree Zero*. Trans. Annette Lavers and Colin Smith. New York: Hill and Wang, 1968.

Bluestone, George. *Novels into Film*. 1957; rpt. Berkeley: Univ. of California Press, 1966.

Eco, Umberto. *A Theory of Semiotics*. Bloomington: Indiana Univ. Press, 1976.

Fell, John L. *Film and the Narrative Tradition*. Norman: Univ. of Oklahoma Press, 1974.

Lindsay, Vachel. *The Art of the Moving Picture*. Rev. ed. New York: Macmillan, 1922.

Magny, Claude-Edmonde. *The Age of the American Novel: The Film Aesthetic of Fiction between the Two Wars*. Trans. Eleanor Hochman. New York: Ungar, 1972.

Manvell, Roger. *Shakespeare and the Film*. Rev. ed. South Brunswick, N.J.: Barnes, 1979.

McConnell, Frank. *Storytelling and Mythmaking: Images from Film and Literature*. New York: Oxford Univ. Press, 1979.

Metz, Christian. *Film Language: A Semiotics of the Cinema*. Trans. Michael Taylor. New York: Oxford Univ. Press, 1974.

———. *Language and Cinema*. Trans. Donna Umiker-Seboek. The Hague: Mouton, 1974.

Murray, Edward. *The Cinematic Imagination: Writers and the Motion Pictures.* New York: Ungar, 1972.

Nicoll, Allardyce. *Film and Theatre.* New York: Crowell, 1937.

Ropars-Wuilleumier, Marie-Claire. *De la littérature au cinéma: Genèse d'une écriture.* Paris: Colin, 1970.

———. *L'Ecran de la mémoire: Essais de la lecture cinématographique.* Paris: Seuil, 1970.

Sontag, Susan. "Film and Theatre." In *Film Theory and Criticism: Introductory Readings.* Ed. Gerald Mast and Marshall Cohen. 2nd ed. New York: Oxford Univ. Press, 1979, pp. 359–77.

Spiegel, Alan. *Fiction and the Camera Eye: Visual Consciousness in Film and the Modern Novel.* Charlottesville: Univ. of Virginia Press, 1976.

Wicks, Ulrich. "Literature/Film: A Bibliography." *Literature/Film Quarterly,* 6 (1978), 135–43. This journal, as its name indicates, is devoted exclusively to the comparative issues of film and literature.

Other major scholarly film journals in English include:

Cinema Journal. Official publication of the Society for Cinema Studies, a professional organization of cinema scholars; specializes in historical scholarship.

Film Quarterly. The oldest extant serious film journal in America; primary emphasis on criticism.

Journal of Popular Film. Film as popular culture; American genre film study.

Quarterly Review of Film Studies. Theoretical and pedagogical; articles on major issues in film study and extensive, serious reviews of new books.

Screen. British journal with a strong Marxist and Freudian bias; consistent applications of semiotic, structuralist, and psychoanalytic methodologies to film, drawing on Brecht, Lacan, Foucault, and Althusser as primary authorities.

Glossary

accommodation: a term from the psychological theory of Jean Piaget, describing how input from the external environment modifies the mediating processes of the subject (e.g., learning to see a constant object even though its size on our retinas varies with distance); see **assimilation**

ambivalence: the coexistence of contradictory impulses toward an object (e.g., love and hate), with one feeling usually repressed

anal: pertaining to that phase of **psychosexual development** in which the **ego** gains mastery over the body and accommodates social expectations; issues involve holding on versus letting go, defiance versus submission

anima: in Jungian psychology, the female personification of the **collective unconscious** in men; see **animus**

animus: in Jungian psychology, the male personification of the **collective unconscious** in women; see **anima**

apologetics: traditionally, the intellectual defense of religion against reasoned objections; now extends to any argument in behalf of religion as an enhancement of life

appellate: (derived from French *appeler* 'to appeal') pertaining to the process of review of a lower court's judgment in a given case

archetype: (1) in folklore study, the original or an analogue of an original type or specimen, which, in nearly all cases, can never be known exactly since it is the creation of several hundred or thousand years ago and has since been substantially modified; (2) in Jungian psychology, archaic mythological type that informs the **collective unconscious**

assimilation: a term from the psychology of Jean Piaget, referring to the active mediating process whereby a subject incorporates an object in the environment for its own cognition and use (e.g., ingesting food or perceiving a distant object); see **accommodation**. (The two modes are complementary but not always balanced—hence the need for adaptation. In children's behavior, Piaget terms an imbalance of accommodation over assimilation, "imitation," and an imbalance of assimilation over accommodation, "play.")

Beschreibung: pseudogenre based on the model of the Homeric description (e.g., the shield of Achilles in the *Iliad*)

carmen figuratum: see **pattern poem**

censor: Freud's earliest characterization of the repressive and distorting force in dreaming; see **repression** and **superego**

collective unconscious: in Jungian psychology, psychical inheritance of racial experience functionally potential in each individual

commedia dell'arte: (literally, 'comedy of art') an Italian Renaissance and post-Renaissance form of comedy without a fixed text but with a plot outline, sustained by the continuous improvisation of professional actors; contrasted to the more traditional comedy of character or situation, known as *commedia erudita* 'erudite comedy'

concrete poetry: poetry concentrating on the physical material from which the text is made, the essential feature being reduced language; poems to be "sensed" rather than read: visual poems to be seen like a painting, sound poems to be listened to like music

condensation: a psychological process in dreaming in which two or more wishes or feelings are compressed into a single image, thought, act, or symptom; see **dreamwork** and **primary process**

cosmology: a comprehensive theory of the origin, development, and structure of the universe

cultural history: in contrast with the history of dynasties, wars, institutions, or ideas; includes artistic as well as cultural life (e.g., Voltaire's *History of Charles XII* [1731] and *The Century of Louis XIV* [1751]); in German, *Kulturgeschichte*

day residue: present-day contribution to the **dreamwork** that combines with an unconscious wish to form the dream

defendant: a person against whom a legal action is brought; see **tort**

defense mechanism: usually unconscious technique by which the **ego** protects itself from, or adapts to, internal and external demands

deictics: linguistic forms that refer to various aspects of the situation of utterance, such as *I, you, here, yesterday, tomorrow*

diachronic: pertaining to changes occurring between successive points in time; historical

Dinggedicht: a poem describing natural or human-made objects (in contrast to **iconic poem**, or *Bildgedicht*, which describes works of art)

displacement: an unconscious shifting of psychic energy or interest from one image, object, or activity to another; an aspect of the **primary process**, and central to the **dreamwork**; a form of **defense mechanism**

Doppelbegabung: multiple talent; an artist creative in various media

dreamwork: the process by which the dream is transformed from latent wish to **manifest content**; see **condensation**, **displacement**, **latent content**, and **primary process**

dystopian fiction: (from the Greek *dys* 'ill, bad, diseased' and *topos* 'place'; sometimes referred to as "negative" or "pessimistic" utopia) the presentation of a possible world that is the nightmarish opposite of perfection; has its origins in the satirical use of utopian fiction in such works as Swift's *Gulliver's Travels* and Samuel Butler's *Erewhon* but to a large extent is a product of twentieth-century pessimism (e.g., Zamyatin's *We*, Huxley's *Brave New World*, and Orwell's *1984*); see **utopian fiction**

écriture: (literally, 'writing') used by some contemporary critics to suggest that literature is not a unique or special form of language or writing, enjoys no privileged status, and is subject to the same conditions of analysis as all other rhetorical forms and modes of communication

eikones: see **iconic poem**

ego: in Freud's structural theory that set of organized psychic functions which evolve from the infant's relations to the external world; a mediating agent between internal demands and external requirements; both conscious and unconscious

ego psychology: the focus of psychoanalytic theory after Freud's *The Ego and the Id* (1923); a theoretical midway point between instinct psychology and **object relations**

ekphrasis: a rhetorical term designating all manner of description, in words, of persons, natural things, and human-made objects, including works of art (Latin *descriptio*)

emblem: a mixed genre comprising a motto expressing a moral idea (Latin *inscriptio*), a graphic illustration (*pictura*), and a poem illustrating the idea (*subscriptio*); also known as device

epistemology: branch of philosophy that investigates the origin, nature, methods, and limits of human knowledge; see **metaphysics**

etiology: study of the causes or origins of things

euhemerism: interpretation of myths as traditional accounts of historical persons and events

examining magistrate: also known as inquisitor; a Continental legal figure, favored by many European novelists, who is charged with conducting an exhaustive pretrial inquiry into any serious criminal matter

existentialism: philosophy derived from the work of Søren Kierkegaard and Friedrich Nietzsche and associated with such modern thinkers as Martin Heidegger, Karl Jaspers, Jean-Paul Sartre, and Miguel de Unamuno; gives priority to the particular conditions of individual human existence rather than to the general essence of universals; its method of analysis, especially in Germany and France, supplied by Edmund Husserl's **phenomenology**

family romance: the fantasy of substitute parents, generated by disillusionment with, or rejection of, real parents; also a denial of **Oedipal** attachments

formalism: a school of literary criticism stressing interpretation based on the structure and texture of a work, originally associated with critics like Victor Shklovsky, Boris Eikhenbaum, and Roman Jakobson

free association: the psychoanalytic technique of uninhibited flow of thoughts, loosening fantasy-reality boundaries and allowing access to **primary process;** Freud's theory of psychic determinism asserts meaningfulness of association

fugue: a contrapuntal musical composition in which one or more themes are repeated or imitated by successively entering voices

functionalism: a sociological theory emphasizing the relation of social forms and activities to purpose

fundamental theme: see **leitmotiv**

Geistesgeschichte: a branch of cultural history that seeks to reconstruct the spirit of a time and to explain all facts by this spirit

genetic: pertaining to or determined by the origin or development of something

genital: pertaining to a psychosexual phase in which libidinal drives are subordinated to genital pleasure

Gesamtkunstwerk: a large-scale work of art (e.g., opera, ballet) to which various artistic media contribute

Gestalt psychology: (literally, 'form' or 'configuration' psychology) a school of psychology that emphasizes the integrated structure of experience, understanding both event and response as complete wholes rather than as collections of discrete elements; examines the pattern-receiving and pattern-constructing qualities of perception

hermeneutics: the study of the presuppositions and rules that govern all forms of interpretation

heuristics: a form of study that concentrates on what can be learned from something

hieratic: pertaining to the maintenance and perpetuation of a cult

hierophany: as used by modern phenomenologists of religion, any manifestation of the sacred

historicism: school of thinking that supposes that all phenomena can be explained strictly in relation to their own historical context and antecedents

homology: structural or functional correspondence between two or more things

iconic poem: a specific literary description in poetry (or prose) or a real or imaginary work of art; known in German as *Bildgedicht*, in Greek as *eikones* (occasionally, *agalmatha*), and in Latin as *imagines*; the Italian *poema immagine*, less specifically, is a general literary description in poetry

iconography: (1) the creation or interpretation of images or pictures that represent the thinking, conventions, and motifs of a given period or culture; (2) the description and classification of "images" in the visual arts (Erwin Panofsky distinguishes between preconographical description [of motifs] and iconographical analysis [of images, stories, and allegories])

iconology: study of icons; a mode of interpreting the data furnished by iconography and of establishing their intrinsic meaning and/or symbolic value

id: in Freud's structural theory, the psychic representation of instinctual drives that seek immediate gratification

identification: unconscious "con-fusion" (that is, fusing together) of one's self with another; part of normal development in a family, essential to the formation of psychic structure

identity theme: a personal style of relation developed in infancy, in terms of which an individual perceives and encounters his or her environment; an unconscious "theme" on which "variations" may be played throughout life

imagines: see **iconic poem**

inquisitor: see **examining magistrate**

investigation: see **preliminary inquiry**

latent: pertaining to a stage of personality development extending from about four or five years of age to the beginning of puberty, during which sexual urges appear to lie dormant

latent content: the unconscious meaning of a dream or fantasy; the original "text" of the dream before its distorted transformation by the **dreamwork**; see **manifest content**

legend: a traditional story about past persons popularly, although not reliably, regarded as historical

leitmotiv: a melodic phrase or figure associated with, and accompanying the reappearance of, a certain idea, person, or situation in a musical work; closely identified with Richard Wagner, who used the term *Grundthema* (literally, 'fundamental theme')

littérature à thèse: (literally, 'thesis literature') used in a derogatory sense by Jean-Paul Sartre, as opposed to *littérature engagée*, to refer to works that "objectively" served the bourgeoisie by defending its "ideologies"; in Italian, *letteratura ideologica,* see *littérature engagée* and *Tendenzliteratur*

littérature engagée: (literally, 'engaged literature' or 'committed literature'; Italian *letteratura impegnata*, Spanish *literatura comprometida*) used before Jean-Paul Sartre to convey the sense of mission of the socially responsible intellectual writer and by Sartre himself to refer to the writer possessed of the superior and tragic awareness that characterizes any authentic act of choice, which is radically opposed to any form of ideological *mauvaise foi* (bad faith and self-deception); see *littérature à thèse* and *Tendenzliteratur*

livre d'artiste: illustrated book that contains original works of art executed by the artist and printed under his or her supervision

manifest content: the dream as remembered and reported by the dreamer; a result of the **dreamwork** transformation of the **latent content**

masque: a dramatic spectacle, popular in sixteenth- and seventeenth-century

England, based on a mythical or allegorical theme and having dialogue generally subordinate to scenic effects

metaphysics: (derived from Aristotle's *meta ta physica* 'the treatise that came after the *Physics*') branch of philosophy concerned with possible final realities underlying the data of experience; see **cosmology, epistemology,** and **ontology**

mimetic: pertaining to the imitation or representation of the sensible or real world as an aesthetic act or in an aesthetic form

morphemes: minimal grammatical units of language

morphology: (literally, 'form of words') the branch of grammar that studies the form of words and their variation according, for example, to tense, person, gender, and number

multiple function: the processes by which the **ego** simultaneously accommodates inner demands (from **id** and **superego**) and external reality, either actively or passively

mutual illumination of the arts: the science of relating works of art executed in one medium to those executed in another, with the aim of demonstrating influences, showing similarities and/or differences, or establishing parallels and analogies

myth: a traditional story containing supernatural elements, set in an undated past and originally held to be sacred

mythographer: a compiler, codifier, and summarizer of myths

object relations: that aspect of psychoanalytic theory which focuses on the subject's relations to others (in contrast to the earlier instinct theory of libidinal tension discharge)

Oedipal: pertaining to a late stage of **psychosexual development,** when the child is attracted to the opposite-sex parent and is hostile to (as well as fearful of) the same-sex parent

oicotype: a local variant of some cultural trait, usually narrative, which for cultural, political, or historical reasons is characteristic of a specific locale; these forms are "at home" (hence *oico*) in specific areas and are felt to be alien in others

ontology: the branch of philosophy concerned with the final nature of existence or being; see **metaphysics**

oral: pertaining to the earliest stage of classic **psychosexual development** (although an undifferentiated "symbiotic" phase is often prefaced), which focuses pleasure/pain at the mouth and identifies the mother with the breast; characterized by two modes: erotic and aggressive (sucking and biting)

oral literature: literature composed in oral performance by persons unable to read or write

overdetermination: images, words, actions, or feelings that have several simultaneous meanings or derive from different levels of the psyche; see **multiple function**

pan-cultural: involving all or a number of cultures

paradigmatic: pertaining to the selection of linguistic elements; also, loosely, pertaining to any model or pattern of which certain particulars can be considered variants

pattern poem: verse in which the disposition of the lines represents some physical object or suggests motion, place, or feeling in accord with the idea expressed in the words (Latin *carmen figuratum*)

phallic: pertaining to an intermediate stage in **psychosexual development** focusing on the penis and ideas of potency (or threats to it) and characterized by self-assertiveness, curiosity, masturbation, and increased sexual fantasies

phenomenology: a philosophy associated primarily with Edmund Husserl that analyzes things as they appear to be in relation to a perceiving mind rather than as they may be in and of themselves

philology: formerly the study of cultures as manifested in their languages and literatures; now, more specifically, the study of the language of ancient texts

phonemes: the minimal segments of sound in a language

phonology: the study of the sound plane of language in its functional aspect, i.e., the identification of the units of sound that distinguish words and the study of the rules governing these units of sound

plaintiff: a party who brings a private legal action, seeking a judicial remedy for a private harm; see **tort**

positivism: a philosophy, originally associated with Auguste Comte, then with Ernst Mach, Ludwig Wittgenstein, and the so-called Vienna Circle, that rejects metaphysics and all abstract or theoretical speculation, and seeks instead to restrict itself to the formulation and analysis of strictly observable and verifiable reality

potential space: an intermediate area of experience and re-creation between infant and mother, expressing both fusion and separation

pragmatics: the study of the use of sentences: what they can be used to do and under what circumstances

preliminary inquiry: the process by which an **examining magistrate** gathers data on a given criminal matter; also called investigation

primal scene fantasy: the child's vision of adult (parental) sexual activity; usually imagined as a mystery of violence

primary and secondary processes: the primary process defined as a mode of cognition and mentation, motivated by unconscious wishes or fears; an aspect of the **dreamwork**, characterized by timelessness, omnipotence of thoughts, **condensation**, and **displacement**; the secondary process, closer to consciousness and the **ego**, identified with rational and logical thought; primary and secondary processes best seen as theoretical extremes; most symbolic expression involves both

prosody: study of suprasegmental aspects of the sound plane of language, such as intonation, pitch, accent, rhythm; also the rules and techniques of versification

psyche: in Jungian psychology, the conscious and unconscious structure of thought, feeling, sensation, and intuition

psychosexual development: the classic theory of instinctual (libidinal) and ego development through stages from infancy through adolescence: **oral, anal** (urethral), **phallic, Oedipal, latent,** and **genital;** modified and elaborated by Erik Erikson, especially, to include later phases of life and relationships

regression: a **defense mechanism;** the avoidance of anxiety by retreating to an earlier stage of development where the **ego** was more competent

repression: the psychological process by which unacceptable desires or impulses are excluded from consciousness and left to operate in the **unconscious**

resistance: a **defense mechanism;** the opposition to knowing unconscious motives

Rezeptionästhetik: the study of aesthetic responses in terms of German **hermeneutics** and **phenomenology;** a tradition developed out of Martin Heidegger and Edmund Husserl by Hans Georg Gadamer, especially, and related specifically to reading by Wolfgang Iser, who relies as well on the phenomenology of Georges Poulet; in Spanish, *receptibilidad estética*

ritual: an action or series of actions performed in a largely prescribed manner on specified occasions and expressing symbolically the shared feelings and attitudes of a group

rondo: an instrumental musical composition or movement in which the principal theme occurs at least three times in the same key, with contrasting themes or sections in between

secondary elaboration: the final process of the **dreamwork** transformation, giving the dream a consciously coherent structure

secondary process: see **primary and secondary processes**

semantics: the study of the meaning of words and their contribution to the meaning of sentences

semiotics: the study of signs and sign systems of all kinds; associated with, among many others, Ferdinand de Saussure, Charles Sanders Peirce, and Umberto Eco

shadow: Jung's term for unconscious subjective components of ego functions (e.g., repressed feelings)

socialist realism: literary doctrine of Marxist inspiration that requires that art reflect the progressive elements in society and thereby contribute to the realization of a better, socialist society

sonata: (1) a musical form consisting of an exposition (i.e., statement of main themes), a development section, and a recapitulation of the main themes; (2) an instrumental musical composition typically of three or four movements in contrasting forms and keys

splitting: a psychological process in dreaming whereby a wish or feeling is attached to, or represented by, more than a single image, thought, act, or symptom

structuralism: investigation of recurrent structures responsible for the production of meaning in a particular cultural activity; an important movement in linguistics, anthropology, and literary criticism; associated with, among many others, Claude Lévi-Strauss, Tzvetan Todorov, Roland Barthes, and Cesare Segre

stylistics: the study of expressive devices of a language or of the expressive choices in a given work or group of works

superego: internalized parental and social attitudes, possessing both a benign aspect (the ego ideal), which rewards good behavior, and a vindictive and punishing aspect capable of instilling guilt

symbolism: in psychoanalytic theory, an unconscious mode of displaced representation, typically away from the body and toward a representing image or object (e.g., from penis to knife or from feces to money), that gratifies an unconscious wish in acceptable form

synchronic: pertaining to a single period or phase, ignoring historical antecedents

synesthesia: a process in which one type of sensory stimulus produces a secondary, subjective sensation linked to another sense organ; "con-fusion" (i.e., fusing together) of the senses

syntagmatic: pertaining to the arrangement of linguistic elements to form larger units

syntax: grammatical rules governing the construction of sentences; the division of grammar concerned with the combination of words into sentences

taxonomy: the science, or laws and principles, of classification

technopaignia: a jeu d'esprit; often used to designate pattern poems, but not exclusively so (e.g., Ausonius wrote a *technopaignion* in which he showed his skills as a verse maker; it consists of ten poems in which each line begins and ends with a monosyllable)

teleology: the explanation of events in terms of ends, goals, and purposes

Tendenzliteratur: (literally, 'tendency literature'; Italian *letteratura tendenziosa*, Spanish *literatura tendenciosa*) a directly and explicitly ideological form of literature, whose origins go back to the first half of the nineteenth century; analyzed by Friedrich Engels, who believed that the more the opinions of an author remained hidden, the better the work of art; revived in Soviet Marxist criticism as "partisanship" or "party-mindedness": representatives of **social realism** were called on to demonstrate their allegiance to party philosophy and policy as unequivocally as possible

testator: the maker of a will or one who has died leaving a will

theology: (derived from the Greek *theos* 'deity' and *logos* 'discourse') traditionally, discourse about God; the realm of philosophy concerned with the nature of God and with God's relation to human beings and the world

titulus: epigrammatic description of a work of art in the form of an actual inscription; common in the Middle Ages

topos: originally an argument that helped to make something acceptable to listeners, sometimes a mnemonic aid; now a literary commonplace, whether an image, motif, or figure or speech; originality, tradition, and imitation all interplay in the study of topoi

tort: a private, as opposed to a criminal, wrong to a **plaintiff** (e.g., through another's negligent act), creating an injury for which the injured party seeks recompense from the defendant

transitional object/phenomena: terms that designate, according to D. W. Winnicott, the intermediate area of experience between oral eroticism and true object relations, involving external objects (e.g., a teddy bear) that are not yet fully recognized as belonging to the external world; the cultural world inherits the space first occupied by childhood transitional phenomena; see **potential space**

unconscious: the descriptive unconscious (or preconscious) refers to memories, information, or skills that can be recalled to consciousness; the dynamic unconscious refers to wishes, fears, and drives that are actively repressed and consciously unknown

ut pictura poesis: 'poetry is like painting,' a phrase from Horace's *Ars Poetica* (l. 361) that has become the basis for a long tradition of critical discussion of the relation between literature and the visual arts

utile et dulce: the belief, derived from Horace's *Ars Poetica* (ll. 333–44), that poetry should be both useful (*utile*) and sweet (*dulce*), should instruct as well as delight; the basis for a widespread critical and artistic tradition that survived into the seventeenth century

utopian fiction: derived from Thomas More's *Utopia* (1516), which gave a name to a mode of thinking and a literary form with an old tradition and a rich future; the name originates from a pun: the combination of the Greek *ou* 'no' and *topos* 'place,' yielding *utopia*, literally, 'no place,' which is both homonymous and synonymous with *eutopia*, from *eu* 'good' and *topos*, or 'the good place'; tradition includes numerous literary depictions of the ideal society; see **dystopian fiction**

valorization: a process whereby the value of something is fixed or secured through appropriation or absorption

Index

317